"It is a reasonable assumption that successful boards will share some common characteristics, as will failing boards. The challenge is to identify these factors before success or failure occur. This book, evidently based on Didier Cossin's years of experience with boards around the world, goes a long way in doing so. The Four Pillars of Board Effectiveness will be an inspiration for many boards and their directors, as they consider how they can further strengthen their governance, enhance their effectiveness and ensure their success."

—**Paul Bulcke**,
Chairman of the Board of Directors, Nestlé S.A; Vice-Chairman,
Board of Directors, L'Oréal; Member, J.P. Morgan International Council

"Didier is one of the true leaders in academia on governance, with extensive practical experience from his engagement with many management teams and boards across the world. His Four Pillars of Board Effectiveness offers a simple yet practical approach to making the most out of the boardroom."

—**Robert Maersk Uggla**,
Chairman of A.P. Møller - Maersk A/S, AP Moller Capital P/S and
Maersk Product Tankers A/S, CEO of A.P. Møller Holding A/S

"This is the bedside book any board member should read and reread. Every page calls into question one's practice and pushes each of us to avoid biases and revisit his/her ways of thinking for the ultimate benefit of the company."

—**Barbara Dalibard**,
Chair of the Michelin Group Supervisory Board

"Recent developments in the financial services industry dramatically illustrate the intimate link between good governance and a company's success or failure, particularly in times of crisis. In his latest book, Didier Cossin sheds light on the design principles and practice that underpin good governance. A catchy and comprehensive textbook for those in charge!"

—**Sergio Ermotti**,
Group CEO and President of the Executive Board of UBS AG

"Professor Cossin has got it spot on. His four-pillared 'temple' of board effectiveness is brought to life with the boardroom adventures of Joanne Marker. One hopes that right-minded and passionate directors or would-be directors will read this book and say 'I want to be a John or Joanne Marker when I grow up!'"

—**Teo Swee Lian**,
Chairwoman, CapitaLand Integrated Commercial Trust;
Independent non-executive Director HSBC, former Member at Corporate
Governance Council of MAS, former Independent Non-Executive Director at
AIA Group Ltd., former Deputy Managing Director Monetary Authority of Singapore

"Effective governance is the cornerstone of quality group decision-making, founded on respect for individual views and freedoms, in their full diversity. Didier's book is an essential read for any organization—be it for-profit, philanthropic, investment, or otherwise—looking to improve its governance practices."

—**Alex Soros**,
Chairman of Open Society Foundations

"An important distillation of Didier Cossin's insight and expertise on effective governance. As a long-time follower of his work, I am glad to see Prof Cossin publish this comprehensive guidebook to governance that transcends both geography and sectors. From stewardship of strategic objectives, to managing and structuring risk, the importance of board diversity and more, the lessons are at once practical and essential for any board member."

—**Peter Maurer**,
President of the Board of the Basel Institute on Governance,
former President of the International Committee of the Red Cross,
Independent Director of Zurich Insurance Group AG

"The foundation of *High Performance Boards* is set in the Values and Character of its members. Didier brings this critical point front and center."

—**Ann M. Fudge**,
former Chairwoman and CEO, Young & Rubicam Brands;
Board Member of Northrop Grumman Corporation

"A masterpiece written by an authority in the field. Impressive, complete dive, and focused. It covers every aspect of governance in a deep and compelling way. I recommend it to every board member."

—**Khaled Al Sultan**,
Chairman of Center for Governance, PIF;
Chairman of Saudi Electricity Company

"This book offers a complete and enlightening review of current board governance practices and challenges. The approach and framework it offers are as pertinent in the east as in the west in establishing high performing boards."

—**Hsieh Fu Hua**,
Chairman, ACR Capital Holdings Pte Ltd;
Chairman, Eastspring Investments Services Pte Ltd,
Board Member of GIC, Singapore and MOH Holdings Pte Ltd.

"Professor Cossin has developed the concept of board effectiveness based on his latest research. Intellectually stimulating, this book provides practical guidance to cope with unique challenges associated with governance of institutions. This book is therefore a must-read for board directors of companies, governmental organizations and NGOs."

—**Kumiko Matsuura-Mueller**,
Former CFO and Director,
Division of Financial Management and Administrative Services,
UNHCR, Director Board of Directors at United Nations Federal Credit Union

"I have known Didier Cossin for 14 years. He has always been close by during my executive and supervisory careers. The experience he has built, through academic research and real-life sharing with likes of "Joanne Marker," myself and others, have allowed him to develop and expand a top-of-the-class, practical and applied science of Corporate Governance. The IMD Global Board Center is today 'the' governance reference for current and potential board members, and this is Didier's greatest achievement. Having managed a number of serious crisis during my supervisory career, I can only recommend Didier's book which is a very up-to-date inventory of the skills required to be an impactful board member or chairperson in today's challenging world."

—**Michel Demaré**,
Chair of Astra Zeneca; Board Member of Vodafone,
Board Member of Louis Dreyfus Company, Chair of the Supervisory Board, IMD

"Didier Cossin brings huge direct experience to bear in his fascinating analysis of what makes a good board. Integrity, hard work, collegiality and independence of judgment matter hugely as personal attributes of board members as does a collective ability to focus on strategy, management support and risk in all its forms matters at the board level itself. And if that sounds easier said than done, read this book. This board member felt wiser and more daunted by the end."
—**Lord Mark Malloch-Brown**,
former President of Open Society Foundations,
former Deputy Secretary General and Chief of Staff, United Nations;
former Minister of State in the Foreign Office

"Board work is demanding. Good governance requires a personal sense of accountability and responsibility from all involved. Didier's work with boards of different organizations in many jurisdictions has helped him author this practical guide that will be of great support to chairs, board members and board secretaries alike."
—**Beat W. Hess**,
Chairman, LafargeHolcim (Switzerland); Vice Chairman Sonova,
Chairman of the Compensation Committee, Nestlé S.A

"Didier Cossin's book explains how Governance can be a key factor for companies' success. It's a must-read for all board members!"
—**Lorenzo Bini Smaghi**,
Chairman, Société Générale; Chairman of the Board of
Directors of Italgas, Board Member, TAGES Holding

"What impressed me most is the comprehensive coverage of every aspect of board work in a way that is solidly grounded in every day's practice in boardrooms around the world. As such, the book is a must read for every aspiring board member, but also has a lot to offer for even the most seasoned board member with a curiosity for learning and continuous improvement."
—**Gerard Kleisterlee**,
Independent Director IBEX LTD, Former Chairman,
Vodafone Group Plc; former Deputy Chair and
Senior Independent Director, Royal Dutch Shell; former Chairman, ASML

"Creating a culture of exchanges and constructive challenges among the board remains one of the most inspiring roles for a Chairman. Making sure that members feel accountable for the sustainable success of the firm must be the overarching purpose guiding this inspiration."
—**Michel M. Liès**,
Chairman, Zurich Insurance; Vice Chairman,
Institute of International Finance (IIF)

"The book is a comprehensive and practical guide to key issues relevant for all boards aiming to improve their decision-making processes. There are many useful takeaways on how to increase the dynamics in the boardroom."
—**Olaug Svarva**,
Chairwoman, DNB ASA (Norway); Chairwoman, Norfund;
Board Member of Investinor and Institute of International Finance (IIF)

"Thank you, Dr Cossin. Board members needed this book for a long time. This work will assist board members to understand their responsibilities better."
—**H.E. Dr. Mohammed bin Hamad bin Saif Al Rumhy**,
Former Minister of Energy and Minerals (MEM) Sultanate of Oman;
former Chairman Oman Oil Refineries and Petroleum Industries Company (ORPIC)

"This book offers valuable insights on what it takes to be an effective board. It facilitates a deeper understanding of the range of challenges and dilemmas that boards are faced with and offers guidance and best practices for how these might be addressed. Didier's elucidation of board structures, processes and culture as key elements of quality board interaction and decision-making is timely and instructive. The checklist at the end of each chapter is a useful reminder of the many dimensions of board effectiveness and provides a quick tool for self-evaluation. This book is essential reference for boards navigating through today's era of uncertainty and greater operational complexity, with the attendant new areas of potential risks and accountabilities."

—**Tan Sri Zarinah Anwar**,
Chairwoman, Institute of Corporate Directors Malaysia,
Advisory Board Member at Securities and Commodities Authority (SCA),
former Chairwoman, Securities Commission of Malaysia

"The free market system has created the largest aggregate economic growth in human history. However, the serious problems created by its excesses and structural limitations have become painfully apparent. Prof. Cossin's granular understanding and insights on enterprise governance, contemporary risks and challenges and, most importantly, his perspective on stewardship are extremely valuable in achieving the maximisation of long-term stakeholder value – the 'holy grail' of modern enterprise. This book is borne out of Prof. Cossin's extensive experience across sectors and geographies – a must-read for committed enterprise directors and trustees."

—**Francis Estrada**,
Chairman of CIBI Information, Inc, Chair of Institute of Corporate Directors

"High Performance Boards is the most insightful book I've ever read on corporate governance. It is a brilliant, comprehensive and thorough practical guide that shows how boards do function, but it is also much more than that: it describes with vivid accuracy and real company cases and real-life anecdotes how boards should really function. A must-read for anyone who wants to look behind the curtain and learn about the actual dynamics in the boardroom and, in particular, about the relationship between the Chair and CEO – one of the most important aspects of Corporate Governance."

—**Pierre Vareille**,
former Chairman of the Board, BIC S.A.; Board Member of Vallourec SA and
Verallia SA; Co-Chairman and Founder, The Vareille Foundation

"High Performance Boards is 'the companion' – the guide you need. Of course, you will find in this book all the dos and don'ts for your daily board work. Professor Cossin takes you well beyond the checklist. More than anything else you will be inspired by the leadership dimension – the moral compass. What you will see in these pages are your values in action as you serve in the boardroom."

—**Diane de Saint Victor**,
Board Member of C&A, former Chairwoman of Compensation Committee,
Altran and former Chairwoman of Nomination Committee, Natixi

"Educational and refreshing to the brain, where page after page relate to something one has experienced. The themes are wrapped up and packaged in a very practical way. Overall, it is not a book to read once then shelve, it is something that directors need to read from time to time to ensure protection from drifting with personal habits."

—**H.E. Abdulsalam Mohammed Al Murshidi**,
President of Oman Investment Authority

High Performance Boards

A PRACTICAL GUIDE TO IMPROVING & ENERGIZING YOUR GOVERNANCE

Second Edition

Didier Cossin

This edition first published 2024

© 2024 John Wiley & Sons Ltd

First edition @2020

The right of Didier Cossin to be identified as the author of this work has been asserted in accordance with law.

Registered Office(s)

John Wiley & Sons, Inc., 111 River Street, Hoboken, NJ 07030, USA

John Wiley & Sons Ltd, The Atrium, Southern Gate, Chichester, West Sussex, PO19 8SQ, UK

For details of our global editorial offices, customer services, and more information about Wiley products visit us at www.wiley.com.

Library of Congress Cataloging-in-Publication Data is Available

ISBN 9781394220380 (Cloth)

ISBN 9781394220397 (ePDF)

ISBN 9781394221332 (ePub)

Cover Design: Wiley

Cover Images: © sorbetto/Getty Images (modified by Wiley)

Author photo: Courtesy of Delia Fischer

Set in 11/13pt, ITC New Baskerville Std by Straive, Chennai, India.

SKY10095387_010625

Contents

About the Author

Didier Cossin is chaired professor of governance at IMD, Switzerland. He is the founder and director of the IMD Global Board Center, the originator of the Four Pillars of Board Effectiveness methodology, and an advocate of Stewardship.

Prof. Cossin currently works with sovereign wealth funds, large corporations, non-profit organisations, families, and institutional investors on governance and stewardship issues. He is an advisor to governments, central banks, regulators, and international organisations across the world.

As an investor, he works with prominent asset owners, and uses governance as an engine of investment performance across asset classes and organisations while regularly engaging directly with investee companies and investment committees. The four pillars and the content of this book are then the model used for board engagement. He also has developed a parallel methodology for governance of investments in complex portfolios that is implemented by institutional investors. He is the author of other books such as *Inspiring Stewardship*, book chapters (such as Governance Risk: A Guide for Investors) and articles in the fields of governance, investments, risks and stewardship. He is also principal author of a proprietary methodology of investment selection on governance that is used in a number of funds.

Prof. Cossin holds a PhD in Business Economics from Harvard University (Robert C. Merton chair), is a former Fulbright Scholar from the Massachusetts Institute of Technology, and is a graduate from ENS, rue d'Ulm, Paris, as well as of Sorbonne University and EHESS.

Acknowledgements

Many have contributed, directly and indirectly, to my work and to this book. Of those that contributed directly, I am particularly indebted to Sophie Coughlan. Sophie, as a leadership specialist, and associate director of the IMD Global Board Center, has helped many of the board interactions I lead and has supported me across many chapters. Abraham HongZe Lu has decades of studies and work with me and has also contributed to the substance of this book, bringing sometimes analytical and mathematical flair to what too many see as soft issues only. This book would not be here without their contribution. I am also grateful for the many others that contributed directly or indirectly to this work: Quentin Dufresne, associate director, who has been a key driver of many programmes at the origin of my board practice, notably the High Performance Boards programme, Martin Kralik, Yukie Saito, Jurgita Domeikaite, Philip Whiteley, Loic Frank, Francesca Vitucci, Julie Poivey, and Richard Eames. And for a personal collaboration that has amplified the performance aspect of governance across portfolios of sophisticated investors on four continents, hence reducing waste and optimising wealth creation for future generations, I am grateful to Elisabeth Bourqui, herself a prominent board member and co-founder of PNYX Group.

Of those that contributed indirectly, I owe a particular debt to the real actors of the governance world, board members, directors, government officials, and investors that have peopled my words and my ideas, for the better or for the worse! They probably are just as happy to not see their name mentioned here, as a chair of one of the largest financial institutions in the world wryly remarked once: 'Being in Didier's writings tells you it's time to go!' I suppose that my critical eye has helped a few towards self-awareness J. For many though, they have been an inspiration of how to drive true governance, and many of them are chairpeople or board members of influential and powerful organisations. I am grateful for all those who shared intimate and confidential situations that make the reality of good and bad governance. Without them, I could not contribute to governance improvements that I know impact the world for the better (and sometimes dramatically and publicly so). The dedication, integrity, and altruism of many is commendable. Some are famous, some are unknown, and all support us towards a better governed world. And indeed I have rarely met individuals that did not want to do better, in all senses of the word better. We, as society, should always support the development and improvement of those that govern us and our organisations, and I hope that through my words, their contribution will be heightened. I am in many ways a go-between, putting in words and concepts what the very best-in-class are naturally doing. This book maps and synthesises what some gifted and dedicated individuals have endeavoured to bring to society through their personal judgement skills. It also introduces key elements of evolution for great governance in a complex and conflicted world.

Preface

Governance, or the quality of decision-making at the very top of organisation, has become central to success. But although an effective board can be a huge asset in this regard, boards often fail their organisation – typically in the areas of risk oversight, strategy, the selection and support of the CEO and senior management, and integrity. Making boards more effective, therefore, is crucial to improving governance around the world.

My own interest in the subject began more than 30 years ago, when I studied the governance of risk. I was fortunate to have many inspirational teachers, including five Nobel Prize winners – one of whom, Robert C. Merton, chaired my PhD committee. In parallel with my mathematical work, I quickly became convinced that the human element is crucial to effective governance, and my interest in psychology, philosophy, and ethics increasingly shaped my approach.

In the decades since, I have worked with boards across the globe to assess and improve governance – in large global companies, sovereign wealth funds, government bodies, international organisations, non-profits, family businesses, and tech start-ups. Over the years, I have developed a systematic approach to increasing a board's effectiveness that rests on four pillars: the quality, diversity, focus, and dedication of individual directors; sophisticated information architecture; well-functioning structures and processes; and healthy group dynamics and board culture. By focusing on continuous improvement across all four dimensions, my methodology has repeatedly shown its ability to transform boards for the better.

Diagnosing governance problems is often relatively straightforward, although in some rare cases the causes can be deep and hidden, especially with integrity failures. Improving governance, on the other hand, is often a longer-term process, requiring a gradual, sustained effort over several years. The growing complexity and conflicted nature of the global geopolitical, social, and economic context means that more than ever, boards need to adapt their own governance practice to anticipate and confront the challenges that lie ahead, to be able to steer the organisation with clarity. This has led to a corresponding shift in board practices, necessitating a shift in emphasis from divergence of views solely to convergence and conviction on dividing or ambiguous topics where useful. Board choices (notably of strategy and CEO) are harder than ever and they need to align with strong and decisive action that benefits the organisation over the mid- and longer term.

This book covers both the diagnosis and treatment of governance problems, and aims to provide directors with a practical guide to making their boards more effective. Part I introduces the Four Pillars of Board Effectiveness methodology that my team and I use to assess governance health. Readers may wish to think of this section as a check-up process. Part II addresses the most common areas of governance failure, and how boards can guard against these. In Part III, we look at the importance of board leadership and the role of the chair in ensuring quality governance. Finally, Part IV is a compendium of best-in-class governance practices, with each chapter covering a specific aspect of board work, and drawing on the insights and discussions on this topic that we have had both inside and outside the classroom.

My colleagues at IMD business school, and especially the team at the IMD Global Board Center, have contributed hugely to the content of this book. So, of course, have the thousands of board members whom I have had the pleasure of working with. I pay tribute to them in this book by describing the board experiences of a character called Joanne Marker (not her real name). The real Joanne, an exceptional woman of great energy and dedication, has softly (and sometimes not so softly) impacted the governance of three of the world's most iconic large-cap companies and one of its most influential philanthropic organisations.

As Joanne's experiences illustrate, good governance is about balance, responsibility, and genuine personal accountability. I therefore hope the following chapters will inspire you and your organisations to even better governance and further success.

Didier Cossin
Lausanne, May 2024

PART I
The Four Pillars of Board Effectiveness

Joanne Marker and Board Service

*A*t age 62, Joanne Marker had been a senior independent director for over 20 years on the boards of many different companies and public organisations.

The previous year, Joanne had taken early retirement from her job as a senior leader at Connect, a major US telecommunications company, where she had worked for more than two decades. Hers had been a rewarding and challenging career, of which she was proud.

Joanne now derived a different kind of satisfaction from her board service at three very different companies: Connect, international pharmaceutical company Ziogen, and engineering multinational SNB. In recent months a few other organisations had extended invitations, and she was currently evaluating each of them.

One morning, an email from her nephew Thorsten popped up on her screen.

> Dear Aunt Joanne,
>
> Exciting news! I just received an invitation to be on the board of Kloetzel & Brothers! First board meeting is next month. I wanted to pick the brain of my favorite board member! Can I take you to lunch at Mario's when you're in town next week?
>
> Yours,
> Thorsten

Thorsten was an ambitious, capable, and educated young man working in investment banking on Wall Street. Joanne had no doubt that he would make a fine board director; his knowledge of the financial markets and banking regulation would certainly be helpful to Kloetzel, a global financial services company. He was bright, energetic, and hardworking – and from what she had heard, had earned a reputation in banking as a name to watch. Still, she found herself remembering a few incidents that made her *wonder whether he had the maturity and self-possession needed for boardroom discussions. She checked her calendar and emailed Thorsten, confirming the lunch.*

***

Joanne cast her mind back to a chilly March afternoon 19 years earlier. She had been in her office thinking about how to improve a distribution partnership for WeCare, the multinational consumer goods company she worked for at the time, when her phone rang.

It was her old friend from business school, Burt Goodman, who was now a mover and shaker at GCD, a major consulting firm. Goodman invited Joanne to join him for the Henry Street Settlement dinner in New York City. 'I'm just not cut out for big gala events, Burt', she had protested.

'Oh come on, it will be good for you', Goodman said. 'Sometimes even an MBA and over 20 years of experience in a major multinational can't match the magic of one lucky dinner conversation.' So Joanne decided to go.

At the dinner, she was seated next to Jordan Wise, the CEO of Amsterdam-based Virtuous Ventures, a major international conglomerate. Their conversation touched upon Joanne's family and career journey to date, and Wise asked her advice on the pros and cons of joint ventures in different emerging markets. Joanne shared her key learnings about each market, as well as the main strategic and industrial dimensions that needed to be considered.

'But doesn't it depend on your partners in the end?' Wise wanted to know. Joanne described the different partnerships that WeCare had developed locally, depending on the distribution channels in place (or not) in different markets.

Two days later, Wise called her with a proposal that took her by surprise. 'How would you like to be on the Virtuous board, Joanne?' he asked her. She had always aspired to board service at some point in her career – but she was only 43, surely far too young to be a director.

Wise explained: 'We're expanding internationally into a new retail business, and we need your international marketing expertise. You can bring in solid knowledge about distribution networks and consumer insight too.' Now Joanne's interest was piqued. She began to ask questions. Wise soon ran out of answers.

Her first meeting with Virtuous Ventures' Chairman Gerald Grossheim was over lunch at the famous Charlie Trotter's restaurant in Chicago's Lincoln Park. Over their first course, Grossheim explained how the company's 11-member board worked, how often it met (four times a year), and his relationship with Jordan Wise (almost daily contact, yet with a certain necessary distance). He also discussed other members of the top team.

Grossheim asked Joanne about the kinds of challenges she had encountered when negotiating with local distributors during international expansions, and about how she had developed an understanding of customers in different markets. Joanne happily described her extensive travels in India, Bangladesh, Thailand, China, and Egypt to talk to WeCare's local sales teams. She had accompanied them on visits, discussing their frustrations and where they saw opportunities, in order to get a sense of the reality on the ground.

Joanne had some questions of her own. While Grossheim sipped his coffee, she asked him:

- *Who was on the Virtuous board? How dedicated were they? What did each bring – and what was his or her unique contribution?*
- *How did board directors ensure they had the information they needed to make decisions? What were the board briefing papers like? Were there other sources of information?*
- *What kind of processes and structures did the board have in place to ensure it was doing things efficiently and professionally? How did it ensure directors have a sufficient board-level view of risk? (Here, Joanne recalled the WeCare board's inability to understand how their growth strategy had exposed her own company to key vulnerabilities.)*
- *What was the Virtuous boardroom culture like? What kind of dynamics were at play? How would the other directors view the contribution of a much younger woman?*

Together, they formulated questions for Grossheim to ask Virtuous Ventures' President of Marketing, including what additional information he could ask for that would be helpful in assessing the company's current global marketing plan.

Outside, they shook hands and agreed to speak again in the coming weeks. 'I hope to be seeing a lot more of you, Joanne', Grossheim said, smiling at her.

Three months later, after a series of discussions and a formal panel interview by the nominations committee, Joanne was appointed as an independent director and began eight years of board service with Virtuous.

***

The following Tuesday, Joanne walked into Mario's and kissed her nephew Thorsten on the cheek. It had been 18 months since she had last seen him. While Joanne sipped her iced tea, Thorsten told her how his favourite professor from business school, Sam Cragnolino, was on the board of Kloetzel and was approaching retirement.

As a member of the nominations committee, Cragnolino had seen the board's needs analysis, which had identified a gap in the area of finance – and investment in particular. The head of the committee had developed a skills and competency matrix, which specified that the candidate should also be young (between 30 and 40), and had then issued an invitation to executive search firms. He also asked the other board members if they had any candidates to nominate. Sam had recommended Thorsten.

James Caspar, Kloetzel's chair, had also screened the candidates proposed by the search firms, and invited Thorsten for a panel interview. The young man's expertise in securing and structuring deals with a series of major clients had attracted Caspar's attention as being something missing from the board's existing skillset – and something they very much needed. Thorsten had made the shortlist and passed the due diligence process, and then met the full board. He had been impressed by the ambition of its members to contribute to transforming Kloetzel.

'I really like what they're doing', Thorsten said to Joanne. 'James seems active and engaged, yet not overbearing. Everyone I talked to seems serious about really building something.' Joanne smiled at his enthusiasm.

'That's great, Thorsten', she said. 'Board service is one of the most rewarding experiences any professional can have during their career, and I think you stand to gain a lot. But tell me', Joanne said, putting down her fork and looking intently at the young man, 'what is it about your experience that leads you to think you could make a meaningful contribution to Kloetzel?'

'I know how companies are thinking about the costs and benefits of major transactions', Thorsten said. 'I could help Kloetzel think about whom they could approach and with what messaging to expand in major markets, which is part of their strategy.'

Joanne asked him about Kloetzel's current performance, and whether there were discrepancies across major markets. Thorsten shook his head. He didn't know the details. He dug in his pocket for a pen to make a note.

She pointed out the difference between board service and an executive director role. 'You're not there to tell management how to do their job', she said. 'You're there to challenge them on the strategy to make sure it's a good one, and to help them to get what they need to be able to do it, and then to check that they actually do it.'

Then Joanne asked Thorsten the following questions:

- People: Who were Kloetzel's current board members? What kind of skills, background, personality, and expertise did they have? How many other independent, non-executive directors were there? What kind of diversity and breadth of experience did they have? And how committed were they?
- Information architecture: What kind of information did he have access to that would help him to support Kloetzel in delivering its strategy and monitoring its risks? Who in his network could help? What kinds of social media was he following?
- Structures and processes: What kind of structures and processes did the Kloetzel board have in place? How were these helping it to stay ahead of regulation trends in the financial services industry? Did the board have a risk committee? An investment committee? Would Thorsten be able to serve on either of these?
- Dynamics: Had he spent enough time with the chair of Kloetzel? Did he like him and his style? What about the other directors? How were the interactions? How did the board engage with the firm's senior executives? And how much passion about the firm could he feel?

'With all due respect Aunt Joanne, aren't you ahead of yourself?' Thorsten asked. 'Won't I have time to figure this out once I'm on the board?'

Joanne thought back to a board she had sat on – an Indian tech company, where she had submitted her resignation after just six months. She wished she had done her due diligence exercise better before joining that board.

'Fundamentally, Thorsten, it comes down to two questions', Joanne said. 'The first is: is this a good board which I want to be part of?' He nodded with vigour. 'The second is: am I good for this board?'

Joanne smiled at the young man. 'Saying no to the wrong board appointment is just as important as saying yes to the right one', she said. 'If you don't think you will be able to usefully contribute, do yourself a favour and save yourself from a world of frustration and pain.'

'Thanks Aunt Joanne', Thorsten said, slumping a little in his chair. 'I guess I have some homework to do.'

1

The Four Pillars of Board Effectiveness

Over the past decade, we have witnessed dramatic and unprecedented developments in business, politics, and society. The main upshot of this has been the growing realisation that governance is the determining factor behind the success and failure of organisations. And with fresh evidence of abdication of duty in the corporate and policy-making spheres emerging on a weekly basis, there are growing demands for better governance in different countries, and for all types of organisations – businesses, governments, NGOs, and many others.

When we refer to governance, we mean the quality of decision-making and implementation at the top of organisations – and the processes to ensure these. Increasingly, boards are seen as having a key responsibility and role as the 'owner' of governance in an organisation. It is their competence, structures, and integrity, and their interactions with CEOs and management teams, that shape the governance DNA of organisations.

Until a few years ago, governance and boards were considered to be well understood, and operating along standard and predictable lines. As a result, the subject attracted relatively little attention from researchers. But the situation changed significantly as more stories of corporate malfeasance appeared in mainstream media, industry publications, and academic journals, inevitably accompanied by the question 'Where was the board?'

Indeed, events during the past decade have made it clear that boards can fail in various ways. They have failed to manage risks, failed to contribute proactively to firm strategy, failed to identify the 'right' team and, in some cases, failed to deal with integrity issues and possibly outright fraud. We will discuss board failures and challenges in more detail in Part II.

Partly as a consequence of these much-publicised and damaging failures, today's boards are eager to improve their performance and to continually fine-tune their effectiveness. They have become more cognisant than ever of their role in supporting their organisations' long-term success by aiming for world-class governance.

So, if business as usual is not an option for boards, what are the main dimensions to target when trying to make a board function better? How do we distil the key factors that contribute to board effectiveness?

In our work over the years inspiring the boards of organisations around the world toward greater success, my team and I have identified four discrete pillars of board effectiveness (see Figure 1.1). These are people quality, focus, and dedication; information architecture; structures and processes; and group dynamics and board culture. We will explore each of these pillars in detail in Chapters 4 to 7.

This simple framework for assessing a board's effectiveness has a deep-rooted underlying rationale, and its practical application has helped to transform boards for the better in many different contexts. These include large publicly traded companies, family-owned businesses, non-profit organisations, governments, and other bodies, across all geographies, and in both developed and developing contexts.

The four-pillar methodology, focusing on systematic and continuous improvement along each dimension, has proven to be a strong asset for all types of organisation.

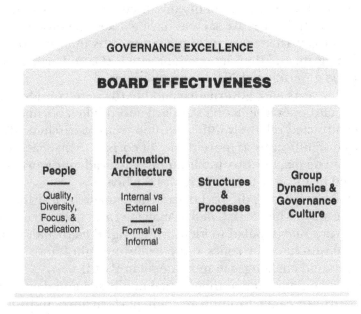

Figure 1.1   Governance Excellence Rests on Four Pillars

The First Pillar: People Quality, Diversity, Focus, and Dedication

A boardroom is a social place, as is business in general. Therefore, the first of the pillars that support a board's effectiveness consists of the people who socialise, interact, learn, make sense of situations, and reach decisions in the boardroom. Their quality, diversity, focus, and dedication are often what makes or breaks a board's ability to perform effectively.

The quality of the board's composition and functioning is crucial. For starters, members of the board and its committees are expected to have the necessary and relevant knowledge. Boards are typically composed of experienced, accomplished individuals from a variety of backgrounds, including top managers, public officials, and education experts. Yet these backgrounds do not automatically give them the knowledge they need to contribute effectively to the work of a specific board.

As we have seen time and again in recent years, having limited knowledge hinders a board member's effectiveness. Whenever a major corporate initiative has run aground, the board members' technical and other specialised knowledge has come under scrutiny. Effective boards therefore ensure that performance and knowledge standards are articulated and tailor-made for individual directors, with the help of matching learning modules and other opportunities. Board members' performance can then be evaluated against those standards.

The quality of the board is further enhanced by its diversity of gender, personality, and opinion. (For a fuller discussion of diversity, see Chapter 19.) In particular, high-quality boards are typically successful at managing their mix of personalities. How many times have we read news stories attributing boardroom confrontations, showdowns, and dramatic exits to a 'clash of personalities', 'incompatible personalities', or, to use a euphemism, 'strong personalities'? The example of Steve Jobs being fired by the board of Apple is just one of many such cases.

To avoid becoming one of these headlines, a board needs to map out, understand, and learn to work with the range of personalities on it. As in all such exercises, this requires tools or 'cognitive handles' that help to capture not only the composition of personalities and the risks involved, but also the configurations that, with a bit of planning and effort, can help to infuse the board with additional vibrancy and strength of performance.

Boards can productively employ and draw on a number of taxonomies in this regard. For instance, personality diagrams highlight board members' introversion or extroversion, their abstract 'big-picture' thinking or orientation to detail, their level of emotional reactivity, and the emphasis they put on competition as opposed to harmony. The well-known NEO Personality Inventory framework describes the 'Big Five' dimensions of personality: emotionality, introversion/extroversion, openness to experience, agreeableness, and conscientiousness (see Chapter 7 on Group Dynamics and Board Culture).

As important as skills and quality are, directors must also be focused and dedicated. Yet these attributes are often missing, in varying degrees, from the boardroom.

Dealing with ambiguities in decision-making is inevitable – in fact, it is a sign that the board is addressing real issues. But when directors misunderstand their roles and functions, their focus suffers. To sharpen and re-energise it, boards would do well to establish their own statement of purpose (often codified as a board charter statement) and define their role in a way that adds value to the company's activities. Boards need to reflect regularly on their involvement and strive to make it firstly distinctive, so that they do not replicate the efforts of other parts of the organisation; and secondly additive, whereby the board builds upon decisions made by the firm.

Well-focused boards know how to distinguish between contexts. From there, they determine whether they should perform a supervisory role or rather offer support or challenge to management. Such boards are ready to be proactive and jump into pre-emptive action when they see signs of risk and recognise that oversight is needed. In other situations, such as during a crisis when the organisation's reputation is at stake, they are just as efficient in identifying and acting on the need to communicate the firm's strategic objectives. In addition, a board's focus can be strengthened by having the right agenda: one that looks more towards the future than the past, and that aims to capture long-term issues while managing short-term matters.

But even high-quality, focused boards will underperform if their members are not fully dedicated to their work and to the organisation. Directors frequently tell me that their board meeting discussions reflect a level of preparation that was 'basic' and 'not in great depth'. A minority of them do report rich and diverse preparation, where board members have diligently read the relevant documentation and obtained external information where necessary. But all too many describe the board members in their organisations as typically 'not very well prepared'. The percentage of directors who have regularly witnessed great preparation for board meetings, with members actively consulting outside sources and analysing information in depth, is in fact small.

A similar picture emerges when we ask board members how many hours of preparation time one hour of a board meeting requires from each director. Typically, more than half of them estimate one to three hours of preparation, around 25% report three to seven hours, and only a minority report seven to ten hours. It is rare to hear of directors spending more than 10 hours preparing for each hour of a board meeting. Worryingly, in fact, a few say that less than one hour of preparation time is required – even though most responsible individuals believe that a director should not sit on more than five boards at once anyway. If five boards are like a full-time commitment, doesn't this mean that one day a week per board is what is needed?

A director's sense of dedication should entail precisely what the word implies: giving freely of one's self, and not just because of the high-powered networking, access to industry information, and higher social status and income that come with the position. And, indeed, there are many directors whose main motivation for joining a board is their desire to contribute to the company's success, and who consider it an honour to serve in this capacity. These are the types of dedicated individuals that boards need to attract and empower: people of integrity, character, and conviction who are ready to speak up and voice their concerns for the greater good of the organisation.

The Second Pillar: Information Architecture

Sophisticated information architecture is key to successful boards. Although this design does not necessarily need to be complex, it should inform the board about all the company's essential activities and the issues facing it, both now and in the future. When considering information design, directors should have three rules of thumb.

First, board members should have as much information on external issues as they do on internal matters. Boards typically think of information as coming from management. Ideally, this will be brief, well-focused, prioritised, and strategic, with executive summaries, key issues to tackle, and options to consider. But directors should also be fully informed regarding external issues, such as reputation analysis, the competitive landscape, customer knowledge, an understanding of shareholders, and technological evolution. Often, however, this is not the case, resulting in boards that do little more than go through the motions. Clearly, there is significant room for improvement. This is highly strategic as boards indeed try to engage more productively on strategy matters, and thus more forward-looking and external-oriented board packages become the standard of quality governance.

Second, directors should have both formal and informal information channels. Formal internal information should be jointly designed by the board and management, with briefings that include financials with forecasts, a CEO report, risk and opportunity maps, analysis of the management gene pool, and a summary of financial analysts' views. In addition, regular communication between management and the board, for example via management letters between meetings, provides further efficient and timely information. Board committee reports are also fundamental in building the depth of knowledge required by directors in specific areas – as long as such reports include analysis of the issues and not just recommendations. It is critical that the board is actively involved in designing the information, including whether that design should change along with the firm, its environment, and its strategy.

At the same time, informal channels of information are key, and need to be cultivated. These channels should be diverse and well-structured, giving board members access to employees and stakeholder networks, links to fellow directors outside board meetings, and connections with management. This might be through a Sunday afternoon barbecue, a coffee during the week, or an early evening call, depending on the board member. Such interactions must strike the right balance, providing board members with greater freedom and inspiration without infringing on management's role.

Third, dedicated directors should aim to receive as much information from independent sources as they do from management. Rather than relying solely on management information, these board members see it as their duty to track down the most useful social media posts, market information, and other sources.

The Third Pillar: Structures and Processes

As governance becomes more sophisticated, its structures have likewise evolved greatly. Board effectiveness is hugely influenced by the quality of the structures and processes organised by the board secretariat and steered by the chair. It is imperative that boards regularly benchmark these against the ideal situation and act to address any divergence.

In the most basic structural terms, the size of the board should be carefully examined, in addition to the necessary number and effective functioning of board committees. The main goal is to ensure that the board's committee structure is pertinent to the current reality of the organisation. There are a number of innovative and inspiring examples in this regard. HSBC had a committee on Financial System Vulnerabilities, which addressed one of the primary strategic issues in banking. It now has a Technology committee, just as essential and now prioritised. In addition, board Innovation committees are becoming increasingly common at companies operating in industries at high risk of disruption. Some time they combine with Technology. Both Procter & Gamble – a global giant in fast-moving consumer goods – and UK-based bank RBS have a Technology and Innovation Committee on their respective boards, for example. Finally, some companies are creating Geopolitical or other topical committees of importance to their success.

As mentioned earlier, beyond its structural 'hardware', a board should radiate a well-managed diversity of personality, experience, gender, and opinion. The independence of board members is crucial too – but so is their structured access to the right individuals. For example, in some organisations the chief risk officer has a dotted reporting line to the chair of the risk committee, or to the chair of the board.

Along with structures, a number of processes need to be in place to ensure that the board systematically addresses the issues within its remit. The list of processes that truly matter includes agenda setting, reviewing and monitoring management performance, CEO succession, stakeholder engagement, audit, regulatory compliance, risk, strategy, ongoing board improvement, and many others.

A strong board will integrate these processes smoothly within its yearly agenda. Below, we briefly discuss four of them: strategy, agenda setting, evaluation, and CEO succession. We then examine board structures and processes more closely in Chapter 6 and other parts of the book.

The board's strategy process is critical to increasing its effectiveness. Strategic board involvement occurs along three dimensions – co-creation, supervision, and support – and good processes will enrich all three. Typically, regular board meetings will complement retreats, and external presentations will add to internal ones. Focused, decision-oriented meetings will complement boards' long-term strategic understanding of the company and its industry. A well-designed board strategy process strengthens the firm's strategy by helping to define it, aligning it with objectives and ensuring commitment. Ultimately, this enables boards to efficiently assess the company's strategic risks and opportunities. We will discuss the board's strategic role in more detail in Chapter 21.

Setting the agenda is another key board process. This necessarily involves a number of balancing acts, such as board-management interaction, consideration of stakeholder issues, clear prioritisation, a focus on key issues, and time management. A strong agenda-setting process will be both strategic, by providing a high-level setting for the following two years, and tactical, by ensuring the board spends its time on the most critical issues.

A third decisive process is board evaluation. When directors are not performing to the standards set by the board, they need to receive feedback clearly indicating this. A poor evaluation process contributes to governance failure, which is why thriving boards engage in a formal assessment procedure. This might be self-assessment or external assessment, and should cover individual directors' roles, dynamics, and performance. A good practice is to utilise technology. Using smartphones or tablets to evaluate board sessions during meetings, for example, provides results in real time and offers an opportunity for careful and dynamic scrutiny in between annual evaluations.

Finally, CEO succession is a critical process that requires ongoing attention and planning. Whether based on an internal or external 'horse race' or search, the process of identifying leadership talent and candidates should focus on the transparency of selection criteria, the fit with the organisation, the quality of the on-boarding process, and the smoothness of the transition.

Hewlett-Packard (HP) provides a good example of difficult successions creating real governance risk. In a period of six years, HP fired three CEOs, resulting in corporate turmoil that negatively affected the company's brand reputation. In one of the cases, the HP board did not meet the new CEO before proceeding with the nomination. This raises questions regarding the process in place, and the implied failure of the board to identify a candidate who would fulfil the company's strategic vision.

The Fourth Pillar: Group Dynamics and Board Culture

The three board effectiveness pillars we have examined so far include focused, dedicated people accessing different types of information and applying this to increasingly sophisticated structures and processes. In keeping with this strongly social, people-centric snapshot, the dynamics within this group of people constitute the final pillar in our edifice. This pillar concerns how board members interact as a group, and what they individually bring to and collectively take away from their discussions. Over time, these dynamics give rise to a specific board culture: a set of customs, practices, and often unspoken rules about 'how we get things done around here'.

As with any group, it sometimes doesn't take much for a board to go down the path of inefficiency and dysfunction. Sleepy, low-energy boards are sadly quite common. And in some cases, dysfunctional dynamics are intentionally used to set a board up for governance failure – for example, through late distribution of meeting documents and not making relevant information available. But some of the more benign board pathologies can be just as destructive. These include the presence of disruptive or dominating members on the board, or a tendency to group-think, where board members avoid any paths less travelled in an effort to ingratiate themselves with the group.

These dysfunctions are often symptoms of a deeper issue, such as a lack of trust or overlapping roles. Governance is enriched by directors' different opinions and constructive dissent; having a critical view of assumptions makes for an effective strategy. Yet some firms appoint directors who are close associates of the company's founder or CEO. They may be prominent figures in their respective industries, but their role on the board is circumscribed by their relationship with a dominant figure in the company.

Interactions between the board and senior management are an important aspect of this pillar. BlackBerry (formerly Research in Motion) once thrived on the long-running partnership and friendship of its two co-CEOs. Once they stepped aside, deep divisions surfaced within the company and the board regarding its flagship product, key technology alliance, and planned China expansion, with the new CEO actively canvassing behind the scenes to kill off some of these flagship initiatives. BlackBerry's share price then plummeted, and its product offerings were considered late to market.

Although conflict is important for an open exchange of views, boards are more effective when discussions remain productive. This can only be achieved if a board makes its rules of engagement clear to all its members and promotes their equal participation and mutual respect. Functional board dynamics can help to avoid conflicts of interest, especially if the board culture emphasises accountability towards relevant stakeholders and is based on openness and constructive dissent (see also Chapter 13). And a culture that ensures board members are connected to reality also reduces the likelihood of them being overconfident.

The chair's role is key in developing a successful board culture. This can be partly formalised in writing in order to be easily shared and understood. An awareness of discussion styles (such as fast thinking, influencing, and the 'false yes') and decision styles (whether autocratic, consensual, or indecisive) is similarly essential in managing group dynamics. We will look at these in more detail in Chapter 7.

Even more fundamentally, boards are now increasingly discussing their common values, and the level of stewardship they want to provide to the organisation. Do board members share the same long-term perspectives? Do they have a common view of their contributions to society, and of their impact on employees, customers, and other stakeholders? This will form the focus of Chapters 20 and 32.

Board effectiveness requires constantly sustaining the four pillars we discussed in this chapter. A board cannot neglect the quality, focus, and dedication of its members. Information architecture needs to be carefully designed in order to optimise its effectiveness. Successful boards continuously improve their structures and work processes as they become more sophisticated. Finally, effective board dynamics, based on a culture that promotes quality discussion, greatly contribute to the strategic coherence of the firm.

Excellence in these areas makes for sustainable success in board practices. Although the four pillars do not constitute a foolproof guarantee against board or company failures, they provide a solid foundation for good governance and help to make organisations more resilient. And as we will see in Chapter 2, good governance is becoming increasingly vital around the world.

CHAPTER

2

Governance Challenges around the World

Governance is the ability to take the right decisions at the top of organisations, and it is fast becoming a competitive differentiator and a driver of performance. In an increasingly chaotic, rapidly changing environment, good governance is vital to giving organisations the wherewithal to make the right choices and the resilience they need to withstand shocks. Governance drives organisations' efficiency, integrity, and social impact, all of which are necessary for sustainable success. Yet there are numerous examples of poor governance, around the world and well into the twenty-first century, in the corporate, public, non-governmental, and inter-governmental domains.

The case of Volkswagen (VW) shows how a rift between the chair and CEO can result in major governance failures. In April 2015, VW Chair Ferdinand Karl Piëch, the 78-year-old grandson of Ferdinand Porsche (who founded Porsche), made the following comment to *Der Spiegel* – online – without forewarning the board: 'I am distancing myself from [VW CEO Martin] Winterkorn.' This caused tension among the board members, who began to speculate whether it would be the chair or the CEO leaving the company. VW's executive committee (as well as supervisory board member Wolfgang Porsche, also a grandson of Ferdinand) urged Piëch to soften his statement, and publicly reiterate his support for Winterkorn. Piëch agreed – allegedly on the condition that the committee recommend that he once again be elected chair of VW's supervisory board when his contract expired in April 2017.

Winterkorn, the company's CEO since 2007, had joined VW subsidiary Audi in the 1980s and had been hand-picked by Piëch, himself a former VW CEO. Piëch initially batted away suggestions that his wife Ursula might replace him at the head of the supervisory board, saying that the position was earmarked for somebody with an engineering background. A panel of six board members that had been established during the crisis concluded that 'in the light of the past weeks, the mutual trust necessary for successful cooperation was no longer there'. Piëch, a representative of the family controlling 52% of VW shareholder votes, resigned from the supervisory board and was replaced by an interim chair.

This infighting was a red flag that foreshadowed the subsequent governance failure at VW. It also revealed the very human side of governance, with the frailties and flaws of the individuals involved.

Later in 2015, the cover up of VW's diesel emissions scandal was made public. The company had installed software in engines just so that they could pass laboratory emissions tests – a practice orchestrated at very senior levels of the organisation. The head of VW's US compliance team, Oliver Schmidt, had briefed executive management about the software in July 2015, and told them that US regulators were not aware of it. But he had been instructed to persist in the deception. NGOs in Europe and then in the United States had suspected the problem much earlier than that, and it was apparently known about within VW for probably two years. The scandal led to an investigation and estimated costs of US$18 billion. According to Alexander Juschus, director at German proxy advisor IVOX, 'The scandal clearly also has to do with structural issues at VW . . . There have been warnings about VW's corporate governance for years, but they didn't take it to heart and now you see the result.'[1]

By 2020, the emissions scandal had cost VW over US$30 billion. In addition, the US Department of Justice had appointed Larry D. Thompson, a former US Attorney General who worked on the prosecutions of Enron executives, to monitor the company. According to the VW website, Thompson would ensure that the Volkswagen Group was fulfilling the conditions of the company's settlement agreement with the US government. These include compliance-enhancing measures, reporting and monitoring mechanisms, and the implementation of an enhanced compliance and ethics programme at the company. Thompson would also be tasked with certifying that VW's compliance programme was able to detect issues such as that involving diesel emissions, and to prevent anything similar from happening again.

In 1920, the average lifespan of a company in the S&P 500 Index was 67 years – longer than average human life expectancy, which then stood at 54 years. But by 2021, things looked dramatically different. Whereas people's life expectancy had increased from 54 to 76, the average lifespan of S&P companies had fallen to just 15–20 years.[2]

---

[1] Bryant, C. and R. Milne (2015). Boardroom Politics at Heart of VW Scandal. *Financial Times* (4 October 2015). https://www.ft.com/content/e816cf86-6815-11e5-a57f-21b88f7d973f
[2] The calculation and methodology is given by Innosight in the 'Corporate Longevity Forecast' available on https://www.innosight.com/wp-content/uploads/2021/05/Innosight_2021-Corporate-Longevity-Forecast.pdf

There are of course much older businesses, some of them hundreds of years old, or even a thousand years in a small number of cases. But many of them are small businesses facing few competitive challenges, such as hotels, wineries, or funeral homes. By contrast, global firms that are more than 300 or 400 years old are extremely rare.

The strong process of natural selection in the business world has spread to NGOs – and possibly to government bodies as well. That process of natural selection is probably at the heart of the success of the capitalistic market system. And in that world of accelerated natural selection, modern governance has become crucial to long-term success.

Scientific Lessons from Natural Selection

Older companies tend to underperform. In order for a company to survive and actually thrive in the long term, it must apply the Darwinian principles of variation, selection, and replication. Just like in the natural world, the most successful firms evolve constantly to adapt to changing conditions, while those that fail to do so become extinct.

It is worth considering variation and replication in a governance context due to the many different models around the world. In terms of ownership structure, for example: there are publicly traded companies; family-, private-equity-, and government-owned firms; non-profits; and members' associations.

One interesting case is how the Communist Party of China governs the country's state-owned assets, and in particular its publicly listed state financial institutions, through the sovereign wealth fund community interest company (CIC) and its dedicated division, Huijin. CIC has developed governance practices that might be useful for large, complex organisations elsewhere. These include having full-time non-executive directors in parallel to Western-style independent directors, and strongly aligning perspectives in the governance of holding groups and subsidiaries. It might well be an inspiration in other parts of the world from a technical governance standpoint, and beyond the political dimension. For example, is it possible that large global financial institutions have become too complex to be governed by part-time independent directors mostly and would professional full-time board members make sense?

Yet the global focus on excellence in governance has only been possible because of earlier success in other important areas: administration, management, and leadership. High-quality administration was developed and systematised as early as the eighteenth century by organisations such as the East India Company. Then quality management to ensure efficiency and better results was systematised in the first part of the twentieth century by business leaders such as Alfred Sloan and Henry Ford. Business schools were then established to educate leaders in management. The second part of the twentieth century saw the systematisation and theorisation of leadership – the ability to engage and energise people at a higher level – through theories developed in the 1970s.

Today, organisations need to go to the next level. Moving from A to B, and energising people towards achieving this result, requires organisations to develop the ability to choose the right objectives and make the right decisions. And this is the essence of governance. With public trust in corporations and leaders at an all-time low, quality governance will be one of the competitive advantages of the future.

At the same time, governance successes and failures stem from the reliance on leadership within organisations.

What is Transformational Leadership?

Of the many types of leadership that have emerged over the past century, transformational leadership is one of the most recent. In the 1970s, James MacGregor Burns defined this in both a political and business context as leadership that enables leaders and followers to raise one another to higher levels of motivation and morality. The more active such leadership is, the more effective it is (Figure 2.1).

In general, transformational leaders:

- empower followers and nurture them through change;
- become a strong model for their followers;

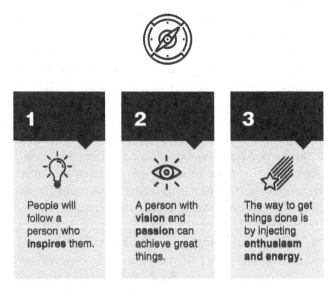

Figure 2.1   Transformational Leadership Principles

- create a vision for the organisation;
- act as change agents for a new direction within the organisation; and
- become social architects.

Should We Trust Leaders?

The transformational leadership model relies strongly on trust, and in particular on employees trusting their leaders. Yet many inspiring and transformative leaders have changed their organisations for the worse instead of for the better. And trust in leaders has been affected by a string of events that have negatively impacted many people's lives and well-being.

One example is the nuclear leak in 2011 at the Fukushima plant of the Tokyo Electric Power Company (TEPCO). Back in 2007, an earthquake had caused a small nuclear leak, and the company's president, Tsunehisa Katsumata, was asked to retire. However, Katsumata then became chair of TEPCO, despite his previous failure to adequately manage this risk.

Another case concerns Chinese company Sanlu, which raised protein levels in baby milk by using chemicals including melamine. The firm's top management was aware of this and informed the board, which included directors from New Zealand. Hundreds of thousands of babies were affected, and Sanlu's board voted to recall all the products in question. However, because the crisis happened just before the 2008 Beijing Olympic Games, the company's chair at the time reversed the board's decision in an attempt not to harm China's reputation. Six babies subsequently died after consuming the milk. After being informed by the New Zealand government, the Chinese authorities intervened. At the time of writing, the chair is in jail and the company no longer exists.

Many other large organisations have been hit by scandals related to governance risk in recent years: Boeing, OpenAI, Wirecard, Goldman Sachs, BP, and Oxfam, to name just a few.

Little wonder, then, that many people are increasingly reluctant to trust government leaders and their decisions. According to the Edelman Trust Barometer, the public has grown more distrustful and sceptical of institutions. Nearly one in three don't trust government leaders. With growing polarisation, employers are becoming the only trusted institution – with over two-thirds saying their CEO is their most trusted institutional leader (as compared with only 41% placing their trust in government leaders.[3]

In addition, economic shifts mean that leaders' unwise decisions can now hurt their organisations even more than previously. The market value

---

[3] See the Edelman Trust Barometer: https://www.edelman.com/trust/2023/trust-barometer

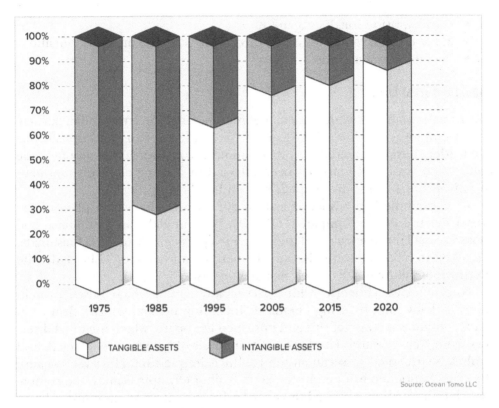

Figure 2.2   Components of S&P 500 Market Value
Source: Ocean Tomo LLC.

of companies is mostly based on intangible assets such as knowledge, good-will, brand, and R&D (Figure 2.2). The quality of decision-making at the top is therefore critical. Intangible assets are typically more sensitive to decision-making than tangible, hard assets are.

The Governance DNA

Corporate governance requires a balance in decision-making between different bodies in order to provide a good counterweight to leadership. The governance DNA entails balancing decision-making power between an organisation's leader, board, and owners at the heart of the triangle (Figure 2.3) and ensuring the quality of decision-making through the participation of all three parties. Any decision that is taken at one corner of the triangle, in isolation from the others, is an example of poor governance. Decisions should ideally be located at the triangle's centre of gravity.

Another principle of governance effectiveness is clarity of roles. The board sets the tone, culture, and objectives; it often chooses the leadership team;

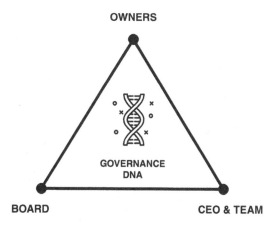

Figure 2.3   The Governance DNA

and it aims to ensure objectives are reached by supervising and supporting the team in place. There are differences in the board's role, of course. In Germany and Holland, for example, the two-tier board system may give more decision power to the management board on strategy (although this gets challenged today for quality governance). In China, the boards of state-owned enterprises do not select the leadership team. Rather, this is the job of the Central Organisation Department, the HR arm of the Communist Party, which also nominates key government leaders including ministers. But even in this environment, balance is key to quality business decision-making, and with clarity of roles, is the essential element of governance. In Scandinavia, we see external board nomination committees, themselves constituted by shareholders, rather than internal nomination committees. And in the United States, the board's chair often has an executive role, which also pushes for a different role to the non-executive board, in terms of oversight and challenge. So across the world, different contexts drive different forms of governance, and some fine-tuning on the role of the board, but the underlying forces to quality governance remain the same.

Good decision-making at the top is the key to governance success, and the underlying force beneath the four pillars. And a strong dialectic process, an exchange of views by dedicated, well-informed, knowledgeable individuals with differentiated perspectives is the fundamental engine of governance. The integrity of decisions is therefore particularly important. This can be reinforced by board members' independence, as well as by overcoming the various conflicts of interest that arise naturally in an organisational context. Diversity, having an open mind, and being able to combine a range of views around key topics are vital for quality organisational decision-making in many contexts. But there is much more to a successful director than that. And this is what we explore in the next chapter.

3

The Successful Director: Values and Character

Board decisions concern large amounts of resources, and impact people within the organisation as well as external stakeholders. This means board directors wield tremendous power. It is key, therefore, that they adhere to a culture underpinned by fundamental values. In turn, they need to uphold board values, and ensure that their behaviour reinforces the board culture.

Along with their power, board members must accept and embrace their responsibility toward the company they serve. This requires having total clarity regarding their role, and the conscientiousness to perform it to the full. Directors need to acknowledge that the board has a duty to oversee the organisation's success. It must also supervise risks that are important for the organisation and impact employees and their families, customers, and society as a whole, often into the next generation.

Accountability is another key value. Board members must be prepared to explain and justify decisions that have been taken, and to be answerable to the company's stakeholders. Being a board director also requires moral authority – the adherence to a set of principles founded on a correct course of action.

Finally, while diverse opinions and constructive dissent need to be heard in the boardroom, it is essential that directors embrace the 'one-voice principle' once a decision has been taken. In other words, they must fully respect the decision and support it within and outside the boardroom. This voice is usually expressed by the chair (although it may not necessarily represent his or her private views).

A board's values set expectations regarding directors' behaviour, and also define what is unacceptable in this regard. Directors should demonstrate independence and integrity, and be committed to enhancing their own knowledge through external support and continuous education. Discussions should be characterised by equal participation and mutual respect, as well as openness and constructive dissent. Zero tolerance for imprudent, unlawful, or unethical behaviour must also be embedded in board culture (see Figure 3.1).

Specific expectations regarding a board member's contributions and responsibilities may vary, partly depending on whether he or she is an executive director, independent director, or a shareholder or employee representative. An independent director of a publicly traded company has different responsibilities to an owner representative and full-time employee on the board of an oil and gas joint venture, for example.

Nonetheless, all directors need to successfully fulfil their three mandates: the duty of care, whereby they undertake their role and responsibility with care, diligence, judgement, and skill; the duty of loyalty, or putting the interests of the company and its shareholders ahead of their own; and the duty of compliance (or obedience) or ensuring that the organisation's actions align with its mission and comply with the law. Board members therefore need a combination of core attributes, including relevant skills and competence, a detailed knowledge of their legal responsibilities, and dedication and focus.

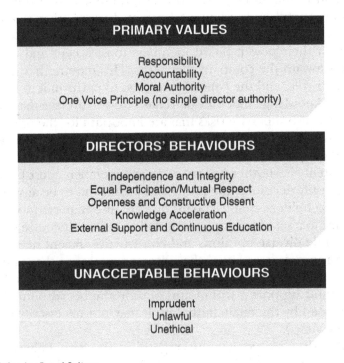

Figure 3.1   Reinforcing Board Culture

Duty of Care

Good judgement is essential for directors to fulfil their duty of care. When this is lacking, the quality of decision-making suffers. Judgement comes from knowledge and intuition, both of which can be improved.

First, individuals must have the necessary knowledge – acquired through education and experience – to make good, considered decisions. Education gives us the technical knowledge to understand complex problems. Curiosity helps individuals to complement their formal education and continue learning, thereby enabling access to a memory bank of information and details that may be relevant to the present.

People also use their individual experiences to draw lessons from the past and apply them to the future, in an integrative process. In some situations, either weak signals or true shocks may prompt us to realise that our knowledge is insufficient, and that we require additional input to evaluate situations effectively.

Specifically, a board member develops an integrative view – in terms of the executive world, he or she may generally put a premium on analysis, when in fact it is synthesis that is badly needed in many contexts. Because a board needs to address many stakeholders toward the long term and the next generation, a certain skill in deriving the essential from many pieces of information is key to board quality.

Intuition is the second key driver of good judgement and depends on individual personality and values. According to the Swiss psychologist Carl Jung, personality consists of both the ego – how we identify ourselves – and the unconscious or shadow side that we are not aware of and have suppressed early in life.

Emotions play an important role in intuition. They affect how we respond to crises, for example, whether we remain calm and hopeful, or suffer anxiety and panic. The other component of intuition is values. These are drawn from our sense of ethics – the moral principles that govern our behaviour – as well as individual integrity. Good judgement is a function of the interplay between internal variables and external factors, summarised in Figure 3.2.

For experienced and well-prepared board members, good judgement often materialises as a well-informed 'gut feeling', or right intuition. This in turn comes from lengthy preparation, going through the right materials, having the right balance, not putting too much ego into the discussions and decisions, being aware of one's weaknesses, and having both the right ethical values and the integrity to withstand pressure. All this feeds into discussions among peers in a confidential and protected setting that result in a collective board decision.

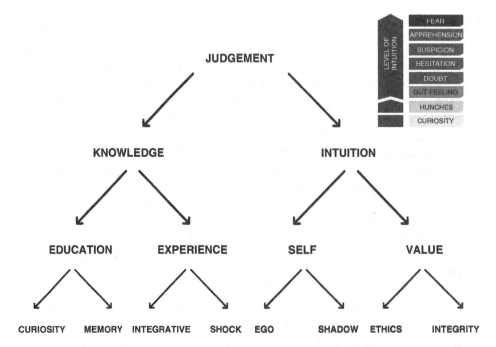

Figure 3.2   The Roots of Good Judgement: Mapping One's Strengths and Weaknesses

Good judgement is especially important today, as boards face increasing external pressures and may have to deal with crises that challenge their decision-making skills. We will discuss crisis management in more detail in Chapter 12.

Duty of Loyalty

Conflicts of interest are rampant in today's world. They arise when directors lose impartiality because of either material interest or a conflict of roles. When directors are in a position that may benefit them, or someone close to them, in any way, then they can no longer make impartial decisions; this is a material conflict of interest. A conflict may also result from one director having different roles, so that their obligations to one company are compromised by those to another. Directors who sit on multiple boards may therefore have a potential conflict if two of these organisations form any kind of relationship.

Another source of conflict is self-interest. When directors focus primarily on maintaining their position, comfort, and income rather than on what is best for the company, they are likely to be highly biased. They may also become compliant and not wish to be unpopular. Again, they lose their impartiality.

Sometimes directors fail to acknowledge conflicts of interest – even to themselves. It is critical that directors think about this honestly, because it has a direct impact on board service. All of us are conflicted, and figuring out these conflicts is part of our duty. We explore the four tiers of conflicts of interest facing boards in Chapter 13. A good rule of thumb is for board members to have a list of their own conflicts of interest: time, money, effort, friends, relationships, financial interests, reputation, social network, and more.

Duty of Compliance (or Obedience)

Board members are also safeguards of the organisational mission. As such they have a duty to ensure that the organisation's activities are well aligned with the organisation's mission. As board members review information, initiatives, investments, and are confronted with decisions, they can be guided by the question: how does this advance the organisational mission?

Central to this responsibility is monitoring the compliance of organisational activities within the applicable legal and regulatory framework. This requires that they stay abreast of all legal and regulatory changes that may impact the organisation's compliance obligations, that they have the right oversight mechanisms in place to prevent unauthorised activities. It also means that board members need to hold themselves and the management to high ethical standards – and to conduct thorough due diligence and investigation in cases of reported misconduct.

Exercising duty of care requires a board with a healthy distance from management, sufficient expertise and diversity, a strong foundation in the organisational values and that take seriously matters of integrity.

Integrity: A Key Characteristic of Board Directors

Directors need to know what is right and have the courage to stand up for it. They also need clarity about their role. In times of crisis, confusion may obscure the right course of action, making individuals vulnerable to mental biases. But board members with integrity devote themselves to doing the job for which they were hired, and conscientiously equip themselves with the necessary knowledge and skills. As such, integrity is a keystone of successful directorship.

For some, integrity means fully adopting the values one believes are right. This requires authentic deliberation about individual values through deep personal reflection, rather than a simple acceptance of social norms. Maintaining integrity means being able to resist engaging in self-deception about whether individual actions are the logical outcome of personal values or some other force (such as fulfilling psychological needs).

Another definition of integrity is the ability to be clear about the boundaries of what is acceptable, and the commitment to stand by these regardless of the consequences. In other words, integrity is the way in which individuals support projects and then loyally commit to them. This is the case with artistic integrity, for example, when artists demonstrate loyalty to their vision and pursue their path, rather than conforming to what others think is right or acceptable or commercially valuable.

There is also a social dimension to integrity.[1] Having integrity means not only standing up for what you believe and defending it, but also recognising that others have their own judgements and convictions. Bullying and coercion are therefore antithetical to integrity, whereas compromise and ambivalence might not be.

Table 3.1 summarises the key behaviours of successful directors.

Table 3.1 Behaviours of Successful Directors – A Checklist

Independence and Integrity
1. Do I say what I mean and mean what I say?
2. Do I speak up when I fundamentally disagree with what someone has said – even if it may result in confrontation or ridicule?
3. Am I clear about my role and legal responsibility as a director? Can I clearly and simply articulate my mandate and responsibility?
4. How do I demonstrate accountability as a director?
5. How do I feel about holding other directors accountable?
6. Am I clear on what personal moral and ethical boundaries I will not cross, no matter what the consequences?
7. Do I feel that I bring a fresh perspective to discussions, a different viewpoint or knowledge set to the other directors?

Equal Participation/Mutual Respect
1. Do I contribute to the best of my ability in the boardroom?
2. How curious am I about the company, what it does? How much time do I spend asking questions and seeking answers to these questions?
3. Do I actively listen to others' contributions and respect their opinion, even if it is very different to mine?
4. Can I understand the perspective of others – even if I don't agree with them?

Openness and Constructive Dissent
1. Am I willing to express my viewpoint, even if I know it will be unpopular?
2. Am I able to land sharp remarks in a positive and respectful way?
3. Are there times when I hold back, due to a fear of how I may be perceived by the other directors?
4. How do I ensure that I am not simply conforming with the group, but checking that my evaluation of issues is sound?
5. How do I feel when others challenge my view?
6. How actively do I challenge others' perspective and underlying assumptions?

Critical Thinking and Framing
1. How do I ensure I am not falling prey to my own biases?
2. Do I consistently reframe decisions presented in relative terms in absolute terms?
3. Do I fear someone or something on this board?

Conflicts of Interest
1. Have I thoroughly considered my different business relationships and roles and how they influence one another (if at all)?
2. How important is the income and status of this board seat? Does it affect my willingness to speak up?

Knowledge Acceleration
1. Do I seek external support when I feel that I need more knowledge in a certain area?
2. How do I ensure that I continue to educate myself on topics that enable me to make an effective contribution, including professional service?
3. Do I actively seek feedback from the Chair or other directors as to my knowledge and competence – and fill in necessary gaps?
4. Do I have a firm grasp on the corporate governance code, pertinent regulations, and social expectation?
5. Do I meet with key stakeholders?
6. Do I regularly meet with other directors, beyond board meetings?

---

[1] Calhoun, C. (1995). Standing for something. *The Journal of Philosophy* 92(5): 235–260. https://www.jstor.org/stable/2940917

Board members' specific legal responsibilities depend on the nature of the organisation and the jurisdiction within which the board operates. But clearly, successful directors need to have good judgement and the integrity to stand by what they believe. During crises, directors need to rise to the occasion, simplify the situation, and have the courage to do what is right.

We will return to the subject of board leadership and values in Chapter 15. But now we will look more closely at the first pillar of a board's effectiveness: people quality, focus, and dedication.

CHAPTER

4

The First Pillar: People Quality, Diversity, Focus, and Dedication

The quality, diversity, focus, and dedication of board members is critical. Directors need to be committed, competent, and qualified, possessing both the expertise and the willingness to contribute. A board that lacks the right composition, does not focus on the most important issues, or whose directors are insufficiently dedicated, is at risk of major failure.

A case in point is the Toshiba accounting scandal, where individual and institutional corruption at the 140 year old Japanese electronics conglomerate went undetected by its board of directors.

Quality and Diversity

Expertise and competence are essential attributes of any high-quality board (Table 4.1). In this regard, skill maps are a useful tool for not only assessing the range of competencies of the current directors but also for specifying the skills, attributes, and even personalities required for effective board work – and for addressing any gaps between the board's current and ideal composition. The fit between the skillset of each member and the board's requirements is what counts. There is no ideal skill map, and typically it should extend beyond professional experience to include personal attributes and personality traits, as exemplified in Table 4.2 at the end of the chapter.

Diversity – of industry, professional background, gender, ethnic background, age, personality, and opinion – also improves the quality of board decisions, in particular when creativity and innovation are required, or simply to overcome blind spots. By bringing in a range of specific types of expertise, diversity can enhance the board's ability to consider different solutions and reframe issues.

Case study: The Toshiba Accounting Scandal

In December 2023, Toshiba ended its 74-year history as a publicly listed company with a US$14 billion leveraged buyout by Japanese Industrial Partners (JIP). This was the conclusion of eight years of turmoil, which started with a major accounting scandal. In 2015, Toshiba admitted to accounting irregularities which had been used to inflate its profits by 151.8 billion yen (US$1.22 billion) between 2008 and 2014. This overstatement represented approximately one-third of Toshiba's pre-tax profits during the period. The revelations, which came just six weeks after the introduction of a corporate governance code in Japan, were a surprise to many because Toshiba had long been lauded for its ethical culture and corporate governance practices. In the early 2000s, the company had hired outside directors and moved to a 16-member board. The company's governance structure was compliant on paper, but competencies and culture were not adequate – as the accounting scandal showed.

Toshiba established an external committee to probe the fraudulent accounting. Its report found that the company's problems resulted from top executives putting intense pressure on subordinates to meet increasingly difficult profit goals, even as demand for Toshiba's products fell during the 2008 global financial crisis. Pressure from senior management often came before the end of a quarter or fiscal year, which may have pushed lower-level employees to postpone losses, push forward sales, and understate costs on long-term projects. Toshiba's auditor, Ernst & Young ShinNihon LLC, failed to detect the improper accounting practices.

The report found that Toshiba's three most recent CEOs were complicit in inflating the company's operating profit. In the wake of the scandal, chief executive Hisao Tanaka immediately resigned. The two previous CEOs, Atsutoshi Nishida (2005–2009) and Norio Sasaki (2009–2013), were forced to resign from the positions that they retained at the company. In total, 8 of the 16 board members resigned.

After the scandal was exposed, Toshiba cut thousands of jobs and sold off its major businesses, such as laptop computers, semiconductors, medical equipment, and consumer-electronics.

Continuing to reel from these events, Toshiba cut its workforce further and continued to spin off troubled assets during the following years. In the aftermath of the delisting, Toshiba retained its CEO, Taro Shimada, while JIP placed members on the board.

Diversity in terms of personality is important on a board, but can be uncomfortable. (One instrument for understanding differences in personality is the NEO-PI Figure 4.1 which we discuss in greater detail in a later chapter on diversity.) Gender diversity is key; boards with more women are likely to explicitly identify criteria for measuring strategy, monitoring its implementation,

Table 4.1 Traditional Board Competencies (Rating from 1 to 10, With 10 Full Expertise and 7 Proficiency)

	DIRECTOR									CANDIDATE				
	1	2	3	4	5	6	7	8	9	1	2	3	4	5
Experience/skill														
Accounting/financial expert														
Governance experience														
Strategic planning														
Innovation and technology														
Digitalisation														
Partnering experience														
Value creation														
Regional experience														
Business transformation														
Prior audit committee experience														
Prior nomination committee experience														
Other committees														
Industry experience														
Investments														
Capital formation														
Capital markets														
Financial services														
Information technology														
Legal and regulatory compliance														
Asset management														
Risk management														
Securities analysis														
Joint venture management														
Human resources														
Cross-cultural experience														
Geopolitics														
Turnaround experience														
Other outliers as required														

Sources: Multiple discussions.

and developing and monitoring a code of conduct, for example.[1] However, poorly managed diversity can sometimes lead to communication difficulties and decreased trust, which are disruptive. Boards therefore need to develop processes to leverage and manage diversity well. We explore how to achieve effective diversity in Chapter 19.

Focus

Even an excellently composed board will underperform if it does not focus on the most important issues. Because their time is limited, boards need to be strategic about their work for the organisation. This means figuring out what matters most, rather than simply having a pre-cooked agenda meeting after meeting. Relying on the charter's definition of the role of the board is therefore not enough. In fact, being proactive in defining the board's role can help directors decide on their priorities. The ability of board members to understand clearly the role of the board in the organisational context, to focus on the right issues, and to prioritise is crucial.

Figure 4.1,[2] which is based on the board of a sovereign wealth fund, outlines the classical roles of the board and the nature of its corresponding

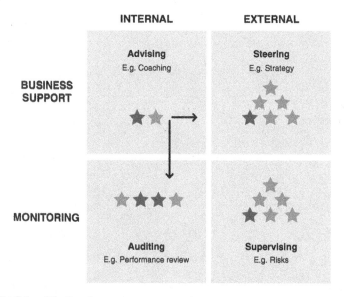

Figure 4.1   The Roles of the Board
Source: Adapted from Strebel (2004)

---

[1] See, for example, Terjesen, S., R. Sealy, and V. Singh (2009). Women directors on corporate boards: a review and research agenda. *Corporate Governance: An International Review* 17(3): 320–337. There is of course a large literature on the topic.
[2] This very useful process for determining board focus is adapted from Paul Strebel (2004). The case for contingent governance. *MIT Sloan Management Review* 45(2): 59–66.

involvement. In general, a board may concentrate more on internal or external issues. Many boards that used to be highly focused on internal matters, including audit and performance review, now spend more time addressing external issues such as regulatory trends and geopolitics. Another dimension to consider is whether the board's primary task is to support the success of management, or to supervise and monitor it. This will depend on the maturity of the management as well as the context of the organisation.

Boards need to achieve on all fronts, of course, but because of time constraints will prioritise what matters most to the organisation. Often, board members will have different views in this regard. By working along a graph like the one shown in Figure 4.1, they can understand their differences and build alignment. In Figure 4.1, members of one board – including three government ministers and other leading chairpersons – put a star in the quadrant they saw as the board's top priority and possibly a second star in their second priority. The exercise revealed a lack of alignment among directors as to where the board should focus its priorities. This was resolved through a session dedicated to improving focus.

Once it has achieved a certain alignment regarding its role, the board can focus on elaborating a list of main tasks. These will then be incorporated into a two- to three-year action plan that will guide the board's work more productively than a traditional passive agenda could. Figure 4.2 highlights some of the typical tasks that boards undertake, while Figure 4.3 summarises the action plan of that sovereign wealth fund board.

Dedication

The most effective board members are more than simply competent and conscientious – they are individuals with genuine passion, energy, and dedication who are not motivated solely by the financial or social rewards of board membership. Board members must spend enough time keeping up to date on relevant issues and preparing for meetings, including through conversations with fellow directors. Norms in terms of preparation time have increased dramatically; according to a KPMG survey, for large organisations, one hour of board meeting requires 17 hours of preparation. As we saw in Chapter 1, many directors spend much less time than this. But the best board members always go the extra mile in their preparation.

The first pillar of board effectiveness is about people, and in particular their quality, focus, and dedication. All three of these dimensions are important, and none are ever perfect, of course. The board's composition needs constant adjustment, by understanding members' weaknesses and addressing them through education and other means. A smart board will seek a strong, dynamic focus on the right issues, and will set a yearly agenda that prioritises

INVOLVEMENT	TASKS
INTERACTIVE	Essence, culture, and core values
INTERACTIVE	Strategic direction and objectives
	Selection of an effective management team, particularly:
INTERACTIVE	• Managing director
SUPERVISORY	• Top management and General management
SUPERVISORY	• Management processes
APPROVING	Policy formulation
SUPERVISORY	Policy application
APPROVING	Organisational Structure
INTERACTIVE	Assuring the availability of financial resources and their proper allocation, financial soundness, long-term success and survival
EXECUTIVE	Effectiveness and continuity of the Board
INTERACTIVE	Monitoring of all facets of operations
INTERACTIVE	Protection and promotion of reputation
INTERACTIVE	Analysis and interpretation of environmental influences
INTERACTIVE	Assuring socially responsible corporate behaviour
INTERACTIVE	Ethical Code and Code of Conduct

Figure 4.2   An Example of Typical Board Tasks

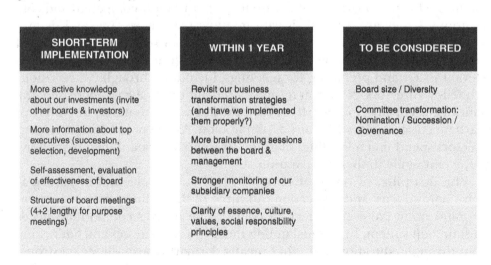

SHORT-TERM IMPLEMENTATION	WITHIN 1 YEAR	TO BE CONSIDERED
More active knowledge about our investments (invite other boards & investors) More information about top executives (succession, selection, development) Self-assessment, evaluation of effectiveness of board Structure of board meetings (4+2 lengthy for purpose meetings)	Revisit our business transformation strategies (and have we implemented them properly?) More brainstorming sessions between the board & management Stronger monitoring of our subsidiary companies Clarity of essence, culture, values, social responsibility principles	Board size / Diversity Committee transformation: Nomination / Succession / Governance

Figure 4.3   A Board Action Plan from a Sovereign Wealth Fund

and caters for these. Finally, dedication needs to be watched constantly, because some are good at faking it. Good board work requires involvement, and not necessarily in a financial sense.

As well as the right people, boards also need to have the right information in order to be fully effective. This is the focus of our next chapter.

Table 4.2 Example of Board Skill Map

The Board Skill Map provides a simple tool with which to assess the knowledge level and personal attributes of your directors across various board critical dimensions. It can be used whether the board has a choice of directors or not (owners' representatives). Personal attributes matter as much as skills. This document is meant to be used for your self-assessment purposes and should be adapted to the organisation. Administering it will offer you an overview of your board's competency, personality, and attribute gaps. This specific skill map was established for a non-profit: a sports organisation specialising in the fight against doping, but the personal attributes could be used in other organisations, including for-profit corporates, technology, oil and gas, financials. Any skill map needs to be adapted to the characteristics of the organisation.

HIGH-LEVEL SKILL MATRIX	Board members								
	1	2	3	4	5	6	7	8	9
Status (e.g. ED/ NED/Independent)									
Director since									
Age									
Board of Director Experience (Y/N)									

KINDLY RATE THE FOLLOWING SKILLS

1 No Knowledge	2 Some Knowledge	3 Good Knowledge	4 Strong Knowledge	5 Expert

SECTOR EXPERIENCE	1	2	3	4	5	6	7	8	9
Sports direct									
Sports related									
Medical direct									
Medical related									
Government/regulatory direct									
Government/regulatory related									
GROUP TECHNICAL SKILLS I	1	2	3	4	5	6	7	8	9
Management									
Accounting									
Legal									
Chemical/biology									

Table 4.2 (*continued*)

	1	2	3	4	5	6	7	8	9
Human resources management									
Communication									
Core technical									
General technical									
Scientific									
GROUP TECHNICAL SKILLS II	1	2	3	4	5	6	7	8	9
Sector – commercial									
Funding									
Government and regulatory affairs									
IT/ Digital									
Legal – anti-doping									
Legal – general									
Marketing									
Risk management									
Strategic planning									
Human resource management									
Financial management/audit									
Other expertise									
PERSONAL ATTRIBUTES	1	2	3	4	5	6	7	8	9
Clear communication skills									
Leadership competencies									
Strategic agility									
Political astuteness									
OTHER ATTRIBUTES	1	2	3	4	5	6	7	8	9
Proactiveness									
Clear moral or ethical boundaries									
Credible as independent voice									
Honesty									
Directness									
Ability to challenge									
Embracing ambiguity and coping effectively with change									
Ability to present the truth in helpful ways									
Network of contacts									

CHAPTER 5

The Second Pillar: Information Architecture

1 *0:30 pm, 4 October: Joanne Marker sat at the desk in her home office, preparing for a board meeting the following week at Cynched, a telecommunications and tech company.*

After going over her notes from the previous quarter, made on the basis of news clippings and her daily Google alerts, Joanne opened the information package from the board portal on her iPad. She highlighted key figures and elements of the firm's strategy, typing her questions as notes into the document. The past quarter's financial results were there, including all the breakdowns, along with notes on broader market trends.

Joanne then clicked open a podcast from the CEO and made a few notes: closure of a plant in Malaysia, possible acquisition of a small social media firm in Berlin, possible restructuring. She read the risk report in detail, questioning whether the provision set aside for a cyber-security breach was sufficient.

A digest of relevant tweets, Facebook posts, and LinkedIn comments also caught her eye – she saw on Glassdoor that a few bitter former employees were badmouthing a product release as being poor quality. Joanne concluded by going through her Hootsuite and checking on RelSci whether she had a direct connection to some of the complainers. She made a note to call her contact in marketing – as approved by the board – to see what the internal chatter was. Saving her notes directly into the document, she logged off the portal.

Joanne remembered receiving her first board package as a new director of Virtuous Ventures back in the early 1990s. It had been a heavy tome of more than 400 pages that had arrived by DHL three days before the meeting. She soon realised it was simply a copy of directors' reports, with in-depth figures from all the country offices. It had taken her days to make sense of the information, and even then she was missing key analysis that would enable her to understand the potential issues. There was nothing on competitors, trends, customer insights, or reputation. The package covered only internal matters, mostly financial, with nothing on culture. And there were no executive summaries of the main documents, nor any prioritisation or summaries of major decisions to be taken.

What a contrast to the crisp, well-prioritised, and thorough package on internal and external issues from Cynched that Joanne had enjoyed working on for the past few hours.

***

For a board to function optimally, directors need to be informed about developments relevant to the business and its key value drivers. They should receive such information through both internal and external channels, and through formal and informal routes.

Board members must continually monitor competitive trends, regulatory and technological changes, and stakeholder developments that may be strategically relevant for the company. To do this, they need to effectively utilise external sources, such as stakeholders and social media, and not rely solely on information they receive internally through the company. Indeed, more and more, forward-looking perspectives (including scenarios) are part of the toolkit of modern boards and allow more pertinent discussions on risks and strategy.

Directors also need to cultivate informal sources of information, for example, through conversations with stakeholders, other board members, and management. Some make a point of visiting subsidiaries or local facilities when they travel, in order to develop relationships with the firm's local operations. Through conversations with people in the field, directors can learn a great deal about how strategy is being implemented, for example.

How Complete is Your Information?

Typically, information architecture is designed by management, who often fail to understand the type of inputs needed to make board decisions. Executives often want to provide too much data, often of an operational nature. They also tend to neglect the design. A good board pack has plenty of graphics and synthetic information. For sure, information for directors should be comprehensive, covering the company's essential activities and the main issues facing the organisation. But it should remain sufficiently high level to allow the board to have an informed discussion without getting lost in the detail. Figure 5.1 provides a quick checklist of some of these information channels and sources.

Boards are increasingly using board portals to streamline information and materials. But although technology is an enabler for communication, it should not be the driver. It is essential that information design be aligned with the board's mandate – which is support and supervision.

Boards should start the process of information design by identifying the conversations they want to have, and then design the architecture accordingly.

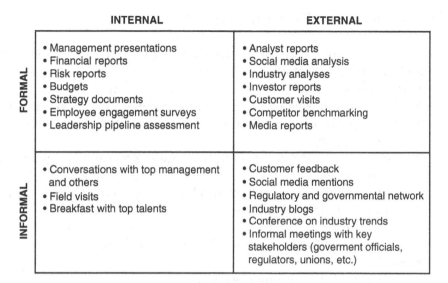

	INTERNAL	EXTERNAL
FORMAL	• Management presentations • Financial reports • Risk reports • Budgets • Strategy documents • Employee engagement surveys • Leadership pipeline assessment	• Analyst reports • Social media analysis • Industry analyses • Investor reports • Customer visits • Competitor benchmarking • Media reports
INFORMAL	• Conversations with top management and others • Field visits • Breakfast with top talents	• Customer feedback • Social media mentions • Regulatory and governmental network • Industry blogs • Conference on industry trends • Informal meetings with key stakeholders (goverment officials, regulators, unions, etc.)

Figure 5.1   Mapping Board Information Completeness

Strategy, performance, and governance should then each be addressed from the perspectives of steering and supervision, respectively, including by asking key questions:

1. Do we have the right strategy?
2. Is our strategy on track?
3. How can we work smarter?
4. What culture and policies do we foster?
5. Will we hit this year's targets without sacrificing our long-term ones?
6. Are we working in the 'right' way?

The aim is for boards to have more focused and productive conversations by ensuring they receive the information they need. To enable this, board packs should be shorter, more focused, and well-prioritised on what matters so that directors can read their pack and fulfil their duties. To ensure that the pack achieves this while still being comprehensive, report writers must produce succinct papers that respond to the board's key questions.

A good board pack will include executive summaries, key decisions to be made, options for the different decisions, priorities in the materials (with a potential ranking from A to C), a summary of former discussions and materials distributed for each decision, elements of external information, and information on softer issues (personal perspectives on culture and conduct from key managers).

Typical components include the following:

- A board briefing that is jointly designed by the board and management and includes, on a yearly rotating basis:
  - circa five to ten pages of financials with forecast;
  - a one to three page CEO report with personal views of key issues;
  - risk/opportunity analysis (three to five tools including maps, sensitivities, scenarios);
  - tracking of key trends of interest, including technology, geopolitics, and sustainability issues;
  - competitors positioning on financials and other value chain dimensions;
  - a brief on gene-pool analysis;
  - culture survey and trends;
  - a summary of financial analysts' or external views;
  - employee/customer surveys; and
  - evolution of the customer proposition.
- Management letter in-between meetings.
- Director outreach summary (plants/technology/audits, individual and group visits).
- Committee reports, including analysis and insights as well as a recommendation.

In my experience, it is too often common practice for management to take the lead in designing board packages with some input from the board, or even to design them alone. As a result, the board often receives incomplete information regarding external issues such as reputation analysis, customer knowledge, stakeholder understanding, and technological evolution.

Although the board is responsible for ensuring that it has complete information, it is still very rare for a board to co-design a package with management. However, such cooperation is essential to produce strategic packages that give the board a suitably high-level perspective and lead to meaningful boardroom discussion. Figure 5.2 provides an example of how to drive a board-pack design process that facilitates the board's strategic role. Building scenarios is also a good practice that helps management and board reflect on what truly matters for the board horizon.

The primary purpose of board meetings is for directors to have productive conversations with regard to company strategy and people, and to supervise key risks, enabling them to make decisions to create long-term wealth for the company. Too often, however, boards spend the majority of their meeting time – frequently between 50 and 80% – listening to management presentations. Although such presentations serve an important function by exposing the board to talent in the management pipeline, they should never take up

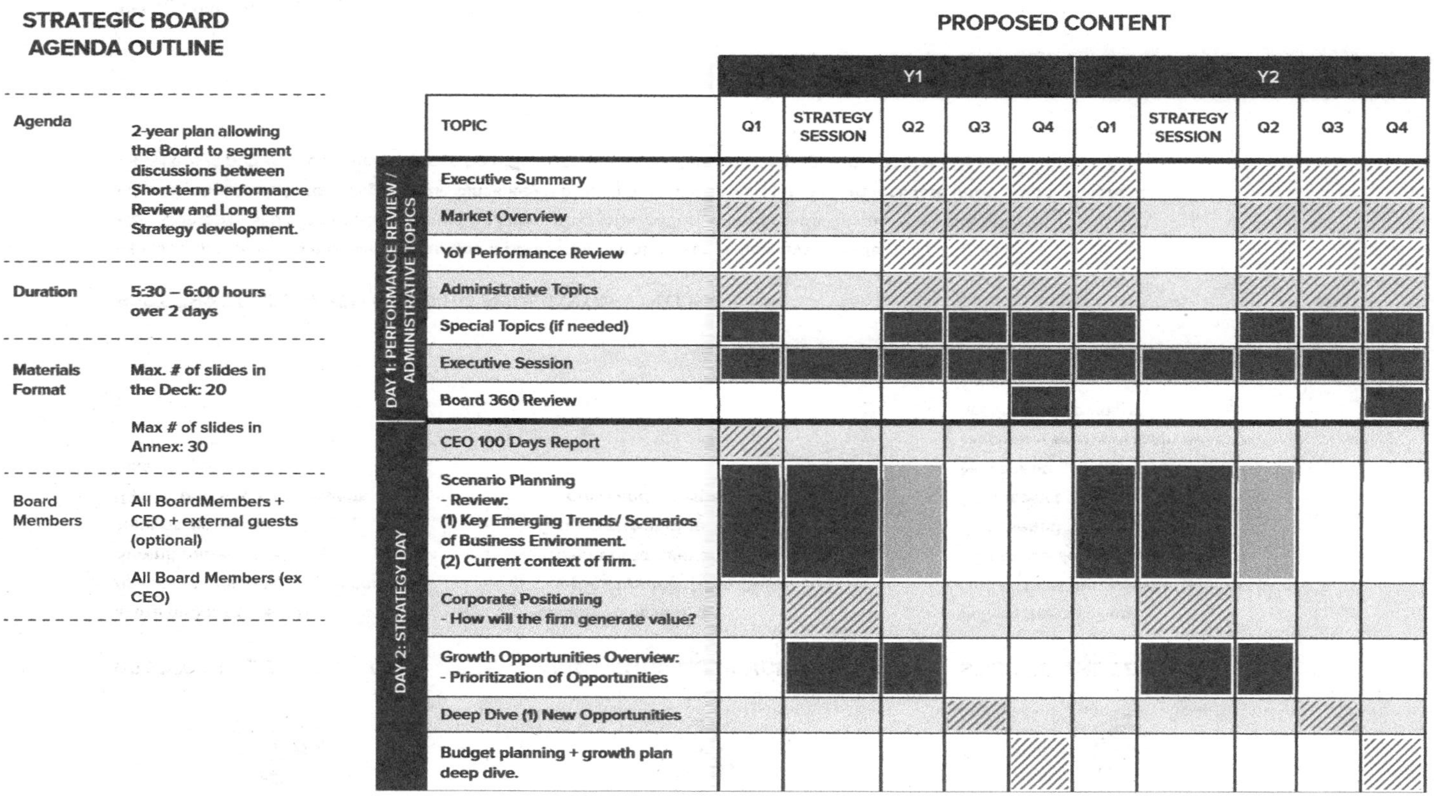

Figure 5.2   Facilitating the Role of the Board at Steering Long-term Strategy

RESPECT THE BOARD'S TIME

Is the paper necessary?

Address questions and be concise

Submit paper on time

Take paper as read

If you don't have the answer, take action!

KNOW YOUR AUDIENCE

Executive or Board?

Set the appropriate context

Present data relevant to the audience

Explain stakeholder impact

Be open and transparent

STICK TO THE TEMPLATE

Follow the guidance

Understand the power of the first page
– Purpose, Action, Sponsor

Comments!

Be succinct

No repetition

Be clear – next steps, timelines and accountable owners

BEST PRACTICES WHEN BUILDING SLIDES (STORYTELLING):

- 1 – Title phrase – Title of slide should be a phrase highlighting key takeaways of slide
- 2 – Content - Slide information should be supporting information to lead reader to conclude title phrase
- 3 – Highlight key texts – Highlight in black key words that reader should jump to, to facilitate information digestions
- 4 – Less is better – too much text can be difficult to follow. Prefer pictures or graphs / tables

Figure 5.3   Best-in-class Board Information

Source: PXNY Group 2024

more than 30% of a meeting (and ideally far less). Having the CEO or CFO prepare podcasts in advance of board meetings, for example, would help the board to use its face-to-face time with management more efficiently.

Limiting presentations to fewer than seven slides and less than seven minutes is certainly good practice. One board I know has cancelled all *in situ* presentations by management to the board. Instead, presentations are sent to directors a few days before, and responsible managers are present at board meetings for direct questions and answers. To encourage this, the board secretary organised a seating plan in which each manager present sits next to an external board member. On another board, to ensure a rejuvenation of information exchange, one of the independent external board members was asked to present specific views on a key dimension to the management, rather than the reverse. Finally, a third board interviews young recruits (typically 20- to 25-year-olds) to get a sense of how company culture is perceived by the younger generation, and to get a feel for the atmosphere. There is thus plenty of room for creativity and originality in reaching a best-in-class information-sharing process (Figure 5.3).

Information architecture is the crucial second pillar of board effectiveness. However, to benefit fully from a rich flow of strategic information, boards also need to have high-quality structures and processes in place. These will be the focus of Chapter 6.

CHAPTER

The Third Pillar: Board Structures and Processes

*T*en days after her lunch with Virtuous Chair Gerald Grossheim, Joanne Marker had been formally invited to an interview with the nominations committee. Three months later, she had attended her first board meeting at Virtuous. Joanne enjoyed the mental challenge of mapping problems from her work at WeCare onto Virtuous, and figuring out the implications for the company's strategy and marketing efforts. As a member of Virtuous' strategy committee, she also enjoyed challenging the CEO on his strategic direction and any risks she thought he had overlooked — such as changing consumer trends and tastes in different geographies.

Joanne soon noticed that certain items were frequently left to the end of the discussion and somehow dropped off the agenda. She therefore suggested to Grossheim that he introduce a two-year agenda-setting process and also institute a standalone board secretary function. The latter worked well on another board Joanne was on, by helping its members to retain focus and have more disciplined discussions.

'A board secretary?' Grossheim said. 'But Gary (the chief legal officer) does this well.'

Joanne explained the value of having a dedicated board secretary who would ensure the quality of all board processes, support the chair in preparing meetings, and provide directors with synthetic overviews that would provide context and set the stage for effective discussion. Grossheim nodded his approval. He was fed up with having to use valuable discussion time explaining and re-explaining things to directors who lacked the necessary background knowledge. He could also see that the board was not running as smoothly as it could. 'OK Joanne, done. What else?'

She suggested an annual strategy retreat to address long-term megatrends, the competitive landscape, opportunities, and threats. She then asked Grossheim to introduce 360-degree evaluations and feedback sessions for directors.

'That's not going to be very popular – especially with a few board members', laughed Grossheim.

Joanne didn't smile. 'Precisely my point', she said.

******

Effective structures and processes enable boards to deliver on their mandate of supervision and support. Indeed, high-performance boards go a step further, innovating and refining these to a more sophisticated level. A relevant committee structure and a good board secretary can be influential in improving the quality of the board's work, while lead directors are playing an increasingly important role.

Processes

Boards must master a wide range of processes in order to be highly effective. A well-designed strategy process, for example, is critical to a board's strategic support function, as we will see in Chapter 21. We also discuss essential risk processes in Part II. Tracking the effectiveness of the board's decisions is important, along with best practices in recruiting, onboarding, educating, and evaluating directors. CEO succession planning is vital too, yet boards often lack expertise in this area and thus avoid discussing it on a regular basis, especially as this is often a sensitive topic.

Following is a non-exhaustive list of key processes for boards. All directors – not only the chair – should have a good sense of how well the board is mastering them.

- Agenda-setting and board session organisation (including decision recording and minutes).
- Management performance review.
- Audit (including board, committee, and management formal relation thereof).
- Regulatory compliance.
- CEO succession.
- Risk thinking, including risk identification, assessment, management, and appetite.
- Strategy.
- Ongoing board improvement process, including evaluation and education.
- Nominations.
- Gene-pool analysis.
- Organisational culture oversight.
- Conduct and ethics oversight.
- Crisis management.
- Onboarding and outboarding.

In addition, digital transformation is becoming a board process for many organisations. A family business may well have a family-board interaction process. In general, a well-specified process for management consultation by board members is also useful.

Board members should ask themselves the following questions:

- How do I feel about each of these processes? Do I have a clear view of each? Is each process complete and detailed enough?
- Do we have the right committees, with the right people on them?
- Are the reporting lines foolproof?

Committee Structure

Having mapped the processes, directors need to consider the implications for committees. They should also consider the legal requirements for committees, as well as their ideal composition in order to shape selection criteria. Committees should always inform board discussions rather than replace them. Although they are tasked with going into greater depth on audit, risk, nominations, technology, or other critical issues such as sustainability, committees do not have decision-making authority. Instead, they systematically report back to the board to help it make better, more informed decisions.

The committee structure needs to be closely aligned with organisational strategy and other requirements. Table 6.1 provides examples from three large organisations.

Table 6.1 Examples from Three Large Organisations

HSBC
- Group Audit Committee
- Group Risk Committee
- Group Remuneration Committee
- Nomination and Corporate Governance Committee
- Group Technology Committee[1]

Coca-Cola
- Audit Committee
- Talent and Compensation Committee
- Corporate Governance and Sustainability Committee
- Executive Committee
- Finance Committee[2]

Singapore Airlines
- Board Executive Committee
- Board Audit Committee
- Board Compensation and Industrial Relations Committee
- Board Nominating Committee
- Board Safety and Risk Committee
- Customer Experience, Technology, and Sustainability Committee.[3]

---

[1] HSBC. (n.d.). Board committees. https://www.hsbc.com/who-we-are/leadership-and-governance/board-committees
[2] The *Coca-Cola* Company. (n.d.). Corporate governance. https://investors.coca-colacompany.com/corporate-governance/board-committees
[3] Singapore Airlines. (n.d.). Board of directors and corporate data. https://www.singaporeair.com/en_UK/us/about-us/information-for-investors/SIA-Director

Board Secretary

The secretary's role is to support the chair in ensuring the smooth functioning of the board. As a minimum, the secretary should ensure that board meetings are called and organised in accordance with organisational requirements (such as the articles of association), and that minutes are accurately recorded and kept on file. The secretary may also need to make sure that the organisation complies with company law requirements, particularly regarding procedures for annual and extraordinary general meetings.

Other secretarial responsibilities include:

- Meetings: sourcing agenda items from the chair and board members; circulating agendas; and circulating decisions made (ideally within 48 hours after the meeting ends).
- Records and administration: keeping up-to-date contact details for the board members; filing minutes and reports; maintaining a database of names and addresses that are useful to the organisation; recording the organisation's activities and tracking future activities.
- Legal requirements: safeguarding the organisation's constitution and other company documents; monitoring legal requirements and organisational compliance in governance.
- Communication and correspondence: responding to and filing all board correspondence; keeping an archive of all company publications; and keeping stakeholders informed of the organisation's governance activities.

Most importantly, the board secretary oversees all the above-mentioned processes, including evaluations, and thus ensures that the board functions smoothly in addition to satisfying legal requirements.

Lead Director or Vice Chair

The lead director role initially emerged in the United States, in particular on boards where the chair and CEO roles were combined. The idea was that this board member would serve as a leader for independent directors and act as a counterweight to the chair–CEO. Many corporate boards inside and outside the United States now have lead directors or vice-chairs, who typically contribute to improved corporate performance in four areas.

Firstly, they take the initiative for improving board performance, often building on evaluations of individual directors and the chair. Secondly, they aim to build a productive relationship between the board and the CEO – smoothing what is sometimes a tense relationship between the chief executive

Abu Dhabi Commercial Bank (ADCB) appointed Simon Copleston, a UK-trained lawyer, as its first-ever group general counsel and board secretary in 2008. Copleston was then instrumental in making the bank a recognised regional leader in corporate governance.

ADCB clarified certain roles between the board and management and revised the board's composition. It took steps to improve the coordination of risk management throughout the bank and restructured the board and management committees. The bank also changed particular shareholder policies and improved their disclosures to put it on par with the highest international standards.

In particular, ADCB:

- adopted a target of one-third independent directors;
- appointed five new board members, including the CEO and directors with additional banking experience;
- clarified the distinction between board and management, emphasising the board's role in monitoring management performance;
- removed directors from the combined executive committee;
- adopted a revised committee structure including Audit, Risk, Nomination / Remuneration, and Corporate Governance committees;
- developed clear terms of reference (TORs) for each, removed management duties (e.g. loan recoveries), and ensured adequate independent composition;
- set three-year terms with the possibility of re-election to ensure a healthy turnover of directors;
- established a formal process for identifying and nominating appropriate directors for approval by the AGM, led by the Nominations Committee; and
- introduced a formal annual evaluation process (internal and external) to assess the board's performance.

In May 2019, as part of a regional wave of consolidation in financial services, ADCB merged with Union National Bank and acquired Al Hilal Bank. The enlarged ADCB became one of the three largest banks in the United Arab Emirates, with around US$145 billion in total assets and a 15% market share in 2023.

Analysts say that the success of the merger will depend on whether ADCB can ensure that its strong corporate governance remains a core part of the merged bank's culture, including in the structure and processes of the new board.

and the board – and to ensure the quality of the CEO–chair relationship where these roles are separated.

Thirdly, lead directors provide leadership in crises when the chair is unable to, such as in a conflict-of-interest situation. Finally, they chair meetings of independent directors (they usually have the authority to call executive sessions), especially when the chair is not independent. This is particularly important when the roles of CEO and chair are combined, and also in family businesses where the chair is a member of the family and the CEO is an external professional. Typically, a lead independent director or vice-chair can help infuse governance in a setting where the family can dominate the board.

As we have seen in the last three chapters, people, information, and structures and processes are all essential to board success. But the dynamics and culture in the boardroom are ultimately crucial. We therefore conclude Part I by looking at this fourth and final pillar of board effectiveness.

7

The Fourth Pillar: Group Dynamics and Board Culture

The quality of board members' interactions is crucial to board success. The ideal board culture will encourage strong debates (the dialectic process) while fostering alignment (finding the path to purpose) based on solid shared values. Traditionally, analyses of board dynamics focused on the individual director as a key building block, examining his or her demographic attributes, personality type, and emotional and cultural intelligence. But although these are of course important, a board is primarily a high-performance work group and a social institution. We therefore need to know more about the board's collective processes and behaviours in order to understand and predict the quality of governance, and the resulting impact on the organisation's performance.

People create meaning through interactions with each other. The effectiveness of their decisions depends on their ability to productively exchange views and challenge one another. As such, healthy board dynamics are an essential foundation for good governance. These include: the ways in which the board handles differences; generates trust; creates the right context for discussions and decision-making; manages conflict; and sets up leadership roles. In addition, directors' participation and contributions during board meetings are key factors in board effectiveness.

Boards need to present a unified front to the outside world in accordance with the 'one-voice principle'. That single voice must be reached after building on true differences in perspectives. These will arise from differences in background, personalities, or simply dynamics. Building on structural arrangements and cultural understandings, the system of interaction between board members must allow for productive exchanges in order to reach agreement on how to move forward.

Executives moving to a director role need to understand the significant change in communication and behavioural style required at board level, because this will be critical to their success in building a portfolio of directorships in the future. Board members must be able to observe and analyse the dynamics at play within a board and understand what kinds of discussion styles and non-verbal behaviour may be resulting in dysfunction.

How do boards exert power and influence? In joining the board, people have their own personal histories, motivations, and agendas to build on and pursue, and specific sets of stakeholders to represent. In this light, the board is a rich slice of not only business and industry but human community and society in general. Whether these dynamics induce dysfunctions, and how strong these dysfunctions are, is key to board work. Red flags as shown in Table 7.1 are a good way to start from consequences and develop awareness of a board's problematic dynamics.

Table 7.1 Red Flags

Red Flags should trigger your Early Warning System as a board member. Presented here are some of the most common indicators of board dysfunction, which frequently point to deeper issues.

BOARD MEETING DISCUSSION STYLE	Yes, this happens frequently	Yes, this has happened	No, this never occurs
↪ Inappropriate allocation of time to critical issues	☐	☐	☐
↪ Sense of pressure to get through the agenda	☐	☐	☐
↪ Rationalisation of poor decisions	☐	☐	☐
↪ Executive debate tending to 'Yes I agree BUT'	☐	☐	☐
↪ Little discussion on how debate could be improved	☐	☐	☐
↪ No opportunity to consider 'What could we do differently next time?'	☐	☐	☐
↪ Difficult issues not sufficiently discussed	☐	☐	☐

INTERACTION WITH MANAGEMENT	Yes, this happens frequently	Yes, this has happened	No, this never occurs
⬚ Debate becomes personalised, not issue-focused	☐	☐	☐
⬚ Dissenting voices marginalised	☐	☐	☐
⬚ Special insights not used	☐	☐	☐
⬚ Stereotyping of third parties	☐	☐	☐
⬚ Consistent lack of contribution	☐	☐	☐
⬚ Focus narrowly on 'own world view'	☐	☐	☐
⬚ Management team is defensive/aggressive	☐	☐	☐
⬚ Long management presentations	☐	☐	☐
⬚ Executive presenting answers rather than options	☐	☐	☐

Understanding Group Dynamics

As with any group, board members don't convene just to sit in a room and be together. They immediately develop dynamic tensions and start forming alliances, whether consciously or semi-consciously. Upon entering the board-room, we can instantly observe some of this emergent tension, and start reflecting on the rules, distances, and authority that are playing out. Are they formal, informal, or culturally defined? Do they follow some unconscious but clearly visible patterns?

The dynamics evolve greatly during a board member's tenure. A sign of health is the ability to transform these dynamics depending on the context or the issue being considered. A solidified fragmentation of the board into groups is one of the most difficult governance situations to resolve.

When people first meet to discuss key issues, the initial, awkward orienta-tion phase is marked by anxiety, the search for a 'safe spot', and attempts to pair up with a peer (Phase I). A board member then goes through the explor-atory phase, often marked by conflict, where they make sense of others', and their own, sense of power, authority, and status, and start to outline the first contours of competition (Phase II). The final phase is a state of cohesion, where board members finally allow themselves to settle into a fully functioning group that builds on a sense of engagement, challenge, intimacy, and communicative disclosure (Phase III) (Figure 7.1). For a board to be functional, each member should proceed as swiftly as possible on this path. As the stakes rise and issues become more complex, that process may need to be renewed.

Throughout these experiments and attempts to settle into an organic structure that is not yet defined but is starting to function, we never lose sight of our faculty of social comparison. Whether we admit it or not, what can drive some of our interactions with our new set of peers is an innate desire to define ourselves versus the others; for example, as superior, to feel 'better than you', or simply as truly distinctive.

Human dynamics are critical to understanding the complexities of how people function and interact with one another.[1] Our role in groups often starts with family dynamics – how we compete, learn, communicate, relate to

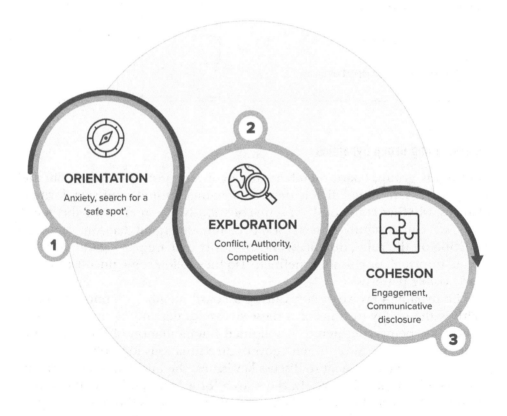

Figure 7.1   Path to a Functional Board

---

[1] For a good example of how to analyse and overcome, see Manzoni, J-F. (2014). Dysfunctional dynamics behind boardroom conflicts. *SID Directors Bulletin* 4.

For Uber, Travis Kalanick was the ambitious, tenacious co-founder and CEO who had made it possible for the company to report gross revenue of US$37 billion in 2017, after only eight years of existence. However, the same attributes created a company culture built on a 'hustle at all costs' approach, which resulted in a spate of serious high-profile lawsuits and scandals and ultimately led to Kalanick's ousting as CEO. This dysfunctional, toxic culture was at the core of Uber's troubles – both within the company and its leadership team, and on the board.

In 2017, Uber commissioned an independent investigation led by former US Attorney General Eric Holder, following the publication of a scathing blog by former employee Sarah Fowler that outlined instances of harassment and discrimination at the company. The subsequent report strongly advocated improved boardroom dynamics in addition to reform of top management. The report sought to improve the board's oversight by ensuring its independence, and advised the board to create an Ethics and Culture Committee 'to oversee Uber's efforts and enhance a culture of ethical business practices, diversity and inclusion . . .'.

Uber's board of directors voted unanimously to adopt all of the report's recommendations. The months that followed saw several steps towards implementing these – the largest being the replacement of Kalanick with Dara Khosrowshahi, the external CEO brought in to improve the culture at the company.

In December 2019, Kalanick disengaged completely from Uber's operations by resigning from the board of directors and divesting his shares. Under Khosrowshahi, despite the layoffs of approximately 3,700 employees in 2020 due to the impact of the Covid pandemic, Uber has demonstrated its efforts to recover.

family members, and develop as human beings. We often carry this 'valency' into other groups throughout our lifetime, which may unconsciously draw us into unproductive dynamics of dependency or dominance. It is important for any director to be aware of what is beneath the surface level of the group – unspoken power struggles or competition, for example – and to confront these dynamics if they begin to block effective exchange or critical thinking.

By applying an understanding of human dynamics to board work, directors can enrich relationships, communicate more effectively, and work together more productively. However, by the same token, competition and comparison is also an inevitable part of these interactions, because people generally want to feel good about themselves through winning. Within a board, this typically means that directors could well be striving to be:

- closest to the chair;
- the one most seen, most heard, most recognised;
- the cleverest board member;
- the most influential board member; or
- better than their predecessor/successor.

Coalitions Within a Board are Inevitable – and they Feed into Politics

If things do not go according to plan in these competitive situations, someone will attempt to pinpoint a specific reason behind the board's lack of success. More often than not, a failure is attributed to a scapegoat, because every group needs someone to blame when things do not go well. To avoid being the scapegoat, people form alliances. When these groups form, or shift suddenly, like in a game of musical chairs, the odd one out will be the scapegoat. Figure 7.2 synthesises directors' perceptions of their own grouping on the board.

Coalitions Within a Board are Inevitable

A common presumption in the management world is that when points of difference arise, they should be considered objectively; everyone should work together in a non-partisan way to deliver the chosen outcome. In this equation, the categories of power and politics are conspicuous by their absence. Yet cogent understandings of politics predate management theory – they have long been developed in disciplines such as philosophy, sociology, literature, and political science. In addition, postmodern theory has taught us to read between the lines, be comfortable with ambiguity, and also listen to what is *not* being said. Meanwhile, management theory and business education for the most part seem to maintain that within organisations, there are no out-of-bounds markers that we cross at our own peril. By contrast, sociology has long embraced the idea that all human interaction involves continual contestation of impulses drawing on science, intuition, and politics.

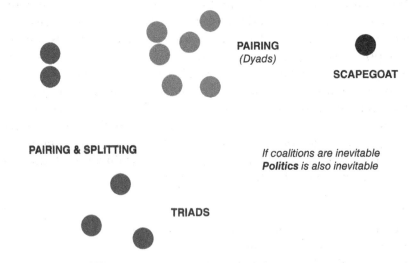

Figure 7.2   Mapping Board Alliances

When executives fail in their new positions, the key factors are the culture and politics they stumbled upon in the new environment – and often not experience, nor even leadership capability. Politics means understanding that we are involved in processes of struggle for limited resources, not simply material or financial, or even power, but struggles for attention, respect – for time and the ability to be listened to carefully in a boardroom discussion, for example; nothing more and nothing less than that.

In healthy boards, such subgroups are floating and never solidified, and members can easily shift from one to the other depending on the issue. In practice, however, splitting up coalitions can often prove to be a challenge – especially if a board's culture needs to be reformed.

As boards become socially differentiated, their politics can give rise to cliques and factions, where several members align in opposition to the rest of the group. Sometimes an elite 'inner board' will form around the CEO or chair. This can be quite common in boards with ethnic, linguistic, political, or tribal differences, for example.

Ecobank Transnational

The pan-African lender Ecobank Transnational (ETI), with a presence in 35 countries and assets of more than US$29 billion in 2022,[2] has been seen as one of Africa's business success stories. However, since the opening the first affiliated bank in Togo in 1985, the path has not always been easy.

In 2014, the board of directors of ETI put an end to a protracted, nine-month battle with the bank's management by ousting the chief executive, Thierry Tanoh. Shortly before this, a shareholder meeting had discussed allegations, first brought to light by the *Financial Times,* that Tanoh had in 2012 agreed a pay rise and a 400% bonus increase with the former ETI chair. Additionally, Tanoh's appointment of the bank's internal auditor in a dual role as his special advisor represented a conflict of interest.

The campaign for Tanoh to step down had been launched by ETI directors, senior managers, former chairs, and possibly South Africa's Public Investment Corporation, a large shareholder. Coupled with Tanoh's denial of any culpability, the resulting developments weakened market confidence in the bank and led to a temporary outflow of deposits.[3] Tensions among different groups of directors (between French and English speakers, and between Nigerians and South Africans, for example) contributed greatly to the board's difficulties in handling the situation. Alleged malpractice by the ETI chair, which made the front pages of international papers, deepened the crisis and increased the board's fragmentation, arguably leading to a decade of underperformance.

---

[2] Ecobank Press Release, 30 March 2023.
[3] www.ft.com/content/a51ad338-a93c-11e3-b87c-00144feab7de

Language is a natural factor around which in-groups converge. On one Swiss board that my team worked with, the chair surrounded himself with fellow German-speaking Swiss (many of whom were also high-ranking military officials), leading to a sense of exclusion among the French-speaking members. The German-speaking Swiss didn't realise this, because they made it a point to always speak French, but the in-group was still perceived as a cultural one.

Although we live in a global era, the tendency to invest social meaning and trust in concepts, structures, and systems is largely a Western tradition. Other national cultures, by contrast, may find more meaning in face-to-face interactions.

The owner of a family business in Southeast Asia, for example, may see many governance structures, including the board itself, as little more than 'window dressing'. The dynamics of his or her national and family culture may dictate that the ties of kinship, religion, and ethnicity trump all other structures, under any circumstances. Even members of this cohort who have willingly set out to take their company public will freely admit that they struggle with the idea of heeding the advice of an independent director, when 'we are the ones who spent the past ten years building this enterprise from scratch'.

Boards Fall into Traps

Due to the high stakes involved, and the overlapping factors of responsibility, seniority, and loyalty, boards risk falling into behavioural traps.[4] These may be tough for a new board member or an outsider to identify, and can be highly damaging to the company and the people involved. Dysfunctional discussion and decision styles can lock boards into three common traps:

- the argumentative/broken relations trap – trust breaks down, and the board becomes dysfunctional;
- the happy family/support trap – everyone is too supportive and does not raise red flags;
- the leader control trap – one or two board members have disproportionate influence.

The checklist in Table 7.2, together with data from a personality study inventory such as that in Table 7.3, can help board members diagnose some of these dysfunctions and the resulting traps.

---

[4] This section as well as the table on discussions styles and decisions styles is strongly inspired by Paul Strebel's work and notably his co-authored article 'How boards get trapped and what to do about it': Paul Strebel, Denise Kenyon-Rouvinez, and Phil Whiteley, Working Paper, IMD 2018.

Table 7.2 Boardroom Discussion and Decision Styles

Boardroom discussions sometimes fall prey to dysfunctional dynamics, often leading to suboptimal boardroom decision styles.

Have you experienced any of the following during your board meetings?

DISCUSSION STYLES	Often	Occasionally	Never
Uncompromising no Members stay closed to the opinions of others, refusing to yield in any way.	☐	☐	☐
Perpetual maybe Discussion never moves beyond possibilities to a point where a clear path of action is adopted.	☐	☐	☐
Failure to reach closure Discussions fail to lead to a clear decision point, remaining entrenched in opposing viewpoints.	☐	☐	☐
Group narcissism/denial Individuals have an inflated love of the board as an in-group, and are often blind to any possible mistakes or shortcomings.	☐	☐	☐
Group think/false yes An excessive desire for harmony and conformity prevents the group from engaging in critical thinking.	☐	☐	☐
Manipulation/influencing One or two group members steer the board toward supporting their personal agenda, exerting influence and other tactics to prevent constructive debate.	☐	☐	☐
Fast thinking Board members move too quickly through the agenda items, not giving sufficient time to considering all angles of an issues; individual members may lack the opportunity to contribute their perspective.	☐	☐	☐

What kinds of decisions does your board tend to make? Have you ever experienced any of the following during board meetings?

DECISION STYLES	Often	Occasionally	Never
Blocking One or two members consistently disagree, finding a reason why a specific course of action won't be successful.	☐	☐	☐
Inaction The board discussion fails to engender a clear decision to pursue a course of action.	☐	☐	☐
Indecisive Further information is needed and more studies conducted before a decision can be taken.	☐	☐	☐
Unanimous consensus A desire to avoid conflict suppresses dissenting board member voices from being expressed or heard.	☐	☐	☐
Majority coalition A majority subgroup forms a dominant alliance, influencing decision outcomes that may be suboptimal.	☐	☐	☐
Rapid/autocratic Excessive dependence on one or two individuals to make decisions – usually quickly.	☐	☐	☐

(Continued)

Table 7.2 (*continued*)

Given our discussion styles and decision styles, might any of the underlying dysfunctions be at work on our board?

DISCUSSION STYLES	DECISION STYLES	UNDERLYING DYSFUNCTION
– Uncompromising no – Perpetual maybe	– Blocking – Inaction	→ Broken relations
– Group narcissism/denial – Group think/false yes	– Indecisive – Unanimous consensus	→ 'Happy family' syndrome
– Manipulation/influencing – Fast thinking	– Majority coalition – Rapid/autocratic	→ Dominated by a strong leader

Do you have further thoughts on discussion or decision styles on your board?

Table 7.3 NEO PI-R: NEO Personality Inventory – Revised (Adapted from Costa & McCrae, 2008)[5]

The NEO PI-R is a measure of the five major domains of personality as well as the six facets that define each domain. Taken together, the five domain scales and thirty facet scales of the NEO PI-R facilitate a comprehensive and detailed assessment of normal adult personality. The NEO PI-R is recognised internationally as a gold standard for personality assessment. Today, reputable developers of personality tests for the occupational market will, as a matter of course, publish data on the relationship of their tests with the five-factor model using one form or another of the NEO as the benchmark. The total amount of recent data from high level academic journals concerning the NEO PI-R underpins its quality.

Description of the domain and facet scales

Neuroticism/emotionality: identifies individuals who are prone to psychological distress.
1. Anxiety: level of free-floating anxiety.
2. Angry hostility: tendency to experience anger and related states such as frustration and bitterness.
3. Depression: tendency to experience feelings of guilt, sadness, despondency, and loneliness.
4. Self-consciousness: shyness or social anxiety.
5. Impulsiveness: tendency to act on cravings and urges rather than reining them in and delaying gratification.
6. Vulnerability: general susceptibility to stress.

Extraversion: quantity and intensity of energy directed outwards into the social world.
1. Warmth: interest in and friendliness towards others.
2. Gregariousness: preference for the company of others.
3. Assertiveness: social ascendancy and forcefulness of expression.
4. Activity: pace of living.
5. Excitement seeking: need for environmental stimulation.
6. Positive emotions: tendency to experience positive emotions.

Openness to experience: the active seeking and appreciation of experiences for their own sake.
1. Fantasy: receptivity to the inner world of imagination.
2. Aesthetics: appreciation of art and beauty.
3. Feelings: openness to inner feelings and emotions.
4. Actions: openness to new experiences on a practical level.
5. Ideas: intellectual curiosity.
6. Values: readiness to re-examine own values and those of authority figures.

Agreeableness: the kinds of interactions an individual prefers from compassion to tough mindedness.
1. Trust: belief in the sincerity and good intentions of others.
2. Straightforwardness: frankness in expression.
3. Altruism: active concern for the welfare of others.
4. Compliance: response to interpersonal conflict.
5. Modesty: tendency to play down own achievements and be humble.
6. Tender mindedness: attitude of sympathy for others.

(Continued)

[5] Costa, P.T., Jr. and R.R. McCrae. (2008). *The NEO Personality Inventory – Revised.* Hogrefe Ltd. The Test People, Oxford.

Table 7.3 (*continued*)

Conscientiousness: degree of organisation, persistence, control, and motivation in goal-directed behaviour.
1. Competence: belief in own self-efficacy.
2. Order: personal organisation.
3. Dutifulness: emphasis placed on importance of fulfilling moral obligations.
4. Achievement striving: need for personal achievement and sense of direction.
5. Self-discipline: capacity to begin tasks and follow through to completion despite boredom or distractions.
6. Deliberation: tendency to think things through before acting or speaking.

Drawing Strength from the Board's Potential

All the board dynamics outlined so far are driven by powerful human forces. Rather than letting these roam free, directors and boards need to learn to manage such influences and prevent them from becoming destructive.

Individual board members should train themselves to follow some basic rules. The chair can facilitate this process by compiling and distributing a common set of 'rules of engagement' or 'ground rules' to help directors channel and conduct discussions in the boardroom.

For instance, board members need to differentiate clearly between a person and his or her opinion, rather than summarily dismissing both because they do not agree with the other's point of view. Our brains use every opportunity to take shortcuts and latch onto 'cognitive handles' that break down, simplify, and help us digest reality. Although these handles help the brain to use information more efficiently, they also come with pitfalls, such as the urge to label and stereotype others.

As a result, we tend to fall back on the duality of the human mind, which produces the 'paradox of the missing middle', transforming subtle differences into dramatic, black-and-white distinctions. In other words, once we categorise, we also polarise. And given how strongly we are invested as individuals in feeling different or superior, we truly see what we want to see. From there, we are also quick to judge – and more often than not, we judge the entire person, not only their behaviour or argument.

The Biblical verse about looking at the speck of sawdust in one's brother's eye while paying no attention to the plank in one's own is not just a moral message – it is a profound observation on human nature. One successful chair I know, for example, urges his fellow board members to always assume the best intentions from each other, and has made this one of his three golden rules in chairing the board.

In addition, directors need to remain clear about their function in the boardroom, and frame discussions accordingly. When problems are framed positively, by presenting options as certain (or absolute) gains, individuals tend to focus more on risk aversion. But with negative framing, which looks at the relative likelihood of losses, individuals are more likely to make riskier choices. Directors have a responsibility to remain vigilant to framing and to challenge the board members to reframe the discussion in absolute terms, rather than relative terms.

Developing Self-awareness

Individual directors also need to ensure that they are not falling prey to flawed thinking, which can result from cognitive biases or from self-deception rooted in a lack of self-awareness. Self-deception leads to individuals refusing to acknowledge a conflict of interest – even to themselves. Honing self-awareness requires regular and honest reflection, as well as a commitment to seeking honest feedback from others to identify one's own blind spots. Tackling cognitive biases, meanwhile, requires awareness and vigilance to maintain rationality in the face of various pressures, and a certain discipline in order to frame problems correctly.

Cognitive Biases: Groupthink

Although many individuals may exercise good judgement in most aspects of their life, cognitive biases may sometimes cloud their thinking and lead them to take decisions or actions in an illogical manner. One major cognitive bias is the psychological phenomenon of groupthink, in which members of a group fail to critically evaluate different viewpoints or courses of action, in order to preserve harmony and minimise conflict.[6] The in-group tends to overrate its own decision-making abilities (or has an 'illusion of invulnerability'), and underestimates those of the out-group. An example of groupthink is the decisions that led to the launch of the Challenger space shuttle, and the subsequent disaster.

Individual directors need to remain vigilant toward possible symptoms of groupthink. According to the US psychologist Irving Janis, these include an inflated sense of the group's power or morality; closed-mindedness (rationalising potential challenges to the group's assumptions, and stereotyping anyone opposed to the group, for example); and pressures toward uniformity (including illusions of unanimity, suppressing dissent, or framing dissent as disloyalty).

Reintroducing productive interpersonal dynamics into the boardroom   When faced with a dysfunctional situation, directors can take steps to reintroduce productive interpersonal dynamics into the boardroom. The key is to align the individual board members' objectives in a constructive fashion, through commitment and shared responsibility. This will involve pre-empting and defusing polarisation while stimulating healthy and constructive exchanges, even managing conflict.

---

[6] Janis, I.L. (1971). Groupthink. *Psychology Today* 5: 84–89.

On political boards, for example, the chair and/or individual members can assume the role of a cultural and political 'translator', bridging opposing views on a particular issue. They can also break up factions by separating political allies when assigning members to activities such as site visits, external meetings, and research projects. It's also useful to poll individual board members occasionally, with external consultants administering this if necessary. And remember that good governance is creative: one Finnish board I know sings together and has a great time. Another leading chair plays the cello and sometimes brings the board together around music.

Similarly, contained conflict can serve as a productive platform to 'get things out in the open' and obtain clarity on individual perceptions and objectives. When properly channelled and managed, this may allow board members to feel strong by making themselves vulnerable. The process will also enable directors to further their technical knowledge (about products, markets, and technologies), cultural awareness (about norms, values, and assumptions), and political sense (regarding alliances, power, and influence).

The leaders in the boardroom are those who can identify the dynamics, conflicts, and emotions and harness them for the betterment of the organisation they serve. They should ask themselves the following questions:

- How well is our board addressing the political issues that should engage its attention?
- How much does the board encourage effective challenging within the board itself?
- How successful has it been in creating a sense of commitment and shared responsibility?

Finally, boards need effective mechanisms for identifying the kinds of challenging discussions that are taking place at different levels of the business, including in the board itself. These can be supported by mentoring or coaching processes that draw out effective performance in all three of the scientific, intuitive, and political dimensions.

If boardroom interactions are healthy and guided enough to produce meaning, then board members will react accordingly. Instead of 'selling their time and expertise', which is impersonal and calculative, they will show creativity, resilience, and caring.

Board Culture

As we saw in Chapter 3, directors have a duty to clearly embody and reinforce board culture through their values and behaviour. The checklist in Table 7.4 will help board members assess the health of their own board's culture – essential for setting the tone at the top.

Barclays' LIBOR scandal highlighted cultural deficiencies within the board as a key contributor to the case. The scandal involved Barclays' manipulation of the London Interbank Offered Rate (LIBOR) to benefit its derivatives trading positions, impacting loans valued at over US$300 trillion globally. This resulted in significant financial losses for Barclays' shareholders, as the bank paid fines totalling US$435 million to resolve cases with regulatory authorities in the United Kingdom and the United States, along with an additional US$100 million settlement to 44 US states.[7] This scandal led to significant harm to its reputation, resulting in the departures of chairman Marcus Agius and group CEO Bob Diamond in 2012.

The Salz Review, an independent review of Barclays' business practices, determined that deficiencies in the organisation's culture were primarily to blame. It highlighted the board's neglect of organisational values, culture, and business practices as contributing factors to the issues that led to the scandal. The report characterised the culture as one that 'tended to favour transactions over relationships, the short term over sustainability, and financial over other business purposes'.[8]

Table 7.4 Reinforcing Board Culture

To what extent do you agree with the following statements with regard to your own board?

No, not at all	To a limited extent	I'm not sure	Mostly, with some exceptions	Yes, this is true
1	2	3	4	5

(1) PRIMARY VALUES:
Each individual on our board is highly committed to these values:

	1	2	3	4	5
a. Responsibility	☐	☐	☐	☐	☐
b. Accountability	☐	☐	☐	☐	☐
c. Moral authority	☐	☐	☐	☐	☐
d. One voice principle (no director authority)	☐	☐	☐	☐	☐

What other values are fundamental for our boards?

(Continued)

---

[7] McBride, J. (2016). *Understanding the Libor Scandal.* The Council on Foreign Relations.
[8] Salz, A. and R. Collins. (2013). The Salz Review. https://www.wsj.com/public/resources/documents/SalzReview04032013.pdf

Table 7.4 (*continued*)

No, not at all	To a limited extent	I'm not sure	Mostly, with some exceptions	Yes, this is true
1	2	3	4	5

(2) DIRECTORS' BEHAVIOURS:
Our directors' unequivocally demonstrate the following behaviours:

a. Independence and integrity

b. Equal participation/mutual respect

c. Openness and constructive dissent

d. Knowledge acceleration

e. External support & continuous education

What other behaviours does your board deem to be critical for its directors?

(3) UNACCEPTABLE BEHAVIOURS/EXECUTIVE LIMITATIONS:
There is zero tolerance for these behaviours by individual board members. We are all clear that any evidence of these behaviours will result in removal from the board.

	1	2	3	4	5

a. Imprudent

b. Unlawful

c. Unethical

Are there additional behaviours which are unacceptable for your board members?

In Part I, we introduced the four pillars of board effectiveness and discussed each of them in turn. The toolkit on the following pages contains checklists for each pillar that will enable directors to measure the health of their board.

In practice, of course, many boards fail, and almost all face major challenges at some point. These failures and challenges will be the focus of Part II.

Summary Table to Part I: The Four Pillars of Board Effectiveness Toolkit

At the forefront of organisations, boards have a key role to play. Governance is a critical driver of success – or failure. In order to assess the health of a board, it is useful to examine the strength of each of its four pillars:

1. People quality, diversity, focus, and dedication.
2. Information architecture.
3. Structures and processes.
4. Group dynamics.

Are you, as a board, delivering to a high standard on these four dimensions? Checklists on each of these dimensions are provided to help you evaluate each pillar in turn.

No, not at all	To a limited extent	I'm not sure	Mostly, with some exceptions	Yes, this is true
1	2	3	4	5

Checklist on People Quality, Diversity, Dedication, and Focus

	1	2	3	4	5
1. The company is close to the heart of every board member.	☐	☐	☐	☐	☐
2. Where do I truly add value to this board?					
3. I am confident in my board colleagues to steer our company in the right direction.	☐	☐	☐	☐	☐
4. Our board has a good level of diversity in terms of abilities, personalities, and competencies.	☐	☐	☐	☐	☐

	1	2	3	4	5
5. I am clear about the role of our board.	☐	☐	☐	☐	☐
6. I am clear about the role of each committee.	☐	☐	☐	☐	☐
7. The agenda has enough focus on the future.	☐	☐	☐	☐	☐
8. My knowledge is on a par with that of the ideal board member for this company.	☐	☐	☐	☐	☐

No, not at all	To a limited extent	I'm not sure	Mostly, with some exceptions	Yes, this is true
1	2	3	4	5

Checklist on Information Architecture

	1	2	3	4	5
1. I know and intimately track the business and its key value drivers.	☐	☐	☐	☐	☐
2. I am well-informed of competitive trends, including regulatory changes, technological changes, and stakeholder evolution.	☐	☐	☐	☐	☐
3. I have enough information independent from management available for my judgement.	☐	☐	☐	☐	☐
4. I have strong informal information processes.	☐	☐	☐	☐	☐
5. I was involved in designing the information architecture, and so were my fellow board members.	☐	☐	☐	☐	☐

Checklist on Structures and Processes

	1	2	3	4	5
1. How well managed are these processes for your board?	☐	☐	☐	☐	☐
a. Strategy	☐	☐	☐	☐	☐

		1	2	3	4	5
b.	Evaluation	☐	☐	☐	☐	☐
c.	CEO succession	☐	☐	☐	☐	☐
d.	Risk	☐	☐	☐	☐	☐
e.	Board education	☐	☐	☐	☐	☐
f.	Stakeholder engagement	☐	☐	☐	☐	☐
g.	Audit	☐	☐	☐	☐	☐
h.	Regulatory compliance	☐	☐	☐	☐	☐
i.	Onboarding/outboarding	☐	☐	☐	☐	☐
j.	When I think about the other processes that are truly important for this board, they are:					
k.	I have a clear view of each of these processes, which is complete and detailed.	☐	☐	☐	☐	☐
l.	We have the right committees and the right people on them.	☐	☐	☐	☐	☐
m.	The reporting lines are foolproof.	☐	☐	☐	☐	☐

No, not at all	To a limited extent	I'm not sure	Mostly, yes	Yes, this is true
1	2	3	4	5

Checklist on Group Dynamics

	1	2	3	4	5
1. My board is energetic.	☐	☐	☐	☐	☐
2. I feel that the contribution of the different board members is strong.	☐	☐	☐	☐	☐
3. The culture of my board provides for well-managed meetings and 'equal participation' in discussions.	☐	☐	☐	☐	☐
4. I genuinely listen to the opinions of others and challenge them, respectfully but without conceding, while maintaining a personal relationship.	☐	☐	☐	☐	☐
5. I make points when I have knowledge or a judgement to offer. My points are short and to the point.	☐	☐	☐	☐	☐
6. I am able to talk to the chair about something that we do not address well, possibly even in his or her own role.	☐	☐	☐	☐	☐

PART II
Board Failures and Challenges

CHAPTER

8

Four Areas of Board Failure

Boards are not infallible: they can fail the organisation that they are in charge of protecting and helping to thrive. My teams and I estimate that 90 to 95% of organisational failures due to board work occur in the following four areas:

1. identifying, assessing and managing risks;
2. strategy;
3. non-executive to executive relations and especially CEO and team selection/support; and
4. integrity.

Board leadership in these areas is particularly important, and failures typically lead to terrible organisational damage. Boards therefore need to be particularly alert to their governance abilities in these domains. The following high-profile examples illustrate the four areas of failure.

A failure to adequately assess and manage risks: In 2008, global financial services giant UBS was the Swiss bank hit hardest by the sub-prime crisis. Due to its risk exposure, the bank wrote down around US$40 billion. The UBS board – which was ultimately responsible – was one of the highest paid in the world and included some of the most influential corporate leaders. Yet it was largely unaware of the risks and unable to deal with them, and its chair, Marcel Ospel, was removed. For example, the board did not have any knowledge of UBS's exposure to the responsible instruments (concentration metrics on the derivatives of choice at the time, so-called collateralised debt obligations or CDOs), despite their contributing 40% of the bank's pre-crisis profits. UBS had a better risk positioning than most investment banks before the crisis (thanks to its massive wealth management outfit). But its lack of risk abilities at board level killed the bank (which was subsequently rescued by the Swiss National Bank).

Strategic failure. The board of Nokia, the Finnish multinational communications company, dismissed the first iPhone as a toy and did not see it as a strategic threat. The firm decided to allocate scarce resources to developing new phones that responded to previous market needs, instead of making devices and an operating system to compete with Apple and the smartphone revolution.

CEO and team selection/support and board–executives relations issues. From 2007 to 2012, the US technology company Yahoo went through a turbulent period with frequent changes in its leadership. Yahoo co-founder Jerry Yang took over as CEO in 2007, but was replaced by Carol Bartz in 2009 after he rejected a lucrative offer from Microsoft to buy the firm. Bartz was fired in 2011 and replaced by interim CEO Tim Morse. Former PayPal President Scott Thompson took over as chief executive the following year, but lasted only four months before being replaced in mid-2012 by Marissa Mayer, a former Google engineer.

Integrity failure. US federal prosecutors pursued criminal investigations into corruption at FIFA, football's international governing body, leading to the indictment of nine FIFA officials in 2015 for offenses related to illegally pursuing personal gain. Despite receiving independent recommendations to reform its governance policies, FIFA did not adopt time limits on board membership, introduce independent directors, provide transparency into its election processes, or adopt best practice conflict-of-interest policies.

Using the checklist in Table 8.1, directors can assess their own board's abilities in each of these four key areas.

The following chapters in Part II focus on two of these areas of failure: risks and integrity. We examine the board's role in strategy, and its relations with the CEO and management team, in Part III, in the context of board best practices.

Credit Suisse Collapse: Scandal and Mismanagement

Once regarded as a paragon of financial excellence, Credit Suisse found itself embroiled in a web of high-profile scandals and governance deficiencies in the years leading up to its demise. The bank was among the world's 30 financial institutions identified as 'too big to fail' by the Financial Stability Board.[1]

(continued)

[1] Financial Stability Board. (2022). 2022 List of global systemically important banks. 21 November. https://www.fsb.org/wp-content/uploads/P211122.pdf

(continued)

Credit Suisse's tumultuous path was marked by the significant Greensill scandal in 2021. The bank had invested US$10 billion of its clients' funds, but was unable to recover them all due to the collapse of the company. This was followed by the collapse of Archegos, resulting in a loss of US$5.5 billion.[2] These incidents underscored failures in board oversight, leading to substantial losses.

In the same year, the Swiss Financial Market Supervisory Authority (FINMA) announced the identification of 'serious organizational shortcomings' within Credit Suisse, during a probe into spying activities involving its COO, leading to the resignation of CEO Tidjane Thiam.[3]

In 2022, Credit Suisse became the first major Swiss bank to stand trial for a criminal case related to money laundering in a Bulgarian cocaine trafficking scheme, resulting in a US$22 million fine.[4] Its reputation suffered further from the 'Suisse Secrets' scandal, revealing accounts linked to criminals and corrupt officials totalling over US$8 billion, despite denials from the bank.[5]

Leadership instability and the board's failure were further underscored by the resignation of Chairman Antonio Horta-Osorio in 2022, following violations of Covid quarantine rules.[6] This period also saw the board receiving substantial compensation packages amid ongoing crises.[7]

The downfall was accelerated by a loss of confidence, particularly fuelled by the bank's inadequate management of its reputation on social media platforms. This mismanagement led to significant client withdrawals from its wealth management sector, culminating in outflows of CHF 111 billion in the final quarter of 2022.[8] Rumours on social media about the bank's financial stability notably exacerbated this bank run.

The cascade of scandals revealed the failures at the board level, in risk management, and in maintaining reputation and client confidence, all of which were instrumental in Credit Suisse's bankruptcy in 2023. It demonstrates how vulnerabilities in these domains can swiftly erode confidence among clients and investors. It may also serve as a warning about the repercussions of neglecting proper governance and ethical conduct.

[2] Allen, M. (2023). Where did it all go wrong for Credit Suisse? 9 February. https://www.swissinfo.ch/eng/business/where-did-it-all-go-wrong-for-credit-suisse-/48269536

[3] SwissInfo. (2021). Credit Suisse punished for corruption and spy cases. 20 October. https://www.swissinfo.ch/eng/business/credit-suisse-punished-for-corruption-and-spy-cases/47042394

[4] *The New York Times*. (2022). Credit Suisse is fined for helping a Bulgarian drug ring launder money, a court said. 27 June. https://www.nytimes.com/2022/06/27/business/credit-suisse-fine-bulgarian-drug-ring.html

[5] France 24 News. (2023). Credit Suisse: A bank sunk by scandals. 19 March. https://www.france24.com/en/live-news/20230319-credit-suisse-a-bank-sunk-by-scandals

[6] Rain, A. (2022). Credit Suisse chair Horta-Osório resigns over Covid-19 breach. SwissInfo, 17 January. https://www.swissinfo.ch/eng/business/credit-suisse-chair-horta-os%C3%B3rio-resigns-over-covid-19-breaches/47267616

[7] Credit Suisse (2022). Annual Report, Compensation. https://www.credit-suisse.com/media/assets/corporate/docs/about-us/investor-relations/financial-disclosures/financial-reports/csg-ar22-compensation-en.pdf

[8] Walker, O. and S. Morris (2023). Credit Suisse: the rise and fall of the bank that built modern Switzerland. *Financial Times*. 24 March 2023 https://www.ft.com/content/072dd83d-232d-4223-9428-801d4437b4f6

Table 8.1 The Danger Zone: Board Failures

When board failures occur, they are typically the result of four different sources of breakdown in board work. Do you recognise any of these in your board?

Non-existent	Weak	Average	Strong	Best Practice
1	2	3	4	5

TECHNICAL RISKS
Extraordinary risks – such as economic risks, societal risks, and technology risks – are a reality. What are some of the significant risks we may not be considering?

How would we evaluate our board's technical expertise in identifying, assessing, and supervising risks and their mitigation?

| 1 | 2 | 3 | 4 | 5 |

STRATEGY
The board's ability to assess and engage on strategy is critical. What are some of the areas of threat to the strategy that the board needs to consider?

How would we evaluate our board's commitment and ability to engage on strategy with the executive team?

| 1 | 2 | 3 | 4 | 5 |

CEO AND TEAM SELECTION/SUPPORT
A frequent area of board failure is its inability to select the right CEO. On many occasions it is not handled proactively or systematically, and left until the last minute.

How would we assess the sophistication of our CEO selection process? How would we rate our board's capability to manage this as an ongoing process?

| 1 | 2 | 3 | 4 | 5 |

INTEGRITY
Integrity failure is another key area of failure, and a very common one. Have we had any recent failures in ethics? If not, we probably aren't looking hard enough! How central is integrity in our board discussions? Any challenges?

How would we rate the strength of our board's commitment to compliance and ethics?

| 1 | 2 | 3 | 4 | 5 |

CHAPTER

Risks and Ensuring the Right Board Risk Philosophy

Risks are a primary board responsibility, and a strong risk philosophy will help boards to be a secure base in this area. The board provides risk back-stops for management and also drives the risk appetite of the organisation. In addition, the board makes major choices regarding mergers and acquisitions, culture, and strategy that drive the fundamental risks of the business. Thus, a well-anchored risk philosophy is important, especially as the world becomes more chaotic and the risks ever more challenging.

As the value of goodwill features more prominently on companies' balance sheets, their responsibilities for managing risk – and especially reputational risk – increase greatly. Not handling this issue properly can have substantial implications, as the case of US theme park chain SeaWorld illustrates.

> In 2013, a US documentary called *Blackfish* was released that criticised SeaWorld's treatment of killer whales. It received much media attention and caused a public outcry against the company. The US Securities and Exchange Commission (SEC) later began investigating fraud charges against SeaWorld for misleading investors about the impact of the documentary on the company. In 2018, the SEC announced that SeaWorld, and its former CEO and Vice President of Communications, would pay more than US$5 million to settle the charges. 'This case underscores the need for a company to provide investors with timely and accurate information that has an adverse impact on its business', said Steven Peikin, Co-director of the SEC Enforcement Division. 'SeaWorld described its reputation as one of its "most important assets," but it failed to evaluate and disclose the adverse impact *Blackfish* had on its business in a timely manner.'[1]

---

[1] US Securities and Exchange Commission. (2018). SeaWorld and former CEO to pay more than $5 million to settle fraud charge. 18 September. https://www.sec.gov/news/press-release/2018-198

All boards should keep the following six principles in mind regarding risks, whether these concern people, markets, operations, safety, demand, or other parts of the organisation's activities.

Risks are everywhere! Many business leaders think about risk too narrowly. True business risks go far beyond the technical risks that risk departments or chief risk officers focus on. They can be external, related to the industry, competitors, customers, the environment, and the economy, or internal, stemming from operations, leadership and decision skills, and personal ethics. Risks can be hard and quantifiable or soft and qualitative. They may be well-defined or ambiguous. Risks are connected to strategy, and to the levels of complacency, discipline, and creativity in the organisation. Boards must therefore develop a specific view of risks, and not rely solely on a management risk report.

Risk techniques will fail. Indeed, they are bound to do so, because if we knew exactly what the risks were, they would not be risks anymore. The goal of risk techniques is thus not to determine precise risk results, but to understand the complexity and sophistication of current risks in order to respond intelligently. This is why 'black-box' risk models don't help boards in their risk work.

For every risk there is an opportunity. Success is about navigating risks, whether the goal is to make money, treat customers and employees well, or cater to shareholders or governments. A challenging wind can in fact carry a well-managed organisation further, while blowing others off course.

The deepest risk is the one within us. Ultimately, it is the ability to make decisions and steer a business in the right direction that matters the most. Each individual has their own risk responsibility, and every board member, manager, and employee owns his or her own risk decisions. This responsibility requires awareness, which in turn drives true success. The biggest risk is not external: it is our own ability to decide in the face of all the other risks.

Risk is positive. What takes you down can take you up. Life is risk. Business is risk. Without risk, there is no movement, opportunity, challenge, or growth. Risk is what makes us choose the right path and the right decision. It is what sends us to the acme of success. The only thing more beautiful than risk itself may be the strength and ability to avoid the risks we choose to avoid, to take the risks we choose to take, and the wisdom to know the difference.

There is no single best way to measure risk. Risk techniques do have value. Sensitivity analyses, stress tests, volatilities, scenarios, and Monte Carlo simulations all look for simple solutions to risks. But any model has deficiencies – from simple (extreme versus moderate risks) to complex (linkages between risks) – that make it incomplete and thus wrong. There is no complete and perfect mathematical measure of risk. These risk-measurement tools can provide guidance and may support executive thinking. But they can fail too, so boards should remain somewhat sceptical.

Because risk measures do not always work, boards should have several frameworks to think about risk. Preparing for risks is more useful to a board than measuring them (or believing it has done so). And developing the right risk culture, with a balance of appetite and aversion, is most useful of all. Risk awareness should be ingrained in the behaviour of everyone within the organisation, with as great a sense of ownership as possible.

With these principles in mind, the next chapter offers practical ways for board members to think about risk.

10

A Board Member's Practical Guide to Risk Thinking

Risk thinking used to be reserved for the back office, and risk reports used to put board members to sleep. Not anymore. The complexity and impact of risk have increased dramatically, and those companies that have developed special skills, flexibility, and acumen in this area have gained a terrific advantage.

We find that best practices in risk are aligned along the following four dimensions:

- **Physical health check** – What are we exposed to?
- **Mental health check** – Are we capturing the right problems?
- **Strategic risk check** – Are we making the right moves?
- **Governance risk check** – Are we well-structured for continued awareness?

Boards must focus on all four dimensions, because slippage in any one of them may doom the organisation to failure or under-performance. When times are good, underperformance is often acceptable because everybody is doing well. But not in more difficult conditions, such as the 2020s, when money has become scarce, the generosity of fund providers is waning, and the competition is becoming tougher. Yet fortunes are often made during precisely these periods when only the fittest survive. And adequate risk fitness is crucial in this regard.

The Physical Health Check: Technical Risks

First and foremost, a physical health check is necessary. Every board should be aware of where the organisation hurts. Ideally, it will also know where major clients and suppliers are feeling pain, which individuals are most vital to the organisation's success and resilience, and which input prices have the biggest impact on the business. In short, a board should know which risks matter most.

I am puzzled by companies that almost seem surprised when they encounter difficulties as a result of volatility in well-known risk factors such as interest rates, currencies, and the prices of oil and other commodities. The high variance of these has long been demonstrated, and the past 30 to 40 years highlight their incredible uncertainty.

Suddenly, risks are converging, interconnecting and complicating each other. For example, bankers' traditional view of risk as residing in markets, credit, or operations has been blown to pieces (and the efficiency of regulations such as the Basel Accords are threatened as well). In the oil and gas sector, volatile oil prices create ripple effects that go beyond revenues and even the organisation itself, touching suppliers, clients, countries, and geopolitics. Furthermore, culture and integrity may now have become a bigger risk than equity markets to any organisation.

Nothing should surprise us anymore. Boards need to revisit their old risk assumptions, open their minds to all risks, and prepare as best they can. This will help to frame minds so that the organisation can react faster, better, and stronger when risks materialise. With that goal in mind, boards should consider adopting a four-step process for mastering technical risks: identify, assess, manage, structure.

Identify your Risks

Identifying risks is too important to be just a bottom-up process, because employees – whether a single person or a department – will often miss the big picture. When one well-known family packaging business started risk reporting to the board, it conducted a large survey of most of its employees. The survey suggested that the major risk – meaning the one consistently rated as having a high impact on each employee – was VAT compliance, which was hardly a major corporate risk. Without input from senior management, therefore, employees' views of major risks may not result in a good view of risk for the whole organisation.

However, the bottom-up approach, and listening to different viewpoints, is still important and should be supported by open lines of communication in the organisation. In April 2007, a risk manager at UBS reported difficulties in the valuation of sub-prime structured products to his boss. This could have been a strong signal to top UBS management and the board. But the chair's office did not take the signal, closed the trader's outfit, and integrated it in UBS's investment bank with little proper risk identification. And as we saw in Chapter 8, we all know how that ended.

Old ways of identifying risks also need to be revisited. The board needs to engage in this; for example, by having an annual session – with management not present – where directors discuss major risks. These could result in simple maps that go beyond risks identified by management, to include risks related to the CEO, as well as cultural, social, geopolitical, and complacency risks.

Assess your Risks

Once the board has identified major risks, it must assess and gain a better understanding of them. Even non-quantifiable risks can be assessed. The assessment does not need to be exact. After all, if risks could be fully assessed, they would not be risks. Rather, the aim is to grow awareness and develop a common language that can be used to communicate and prepare for these risks.

There are many risk-assessment tools, and I recommend that boards use several for large or sensitive investments. Sensitivity analyses (tornado diagrams or spider diagrams), scenarios, and Monte-Carlo simulations are all useful tools, with different levels of granularity and ease of use. Verbal assessments by those closest to risk are also helpful. A simple scoring system will help the board agree on priorities and address differences in risk perceptions between members. The goal is not to increase paperwork, but rather to raise awareness of the potential impact of the identified risks. We will discuss advanced risk techniques for board members in more detail in the next chapter.

Risk Appetite from the Board   Companies face critical decisions about how to allocate their capital, liquidity, and other resources to effectively manage risks and optimise returns. At the heart of these strategic choices is the concept of risk appetite, a crucial factor in guiding companies through the uncertainties of market dynamics and the pursuit of long-term value creation.

Risk appetite refers to the amount and type of risk a company is willing to accept in pursuit of its strategic objectives in its quest for long-term value creation. Contrasting this, risk tolerance sets the thresholds that define the maximum level of risk a company is ready to tolerate, thus establishing clear boundaries that its activities should not exceed. Together, they provide insight into the company's stance on risk-taking and its adaptability to the continually changing business environment.

Typically, a Risk Appetite Statement (RAS) is issued by the board of directors. RAS specifies the particular types and amounts of risk appetite and tolerance. Figures 10.1 and 10.2 provide examples of two risk appetite statements.

Establishing the risk appetite serves a purpose beyond merely setting limits; it also delegates the authority of risk-taking. The risk appetite statement from the board sets parameters within which innovation initiatives can proceed without requiring explicit board approval, as long as they fit within the

	HIGH	MEDIUM	LOW
Supply, demand, and prices of commodities		✕	
Currency exchange (FX) rates			✕
Geopolitical, permits and licences to operate	✕		
Laws and Enforcement		✕	
Liquidity			✕
Counterparty credit and performance			✕
Operating			✕
Cyber			✕
Health, safety, and environment	✕		
Climate change	✕		
Community relations and human rights			✕

Source: Based on Glencore Annual Report 2021.

Figure 10.1   Example of Risk Appetite Statement 1
Source: Based on Glencore Annual Report, 2021.

predefined risk appetite. This approach promotes a culture of responsible risk-taking, empowering innovation within defined risk levels.

Beyond merely drawing lines around permissible risk, clarifying the risk appetite opens doors to strategic opportunities while ensuring a clear understanding of the associated risks. As such, the risk appetite contributes to making more informed decisions and fostering long-term value and innovation.

Manage your Risks

Managing risks does not mean eliminating all of them. Organisations may at times be too conservative, and in those cases management's concern with board prudence is justified. Investors and stakeholders expect risk-taking in pursuit of success. Organisations should eliminate only those risks that are not core, or that are too negative, and then manage the remaining risks with full transparency.

For example, a gold-mining company that does not fully disclose its price hedging may be misleading investors that bought the stock for its gold-price

1. Organic growth

We will rigorously pursue divisional organic growth strategies to meet our market growth objectives.

2. Mergers and acquisitions (M&A)

We will actively pursue M&A opportunities that enhance our strategic platform subject to meeting investment criteria.

3. Returns and profitability

We will not pursue growth at all costs, and expect high margins, strong returns on capital and working capital discipline together with cash generation.

4. Capital allocation

We will encourage capital expenditure in pursuit of our growth ambitions subject to Internal Rate of Return (IRR) hurdles and capital structure targets.

5. Capital structure

We are prepared to use leverage in pursuit of our growth agenda and will actively seek low cost debt to fund the Group but, recognising cyclicality in our end markets, will maintain significant headroom against our financial covenants.

6. Reputation and brand image

We will avoid/manage situations or actions that could have a negative impact on our reputation and brands. We aim to be transparent with all of our stakeholders unless prejudicial to our collective interests.

7. Safety, Health and Environment (SHE)

We will not undertake or pursue activities that pose unacceptable hazard or risk to our people, the communities in which we operate, or the broader environment.

8. Country presence

We are prepared to enter new countries which offer opportunities for growth consistent with our overall strategy. We will not enter, or will exit, countries which present a high risk of harm to our people, damage to our reputation, or breach of international sanctions.

9. Innovation

We will invest in technology, research and development to innovate our customer offering allowing us to maintain and expand our market share.

Source: Extracted from Weir Group Annual Report 2017

Figure 10.2   Example of Risk Appetite Statement 2

Source: Extracted from the Weir Group Annual Report, 2017.

exposure. The best risks to manage technically (with hedging) tend to be those that create more downside than upside. A good example is airlines' exposure to fuel costs, because an airline has more to lose when oil prices are very high than when they are very low. In 2022, British Airways' parent company, IAG, revealed that its fuel hedging initiative held a value of around US$1.2 billion, offering some relief against escalating oil prices. Similarly, Southwest and Air France-KLM announced potential gains of approximately US$1 billion each through their hedging strategies.[1] This shows that hedges can have a strategic dimension. An easy rule of thumb for assessing whether a hedging programme can be valuable is to ask whether the risk is asymmetric: Is there more to lose than gain from the underlying risk, or vice versa?

Thus, for any risk management programme, boards should ask two questions. Firstly, does it truly create value for shareholders, or rather create comfort for managers? Secondly, does the risk management programme depend on the timing of its implementation? If it does, then it is speculative. In that case, the board should ask management how good they are at speculation.

Structure your Risks

Finally, organisations have had considerable success in recent times with structuring – or sharing – risks. This entails identifying different risk exposures in a company's network of relationships (including with investors, clients, and suppliers) and agreeing to share the risks with those least sensitive to them, to create value for all. This principle has often been used in joint ventures and acquisitions (with earn-outs), as well as in commercial contracts. It has become part of digital transformation and of business transformation more generally.

For example, Syngenta, one of the world's largest producers of fertilisers and pesticides, has boosted its Latin American business by providing farmers in the region with yield guarantees. The high-risk farmers (who typically default in bad times) are thus able to pass on some of their risks to the company. Syngenta, in turn, can have its aggregated exposures hedged via a commodity trader. In this way, the company obtains more business, with less credit risk (since the 'insured' farmers will probably be more likely to pay), and typically at higher prices for its products. The company has since applied this practice to the United States, Eastern Europe, and Russia. In times of turmoil, with parties so sensitive to risk, smart risk structuring can make an important difference.

Once the board has completed its physical check of technical risks, it needs to address the mental, strategic, and governance steps of the risk process.

---

[1] Longley, A. and D.K. Kumar (2022). Airlines set to save billions with fuel hedges amid $100. Bloomberg UK, 3 August. https://www.bloomberg.com/news/articles/2022-08-03/airline-fuel-hedges-set-to-save-billions-for-some-with-100-oil

We discuss these briefly in this chapter, and in more detail later in the book. It is important to note that deep investigation in these areas can also create much value.

The Mental Health Check: Behaviours

'Real knowledge is to know the extent of one's ignorance.'

Confucius (551–479 BCE)

Boards are at the heart of risk governance. By their nature, risks cannot be fully and exactly measured. The real question proficient directors should ask, therefore, concerns the board's *attitude* to risks.

Market sentiments, fads, and even so-called global trends have taken many by surprise; these are well-known risk factors. Markets may be somewhat irrational, but they are simply a reflection of people, possibly even of ourselves. Can boards, therefore, look at their own failings?

As we saw in Chapter 7, we now have a good view of typical behavioural risks related to dysfunctional group dynamics and board culture. As an exercise, board members should assess and test themselves for the following nine behavioural risks. These are the ones I see most frequently on boards (many others are available in the general literature on mental biases):

- **Herd behaviour and groupthink:** Is your organisation following the herd? Are you as a board member doing the same and engaging in groupthink? There is something biological about living in agreement with others. It is typically much safer to be wrong with others than wrong alone. But although this behaviour may be safe for the individual (look at those who profited from the pre-financial-crisis era, for example), it does not contribute to the organisation's long-term performance and social responsibility. Boards should therefore re-visit past decisions, successful ones as well as failures, in this light. Much governance work is about overcoming this classical mental bias, including through diversity in all its forms.
- **Optimism:** Senior management tends to comprise individuals with an optimistic bias. Indeed, optimism is typically better liked and more successful socially. It also supports modern leadership practices of motivating and energising employees. Finally, optimism helps resilience in the face of difficulties typically faced by top management. The ideal board member, by contrast, could well be slightly paranoid. In both cases, a reality check may be warranted.
- **Overconfidence:** The best professionals acknowledge that predicting oil prices is close to impossible. The same can be said for currencies or markets. Yet many of us start believing our own views. Do we truly know

how little we know? Perhaps not surprisingly, most of the senior managers and board members, including government ministers, with whom my teams and I have administered a simple test of overconfidence tend to show strong overconfidence. This is not negative per se, because overconfidence may bring strong motivation and energy to an organisation. One does not lead others without a certain level of confidence. But when crucial decisions are taken, it is best to hold overconfidence in check. Governance concerns key decisions for the organisation, including strategy and mergers and acquisitions. Board members should therefore check themselves for possible overconfidence.

- **Dunning–Kruger Effect:** People with substantial, measurable deficits in their knowledge or expertise lack the ability to recognise these (see Figure 10.3). The Dunning–Kruger effect illustrates that people tend not to recognise their lack of ability at first, basking in a form of illusory superiority, but become more aware of it as their knowledge increases. As a result, board members may think they are performing competently when they are not. This is particularly problematic for board members who are asked to make key decisions on matters beyond their expertise. Cultural diversity in the boardroom can help to overcome this effect, because the effect varies across cultures, as long as competency in the boardroom remains a priority.

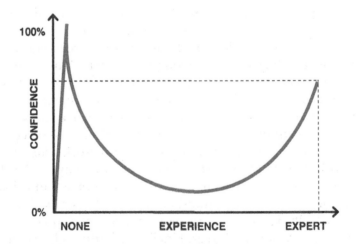

Figure 10.3   The Dunning–Kruger Effect

Source: Adapted from https://www.optimaloutsourcing.co.uk/the-risks-of-the-dunning-kruger-effect/[2]

[2] Zawadka, M., A. Graczyńska, A. Janiszewsa, A. Ostrowski, M. Michałowski, M. Rykowski, and P. Andruszkiewicz (2019). Lessons learned from a study of the integration of a point-of-care ultrasound course into the undergraduate medical school curriculum. *Medical Science Monitor* 2(25): 4104–4109.

- **Belief perseverance or Tolstoy Effect:** This is well expressed by the great Russian writer's quote: 'The most difficult subjects can be explained to the most slow-witted man if he has not formed any idea of them already; but the simplest thing cannot be made clear to the most intelligent man if he is firmly persuaded that he knows already, without a shadow of doubt, what is laid before him.' Have you figured out the business or the world in such a smart way that you find it hard to challenge your views, despite the large shifts that are happening? If so, are your views steady or rigid? Most of us do not adapt fast enough; we do not have the flexibility. We have developed sophisticated heuristics to understand the systems we work in, which have probably been successful so far. But as the environment changes, these heuristics become obsolete and our decisions become challenged. How fast can you adapt to the new environment we are facing? Do we still expect the old times to come back? If so, it's time for a reality check.

- **Confirmation bias:** Our thoughts, opinions, beliefs, and world views are based on years of experience, reading, and rational, objective analysis. Unfortunately, these years of sampling information may have been subject to confirmation bias. We may always have implicitly paid more attention to information confirming our implicit views on ambiguous topics – such as what constitutes a great CEO, effective compensation structures, and the social impact of business.

- **Hindsight bias:** There is a tendency to overestimate one's ability to have predicted an outcome that was not easy to predict, once that event has happened. This manifested itself clearly after the Russia–Ukraine War broke out in 2022; few had foreseen it accurately, yet many subsequently thought they had done. Are you the type that tends to think 'I told you so. I knew it'? If so, are you looking back in time truthfully, or are you second-guessing how you would have reacted based on today's situation?

- **Anchoring:** Do you tend to anchor to values and numbers, even unconsciously? This bias particularly affects key decisions such as acquisitions, when board members may hold on to one number despite having a better understanding of synergies, integration challenges, or changes in context. Directors may intellectualise these changes and differences, but still typically come back to their original 'anchor' values.

- **Representativeness:** Giving a shape to highly uncertain processes also reassures the mind. Relying on patterns is the last of the typical biases we are most concerned with. It happens notably in cyclical activities (but aren't they all?). Do you believe that markets will come back up because they always do? Do you believe the cycle is four to five years, as it traditionally has been? Are you looking for some pattern to repeat itself? This may not be productive. Sometimes, life-altering changes happen – such as the Russian Revolution or the development of artificial intelligence – and change the world in such a way that past patterns do not return.

All of these behavioural patterns limit directors' awareness of risks and opportunities. Good governance can overcome these mental biases through the best practices described elsewhere in this book. These include boardroom diversity, effective processes, and good dynamics among directors, as well as between management and the board. Having a diversity of perspectives is particularly important to overcome limiting behavioural factors such as these, as we will see in Chapter 19.

The Strategic Risk Check

As major shifts happen, strategies need to be revisited. Holding on to past strategies does not make sense. But developing new ones, or adjusting to the markets, can be challenging. Strategic thinking is complex, and building strategies requires much work, such as improving client and competitor awareness and building on the organisation's core distinctiveness. Nonetheless, there are ways for boards to test strategic choices for their pertinence and thus overall risk.

Typical Strategies

Categorising strategies can help. Ohlsson and Strebel's framework,[3] for example, puts all big strategic moves into five categories:

- Going for growth, such as when rolling out a product.
- Restoring profitability, as when a company needs restructuring.
- Finding a new game, when a company attempts to reinvent itself.
- Relaunching growth, when a company levers its distinctiveness to differentiate itself from competitors or substitutes.
- Realignment, when a company realigns its value proposition to its customers through a revised value chain, with capability development; for example, with process efficiency.

Strategic Risk Assessment

Once the strategic move is well-identified, whether along the dimensions proposed above or others (and this can be done for clients and suppliers as well),

---

[3] Strebel, P. and A-V. Ohlsson (2010). *Smart Big Moves*. FT Prentice Hall.

the board needs to question whether the strategy is the right one. Overall, the right moves will confront three key strategic risks:

- Strategic Risk 1: Does the strategy lever the company's distinctiveness, that is, its objectives, values, culture, and capabilities, in terms of skills and resources; and lever its resources, in terms of assets, clients, and partners, as well as match its social footprint?
- Strategic Risk 2: Does the strategy fall into psychological traps, including beliefs such as 'we can beat the competition', 'we know what the customer needs', 'we never admit defeat', or 'we always move forward'?
- Strategic Risk 3: Does the strategy address significant market opportunities or is it too marginal to have an impact?

Boards should first assess the strategy and the proposed move by establishing measures or at least perspectives on each sub-risk category. They should then assess competitors' moves, customers' needs, and value chain opportunities. Each dimension can thus be assessed to establish a strategic risk evaluation (Figure 10.4).

Figure 10.4   Strategic Risk Assessment for Boards
Source: Adapted from Strebel & Ohlsson (2010).

The board will then address execution of that strategy, probing how management intends to achieve the goals, what principal moves have been selected, how people across the organisation will engage in the strategy, and what the fall-back options are. Execution is of course itself a key risk, while of a different nature to the strategic risk analysed here.

Even smart strategies can fail, perhaps because the environment changes or competitors move unexpectedly, or because they were not well executed. Organisations and their boards may then need to align again, revisiting all previous risks. High-quality boards will recognise this. Remaining open to such moves is part of the awareness provided by solid governance. This brings us finally to governance risk.

The Governance Risk Check

Leaders fail, organisations drift, and environments change. Leaders are human, and although the selection process may be rigorous, good leaders in some circumstances may prove to be bad ones in others. Organisational culture changes, corporate conscience deteriorates, integrity gets lost, the context changes. The problem comes when governance is too weak to recognise and address these threats fast enough. This is where governance risk arises.

In order to control for that risk, governance rules need to apply. These should not constrain, but rather make sure that leadership failure, organisational deterioration, and contextual changes, when they happen, do not become too costly to the organisation.

Boards in any organisation can self-check for well-known governance risk factors. In particular, these include:

- a poorly defined role of the board;
- a domineering CEO (or chair);
- an inefficient board: size, independence, personalities, the role of outsiders, and the structure of board committees all matter;
- conflicts of interest at board or senior management level;
- compensation schemes that have strong side effects;

In January 2019, the share price of China Traditional Chinese Medicine Holdings (China TCM) plunged after an independent non-executive director resigned, accusing the company of governance shortcomings. In an open letter to China TCM shareholders, Zhou Bajun said he would resign owing to the company's governance problems, in a rare public spat over a board position at a listed Hong Kong company. Zhou alleged that China TCM failed to keep proper records and written minutes of board meetings after its Hong Kong-based external company secretary stopped attending them. Zhou also said the company had yet to convene a meeting involving its strategy committee, of which he was one of five director members, since it was formed five years earlier.

- a board that is not well aligned with its mission (whether supervisory, strategic, connecting or hands-on); and
- a poor governance culture (values, understanding, and dynamics).

Good governance should be maintained even when things go well. In fact, this is the best time to make improvements, because it is usually less hectic than when things are not going well.

When organisations have done their physical and mental risk checks, have smart strategies in place, and the structures to ensure good governance, then they have a sound basis for success even during difficult times. In fact, these become times of re-incubation, when a company's distinctiveness becomes deeper and new opportunities fuel success. This is hard work, but while being a bitter pill to swallow, a recession can turn into a true medicine for such an organisation.

Good risk thinking for the board should thus not stop at classical physical risk, such as input costs and product prices. Given increased social, technological, and geopolitical uncertainty, mental biases or psychological risks compound the physical risks. All of these need to be addressed through the right strategies, and thus strategic risk assessment completes the analysis. And as strategy has become more challenging than ever by changes in the environment, keeping governance healthy and spotting the key governance risks is part of good risk thinking too. In this chapter, therefore, we have offered a mapping of high-quality risk thinking for a board.

Yet increasingly, board members must have an awareness and understanding of technical risks that go beyond the checks we have discussed in this chapter. We now turn our attention, therefore, to more advanced risk techniques.

Current boards are engaging much more in significant scenario planning than in the past to address the impact of context on risks and strategy at large. Indeed the world of risks and strategy have come closer together for high-level board thinking.

In November 2023, Sam Bankman-Fried was convicted of embezzling US$8 billion from cryptocurrency exchange FTX, which collapsed in bankruptcy. Newly appointed CEO for FTX in bankruptcy John Ray called it 'a complete failure of corporate controls and such a complete absence of trustworthy financial information'. When Bankman-Fried pitched to Social Capital during a US$17 billion fundraising round, the idea of forming a board was raised, but the proposal was vehemently rejected. Despite lacking a board, ESG ratings company Truvalue Labs awarded FTX a higher score on 'leadership and governance' than Exxon/Mobil.[4]

---

[4] Sam Bankman-Fried Becomes an ESG Truth-Teller. *Wall Street Journal*, 17 November (2022). https://www.wsj.com/articles/sam-bankman-fried-esg-truth-teller-ftx-cryptocurrency-crash-11668723808

Boards and Scenarios

The benefit of scenario planning lies in its ability to foster a deeper understanding of potential uncertainties, allowing board members to anticipate a wide range of possible outcomes. As such, scenarios enable boards to understand emerging risks, which cannot be fully captured by other risk tools, and prepare contingency plans.

In a leading renewable energy company the board evaluated three long-term scenarios prepared by the management, detailing possible futures influenced by existing trends and strategic foresights:

1. Net-zero Emissions Scenario: This envisioned advanced economies achieving net-zero emissions through strong environmental policies and a substantial shift to renewable energy, significantly cutting oil demand.
2. Climate Fatigue Scenario: This scenario depicted a future where economic difficulties and rising costs weaken climate action enthusiasm, with protectionism and inconsistent global policies obstructing the adoption of green technologies.
3. Technological Innovation Scenario: This scenario spotlighted a future where technology breakthroughs (on hydrogen and others) drive a global shift towards sustainable energy solutions, marking a departure from current energy sources.

The board, however, found these scenarios to be conventional, following the patterns of best-case, worst-case, and base-case scenarios without delving into deeper and critical external factors. Boards must expand their risk identification efforts beyond conventional risk frameworks, incorporating an extensive range of long-term scenarios and evaluating their potential consequences.[5]

Following the board discussions, the decision was made to disregard the Net-zero Emissions Scenario as overly optimistic. Instead, the focus shifted to the rest of the two scenarios. The Climate Fatigue Scenario was treated as a base-case scenario, while the Technological Innovation Scenario addressed technological uncertainties across specific exposures of the firm.

In both scenarios, the board scrutinised crucial aspects such as competition, regulatory shifts, evolving customer and investor preferences, as well as advancements within the industry. Additionally, they deliberated on the company's future direction and potential organisational adjustments.

---

[5] Heikkinen, K. et al. (2023). When scenario planning fails. *Harvard Business Review*, 21 April. https://hbr.org/2023/04/when-scenario-planning-fails

11

Elements of Advanced Risk Techniques for Board Members: From Quants to Cyber

As guardians of key stakeholder interests, board members need to develop a broad working knowledge of advanced risk-assessment techniques. Only then can they be confident that management is choosing the right path.

Although the current narrow focus on compliance is warranted in the wake of recent corporate scandals, it has distracted the business world from the broader purpose of corporate governance: ensuring a balanced risk/return trade-off for all stakeholders. Boards and managers need to return to a wider view of corporate health and sustainability, including in the risk techniques they use.

Corporate governance generally, and boards specifically, have multidimensional responsibilities in steering top management towards the right risk choices. Boards should:

- systematically monitor the risk situation of the company to identify and evaluate multiple sources of risk;
- understand and influence management's risk appetite;
- take a portfolio view of corporate risks;
- be apprised more specifically of the major risks (or risk combinations) that could significantly alter business perspectives;
- evaluate how management has embedded risk management within the corporation, asking organisational questions such as 'Do we need a chief risk officer?' and technical questions such as 'Which tools are being used?';
- implement joint decision-making procedures for major deals, such as acquisitions and significant investments.

Well-informed risk thinking, as opposed to pure risk avoidance, has become an essential aspect of good corporate governance. True, boards tend to be conservative on risks. But avoiding risks is a risk by itself, as opportunities usually come with risks attached. Some companies, most notably in the financial and oil and gas industries, have developed sophisticated risk assessment tools. Yet, even at international banks and insurance companies, boards have failed. Risk models can become 'black boxes', hiding the complex reality from board members with limited technical understanding of risk issues.

Boards that want to rise to the challenge of broader risk thinking must therefore have a solid understanding of the latest risk-assessment and risk-management techniques.

The Why and How of Quantitative Risk Assessment for Boards

Risks can never be assessed exactly, so why should boards and organisations make any effort regarding quantitative risk assessment? Yet even when such techniques are not as objective as they look, they still offer four advantages in particular beyond informal risk discussions.

Firstly, quantitative techniques foster risk thinking, and help boards and management identify major risk drivers. Consider the impact of changes in oil prices on a car manufacturer such as Ford. The oil price affects a number of variables in the complex web of today's economy, including renewable pipeline and production, government subsidies, secondary energy prices, the cost of inputs for production, and consumer demand for fuel-guzzling cars versus hybrid or electric models. It also affects inflation – and, therefore, the interest rates that drive demand for cars by altering leasing or borrowing costs.

In other words, the impact of oil-price changes on car sales is manifold, especially in an industry where financial services often contribute between 50 and 100% of profits. Resilience to interest-rate changes – as determined by financial leverage, cash flow, protection from exchange-rate volatility, exposure to consumer or supplier default risk, and so on – is vital to the company's competitive position.

Awareness of this web of risks, and how they come together, is essential in understanding management's decisions and, possibly, challenging them. The portfolio view becomes a necessity at board level – and simple numbers help clarify the thinking. What is the company's sensitivity to oil prices in the context of its costs? How do funding costs increase when interest rates go up or down by 1%? And how many sales would the company lose?

Secondly, quantitative techniques clarify risk issues by creating a common language. They encourage clearer communication between managers and the board, and within the board; allow board members to understand management's risk appetite; and stimulate risk understanding by objectifying subjective viewpoints. For example, I have seen two board members assessing the same project, with one viewing it as very risky and the other as moderately risky, although both agreed that the probability of the project failing was around 10%. Their different assessments reflected their personal levels of risk aversion, rather than any objective risk evaluation.

Thirdly, metrics encourage better risk management by helping board members to focus on major risks. Without a clear scaling of risks, boards and even management can be overwhelmed by their breadth and complexity. As a result, they may tend to focus on classic risks, such as currency risk, rather than analysing those that truly impact the business, such as a dramatic loss of market share.

Finally, well-designed quantitative models can help businesses price risks. For example, Moody's KMV model helped investors, lenders, and corporations adopt tools to measure and manage credit risk. Its EDF™ (Expected Default Frequency) credit measure dramatically changed the way credit risk was priced throughout the world. And its LossCalc™ became the first commercially available predictive model of Loss Given Default (LGD).

Classical Quantitative Techniques

The most basic risk assessment techniques start with a sensitivity analysis showing how one value dimension is sensitive to one risk driver, sometimes done within a so-called 'tornado of sensitivities'. It is surprising how many corporations do not even use this simple method to evaluate risk.

For example, most investment bankers these days present an acquisition analysis with cross-sensitivities to the cost of capital and growth rates. Most of the time, a normal spread on the sensitivity analysis will bring out negative perspectives on the acquisition. Yet many boards have approved such deals without paying attention to these, and without questioning future drivers of growth and costs of capital.

> Royal Dutch Shell's acquisition of BG Group in 2016 was driven on the valuation side by strong oil price and growth assumptions. Shell paid US$53 billion to transform the company into a more specialised group focused on the rapidly growing liquefied natural gas (LNG) market and deep-water oil production. The acquisition price was highly sensitive to the oil price – the deal seemed to assume that the price for Brent crude would reach US$90 a barrel by 2018 from less than US$45 in 2016. Yet the average Brent crude price in 2018 was only US$71 a barrel. Analysts at large were sceptical about the financial merits of the deal, notwithstanding its strategic interest.[1] M&As at large fail to create value to the buyer in a majority of cases, despite an overwhelming proportion of them being approved by boards with little or no challenge to the management's optimism.

---

[1] Hughes, C. (2019). Shell still isn't earning enough money. Bloomberg UK. 31 January. https://www.bloomberg.com/opinion/articles/2019-01-31/royal-dutch-shell-still-isn-t-earning-enough-money

However, sensitivity analysis methods are poor (if not altogether inadequate) at jointly evaluating multiple risks. Neither do they allow for the assessment of extreme risks. Scenarios are a good way to encompass multiple and extreme risks. This technique is a step above simple risk identification and basic sensitivities, but remains highly subjective.

The Monte-Carlo simulation has brought the world of scenarios to a new, scientific age, by combining hundreds, possibly thousands, of probability-weighted scenarios into one result – potentially giving boards a clear overview of the risk situation. The technique is used frequently in engineering and banks, but is less common elsewhere, although modern software has made it user friendly. Banks, for example, are switching their Value at Risk (VaR) models, which assess the probability of a certain level of loss or profit, to a Monte-Carlo basis. Since banks make money out of risk-taking, being able to evaluate and measure risk is a core competence. Engineering firms and oil and gas companies use this technique with their P10, P50, and P90 probabilities, meaning the probabilities of reaching a defined outcome (at 10%, 50%, or 90%).

Specific tools to address particular situations have also been developed. For example, option pricing, which is used to calculate the theoretical price of an equity option, has been particularly successful at assessing the economic exposure to specific risks – such as those related to currencies, interest rates, oil price, or credit and corporate default. As a result, corporations can now provide the board with the precise cost (and value) of a hedging programme, or a more precise default risk for a major supplier or customer. This is all the more important given the trend for outsourcing. Similarly, the impact of external or strategic changes on funding costs can be assessed much more precisely.

A good board can expect interesting assessments from these tools. For example, when considering a major joint venture, acquisition, or supply agreement, the board can use an assessment of the credit risk of the other party to challenge a deal. Better still, it may want an assessment of how the joint venture would affect the company's own position.

In addition, the derivatives markets are providing a wealth of information besides commodity and stock price movements, through futures, forwards, swaps, and options. Credit default swaps, which allow an investor to buy protection against a corporate or sovereign default, can give an assessment of a country's risk for a company thinking of opening a new plant there. A board could easily compare possible investments in Thailand and Brazil, for example, despite the long distances involved and the complexity of the two economies.

Hard-to-quantify risks Strategic risks are often so complex that even modern tools, such as game theory, are poor at assessing them accurately. Nonetheless, the board needs to assess strategic and other hard-to-quantify risks in order to have a proper overview. In the case of customer demand risk, for example, what is the risk of a major downturn? More importantly perhaps, how does the board and the organisation prepare for that risk? Is the company being run to simply enjoy the good times, or can it handle the hard knocks as well? Better, can it take advantage of a downturn to gain business from competitors? Or is a digital transformation disruptive enough to the industry to warrant the investment?

Integration of Risks

Financial institutions have become highly sophisticated at integrating different market risks into their models. Some corporations use a VaR related model, cash flow at risk (CFaR), which assesses the probability of the firm having a cash flow below a certain level. However, these models do not encompass all risks – how many of them can combine commodity price and credit risk, and operational and strategic risks, with standard financial risks? Dependencies between these risks make them extremely complex, although the latest tools, such as copulas, which assess how risks move together, may bring greater awareness in this regard. For now, however, even the most complex risk models cannot integrate all factors and their interdependencies. Board members need to be aware of that fact.

Unfortunately, as risk models become more complex, they also become black boxes to most board members. And that makes these models a risk in themselves. Often, simpler thinking may then prevail, at least for the less risk-aware board member.

In general, with integrated risk thinking, we are getting to the point where boards will rely more on their business sense and the corporation's processes than on complex risk models. Nonetheless, an awareness of all dimensions of risks, assessed whenever possible with quantitative techniques, will help the best board members to have a more accurate sense of the business.

The Outcome of Risk Assessment

Once a corporation has adequately assessed risks, its board can be more confident that management is doing a good job of taking and managing them. Should an airline take on oil-price risk? Should a German luxury car manufacturer take on the risk of the euro/dollar exchange rate? Although absolute yes/no answers are often given, more sophisticated choices are often the winners and will reveal management's abilities to the board. For example, a company may decide to cap risks that could put it in jeopardy rather than hedge the whole risk. Or it may decide to take on the risks and inform investors accordingly so that these risks are transparent.

In a complex global company, any risk programme should be designed with value creation in mind. Often, a company creates value when it provides customers with added value or strengthens a competitive situation. Structuring risks has become the name of the game for top-quality management.

In the mid-1980s, Disney was heavily criticised for hedging the yen royalties of its Tokyo theme park when the US dollar was at its peak, thus depriving shareholders of valuable foreign-exchange gains when the dollar subsequently weakened. Disney's assessment was that the currency markets were quite far from the Mickey Mouse business, its core competence. It is hard to assess what the value of currency management to Disney shareholders could have been. On the other hand, Vodafone has chosen to minimise foreign-exchange hedging, saying that its exposures are quite transparent and that shareholders are aware of the risks they take (and can diversify or hedge on their own). Companies have different personalities and policies in this regard. Transparency will help shareholders (and other stakeholders) make the right choices.

Companies must be aware of the risks that will inevitably accompany innovative business models. For example, Schlumberger, a leading oil-services company, has complex projects in which it shares revenues with clients, instead of going for straight sales. This move has created new opportunities that enhance profitability – but also lead to new and/or higher risks. A good understanding of the risks taken may lead to new risk management programmes, such as hedging for oil-price risk.

Structured deals in acquisitions (such as earn-outs, in which the purchase price is paid from the earnings realised after the acquisition) have become commonplace. Few acquisitions can justify being straight deals any more. Instead, the price is structured to share the risks more evenly between buyer and seller, for example by having sharing agreements (in which upside is shared) or support agreements (in which downside is shared). Typically, sharing structures are like call options (the option to buy), while support agreements are like put options (the option to sell). Basic option thinking is thus also important for board members' risk assessments. For example, cement producer Holcim has been building its global presence through joint ventures followed by acquisitions, while its major competitors have grown through outright acquisitions. This is typical risk thinking: in a high-risk environment where delays are not particularly costly, why not get a foot in the door with an option to expand? The option is all the more valuable when the risk is higher (as option traders know well). Boards with that basic understanding can effectively supervise a company's acquisition programme.

Just as a patient is unlikely to accept being operated on with medical technology from the 1980s, so companies today require board members who have a solid grasp of modern risk evaluation and management techniques. Short training courses, coaching, and some reading will take most directors a long way. Rather than acquiring an in-depth understanding of technical subtleties, board members should look to leverage their deep knowledge of business to engage in the competent risk thinking required by modern organisations. Applying these methods in new areas remains a constant challenge. The current risk area of attention is cyber, at the crossroads of tech, social, and geopolitical risks.

Cyber Risk

Cybersecurity is not just about technology. Innovation, processes, and intellectual property have virtual elements which need to be protected. One key element in the property paradigm shift is that digitalisation changes the definition of ownership. Typically, in the real world, ownership is linked with a physical object. When we go digital, we can first ask ourselves what 'owning data' means.

The question is even more important about owning private data. For example, you might have to communicate your data, such as date of birth. It may be your data, but not just yours. It's also shared. What about data that are aggregated? For example, the aggregated data used for cancer treatment. Do you own the data extracted from what is partially from you, partially from somebody else, or what? Finally, what does it mean when your data is stolen? Basically, you have secret information. If somebody has stolen it, you still have it, but it's worth less, because somebody else has it.

So, access to data becomes as or more important than ownership.

The concept of ownership for the digital domain needs to be reviewed. It is more about ruling and protecting the way data:

- Is stored (how and for how long)?
- Can be accessed (by whom)?
- Can be used (for what and by whom)?
- Can be aggregated with other's data (for what and by whom)?

In its early days the internet was the I4H (internet for humans). We had two separated worlds: the real world and cyberspace. This has fundamentally changed. The first element is that cyber-attacks can reach the real world, including money. Not only is the technology increasing, but risky behaviours are as well: critical functions of society are internet based, such as payments via the internet. Personal data is digital and communicated via emails and social networks. At the same time, technology is moving fast and offering new hacking capabilities. Our laws have borders and are slow to react, while hackers are fast and borderless, and sometimes state sponsored.

In cyberspace,[2] all countries are neighbours, sometimes even embedded. A service provider, a bank, a financial institution, or any company, may need 24 months of development to launch a new product or solution. Then there may be nine months of integration, six months of testing, and then about five years of operation. A hacking system may be able to exploit any time during the five years of operation. A hacker will attack a seven year-old system with the latest technology. The risk is asymmetrical. Thus, it's important to design evolving solutions fast enough to address the hacking risks. A successful approach against hackers will combine:

1. Secure technology:
   a well-designed secure architecture;
   secure system components (not too many holes);
   excellence in implementation.
2. Active monitoring:
   cyber monitoring;
   operations in the field (identify the person and where the attacks are from and see what has happened).
3. Proactive response:
   upgrading the solution;
   cyber counter-measures (basically destroying pirate devices);
   legal actions (not always possible depending on the jurisdiction).

Most systems have vulnerabilities that are not discovered early but are discovered with time. What is important is constant monitoring, and thus culture and conduct become an important element of risk management, which cannot be seen only as technical. Which types of attacks have appeared at your premises and at others? If you have no or little awareness, you probably are not fulfilling your cyber risk responsibilities as a board member. Not only is this a way that the company can anticipate where the hackers are looking and what they are searching for, but more importantly it engages you on awareness of the level of risk and preparedness in your organisation.

Finally, cyber is less and less about instantaneous attacks and more and more about compromised systems and personnel over long time periods. The technical side of cyber matters and boards need to gain technological expertise but cannot consider their responsibility limited to this technical knowledge acquisition. They also need to fulfil their responsibility by accomplishing the usual tasks: assess whether the culture is prone to individuals that

---

[2] I am grateful for presentations by and discussions with André Kudelski for many of the insights on cyber in this chapter.

would compromise the organisation's security, support values and systems that enhance security and monitor both efforts and failures of management.

In 2019, the US National Security Agency (NSA) and the United Kingdom National Cyber Security Centre (NCSC) released a joint advisory[3] on advanced persistent threat (APT) group Turla – widely reported to be Russian and also known as Snake, Uroburos, VENOMOUS BEAR, or Waterbug. Turla uses the malicious Neuron, Nautilus, and Snake tools to steal sensitive data and hide behind various foreign states APT infrastructure and resources, thus appearing first as foreign state attacks.

Waterbug's campaigns have involved a range of new tools including custom malware, modified versions of publicly available hacking tools, and legitimate administration tools. The group has also followed the current shift towards 'living off the land', making use of PowerShell scripts and PsExec, a Microsoft Sysinternals tool used for executing processes on other systems.

Turla was able to contaminate government offices including ministries, embassies, as well as multinational organisations and corporates across many countries in Europe, South East Asia, Middle East and Latin America. Compromission lasted for years and was supported by staff in some cases.

How boards identify, assess and manage risk is crucial. But as we will see in the next chapter, they often face their ultimate test in a crisis.

Cybersecurity and board

In 2023, the US Securities and Exchange Commission instituted a mandate for public companies to disclose material cybersecurity incidents and detail their risk management strategies and governance. This directive ensures a standardised framework for reporting on cybersecurity issues, thereby offering investors deeper insights to make more informed decisions. These disclosures are mandated to be integrated in the company's annual report.

The regulation extends to the governance level, requiring the board of directors to provide oversight of risks arising from cybersecurity threats. According to a survey by Diligent Institute, 48% of boards are participating in educational programmes related to the new cybersecurity disclosure regulations.[4] Furthermore, another report highlights that 73% of board members prioritise cybersecurity as a priority for their board.[5]

---

[3] National Cyber Security Centre. (2019). *Cybersecurity Advisory*. https://media.defense.gov/2019/Oct/18/2002197242/-1/-1/0/NSA_CSA_TURLA_20191021%20VER%203%20-%20COPY.PDF

[4] Diligent Institute. (2023). *What Directors Think*. https://www.diligentinstitute.com/wp-content/uploads/2023/08/What-Directors-Think-2023-Still-Taking-Care-of-Business.pdf

[5] Proofpoint. (2023). *Cybersecurity*. https://www.proofpoint.com/sites/default/files/white-papers/pfpt-uk-wp-board-perspective-report.pdf

In 2023, legal action was taken against the software firm SolarWinds and its Chief Information Security Officer, Timothy Brown. They were accused of misleading investors by concealing security vulnerabilities during a significant cyberattack on the US government.[6] Internal communications revealed that Brown was aware of cybersecurity risks and vulnerabilities, but failed to raise them within the company. In presentations prepared by Brown in 2018 and 2019, it was stated that the 'current state of security leaves us in a very vulnerable state for our critical assets'. Further, an internal document shared with Brown in 2020 mentioned that 'the volume of security issues being identified over the last month has outstripped the capacity of Engineering teams to resolve'.[7] This is the first case where the US Securities and Exchange Commission has charged a public company with a fraud charge over cybersecurity disclosure issues.

---

[6] Prentice, C., J. Stempel, and R. Satter. (2023). US SEC sues SolarWinds for concealing cyber risks before massive hacking. Reuters. https://www.reuters.com/legal/us-sues-solarwinds-court-records-2023-10-30/

[7] US Securities and Exchange Commission. (2023). *SEC Charges SolarWinds and Chief Information Security Officer with Fraud, Internal Control Failures.* https://www.sec.gov/news/press-release/2023-227

CHAPTER 12

Crisis Management

8 July – Joanne Marker had recently received an email from a search firm asking if she would be interested in joining the board of RGen, a major infrastructure firm. One of the first questions she had asked the company's chair, Mauro Wright, was what their crisis management plan was in the event that disaster struck. She clicked open Wright's email:

> *Dear Joanne,*
> *I know that your Virtuous experience may have been a traumatic one. Attached you will find our plan, should anything happen to me or to Roger (the CEO). I hope you will find this satisfactory.*

The attachment was a rather generic crisis management plan.

Joanne frowned, remembering the morning of 12 April the previous year. She had awoken at her usual time of 5:00 am. While making coffee in her kitchen, she reviewed the Google alerts on her phone. As she scrolled through, one piece of news gave her pause: there had been a helicopter crash in Brazil. She knew that the Virtuous Ventures executive team had recently held a retreat following a major client meeting in Sao Paulo. With beads of sweat forming on her brow, Joanne opened the article. Her worst fear was realised: it was the Virtuous team on board the fateful helicopter. She phoned Adrian Holmes, the lead director. He agreed to call an extraordinary board meeting for the following morning.

Joanne knew that initial details of the accident might be sketchy and contradictory, and would likely take days to trickle in. But time was not on the Virtuous board's side. To begin with, being physically present near the site of the accident in Brazil was, under the circumstances, the only way to gather reliable information. Furthermore, it was symbolically and morally important that the board not deliberate on a human and organisational tragedy of this scale from thousands of miles away. Among other considerations, someone had to be on the ground to thank personally the first responders who had risked their lives in the aftermath of the helicopter crash.

At the top of the extraordinary board meeting's agenda should be establishing who was in charge. Being a director is not automatically the same as being a crisis controller, and precious time could be wasted if several directors were to jostle for some degree of control, instead of focusing on the crisis at hand. Virtuous' business continuity plan should stand the board in good stead, at least as a departure point for setting up working teams to tackle the crisis, and dividing their responsibilities between gathering information and acting on that information to make decisions. Each team would have a leader and a deputy, and would comprise a mix of board members, staff, and possibly external stakeholders such as regulators and insurers.

Inevitably, in the raw days after a fatal tragedy, time was running against the board and its crisis response, no matter how judiciously and meticulously crafted it was. Because there was so little time to work with, immediacy would often overrule everything. It seemed to take just one hour for social media reactions to the crash to spread. Nevertheless, an hour should be enough time for well-structured teams to clearly identify the issue. And after another hour inside Virtuous' communications war room, initial communications had taken shape, soon followed by a first set of public responses.

The toll that the Brazil disaster had taken on Virtuous' executive team made it even more important for the board to get on the front foot in managing the organisation's response. There were stakeholders to reach out to with carefully crafted, reassuring, and appropriate messages. There was understandable pressure, even duress, applied by shareholders, authorities, and the general public, as well as families affected by the tragedy. And while the human aspect of the disaster unfolded and continued taking its toll, there was a company to be run. For the time being, board members and company officers, led by the chair, would be responsible for day-to-day operations.

The stakeholder outreach included the media, because an air crash with international implications was guaranteed to grab headlines instantly. Arranging a company press conference would not only help to shape the flow and focus of information to the media; it would also project a strong sense of leadership and unity from the Virtuous board in the face of a major setback. This was to be followed by daily briefings on the situation. And despite its best efforts, the company would no doubt also find itself having to respond to criticism about its information and accessibility, and its help for the executives' families.

The Brazil events were not something a director could ever be fully prepared for psychologically and emotionally. But notwithstanding the grief and personal trauma they all shared, the Virtuous board members would quickly have to come to terms with what had happened, and make sure that the executives' families were assisted in coping with their loss. The board would also soon have to consider the event's financial ramifications. Analysts were expecting urgent updates on what financial impact on Virtuous they should expect. Conference calls were set up to assure investors that the company's financials were in good shape, and to inform them that Virtuous may need to nominate its group controller as chief financial officer on an interim basis while the CEO succession unfolded, with the chair taking a temporary executive role.

XYZ, Virtuous' global PR and communications partner, had drafted a guidebook on crisis preparedness. This outlined specific, practical sets of messages and communication channels to prioritise in different circumstances, with a dedicated social media overview including the main actors and influencers. Although these crisis management blueprints would not always be applicable or appropriate to actual, real-life situations, they were invaluable as cues and handles for the Virtuous board to grab on to. In addition, the guidelines were a tremendous time-saver in a situation when having to design a crisis approach from scratch would have been guaranteed to cast the company in a negative light. In particular, the blueprints provided valuable guidance on identifying the best and most appropriate channels of communication between the board and management; between management and shareholders, employees, customers and stakeholders; and with law enforcement authorities and regulators.

In the midst of this frenzied communication, Joanne also understood that no amount of preparation could provide the authenticity of a human touch. This could only come from drawing on one's personal values – as well as, in part, those of the board and the organisation – and allowing them to resonate with the tragedy and drama. This would not always align neatly with the plans and blueprints, but it would give the board's actions the moral centre and human depth that the circumstances called for. She had a thought for those who were close to Amin, the CEO, his family, his collaborators, and the sudden tragedy hitting them. She knew him closely, but it was the same for everyone who was right there with him. She felt like crying.

Joanne was mature enough as a director to see the crisis response as her personal responsibility. It was a role she was not unfamiliar with: 20-plus years of serving on boards of companies and public organisations saw her ride out a number of outsized crises, and remain calm amid great turmoil. She knew well that the task facing the Virtuous board could never be done by one person. What's more, the board would have to move heaven and earth in its response to the tragedy, and would still have the value and quality of its decisions scrutinised. This situation would relentlessly test the mettle of each director. But if the Virtuous board was functioning well before the crisis, a test on this scale should help it to emerge even stronger, with more trust and goodwill to carry it through future crises.

In Chapter 3, we pinpointed judgement and integrity as the main qualities that can make or break the performance and tenure of directors and boards. We also said that these attributes may be severely tested in a time of crisis.

The cautionary tales of boards caught out and paralysed by the scope and velocity of events – be they related to company finances, products or clients, social impact, cyberattacks, or dramatic developments within the board itself – have been widely publicised. A crisis can ensue because of threats to a company's value or reputation, or even to its very existence. These often transcend the operational level and involve shareholders, regulators, and law enforcement agencies. Crises can also revolve directly around board members, for example through controversies in exercising leadership, or nominating and removing senior executives.

Crisis as a Turning Point

Like many words of Greek origin, 'crisis' in its original sense is largely devoid of negative connotations. Ancient physicians including Hippocrates used the term *krisis* to describe a 'turning point' or 'deciding point' in the progression of a patient's disease, after which things could go either way. In today's usage, the meaning of 'crisis' has shifted more toward 'dislocation', but the fundamental if hidden sub-text of being subjected to a decision, of making a choice, remains; in many situations, a crisis is what we make of it. It is a time of decisions.

Boards can and should play a critical role during times of crisis, even if only by acting as a safe base for management. In fact, it is *especially* when unforeseen situations shake the organisation's very foundation that it becomes essential for the board to assume its key responsibilities. This is precisely when the board is expected to shine.

Boards can also help to make their organisations more resilient through preventing, managing, and responding to crises. How, then, can boards groom the judgement skills and rational outlook of their members and management? Can a board prepare for dealing with a crisis before it hits?

There is Work to be Done in Peaceful Times

There is never a better time to start preparing for a crisis than when a company is sailing smoothly. Doing the groundwork required to build resilience is a key weapon in this pre-emptive battle. Boards should begin with risk analysis and management using robust tools and methodologies, as we discussed in Chapters 10 and 11. Extreme risk preparation on an annual basis is also useful.

The current environment, in which 'the only certainty is uncertainty', has popularised a number of techniques that facilitate scenario planning. Among these, 'black swan' simulation is one such 'scenalysis' tool. The term 'black swan' appeared in the aftermath of the 2008 financial crisis to describe random, highly improbable (and therefore unexpected) events which, when they do occur, result in catastrophic consequences.

The dotcom meltdown, 9/11, the sub-prime housing loan collapse, and the 2019 trade wars were each black swans in their own right, as virtually none of the credible sources of economic and political forecasts saw them coming. Black swan simulation tools allow the user to experiment with various real-time variables in order to anticipate even extreme outcomes, the probability of which can only be estimated rather than measured. A simple simulation of such an event can help boards prepare themselves and be readier (rather than ready) for when it occurs.

Communication Principles

Learning to imagine the unimaginable and simulate our environment around it is an increasingly useful skill and mindset. When crisis does hit, however, taking action – even when this is anticipated, premeditated, and carefully rehearsed – is only part of the challenge. Equally importantly, the organisation – and its board, when necessary and productive – *must be seen and heard taking decisive action.* This includes sharing accurate and up-to-date information, elaborating on the company's decisions and projected outcomes, reassuring internal as well as external stakeholders, and seeking assistance and support from public agencies if necessary.

All of these activities seem self-explanatory. Yet without preparation, making them happen 'on the day' will be next to impossible. In the wake of truly cataclysmic events when every minute counts, the public will very likely be in an anxious mood, and hungry for information. Any silence or indecision from the firm in question – and its board – will be deafening. News audiences will speculate the worst, and fundamentally question the organisation's values, leadership, and management competence. Reputation and goodwill that took decades to build may be washed away in one fell swoop.

Preparedness is the key. With sound preparation and planning, one email or call should be enough to set a pre-planned crisis response in motion immediately. Crisis teams will assemble, with each member assuming the specialised task he or she has been trained to handle. Predetermined ad hoc task forces will address stakeholders, call a press conference, engage with the media, issue press releases, track key social media, and react quickly to posts. Guidelines, tool-kits, and written scripts will help automate and coordinate the procedural aspects of the response. Initially, details of the event that precipitated the crisis may be trickling in little by little; likewise, finalising the exact wording of the messages to go out may require a bit of time. But that time will be more productive if the question of 'who does what' has already been clearly decided.

Herbert Wigwe, chief executive of Access Bank, one Nigeria's largest banks, was killed on 11 February 2024, when his helicopter crashed in the Mojave Desert, California, killing all six people aboard. Two days later, Abubakar Jimoh, chairman of Access Holdings announced the appointment of Bolaji Agbede as the Acting Group CEO of the Company.

Not all of this has to be tackled in house, or by the board itself. An external communication partner can be helpful in putting the necessary processes and channels in place. They will come up with coherent sets of scenarios, outreach roles, and messages targeted at specific audiences. This may go a long way towards bolstering the organisation's resilience in the face of crisis. The external partner (for whom dealing with crises may be their bread and butter) can also lead the effort to design what is essentially a new language for dealing with dramatic, unexpected events unfolding inside or outside the company.

All this preparation, and the resulting tools and techniques, will stand board members in good stead, and help them to cope with the shock of being thrust into the spotlight by stakeholders and especially media. It is better for boards to stick to the 'one-voice principle' and keep any dramatic discussions behind the scenes.

Another Powerful Weapon: Gathering Information

Having sleek and quickly assembled crisis management teams in place can ensure that a firm doesn't lose the war on day one. But this may not be quite enough. For sure, reading from a script is always better than an information blackout. Yet to be credible and reassuring in a crisis, the firm's leadership, including the board, must be able to contextualise and present often conflicting information. It helps, therefore, if the company and the board have been continually gathering relevant information over the past few years – as already discussed in Chapter 5. This includes data on the company, its market and operating environment, client needs, competitor trends, and stakeholder motivations. In many scenarios, what is typically referred to as 'external pressures' can be usefully redefined as information. Indeed, weak signals, complaints, and reputation hits become magnified in times of crisis and a board that has paid attention to all these smaller signals has a better chance of going through the crisis easily. For example, a culture that is strongly under financial pressure may well create a crisis linked to small savings with large safety or health impact. A board that spots this early and maps responses and balances the organisation has better chances of getting through the crisis.

In an environment of pervasive uncertainty, directors should also get information from regular conversations with people at all levels of the organisation, including executives, workers on the shop floor, and also customers. These discussions can give directors a real feel for what is happening 'out there', which in turn may help them to foresee and react to a future crisis.

Many of the spectacular boardroom failures we describe in this book share one essential ingredient: the directors' failure to grasp what was going on in the trenches. Ad hoc internal surveys, client feedback, social media scans, and informal testimonials can all be of great value in helping directors build up a nuanced, three-dimensional view of the organisation and the world in which it functions.

Bernard Looney resigned as CEO of oil giant BP in September 2023. Having spent his career at BP, Looney was less than four years into his tenure after admitting that he failed to fully detail relationships with colleagues. He departed the company immediately after his resignation. The company informed investors that Looney 'did not provide details of all relationships and accepts he was obliged to make a more complete disclosure'. Further, it stated that Looney disclosed 'a small number of historical relationships with colleagues prior to becoming CEO' during a review last year, triggered by information from an anonymous source.

In the event of a crisis, having had all-round access to information will help a company's board to make tough decisions and weather the situation through a managed response. Dealing with a crisis in a purely reactive way, and only when compelled to do so by external circumstances, is no longer acceptable. Such an approach undermines confidence in the company's operations, leadership, and integrity – which is hardly surprising. If a stakeholder cannot trust one part of the organisation, such as its publicity engine or the board's handling of a crisis, then why should it trust anything else? Once goodwill and confidence have been undermined, they may be impossible to restore.

By contrast, a focused, dedicated, and energetic board will include directors who see crisis preparedness as a personal responsibility. They will readily assume a public role and take centre stage when circumstances call for it (which is rare, as the board acts as the safekeeper of organisational integrity and communicator of last resort). Because a crisis will inevitably bring out the

In 2022, the US Department of Justice revealed a fraud of US$250 million, which exploited a federally funded child nutrition programme during the COVID-19 pandemic. Among the 47 defendants, Aimee Bock, the founder and executive director of Feeding Our Future, is accused of overseeing this massive fraud scheme, providing false assurances when facing the scrutiny from the Minnesota Department of Education. Across six separate indictments and three criminal informations, the defendants were charged with money laundering, conspiracy, wire fraud, and bribery.

'These defendants exploited a program designed to provide nutritious food to needy children during the COVID-19 pandemic. Instead, they prioritised their own greed, stealing more than a quarter of a billion dollars in federal funds to purchase luxury cars, houses, jewelry, and coastal resort property abroad', stated US Attorney Andrew M Luger.[1]

---

[1] US Department of Justice. (2022). US Attorney announces federal charges against 47 defendants in $250 million feeding our future fraud scheme. Office of Public Affairs. 20 September. https://www.justice.gov/opa/pr/us-attorney-announces-federal-charges-against-47-defendants-250-million-feeding-our-future

best and the worst in board members, they need to prove themselves competent and in charge. A sense of urgency and good timing is also critical. Many crises have shown that delayed reaction, lack of reaction, or overreaction may prove to be a magnet for negative press coverage, which ultimately becomes more damaging than the crisis itself.

A Crisis Will Shed Light on Boardroom Fissures

One of the main themes of this book is the intrinsically social nature of the boardroom, and of governance and business in general – something that is often underestimated. Directors do not come to the boardroom just to attend meetings and dispense guidance. As in all social settings and gatherings, they piece together formal and informal narratives, interact and make sense of things, arrive at new meanings, and create stories. Whenever divisions and schisms within the board have been papered over, they are bound to be exposed, sometimes painfully and embarrassingly, once a crisis erupts. Crises often cast board members in unfamiliar roles that are quite distinct from those assumed by management, and any disharmony can become glaring under the media spotlight.

When the same type of aircraft from the same manufacturer, flown by two different airlines, crashes twice within five months, killing 346 people, big questions arise about the company and the people responsible for running it. Boeing, the manufacturer of the 737 Max aircraft that crashed in October 2018 (Lion Airways) and March 2019 (Ethiopian Airlines), has faced an intense investor backlash since the crashes.

Leading shareholder advisory firms – Institutional Shareholder Services and Glass Lewis – demanded changes to Boeing's governance structure. The dual role of the company's CEO and Chair Dennis Mullenburg was questioned. ISS advised Boeing that 'Shareholders would benefit from the most robust form of independent oversight to ensure that the company's management is able to regain the confidence of regulators, customers and other key stakeholders.'

Some board members sat together on two other prominent boards, prompting considerations of a network effect of 'old boys club' and the chance that the board was in a comfort zone rather than truly challenging the management on risk issues and its ability to deal promptly and effectively with the crisis.

Finally, Boeing's board did not have a risk committee at the time of the crashes. Risk was instead under the purview of the audit committee, prompting Glass Lewis to recommend the removal of Lawrence Kellner, the committee's chair.

'Considering the loss of lives in the accidents, the reputational harm to the company, and the negative impact on future sales of the aircraft, we believe these incidents indicate a potential lapse in the board's oversight of risk management', Glass Lewis said in a report to clients ahead of Boeing's annual meeting in Chicago on 29 April 2019.

In the past few years, numerous companies and their external advisors have described the many rounds of approvals, comments, and reviews behind their crisis management blueprints – some of which run to hundreds of pages. This is a laudable and encouraging trend, which should greatly reduce the risk of future corporate crises taking on the scale of earlier ones such as the BP oil spill of 2010. These blueprints are even more effective when they take into consideration culturally specific modes of communication, reporting lines, and other intricacies of the board's interaction with the C-suite. On the other hand, placing too much focus on the formal, ritualistic aspects of drafting a plan – as often happens in organisations and bureaucracies – may lead to a false sense of security, and a feeling that 'as long as it is written down, it will work'.

Notwithstanding the limitations of the formal, hard-wired aspects of crisis management, the board's structure can in itself be a good source of resilience in decision-making – especially if it systematically prevents conflicts of interest. The alternative, with personalities in the thick of a crisis outwardly projecting ambiguous and at times conflicted roles – has proven to have far-reaching negative ramifications.

In 2016, as Volkswagen reeled from its emissions cheating scandal, the elevation of the company's chief financial officer to be the head of its supervisory board led to further embarrassment. Critics said this was tantamount to handpicking someone who had been directly complicit in the scandal and giving him the task of defusing and investigating the situation.

The restructuring of Tesla's board in 2018, which followed seemingly erratic communication from CEO and Chair Elon Musk about possibly taking the company private, was also controversial. As part of a settlement with the US Securities and Exchange Commission, Musk was forced to step down as Tesla's chair. However, the board was still dominated by the famous CEO (who is also the company's largest shareholder). Despite calls for an independent chair who could exert some control over Musk, the board chose an independent director who had not strongly counteracted him before.

Procedure vs Authenticity

For directors in particular, rising to the occasion during a crisis requires a lot more than following 'what's in the manual'. Whereas an overwhelming series of events may lead management to frame and view problems in narrow – typically technical or legal – terms, the board's challenge will be to reassure shareholders and other groups of stakeholders with measured, appropriate messages. To reassure and resonate with these audiences, such messages must be seen as authentic. They will therefore need to be rooted in directors' personal sense of courage, character, empathy, and breadth of vision, rather than plucked from 'how to' guidelines. In other words, board members must live their own values in addition to those of the organisation.

One of the reasons why many Morgan Stanley employees escaped harm during the 11 September 2001 World Trade Center attacks was that the firm's head of security Rick Rescorla had indeed 'seen it before', albeit on a smaller scale. Rescorla had been appalled at the evacuation effort he witnessed during a previous bombing at the Center in 1993. He therefore made sure that in the years afterwards, employees diligently prepared and practised for another evacuation in the future. His preparedness and the procedures he implemented reportedly saved many lives on 9/11 (although sadly not his own) in the immediate aftermath of the attack on the South Tower.

No single individual can provide this deep alignment with a company's ethics, empathy, and social values. Gaining and maintaining trust, or rebuilding it in the aftermath of cataclysmic events, requires strong and sustained board leadership through values, integrity, and good governance. Empathy, professionalism, and experience are always fundamental to good board work, but become especially valuable during crises. In this respect, a board member with direct experience of previous crises can be a highly useful asset to the organisation.

Communicate Your Way to Rebuilding Trust

Organisations will draw on other less tangible – but equally crucial – assets in times of crisis. These include trust, reputation, and goodwill, and need to be accumulated and cultivated all year round. When a company has failed to establish a sufficiently deep pool of trust with clients, partners, or the general public, there will be a strong propensity to believe news that casts it in a negative light.

How can companies build trust, or recover from a perceived trust deficit? Effective communication goes a long way – if what the organisation says is genuine and compelling. They may choose to communicate their vision, generate a sense of urgency about implementing new initiatives, or simply share stories of their successes and accomplishments ('do well – and also let them know you've done well!').

Importantly, building and rebuilding trust must be a targeted effort, as proposed in Figure 12.1. Boards should have a view of the organisation's likely allies and champions. These can include opinion leaders and experts who can bestow credibility on the company's efforts; network leaders (the 'old-timers' or 'movers and shakers') who exert informal influence; and social leaders who can extend support. Benchmarking exercises and satisfaction surveys with different stakeholders can help to send out powerful signals about challenging the status quo. Do we have the right allies, in government, in unions, in customers' associations? Having mapped these out, and coupled with a few quick wins, strong management of the crisis can create a sense of positive

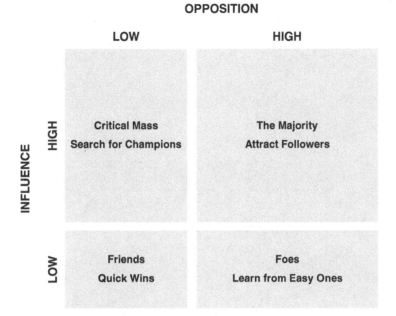

Figure 12.1   Mapping Influencers for Rebuilding Trust

momentum. But if a company has not continuously built a sense of reciprocity and goodwill with all partners, any effort aimed at regaining trust may come across as self-serving and calculating. It is healthy to ask for support – provided the organisation has already established a strong foundation of goodwill.

There is a growing expectation that organisations and their boards will not only know what to do in a crisis, but will emerge from it battle hardened and stronger than before. To handle a crisis in a way that strengthens its reputation, a company needs to draw deeply on existing organisational values and competences. In preparing for, responding to, and recovering from a corporate crisis, the board cannot remain in the comfort zone of an oversight mode. In normal times, crisis preparation should be a regular, yearly exercise for directors, involving the fine-tuning of relevant processes and information.

When emerging from a crisis, organisations may understandably just want to return to normal and regain a feeling of control. In such circumstances, reflection and introspection may not be top of management's list of priorities. But this is precisely where the board can display meaningful leadership by nudging management to draw out the most important lessons from the crisis – including crisis planning, risk management, and how to rebuild trust.

The remainder of Part II focuses on a second major area of board failure: integrity. In the next chapter we look at the responsibility of directors to deal with conflicts of interest, before concluding this section by examining the board's critical role in overseeing fraud risk.

CHAPTER

13

The Four Tiers of Conflicts of Interest*

Addressing conflicts of interest with integrity is at the heart of the personal responsibilities of a leading board member. Although to some degree ever present, such conflicts can be dealt with efficiently and with awareness. Mapping them, accompanied by a personal (or public) register, can certainly help. We can distinguish four tiers of conflicts of interest (see Figure 13.1).

A **tier-I conflict** is an actual or potential conflict between a board member and the company. The concept is straightforward: a director should not take advantage of his or her position. As the key decision-makers within the organisation, board members should act in the interest of important stakeholders, whether the company's owners or society at large, and not in their own. Major conflicts of interest could include, but are not restricted to, salaries and perks, misappropriation of company assets, self-dealing, appropriating corporate opportunities, insider trading, and neglecting board work. All directors are expected to act ethically at all times, promptly declare any material facts or potential conflicts of interest and take appropriate corrective action.

Tier-II conflicts arise when a board member's duty of loyalty to stakeholders or the company is compromised. This would happen when certain board members exercise influence over the others through compensation, favours, a relationship, or psychological manipulation. Even though some directors describe themselves as 'independent of management, company, or major shareholders', they may find themselves faced with a conflict of interest if they are forced into agreeing with a dominant board member. Under particular circumstances, some independent directors form a distinct stakeholder group and demonstrate loyalty only to the members of that group. They tend to represent their own interest rather than that of the company.

---

* This chapter was initially written as an article with Abraham Lu.

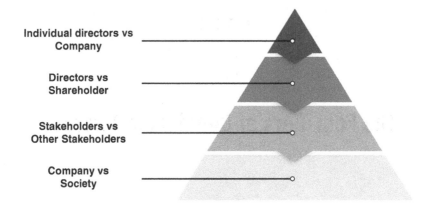

Figure 13.1   The Four-tier Pyramid of Conflicts of Interest

A **tier-III conflict** emerges when the interests of stakeholder groups are not appropriately balanced or harmonised. Shareholders appoint board members, usually outstanding individuals, based on their knowledge and skills and their ability to make good decisions. Once a board has been formed, its members have to face conflicts of interest between stakeholders and the company, between different stakeholder groups, and within the same stakeholder group. When a board's core duty is to care for a particular set of stakeholders, such as shareholders, all rational and high-level decisions are geared to favour that particular group, although the concerns of other stakeholders may still be recognised. Board members have to address any conflicts responsibly and balance the interests of all individuals involved in a contemplative, proactive manner.

Tier-IV conflicts arise when a company acts in its own interests at the expense of society. The doctrine of maximising profitability may be used as justification for deceiving customers, polluting the environment, evading taxes, squeezing suppliers, and treating employees as commodities. Companies that operate in this way are not contributors to society. Instead, they are viewed as value extractors. Conscientious directors are able to distinguish good from bad and are more likely to act as stewards for safeguarding long-term, responsible value creation for the common good of humanity. When a company's purpose is in conflict with the interests of society, board members need to take an ethical stand, exercise care, and make sensible decisions.

Tier-I Conflicts: Individual Directors vs Company

Directors are supposed to 'possess the highest personal and professional ethics, integrity and values, and be committed to representing the long-term interest of the shareowners'.[1] However, in many cases, shareholders have sued

---

[1] General Electric Company. (2016). Governance Principles, p. 1.

directors for taking advantage of the company. An actual or potential conflict between a board member and a company is called a tier-I conflict.

A company is normally considered as a separate legal entity that is independent from its directors, executives, and shareholders. Powerful directors, such as founders or dominant shareholders, can be accused of misappropriating company assets if they are found stealing from their own company; directors who trade on the basis of material, non-public information can be sued for insider trading; those caught accepting bribes or working for competing companies may be asked to resign; and directors who sign agreements on behalf of the company that mainly contribute to their own enrichment may be charged with self-dealing.

For example, the case of Guth vs Loft Inc in the United States in 1939 addressed the issue of individuals pursuing business opportunities for self-enrichment. The president of Loft, who was also the owner of Grace Corp, was found to have used Loft's capital, credit, facilities, and employees to acquire and grow Pepsi Cola for himself rather than for Loft.[2] In the language of the court, 'corporate officers and directors are not permitted to use their position of trust and confidence to further their private interests'.

When board members fail to dedicate the necessary effort, commitment, and time to their board work, it can result in a conflict between them and the company. Because directors often serve on multiple boards, they may not be able to allocate sufficient time to governing any one firm. According to the Spencer Stuart US Board Index in 2023, approximately 20% of S&P 500 boards do not impose a limit on the number of board positions.[3] Stuart Crainer and Des Dearlove have described how directors who were unable to devote enough time to a board 'stuffed the document in their briefcases, all 200 pages or so, and leafed through them in the taxi to the meeting. They extracted, at random, a paper, formulated a trick question and entered the meeting room ready to fire. After all, board work is a power game'.[4] Lack of effort, focus, and dedication are types of conflicts of interest that have not yet received the systematic attention they deserve.

It is well understood that tier-I conflicts arise when directors take advantage of their positions. But when they lack commitment and dedication to their duties, the conflict of interest is somewhat more subtle and much less obvious. Companies need to issue guidelines regarding directors' conflicts of interest and ensure that they follow these rules and act in the interest of the organisations they serve.

---

[2] Kershaw, D. (2005). Does it matter how the law thinks about corporate opportunities? *Legal Studies* 25(4): 533–538.

[3] Spencer Stuart. (2023). Spencer Stuart US Board Index.

[4] Crainer, S. and D. Dearlove (2008). Boards of deflectors. *Business Strategy Review* 19(1): 59–63.

Companies can self-assess their exposure to tier-I conflicts by asking the following questions:

- Has the company previously experienced situations in which individual directors have taken advantage of the company through compensation, self-dealing, stealing, insider trading, accepting bribes, or appropriating opportunities for personal benefit?
- How could negligence of, or lack of commitment to, board work present a conflict of interest?

Having clear guidelines, expectations, and standards, including the signing of a code of conduct at the time of a director's appointment, are all helpful.

Tier-II Conflicts: Directors vs Stakeholders

To whom do board members owe their loyalty? This depends very much on law and tradition, and on the prevailing legal system and social norms or the company's specific situation. For example, directors might declare that they owe their duty of loyalty to shareholders, the company itself, certain stakeholders (customers, employees, or society), or other board members, or a combination thereof.

The Institutional Loyalty of Board Directors

In the United States, directors often consider that they have a duty of loyalty toward the company's shareholders. The idea of maximising shareholder value has been a strong concept in the past, with the view that executives and directors should focus solely on creating value for shareholders. Others argue that since directors and executives are paid by the company, they are employees and should thus focus on the interests of the firm rather than on those of the shareholders. Still others consider that all stakeholders should be considered, with a prioritisation that is both strategic and made explicit. And finally, some consider that to truly maximise long-term shareholder value, all stakeholders need to be taken into account.

According to experts such as the late Lynn Stout, a former professor of corporate and business law at Cornell Law School, shareholder value maximisation is a choice, not a legal requirement. The assumption that shareholders are principals and that directors are their agents is legally incorrect. Corporate law clearly states that shareholders cannot control directors or executives. They have the right to vote on the positions of the directors of the board, and to recover damage compensation from directors and executives if they are found to have stolen from the company, but they have no right to tell executives how to run the business.[5] After all, shareholders are only owners of a financial claim on the assets of the firm, and not the owners of the assets themselves. They rank among other financial claimants in that way.

Being loyal to shareholders is, in any case, easier said than done. Shareholders come and go, and their interest in the company is limited to their shareholding period. Their interests vary depending on their investment horizon, degree of diversification, and investment strategy. Given the many types of shareholders, reaching a consensus for all of them is a daunting task. Individuals and families who invest for their retirement or to fund future expenses are often represented by institutional investors such as sovereign wealth funds, banks, hedge funds, pension funds, insurance companies, and other financial institutions. These powerful representatives interact with board members frequently and exercise most of the pressure, but when they put their own interest before that of the ultimate shareholders, interests could be misaligned. For example, the representatives may be striving for short-term personal gain or compensation while the ultimate investors may want the same as all other stakeholders: the creation and preservation of the corporation's long-term sustainable wealth.

If maximising shareholder value is a widely accepted norm, then board members would be better positioned if they announced that their loyalty lay with the ultimate shareholders. This would lead them to become stewards of the company, and reduce the risk of their being distracted by proposals that generate immediate stock returns but endanger the long-term prospects of the company.

A 2023 study by the European Union on directors' duties emphasised the need for directors to consider not only short-term shareholder value but also the long-term interests of the company.[6] All board members, including shareholder representatives, are required to balance the interests of all stakeholders with the long-term prospects of the company. To help ensure this, the composition and independence of the board of directors are often defined in national corporate governance codes.

For example, according to the Swedish Corporate Governance Code, 'boards of Swedish listed companies are composed entirely or predominantly of non-executive directors'. The Code also states that a majority of the members of the board should be independent of the company and its management. Although at least two members must also be independent of the company's major shareholders, it is still possible for these shareholders to

---

[5] Stout, L. (2012). The problem of corporate purpose. *Issues in Governance Studies Legal Studies* 48: June. Washington, DC: The Brookings Institution.

[6] Study on directors' duties and sustainable corporate governance (2020). European Union.

appoint a majority of members with whom they have close ties.[7] According to the Code, some directors could also have links with minority shareholders, management, or other stakeholders. These ties with various stakeholder groups potentially create divided loyalties for directors.

Table 13.1 is an example of the type of questionnaire that would help to assess directors' independence.

The laws of some countries require stakeholder representatives on boards to serve the interests of their respective principals in some situations. For example, bank directors who are appointed to the board when a company is in financial distress must be loyal to their bank, which lent money to the firm in question. While it may be perfectly legal for such interested parties to be members of the board, it can help if each stakeholder group puts their ultimate objectives on the table before starting negotiations. This allows minority shareholders to have their perspectives heard, which in turn may make majority shareholders more inclined to balance their own interests with those of others.

The Influence of Domineering Board Members on Others

Both independent and interested directors can potentially be influenced by powerful CEOs, chairpersons, or other directors. Board members may also forsake their institutional duties out of personal loyalty to the CEO or chair.

Table 13.1 Director's Independence Questionnaire

Directors are often requested to answer the following questions to self-assess their independence.	
Are you a substantial shareholder or an officer of, or otherwise associated directly with, a substantial shareholder of the company?	Yes/ No
Have you, within the last five years, been employed in an executive capacity by the company or another group member, or been a director after ceasing to hold any such employment?	Yes/ No
Within the last five years, have you been a professional advisor or a consultant to the company or another group member, or an employee materially associated with the service provided?	Yes/ No
Are you affiliated with a material supplier or customer or other related parties of the company or another group member, or an officer of or otherwise associated directly or indirectly with a material supplier or customer or other related parties?	Yes/ No
Do you have any material contractual relationship with the company or another group member other than as a director of the company?	Yes/ No
How many years have you served on the Board and do you believe that this time is such that it could reasonably be perceived to materially interfere with your ability to act in the best interests of the company?	Yes/ No
Do you have any interest or any business or other relationship which could, or could reasonably be perceived to, materially interfere with your ability to act in the best interests of the company?	Yes/ No

Source: Adapted from multiple publicly listed boards across different geographies.

---

[7] Swedish Corporate Governance Board. (2015). The Swedish Corporate Governance Code. p. 9.

One way directors can determine whether they have been overly influenced is by asking themselves, 'Have I been influenced or manipulated in order to agree with others?'

Persuasive influence often comes from people holding the combined role of CEO and chairperson, as they can sway other board members' compensation. Even if a board primarily comprises independent directors, it may not be able to remain truly independent from the management. If most of the board members generate a significant total income from board compensation packages, their independence may be at risk if they are not willing to sacrifice their standard of living for the integrity of their decision making.

Personal, family, and professional relationships can also potentially affect an independent director's judgement. The social connections between directors and CEOs or chairpersons cannot always be thoroughly checked. For example, retired CEOs may remain as chairs of their companies' boards, and many of the directors may owe their jobs to them. Or the CEO may invite close friends to join the board as directors. In both cases, the directors in question may be influenced by a sense of loyalty or duty, even if the CEO or chairperson is not acting in the best interests of the company, its shareholders, or other stakeholders. Independent directors may be reluctant to contradict the views of a CEO or chair to whom they felt they owed their loyalty and may instead either comply or step down from their role.

Chanda Kochhar, the former high-profile CEO of India's ICICI Bank, was charged on 24 January 2019 by the country's Central Bureau of Investigation with allegedly defrauding India's third largest lender. It is alleged that Kochhar misused her position to sanction loans, thereby cheating the bank of approximately US$242 million.[8]

ICICI Bank found its former chief executive guilty of violating internal bank policies and professional misconduct, following a lengthy investigation. The quid pro quo activities were first uncovered in 2016, when a whistleblower accused Kochhar of nepotism and favouritism. The whistleblower alleged that ICICI had granted loans to the Videocon group and 12 of its subsidiaries, allegedly in violation of the bank's lending policies, in exchange for an investment by the group's owner Venugopal Dhoot in NuPower Renewables – a business owned by Kochhar's husband.

The bank said it would treat Kochhar's resignation as CEO in October 2018 as a termination and would recover all bonuses paid to her between April 2009 and March 2018, estimated at millions of dollars.[9]

---

[8] Anand, N. (2019). One of India's most celebrated woman bankers is booked on a $242 million fraud case. https://qz.com/india/1532625/icici-banks-kochhar-kamath-booked-by-cbi-in-videocon-fraud-case/

[9] BBC News. (2019). Chanda Kochlar. 1 February. https://www.bbc.com/news/world-asia-india-47067863

Boardrooms are dynamic places where heated discussions occur. Those occupying positions of power, such as the CEO and the chair, may manipulate directors into agreeing with their preferred decisions by using psychological tactics. Tone of voice and eye contact, for example, can orient the discussion, rebuff criticism, or intimidate others. This happens even in sophisticated large-cap company boards. In some cases, board members may feel as though they are being victimised or manipulated, while those dominating the discussion may just think they are leading a dynamic interaction. Such unbalanced dynamics, including superiority and inferiority complexes, reduce the effectiveness of board discussions and prevent independent directors from exercising their duty.

Board Directors Organised as a Self-interested Stakeholder Group

Regulators and researchers have argued that boards should include a greater number of independent directors to ensure that business decisions are not disproportionately influenced by powerful stakeholders. The Spencer Stuart Board Index 2023 survey confirmed that S&P 500 boards elected 388 new independent directors, a 14% increase in a 10-year period.[10]

The growing tensions between independent directors and management are causing independent directors to form distinct stakeholder groups, which are often recognised by regulators. Such coalitions are growing in power and authority as independent board members increasingly remain loyal to each other in the boardroom, subjugating the interests of the organisations they are supposed to represent to their own. In other words, these stakeholder groups have their own motives and interests, and the strategic decisions they make could benefit themselves rather than the organisations they are paid to serve.

In certain countries, unless otherwise specified, directors decide what their salary, shares, and options will be. If no independent body such as a shareholder committee or a regulator oversees the compensation of directors, this can easily lead to a direct conflict of interest with the company. In the 2015 case of Calma vs Templeton, the Delaware Chancery Court in the United States allowed a claim that challenged the directors' stock compensation from going forward because it was considered 'excessive'. The compensation plan limited the number of shares to one million per year per participant, which represented a value of US$55 million at the time of the lawsuit. The court determined that the entire decision process for compensation was unfair because the awards to the outside directors were decided by the recipients themselves.[11]

---

[10] Spencer Stuart (2023). Spencer Stuart US Board Index.
[11] Katy, D. and L. McIntosh (2105). Dealing with director compensation. *New York Law Journal* (21 May).

In a *Harvard Business Review* article entitled 'What CEOs really think of their boards', one CEO was quoted as saying, 'They like their board seats – it gives them some prestige. They can be reluctant to consider recapitalization, going private, or merging – "Don't you know, we might lose our board positions!" I have been shocked by board members saying, "that would be an interesting thing to do, but what about us?"' Another CEO was quoted as saying, 'In one situation, we had a merger not go through because of who was going to get what number of board seats . . . It is still the most astounding conversation of my life.'[12] In another case, the chair of a large European bank was invited to sit on the board of a large-cap industrial while the CEO of that firm came to be on the board of the bank. Exploring the legitimacy and productivity of such an arrangement is certainly worthwhile.

High compensation does not always have the intended positive effect. The more compensation directors receive, the greater is their personal desire to be re-elected. As a result, they increasingly focus on remaining on the board, enjoying their status and fame, boosting their compensation further, and obtaining more directorships on other boards.

The structure and level of directors' compensation varies internationally. According to the German Corporate Governance Code, the compensation of supervisory board directors should be fixed, with performance-based compensation aligned to the company's long-term objectives.[13] Even though the Code does not explicitly mandate a combination of cash and shares, at Deutsche Bank, 25% of the directors' compensation was converted into shares of the company based on the average share price during the last 10 trading days of the year.[14]

In China, state owners oversee the compensation of both executive and non-executive directors, which effectively eliminates the possibility of self-dealing. At ICBC, the modest pay still attracts high-quality independent directors, especially those with positive character traits such as conscientiousness, integrity, competence, judgement, focus, and dedication, which cannot be encouraged or discouraged solely with money.[15]

Questions aimed at reflecting on tier-II conflicts of interest could include:

- In our legal system, to whom do board members owe their duty of loyalty?
- Can we define whether, in our specific context, loyalty to shareholders or loyalty to the company is paramount? Are there minority shareholders to be concerned about?

[12] Sonnenfeld, J., M. Kusin, and E. Walton (2013). What CEOs really think of their boards. *Harvard Business Review*, April.

[13] German Corporate Governance Code. (2022).

[14] Deutsche Bank. (2022). Annual Report.

[15] Cossin, D. and H.A. Lu (2012). The ICBC Path to Chinese Governance. IMD Case No. IMD-1-0327.

- If a director claims to owe his or her duty of loyalty to shareholders, would one be able to specify who the shareholders are? Are they fund managers or activists, large shareholders on the board, minority shareholders not on the board, or the ultimate shareholders?
- If we directors claim allegiance to company stakeholders, do we have a good mapping of our stakeholders?
- Can a director be fully independent when the CEO or chairperson decides on the compensation and succession of board members?
- If a director is independent, can we specify who they are independent from (for example management, shareholders, other stakeholders)?
- Are we aware that directors can form coalitions and leverage their full control of the board to benefit one another in an 'I'll scratch your back, you scratch mine' type of relationship?

Tier-III Conflicts: Stakeholders vs Other Stakeholders

Board members have another duty: exercising due diligence and good judgement when making decisions. In Germany, duty of care is a legal obligation. The law states that 'executive members have to exercise the care of an ordinary and conscientious business leader'. In the United Kingdom, ignorance can be deemed criminal for directors of financial institutions. Directors have a fiduciary responsibility to the company from the moment they are recruited, and they are expected to display a high standard of expertise, care, and diligence by gathering as much information as possible and considering all reasonable alternatives in order to make sensible decisions.

The trust placed in directors gives them maximum autonomy in decision-making, and decisions are not questioned unless they are deemed irrational. This business judgement rule protects directors from potential liabilities, as their decisions are not tainted by personal interest. Although directors are not allowed to act in their own interests, they can promote the interests of a particular stakeholder group against the company, or the interests of one group of stakeholders against another, or they can favour one subgroup over another within the same stakeholder group. It is up to directors to make wise decisions when stakeholders are in conflict.

If a board is composed of interested directors who remain loyal to their respective stakeholders while building effective board work, then stakeholder representatives need to cooperate and find the optimal coalition to address common interests. Directors must keep in mind the interests of weak or distant stakeholders to ensure their interests are not overlooked.

Conflicts of Interest between Stakeholders and the Company

A company can be seen as an aggregation of stakeholders bound together by economic interest. All stakeholders expect to receive a sizable slice of the pie in exchange for their input. Each group of stakeholders has a different contractual arrangement with the company and distinct motives, which means they will be more likely to push for decisions that benefit themselves first and foremost. For example, creditors, such as banks, will prefer the company to play it safe in order to maximise the chances that it will pay off its debt, but this low level of risk-taking could hurt the company's long-term growth potential. At the other end of the spectrum, shareholders can benefit from the successful outcome of a risky project while their losses are limited to the amount of their investment, so they are more likely to encourage risk-taking, even if it means putting the company's survival at risk.

Employees receive cash compensation plus benefits. By negotiating above-average compensation for workers, unions put the profitability of the company at risk. Companies have gone bankrupt as a result of out-of-control labour costs. In 2008, for instance, workers at GM, Ford, and Chrysler were among the most highly paid in the United States with over US$70 an hour in wages and benefits once retirement benefits were included in the calculation. This was considerably higher than the average hourly labour cost of US$25.36 for all private-sector workers, and the three car manufacturers were paying about US$30 an hour more than their Asian rivals operating in the United States.[16] GM and Chrysler declared bankruptcy, whereas Ford managed to survive without bailout funds. Eventually, all three recovered by adjusting labour costs to be more or less in line with those of their competitors, which they did by creating private trusts to finance the benefits of future retirees.

As a result of the financial difficulties that many companies encountered during the 1980s and early 1990s, some US firms allowed labour unions to designate one or more members of the board of directors, a practice well developed in some European countries. The first major US company to elect a union leader to its board was Chrysler in 1980. Board members representing unions have a delicate balancing act to play, and they need to be aware of the potential conflicts of interest inherent in their role. On the one hand, if they push for high wage increases, they could lead the company into difficulties and negatively affect all stakeholders in the long run. On the other hand, if they agree to substantial wage reductions, they would hurt the workers they are supposed to defend and represent.

Consumers and customers depend on companies for the reliable supply of products and services. When a firm changes its pricing strategy, this can potentially have serious repercussions for consumers. In September 2015, Turing Pharmaceuticals raised the price of Daraprim – a 62-year-old drug for the treatment of a life-threatening parasite infection – from US$13.50 to US$750 per tablet. For some patients, treatment became unbearably expensive, and

---

[16] Sherk, J. (2008). UAW workers actually cost the big three automakers $70 an hour. *Heritage*, December.

hospitals were forced to use less-effective alternatives to limit costs. Martin Shkreli, the 32-year-old founder and chief executive of Turing, said, 'This is still one of the smallest pharmaceutical products in the world . . . It really doesn't make sense to get any criticism for this.'[17] But in December 2015, Shkreli was arrested for 'repeatedly losing money for investors and lying to them about it, illegally taking assets from one of his companies to pay off debtors in another'.[18]

It is challenging for directors to decide which stakeholder group to prioritise when it comes to value distribution and slicing the pie. Only integrity and good judgement skills can help in the many ambiguous situations that boards face. In conflicts, customers can hurt companies, and companies can harm the interests of customers. Closely involved stakeholders, such as creditors, employees, top management, and shareholders, all have motives to push for decisions that benefit themselves but may potentially hurt the company's interests in the long run.

Conflicts of Interest between Different Classes of Stakeholders

Conflicts can arise between different groups of stakeholders, such as shareholders and creditors. Creditors, such as banks, play an important role in corporate governance systems. In some countries, they not only lend to firms but also hold equity so that they can have board representation. In the United States, regulations prevent banks from dealing with debt–equity conflicts through equity ownership as they are not allowed to hold stakes in a firm to which they lend (note that this can get confused with modern asset management). With the Federal Reserve's quantitative-easing programme, share buybacks became the preferred way for companies to boost their stock prices for the benefit of shareholders. In 2015, S&P 500 index companies returned more money to shareholders through share buybacks and dividend payments than they earned. Some of them even borrowed money to pay dividends. This represents a direct transfer of value from creditors to shareholders, since a higher level of debt increases the probability of default and reduces the value of the creditor's claim on the assets of the firm.

Executives may sometimes act controversially in the name of shareholders' interests. Lou Gerstner had a record of fixing ailing companies and was credited with rescuing IBM through tough decisions, including

---

[17] Pollack, A. (2015). Drug goes from $13.50 a tablet to $750, overnight. *The New York Times*, 20 September.
[18] Smythe, C. and K. Geiger (2015). Shkreli, drug price gouger, denies fraud and posts bail. *Bloomberg Business*, 17 December.

massive layoffs. One major change took place in 1999, when IBM under Gerstner shocked long-term employees by overhauling its pension plan to help cut costs. In 2002, Gerstner ended his tenure with an annual salary of over US$1.5 million, an annual pension of over US$1.1 million, and over US$288,000 in deferred compensation in 2001 alone.[19] IBM employees later filed a class-action lawsuit over the pension changes, and in 2004 the company agreed to pay US$320 million to current and former employees in a settlement.[20] If an executive's compensation is linked to cost savings on the back of employees, the two groups are considered to be in a conflict of interest.

Even when executives proclaim that they are dedicated to shareholders' interests, the fact that they try hard to minimise shareholder involvement in corporate governance shows there is a conflict of interest between the two groups. In a 2013 referendum, Swiss voters passed a popular measure 'against corporate rip-offs', which allowed shareholders to control the transparency and format of top executives' income and called for jail time for non-executive directors who would not comply. The reform, which was approved by 67.9% of voters, stipulated that the shareholders of all publicly listed Swiss companies must elect all the members of the firm's remuneration committee, and that all board directors are subject to annual re-election. Supporters spent CHF 200,000 to promote the initiative, while opponents spent CHF 8 million trying to block it. The initiative made it compulsory for shareholders to vote their shares. This Swiss referendum was a strong social response to the conflict of interest between executives and shareholders, and between executives and society at large.

The initiative was launched by businessman Thomas Minder, whose own story illustrated how entrenched executives could damage all other parties to benefit themselves. Minder's company, Trybol, supplied cosmetics to Swissair, and suffered significant losses when the airline went bankrupt in 2001 due to a failed expansion strategy. Before the bankruptcy, it was made public that Swissair's top executive was to receive a golden parachute totalling CHF 12.5 million. Minder was so angry that he started the 'anti-rip-off' initiative.[21]

Could certain stakeholder groups, such as management, creditors, or shareholders, benefit specifically from corporate decisions that could potentially hurt other stakeholders? The answer is yes when the value increase for one class of stakeholder is directly linked to the value reduction of another.

---

[19] 'IBM in the Gerstner Years: An Employees' Perspective,' IBMEmployee.com (April 2002).
[20] Johnston, D.C. (2004). IBM employees get $320 million in pension suit. *The New York Times*, 30 September.
[21] Schneider, M. and E. Wolff (2013). Swiss referendum against rip-offs, 2 March. wsws.org

In January 2023, Hindenburg Research, a short-selling research firm, released a report alleging fraudulent and unethical practices by the Adani Group. These allegations ranged from stock manipulation to improper use of tax havens and environmental degradation. Consequently, Adani Group's stock prices plummeted, and triggered a regulatory investigation. The Adani Group scandal brought forth several governance issues including lack of transparency, close ties with the government, potential conflicts of interest, and inadequate oversight. The Adani family's influence within the company, related party transactions benefiting insiders, and the environmental impact of the Group's operations were all areas that were being investigated. At the time of publishing, the SEBI had not concluded its investigation. However, the damage to Adani's reputation resulting from lack of transparency, as well failure to disclose conflicts of interest (even if only perceived), was significant.

Conflicts of Interest within a Group of Stakeholders

In closely held companies, large shareholders can use their control power to exploit minority shareholders. Directors may be influenced by the controlling shareholder sitting on the board. Using their representation on the board, these shareholders influence capital structure, dividend policy, and investment strategy, or their position with regard to mergers and acquisitions, and might well be in conflict with other shareholders.

In May 2015, Volkswagen AG's 20-member supervisory board included only one independent director. The founding Piëch and Porsche families dominated the board in alliance with labour unions and the state of Lower Saxony. As we saw in Chapter 2, Volkswagen Chair Ferdinand Karl Piëch made the following comment to the media without the board's knowledge: 'I am distancing myself from [Volkswagen CEO Martin] Winterkorn.'[22] These words further inflamed a decades-long battle between the two shareholding families behind Volkswagen and Porsche. Piëch probably instigated this controversy with the intention of extending his influence as a controlling shareholder. But during the shareholder showdown, Winterkorn won the support of some of the other members of the Porsche family, labour leaders and the state of Lower Saxony. After losing the battle, Piëch resigned as chair. However, just a few months later, Winterkorn himself had to resign as CEO amid the Volkswagen emissions scandal.

The Volkswagen case shows that it is difficult even for the board of a sophisticated, large-scale enterprise (with 670 000 employees and €200 billion in revenue) to optimise the interests of shareholders when these conflict.

---

[22] Hawranek, D. and D. Kurbjuweit (2015). Blood feud: behind the scenes of Volkswagen's dynastic battle. *Spiegel Online International*, 6 May.

In practice, when most directors on a board are shareholders or stakeholder representatives, infighting becomes a common issue. Minority shareholders are vulnerable when the controlling owner attempts to squeeze out the other shareholders and gain control of more corporate resources, for example by buying, selling, or leasing assets at non-market prices.

Conflicts within groups of stakeholders are not limited to shareholders. Creditors on boards could have an unfair advantage over other creditors if they use insider information to shield themselves from potential trouble and hurt other classes of debt holders, especially when the firm is in financial distress. Employees can be in conflict with customers' interests. Even customers can be in conflict with society's interests.

The following questions can help directors reflect on tier-III conflicts of interest:

- Is a key stakeholder group pushing for decisions that may benefit them but potentially hurt the interests of the company in the long run?
- How aligned or misaligned are our shareholders, and on which matters?
- How can the pie be divided when there are conflicts of interest between different classes of stakeholders, such as shareholders vs customers, executives vs employees, or executives vs shareholders?
- How can conflicts of interest between subgroups of one particular stakeholder group be dealt with?
- How can I as a director make a wise decision when stakeholders have conflicting incentives and goals?

Tier-IV Conflicts: Company vs Society

How a company views its purpose will affect its notions of responsibility, accountability, and how it creates value. Business ethics have been discussed since the market economy emerged more than 750 years ago.[23] In general, companies and society are not in conflict. Corporations contribute to society by inventing new technologies, fulfilling consumers' demands for goods and services, and creating jobs; society creates the conditions that allow companies to harness their potential for the common good of humanity.

In 1981, the Business Roundtable, an association of chief executive officers of leading US companies working to promote sound public policy, stated that 'Corporations have a responsibility, first of all, to make available to the public quality goods and services at fair prices, thereby earning a profit that attracts

---

[23] Vogel, D. (1991). Business ethics: new perspectives on old problems. *California Management Review* 33(4): 101–117.

investment to continue and enhance the enterprise, provide jobs, and build the economy', and that 'the long-term viability of the corporation depends upon its responsibility to the society of which it is a part. The well-being of society also depends upon profitable and responsible business enterprises'.[24]

Executives initially accepted this definition of the responsibilities of companies. However, their stance changed dramatically in 1997, when the Business Roundtable redefined the purpose of a corporation in society as being 'to generate economic returns to its owners', adding that if 'the CEO and the directors are not focused on shareholder value, it may be less likely the corporation will realise that value'.[25] Board members soon came under pressure to admit that the sole purpose of corporations was to maximise shareholder value.

If not managed properly, maximising returns for shareholders can strip value generation from other stakeholders – for example, by deceiving customers, defaulting on payments to creditors, squeezing suppliers and employees, and evading taxes. Indirect harmful effects on society include shaping the rules of the game (such as through lobbying to change a law, tax and accounting rules, monopolisation, and subsidies), pollution, market manipulation through collusion, and limiting the opportunities for future generations to improve their lives. Such behaviour may well increase payoffs to shareholders in the short term but will lead to the eventual demise of the corporation and the total destruction of long-term shareholder value. Extracting value from society is no recipe for long-term success.

The only class of stakeholders that benefits from this short-term value maximisation are chief executives enjoying high compensation, severance packages, and golden parachutes. According to *Equilar*, the median tenure of CEOs of the 500 largest companies in the United States (S&P 500) was 4.8 years as of 2022.[26] When a CEO believes they could be dismissed at any time, they may be more inclined to take decisions that maximise their own income in the short term in the name of maximising shareholder value. If all CEOs behave in this manner and boards allow it, companies will end up doing more harm than good to society.

In a study for an earlier book on stewardship that I co-authored, companies potentially ranking highly on this dimension used a broad vocabulary in their annual 10-K reports to the US Securities and Exchange Commission to describe their relationships with other stakeholders. They used words including *air, carbon, child, children, climate, collaboration, communities, cooperation, CSR,*

[24] Yang, J.L. (2013). Maximising shareholder value: the goal that changed corporate America. *The Washington Post*, 26 August).

[25] Montier, J. (2014). The world's dumbest idea. GMO White Paper, December.

[26] Chen, J. (2023). Equilar, Inc., July.

culture, dialog, dialogue, ecological, economical, environment, families, science, stakeholder, transparency, and *well-being*. This mirrored their long-term approach to building rapport with local communities and broader society.

By comparison, companies potentially ranking low in terms of stewardship used words like *appeal, arbitration, attorney, attorneys, claims, court, criticised, defendant, defendants, delinquencies, delinquency, denied, discharged, enforceability, jurisdiction, lawsuit, lawsuits, legislative, litigation, petition, petitions, plaintiff, punitive, rulings, settlement, settlements*, and *suit*. This indicates that companies rarely benefit from bad actions in the long run, as costs will come back to them in the form of litigation, sanctions, fines, or public humiliation.[27]

The aftermath of the 2008 financial crisis demonstrated that greed does not pay. From 2008 to 2015, 20 of the world's biggest banks paid more than US\$235 billion in fines for having manipulated currency and interest rates and deceived customers. For example, Bank of America alone paid approximately US\$80 billion while JP Morgan Chase paid up to US\$20 billion. These fines were intended to deter further wrongdoing and to change corporate culture.[28]

Society and various stakeholders place their trust in boards to run companies, and they hold them accountable for doing so. Directors need to understand that a company cannot prosper if it is in conflict with society, even if some stakeholders may maximise their short-term profits. Furthermore, because board members have the power and authority to recruit, monitor, and support management, they are on the front line when it comes to changing the company's culture. In particular, this can include moving away from a short-term focus to considering the long term when resolving potential conflicts between the company and society.

Self-assessment questions to ponder with regard to this last dimension include:

- Why does our organisation exist?
- How does it create value?
- Is our company a contributor or a value-extractor in society? Where does it extract value? Where does it contribute?
- Do we have the courage to take an ethical stand when our company is in conflict with society?

A company is the nexus that links the interests of each stakeholder group within its ecosystem. The board is the decision-making body, and its successes

---

[27] Cossin, D. and O.B. Hwee (2016). *Inspiring Stewardship*. John Wiley and Sons.
[28] Dzimwasha, T. (2015). 20 global banks have paid \$235bn in fines since the 2008 financial crisis. *International Business Times*, 24 May.

and failures depend on the ability of directors to understand and manage the interests of key stakeholder groups. Decisions at the board level should be ethical and reasonably balanced.

Boards need to have a specific policy in place for dealing with **tier-I** conflicts of interest between individual directors and the company. This policy needs to specify processes for dealing in an open and transparent way with major actual and potential conflicts, such as misappropriation of assets; insufficient effort, focus, and dedication to board work; self-dealing and related transactions; insider trading; and taking advantage of corporate opportunities. If possible, the policy should be signed by all directors and updated regularly, and conflicts of interest should be declared at each board meeting. A register of potential conflicts is also helpful.

To deal with **tier-II** conflicts, directors need to disclose their relationships with stakeholders. This gives them an opportunity to declare in advance who they represent. Even if the law requires all directors to represent the interests of the company, identifying their connections with specific stakeholder groups improves transparency and avoids the risk of conflicts of interest. It is also crucial to specify who nominates new directors, who decides on their compensation, how the pay structure and level are determined, and how pay is linked to performance and function. In performing their duties, all directors need to put aside their ego, follow rules in discussions, respect others, and avoid toxic behaviours in the boardroom. Coalitions can be beneficial when they aim to act in the best interest of the company, but can be harmful when they are formed with the aim of dominating the board or benefitting a particular stakeholder group.

Tier-III conflicts of interest can be minimised when directors and boards 'slice the company pie' properly in an effort to support cooperation and avoid retaliation, fines, infighting, or legal actions. Wise decision-making requires understanding deep-rooted conflicts between stakeholders and the company, between different stakeholder groups, and within a stakeholder group. No company can truly prosper without the input of each stakeholder group: responsible shareholders, understanding debt holders, innovative employees, satisfied customers, happy suppliers, great products and services, friendly communities, and effective and efficient government.

Tier-IV conflicts between the company and society are not only philosophical but can also have real impact. Solving them requires directors to act as moral agents who are able to distinguish 'good' from 'bad'. Do companies compensate stakeholders because they are useful or protected by law, or because they contribute to the success of the company? Should firms consider the interests of future generations who have not directly contributed to profitability and who are not represented on the board? Should companies make corporate sustainability investments because they are popular, because they portray the business favourably and increase profitability in the long run, or because they are a way to show true gratitude to all?

Good governance starts with the integrity and ethics of every director on every board. Directors have a moral obligation not to take advantage of the company, but rather to be loyal to it, make wise decisions, neutralise conflicts among stakeholders, and act in a socially responsible way. An ethical board sets the purpose of the company, which in turn influences all its dealings with stakeholders. The four-tier pyramid summarising the different levels of conflict of interest can help board members anticipate and identify potential conflicts, deal with these, and make sensible decisions to chart the company's future course.

In the concluding chapter of Part II, we will stay with the theme of integrity and assess the board's role in preventing high-level fraud.

14

High-level Fraud and Active Board Oversight

In September 2016, Wells Fargo reached a settlement with US regulators over alleged sales abuses at the bank, agreeing to pay US$185 million in fines and US$5 million to customers. In a fraud that extended over five years, Wells Fargo employees opened 1.5 million bank accounts and applied for 565,000 credit cards in their customers' names without the latter's knowledge. The objective was to meet sales targets for employees and generate fees for the bank. Democratic presidential candidate Hillary Clinton called the account openings 'outrageous behaviour'. During a Senate Banking Committee hearing, Senator Elizabeth Warren drilled Wells Fargo Chair John Stumpf pointedly on ethics and accountability in what has become a reference questioning,[1] and concluded:

---

[1] At the September 2016 Senate Banking Committee hearing, Senator Elizabeth Warren questioned John Stumpf, chair and CEO of Wells Fargo, about the unauthorised opening of customer accounts. This refers to accountability and responsibility and the questions that can be asked in a powerful interrogation.

Warren: Mr. Stumpf, Wells Fargo's vision and values statement, which you frequently cite says: 'We believe in values lived not phrases memorized. If you want to find out how strong a company's ethics are, don't listen to what its people say, watch what they do.' So, let's do that. Since this massive years-long scam came to light, you have said repeatedly: 'I am accountable.' But what have you actually done to hold yourself accountable? Have you resigned as CEO or chair of Wells Fargo? **Stumpf:** The board, I serve – **Warren:** Have you resigned? **Stumpf:** No, I have not. **Warren:** Alright. Have you returned one nickel of the millions of dollars that you were paid while this scam was going on? **Stumpf:** Well, first of all, this was by 1% of our people. **Warren:** That's not my question. This is about responsibility. Have you returned one nickel of the millions of dollars that you were paid while this scam was going on? **Stumpf:** The board will take care of that. **Warren:** Have you returned one nickel of the money you earned while this scam was going on? **Stumpf:** And the board will do – **Warren:** I will take that as a no, then. Have you fired a single senior executive? And by that, I don't mean regional manager or branch manager. I'm asking about the people who actually led your community banking division or your compliance division.

You should give back the money that you took while this scam was going on and you should be criminally investigated by both the Department of Justice and the Securities and Exchange Commission. This just isn't right.[2]

Fraud happens. According to Kroll's 2023 global survey of 400 senior executives worldwide, 69% of respondents anticipate a rise in financial crime risk within the upcoming 12 months.[3] And according to the 2022 Global Fraud Study by the Association of Certified Fraud Examiners (ACFE), the median estimate of fraud loss was 5% of revenues. Applying this percentage to the 2022 Gross World Product of US$101.33 trillion gives a projected potential total fraud loss of up to US$5 trillion worldwide.[4] Fraud is a significant threat to organisations – large frauds have driven companies into bankruptcy, wiped out billions for investors, and cost numerous employees their jobs.

Who is responsible for the governance oversight of fraud control – the board, management, internal and external auditors, or everyone in the organisation? In the case of Wells Fargo, the chair and management blamed employees rather than the organisation's culture – the bank fired 5,300 people in connection with the improper account openings. Investors in Wells Fargo had previously questioned the bank's governance practices and called for it to split the roles of chair and CEO. The bank answered that its governance structure already provided effective independent oversight of management. 'How can they argue against my proposal now? Where is the board? Where is the audit committee of the board? It appears they go to the meetings, they pick up their cheques and they go home', said Gerald Armstrong, an activist investor.[5]

Regulatory changes have made boards and management increasingly responsible for fraud control. An active board will not shy away from its responsibility to oversee fraud risk. In fact, the board has a critical role in

---

Stumpf: We've made a change in our regional, to lead our regional banks – **Warren:** I just said I'm not asking regional managers. I'm not asking about branch managers. I'm asking if you have fired senior management, the people who actually led the community banking division, who oversaw this fraud or the compliance division that was in charge of making sure that the bank complied with the law. **Stumpf:** Carrie Tolsted – **Warren:** Did you fire any of those people? **Stumpf:** No. **Warren:** No. OK, so you haven't resigned, you haven't returned a single nickel of your personal earnings, you haven't fired a single senior executive. Instead, evidently your definition of 'accountable' is to push the blame to your low-level employees who don't have the money for a fancy PR firm to defend themselves.

[2] Full transcript widely available, for example on https://www.entrepreneur.com/article/282737.

[3] Kroll. (2023). 2023 Fraud and Financial Crime Report.

[4] Association of Certified Fraud Examiners. (2022). Report to the Nations on Occupational Fraud and Abuse.

[5] Foley, S. and A. Gray. (2016). Activist pushes for shake-up at Wells Fargo. 14 September. https://www.ft.com/content/07f4bae0-7a88-11e6-ae24-f193b105145e

dealing with organisational frauds committed by senior executives or directors, setting the tone at the top, and ensuring a strong ethical culture within the organisation. This chapter provides directors and boards with an oversight framework for predicting, preventing, detecting, and remedying fraud risk, as well as some questions aimed at encouraging senior executives to work on fraud control effectively.

Why Does High-level Fraud Happen?

In the study of the psychology of criminal behaviour, the differential association theory developed by Edwin H. Sutherland is instrumental in explaining what drives a person to commit crime. People used to believe that criminal behaviour was inherited. Sutherland, however, proposed that such behaviour is learned via interaction with others – individuals learn the techniques, drivers, motives, attitudes, and rationalisations for criminal behaviour. In this view, an individual could commit crime if the perceived rewards for being law-abiding are exceeded by the perceived rewards for law-breaking. As a criminal and immoral activity, fraud is an inevitable part of society.

The ACFE has developed the Occupational Fraud and Abuse Classification System, also known as the Fraud Tree. The three major categories of occupational fraud are asset misappropriation, corruption, and financial statement fraud. Asset misappropriation includes skimming, theft, asset misuse, and larceny. Corruption includes conflicts of interest, bribery (kickbacks and bid rigging), illegal gifts, and economic extortion. And financial statement fraud includes over- or understating assets or income, and non-financial components such as inventories. In the ACFE's 2022 report, asset misappropriation occurred in more than 86% of all cases reported, but with the lowest losses among the three categories. Financial statement fraud, meanwhile, was involved in less than 9% of the cases, but caused a median loss of US$593 000. Corruption fell in the middle in terms of both frequency and losses.

For ease of discussion, we can divide fraud into two categories: occupational and organisational. *Occupational* fraud happens when someone takes advantage of their position to break the rules for personal gain. For example, an employee might steal money from the cash register, a head of purchasing could take bribes or kickbacks to favour a particular supplier, one professional might send bills for hours not worked, and another could falsify documents or receipts for their own financial gain.

While studying embezzlement, Donald Cressey identified three elements of fraud motivation: opportunity, motivation, and rationalisation. Together, these form a 'fraud triangle' (see Figure 14.1).[6]

---

[6] Cressey, D. (1953). *Other People's Money: A Study in the Social Psychology of Embezzlement*. Glencoe, IL: The Free Press.

Cressey proposed that a potential fraudster would not commit fraud unless there was an opportunity – in the form of weak internal controls and the technical capabilities required to commit the fraud. The second element of the fraud triangle is the feeling of pressure, which can be real or imagined and drives the actual motivation to act. Examples include supporting a struggling family on low pay, high amounts of personal debt, unexpected medical expenses, family issues such as divorce, extramarital affairs or problems with children, as well as compulsive behaviour such as gambling, and alcohol or drug abuse. The final element – rationalisation – refers to how a potential fraudster justifies their actions before committing the fraud. Examples include 'I will pay back', 'They owe me', 'I earned it', 'I need it more than they do', 'It's only fair', and 'God will forgive me'. The fraud triangle became the most widely known theory of occupational fraud, in which all the elements – opportunity, pressure, and rationalisation – must be present for a fraud to happen.

Organisational fraud happens when senior management, board directors, or chairs commit fraud using the company itself. At Enron, WorldCom, and Tyco, for example, people at the highest levels of the organisation bent the rules or covered up sophisticated frauds. Organisational fraud destroys a company's reputation and shatters trust with stakeholders, including investors and employees, who are left to suffer when a fraud leads to bankruptcy. In the ACFE's 2022 study, only 23% of frauds were committed by owners or executives, but the median loss was US$337,000. Employees and managers were more likely to commit fraud, but the losses were lower – US$50,000 in the

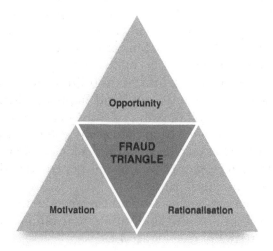

Figure 14.1   The Fraud Triangle
Source: Adapted from Cressey 1978.

In February 2018, the CEO of Switzerland's third largest bank – Raiffeisen Bank – Pierin Vincenz was accused of illegally enriching himself by making personal investments in two Raiffeisen subsidiaries, Aduno and Investnet. Raiffeisen Bank also joined the criminal probe as a complainant. Vincenz, who headed Raiffeisen from 1999 to 2015 during a period of expansion, was forced to step down from various other business roles as the investigation began. He resigned as chair of Swiss insurance group Helvetica and relinquished a similar position at power group Repower. He was also chair at Aduno during the period under investigation. Zurich's attorney general investigated the former Raiffeisen boss for potentially improper business management – including cashing in on company takeovers of the credit card company Aduno and the investment company Investnet. Vincenz's successor resigned in the aftermath of the scandal, stressing the impact of misbehaviours in an organisation.

case of employee fraud, and US$125,000 for managers. In one business school study, 56% of CFOs reported that the CEO had pressured them to misrepresent accounting.[7] And almost 70% of US SEC enforcement actions involving fraud reveal CEO participation.[8]

Boards need to be aware that although executives and owners commit around 20% of frauds, these tend to be more costly. This is because high-level fraudsters have greater access to assets and more authority to evade or override anti fraud controls. In addition, their schemes are generally harder to detect and last longer. This chapter proposes a predictive model to help directors understand the four preconditions of organisational fraud: injustice, lax oversight, a problematic culture, and financial illiteracy. Figure 14.2 provides a model of causes that may lead to board-level fraud.

Injustice

Unbalanced value distribution favouring a particular stakeholder group often leads to value extraction and organisational fraud. In the United States, in an attempt to enforce the alignment of executive and shareholder interests, corporate boards often reward executives with shares and options. Not surprisingly, maximising shareholder value then directly translates into maximising profitability and share prices for personal financial gains. In many cases, incentivised executives become financial engineers and employ deceptive accounting techniques to boost stock prices. Former Enron CEO Jeffrey Skilling, for

---

[7] Feng, M., W. Ge, S. Luo, and T.J. Shevlin (2010). Why do CFOs become involved in material accounting manipulations? (12 May 2010). AAA 2009 Financial Accounting and Reporting Section (FARS) Paper.
[8] Annual report, Division of Enforcement, SEC, 2018.

Figure 14.2   Fraud Risk at Board Level

example, controlled the company's accounting procedures to 'massage' earnings and meet analysts' expectations.

Other corporate scandals involved more than accounting tricks. Mark Whitacre and other executives at Archer Daniels Midland Co conspired with other companies to fix the global price of some chemicals. 'With my base salary and stock options combined, my total compensation was in the seven figures', Whitacre said. 'Much of my compensation was in stock options, where there was much incentive to increase company earnings to drive the stock price upward as fast as possible.'[9]

Should boards and executives maximise shareholder value? Many people would answer yes, because shareholders are often considered the owners of the company. But others disagree. Martin Lipton, founding partner at Wachtell, Lipton, Rosen & Katz, has argued with William Savitt that 'Shareholders do not "own" corporations. They own securities – shares of stock – which entitle them to very limited electoral rights and the right to share in the financial returns produced by the corporation's business operations [. . .] Shareholders possess none of the incidents of ownership of a corporation – neither the right of possession, nor the right of control, nor the right of exclusion – and thus "have no more claim to intrinsic ownership and control of the corporation's assets than do other stakeholders"'.[10]

---

[9] Connor, J. (2010). Archer Daniels Midland: price-fixer to the world. Purdue University Working Paper.
[10] Lipton, M. and W. Savitt (2007). The many myths of Lucian Bebchuk. *Virginia Law Review* 93: 733–758.

In 2020, Germany faced one of its most significant instances of fraud involving Wirecard, once revered as a prominent entity in European fintech. The company's collapse was precipitated by a shocking €1.9 billion accounting fraud, uncovering widespread deceit, including fabricated transactions and exaggerated revenues. Reports suggest that the CEO, Markus Braun, instructed the manipulation of accounts and the creation of false revenues.[11] Braun, along with other top executives, is facing charges including fraud and market manipulation, potentially leading to a maximum sentence of 15 years' imprisonment upon conviction. 'The Enron of Germany' triggered serious questions about the effectiveness of regulatory oversight, particularly the role of the Federal Financial Supervisory Authority (BaFin) and the Wirecard's auditor, Ernst & Young.

Directors do not have a legal responsibility to maximise shareholder value first and foremost. Instead, the role of the board is to seek what is best for the company itself, which requires balancing the interests of all stakeholders. If not managed properly, maximising returns for shareholders – for example, by manipulating accounting, deceiving customers, defaulting on payments to creditors, squeezing suppliers and employees, and evading taxes – can strip value generation from other stakeholders. Injustice in value distribution among stakeholders is thus a rich source of organisational fraud.

Lax Oversight

In theory, the board is elected by shareholders and is the highest authority in the company under the AGM. The board appoints, directs, supports, challenges, and removes the CEO, and serves as a check on the chief executive in order to protect the interest of the company. However, the board's oversight could be compromised in many situations.

Sometimes, directors fail to exercise oversight even when the CEO or chairperson is not acting in the best interests of the company, its shareholders, or other stakeholders. 'At Tyco, for example, some of the "independent" directors depended directly on the company for the bulk of their income, while at WorldCom many of the directors owed their wealth to Bernie Ebbers, the now disgraced and jailed CEO. At Parmalat, the board was comprised mainly of family or friends. Such boards are unlikely to be effective.'[12] Directors who

---

[11] Amann, C. (2022). Wirecard witness admits guilt but pins German fraud on ex-CEO. 19 September. https://www.reuters.com/business/finance/wirecard-witness-admits-guilt-pins-german-fraud-blame-ex-ceo-2022-12-19/#:~:text=MUNICH%2C%20Dec%2019%20(Reuters), Markus%20Braun%20at%20its%20core

[12] Hamilton, S. (2008). Who controls the CEO? IMD Tomorrow's Challenge. June.

contradict the views of such a CEO or chairperson may end up either complying or stepping down from their role.

Some corporate CEOs have achieved celebrity status and become superstars with the aid of the media. They are often self-promoters with many followers. In a *Harvard Business Review* article, Rakesh Khurana highlighted the risk of relying on charismatic leaders. 'Enron's board of directors also bent to the will of its charismatic leader when it agreed to suspend its code of ethics to allow top executives to participate in the off-balance-sheet partnerships', he wrote. 'As Skilling's example illustrates, charismatic leaders reject limits to their scope and authority. They rebel against all checks on their power and dismiss the rules and norms that apply to others.'[13] Charmed into a false sense of security by the CEO's charisma and drive, the board does not challenge him or her on major decisions and becomes passive.

Independent directors without ties to the company may take a hands-off approach to overseeing the CEO, allowing him or her to make major decisions. Boards in the United States typically include a high percentage of independent directors. Although prominent in other fields, they may lack detailed operational knowledge about the company. They have to rely for information on the CEO, who may bury key facts in huge board packs. Such a board may not be able to exercise proper fraud oversight, especially if the CEO is also the chair.

Problematic Culture

A fish rots from the head down, as the old saying goes. Likewise, when a company fails, poor leadership is usually the root cause.

In 2002, a *Business Week* article described Tyco's then CEO Dennis Kozlowski as a 'corporate tough guy, respected and feared in roughly equal measure'.[14] Kozlowski was equally tough in fighting his way to the top of the company. After his aggressive acquisition strategy clashed with the more conservative instincts of former CEO John Fort, he persuaded Tyco's board of directors to side with him. Fort had to resign as CEO and chair, and Kozlowski took over. But Kozlowski and Tyco subsequently became household names after he was sued for misappropriating over US$100 million of company funds for himself. This included more than US$1 million for a lavish celebration of his wife's birthday, as well as having Tyco pay for his US$30 million New York City apartment, equipped with US$6,000 shower curtains and US$15,000 'dog umbrella stands'.

---

[13] Khurana, R. (2002). The curse of the superstar CEO. September. https://hbr.org/2002/09/the-curse-of-the-superstar-ceo

[14] The rise and fall of Dennis Kozlowski. Bloomberg Business Week (December 2002).

The 'tone at the top' determines the ethical standards for the whole organisation, not least because boards and executives tend to hire people similar to themselves. If the company's leaders set a ruthless tone, its employees will be more inclined to have the same values. This will very often result in office bullying and a culture of corporate fraud.

'When I worked at Wells Fargo, I faced the threat of being fired if I didn't meet the unreasonable sales quotas every day, and it's high time that Wells Fargo pays for preying on consumers' financial livelihoods', said Khalid Taha, a former employee.[15] When Wells Fargo executives put pressure on their employees to meet unrealistic goals for cross-selling products, they bore a deep responsibility for how these employees pursued their targets – including through improper practices.

Pressure plays a major role in increasing the risk of fraud. Many regarded the autocratic management style of former Volkswagen CEO Martin Winterkorn as one of the factors that led to the emissions scandal that has cost the company some €28 billion to date. Winterkorn did not like failure, and the pressure on managers was unusually high. Several former VW executives have said that Winterkorn's style fostered a climate of fear. 'There was always a distance, a fear and a respect . . . If you presented bad news, those were the moments that it could become quite unpleasant and loud and quite demeaning', said one employee.[16]

Supremely selfish top executives are not too difficult to identify. These individuals are often greedy and demand money, titles, status, authority, perks, position, power, or services; they are arrogant and rude, at least to some; and they feel entitled.

Some boards believe that strong leaders need to have extreme traits, such as being overconfident, egocentric, ruthless, bold, tough, or selfish. But this is a stereotype. There is also a kind of leadership that speaks softly and gets things done cleanly and firmly. These leaders know where they are going, carefully think through how to get there, and execute precisely. Colman Mockler, the CEO of Gillette from 1975 to 1991, transformed the company, generating strong growth and returns for shareholders. Mockler was quiet, humble, gracious, and shy of publicity, and declined most requests to be interviewed and photographed. Yet no one could mistake his modesty for weakness.

It is crucial for boards to set an ethical example by reining in egocentric executives and balancing the character weaknesses that most CEOs have.

---

[15] Levine, M. (2016). Wells Fargo Opened a Couple Million Fake Accounts. Bloomberg, UK, Opinion. https://www.bloomberg.com/opinion/articles/2016-09-09/wells-fargo-opened-a-couple-million-fake-accounts

[16] Cremer, A. and T. Bergin (2015). Fear and respect – Volkswagen's culture under Winterkorn. 10 October. https://www.reuters.com/article/uk-volkswagen-emissions-culture/fear-and-respect-vws-culture-under-winterkorn-idUKKCN0S40MN20151010

Getting the right people on board can create a healthy corporate culture based on trust and discipline. The wrong people, however, can instil a toxic culture based on fear and greed.

Financial Illiteracy

Directors often see themselves as generalists. They pay significant attention to important board topics such as leadership, strategy, innovation, or relations with the CEO, but tend to regard accounting and finance as a 'technical' subject for specialists. As a result, financial illiteracy is rampant on corporate boards. (In the hope of changing this state of affairs, Chapter 16 provides a primer on finance essentials for directors.)

Running a business without understanding basic financial and accounting concepts is dangerous, because it creates opportunities for executives to manipulate financial results and commit fraud. Boards lacking specialised knowledge cannot prevent, detect, or intervene in fraudulent activities effectively.

Financial illiteracy at board level is a lesson learned hard. After the Enron scandal, the SEC and other US regulators tightened the criteria for membership of boards and audit committees of public companies. Audit committees are now required to consist of independent directors, with at least one member being a 'financial expert'. This is defined as a person with fluent knowledge of US Generally Accepted Accounting Principles (GAAP), who has experience preparing, auditing, analysing, or evaluating complex financial statements in depth, and understands internal controls, financial reporting procedures, and audit committee functions. Every public-listed company board should have sufficient accounting and auditing expertise to provide effective fraud oversight.

However, independent directors who are financial experts may lack the specific industry knowledge to check intricate and carefully concealed insider misconduct. And although boards and audit committees may comply with the financial expert requirements, effective fraud oversight lies in the nuances of structures and processes. If internal control mechanisms and external auditors report functionally and administratively to management, rather than to the board or audit committee, this weakens the independent check on executives. The same is true if independent expert directors cannot freely meet employees, customers, and suppliers and have to rely on information from management.

By comparison, privately held companies generally have fewer or less comprehensive reporting requirements and transparency obligations. Financial literacy on boards and audit committees is not a legal requirement for private firms, which may lead to similarly large scandals.

Theranos, a privately held Silicon Valley start-up, was valued at US$9 billion in 2015 because of its 'breakthrough advancements' in blood-testing technologies. The company claimed that its technology would enable laboratories to run medical tests with a finger-prick of blood. Theranos' original board consisted of retired government officials with no medical or technology experience, and no accounting or auditing expertise. Theranos' former CFO Henry Mosley had been fired in November 2006 after questioning the company's honesty and the reliability of its technology, and since then Theranos had only had a corporate controller. The company failed to prove its scientific claims, and its technology was seen as a fraud following civil and criminal investigations by US authorities in 2018. This led to widespread condemnation, culminating in the 2022 conviction of its founder and CEO, Elizabeth Holmes, along with her partner and Theranos' president and COO, Ramesh 'Sunny' Balwani, for defrauding investors.

How to Create an Effective Oversight Environment

The importance of boards actively managing the risk of high-level fraud cannot be overstated. Board members' proactive insights on the roots of corporate conflict help to shape a fair system, and the tone from the board sets the foundation for an ethical culture. Moreover, by strengthening oversight capabilities and frameworks, the board can act as a strong deterrent to high-level fraud. Potential fraudsters will be less likely to misbehave if they realise that they will be caught sooner or later.

With high-level fraud, prevention is always better than a cure. This is why boards must deal effectively with injustice, lax oversight, culture, and financial illiteracy. An active board therefore takes responsibility for broadening the notion of conflict of interest, building an appropriate oversight framework, creating a great corporate culture, and strengthening its own oversight expertise (see Figure 14.3). These steps are crucial for preventing potential high-level fraud, mitigating fraud risk, and guarding against any potential fraud losses.

Preventing Injustice: Broaden the Notion of Conflict of Interest

The notion of conflict of interest should be widened to include situations when a board member's duty of loyalty to stakeholders or the company is compromised. As we saw in Chapter 13, this can happen when some directors exercise influence over others through compensation, favours, a relationship, or psychological manipulation. Even directors who describe themselves as independent may face a conflict of interest if they are forced into agreeing with a dominant board member. And sometimes, independent directors may form a distinct group and represent their own interests rather than those of the company. Situations such as these increase the risk of fraud.

Figure 14.3   Creating an Effective Control Environment

Broadening the concept of conflict of interest helps board members to uncover potential injustice. Directors must deal with injustice when the interests of stakeholder groups are not appropriately balanced or harmonised. Conflict of interest and resulting injustices are a major source of high-level fraud. Board members must therefore address any conflicts responsibly and balance the interests of all individuals involved. When a company's purpose is in conflict with the interests of society, directors need to take an ethical stand, exercise care, and make sensible decisions.

Preventing Lax Oversight: Build Appropriate Frameworks

Boards fail when they do not have a formal and well-executed oversight process. Directors should begin by asking themselves what the ideal oversight mechanism should look like. For example, if an audit committee is not truly independent from management, its evaluation of high-level fraud risk cannot be effective. Direct reporting to the audit committee is thus important.

To ensure adequate controls on high-level fraud, a board needs to give special attention to the accountability matrices, reporting design, and oversight effectiveness of the audit committee. This should include discussions about the internal audit reporting line. Although there is no universal rule, it is not uncommon for a company's internal audit team to report both functionally and administratively to the CFO. But that raises questions regarding the credibility of the internal audit process.

In most cases, internal audit reports functionally to the audit committee but administratively to a C-suite executive. According to a 2023 Institute of International Auditors (IIA) survey, 72% of chief audit executives (CAEs) of publicly traded organisations said they reported administratively to the CFO.

Functionally, the majority of CAEs reported to the full board or its audit committee.[17] Former IIA President and CEO Richard Chambers said, 'The higher up in the organization a CAE reports, the more objective that individual can be in overseeing audits of tough areas of responsibility and the more independent the internal audit function becomes in the eyes of stakeholders. It enhances the credibility of the CAE and the internal audit function across the rest of the organization.'

Although there are differences in administrative and functional reporting structures across sectors, reporting to the CFO may not shield the company from board-level fraud. Directors must have a process for identifying and assessing such high-level fraud.

Here, it may help to borrow from Eastern supervision practices, and in particular the more complex process in China, where a board of supervisors works alongside the board of directors. The board of supervisors is normally composed of five to seven stakeholder professionals, some of whom are full-time onsite supervisors. By attending board of directors meetings as non-voting delegates, supervisors can monitor the performance of directors and senior management, the overall activities of the company, and decisions that affect the firm in the short and long term. Monitoring is based on criteria such as work attitude, behaviour, capacity to fulfil one's duties, and overall contribution, as well as any activities related to fraud. In addition, retiring and departing directors, and members of senior management, have to undergo an auditing process led by the board of supervisors. By periodically and systematically evaluating senior management and board directors, the board of supervisors creates appropriate checks and balances at the very top of the organisation.

In Chinese state companies, the board of supervisors is integrally involved in identifying high-level fraud, determining the company's fraud risk process, and ensuring that the actions of directors and senior management are aligned with the company's interest and strategy. As shown in Figure 14.4, internal auditors report primarily to the audit committee, with a secondary reporting line to senior management and the board of supervisors. Active oversight by the audit committee and the board of supervisors serves as a deterrent to high-level executives and directors engaging in fraudulent activity. Given the devastating consequences of high-level fraud, a Chinese-style board of supervisors charged with governance in this area might be an alternative to Western practices.

Organisational design and reporting structures are the fundamental elements of an anti-fraud oversight mechanism. It is crucial to define clearly who is responsible for which level of fraud management, and then to establish

---

[17] The Institute of Internal Auditors. (2023). North American Pulse of Internal Audit.

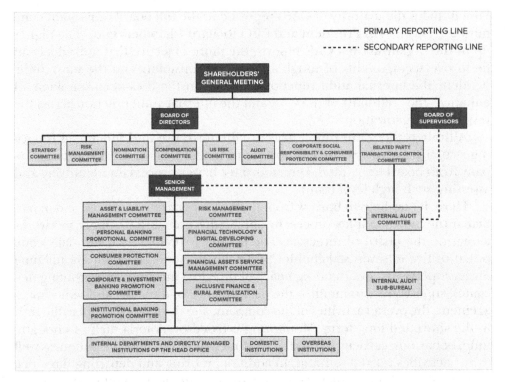

Figure 14.4   Corporate Governance Framework of Industrial and Commercial Bank of China (ICBC)
Source: With permission of ICBC, 2016.

control mechanisms that fit with their respective responsibilities. The message must be that no one, including board directors and CEOs, has the authority to commit fraud. Fraud risk management activities and control mechanisms might include, but are not limited to:

- an anti-fraud policy that defines the specific responsibilities for fraud management within the organisation;
- the ownership of fraud risks at different levels;
- the reporting lines of crucial functions such as internal audit, fraud examination, risk, legal, compliance, human resources, and security;
- the fraud detection methods and controls for all employees, including high-level executives and directors;
- the levels of access to fraud-related information;
- an ongoing monitoring process that is revisited regularly;
- the current development of fraud detection technologies;
- the establishment of a confidential hotline, online form, or email system to receive tips from all stakeholders;

- the overall protocols to deal with fraud-related issues in a timely way;
- an environment of safety for employees to report misconduct;
- rewards and protections for whistleblowers;
- the disciplinary measures for ethical violations.

Preventing Toxic Behaviours: Create a Positive Culture

Tight control mechanisms alone are not enough to make a company fraud resistant. In addition, the board of directors must create an atmosphere of zero tolerance for fraud, and actively foster a culture of 'doing the right thing'. These days, the corporate world is moving away from the narrow rules-based compliance of checking 'dos and don'ts', towards a values-based approach focused on integrity (see Figure 14.5, which was provided by Diane de St Victor, a key executive involved in tackling such issues). This requires judgement, and not only rules, to define the right culture. Board members should ask whether a corporate action passes their own personal integrity test.

The tone at the top is the ethical atmosphere created by the company's board and senior management and has a trickle-down effect through the organisation. The board has the responsibility to encourage ethical behaviour, and to empower internal and external stakeholders to meet these standards all the time.

Compliance	Conduct / Integrity
Following the rules so we don't get in trouble	Following our framework because it's the right thing to do
Enforcing policies as a measured target	Rules are internalised and turned into standards of conduct
Telling people what they should not do	Fostering an environment where people identify what they should do
Controlled by sanctions	Supported by personal and company character / values
Success measured by how well we follow the rules	Success measured by how well we integrate integrity into our business, leading to acceptable conduct
Can be delegated	Taking personal responsibility
Knowing what is right	Doing what is right even if no one is looking

Figure 14.5   The Evolution from Compliance to Conduct and Integrity
Source: Adapted from Diane de St Victor.

Yet this is only a starting point. It is not enough for boards or executives simply to hand out a written code of ethics for others to comply with. They have to 'walk the talk' and demonstrate their commitment to ethical behaviour through their words and actions. They have to communicate what is expected of employees, make clear their intolerance for dishonest and unethical behaviour, and lead by example. To make this work, boards need to monitor and assess the actual tone that senior executives use when motivating employees or communicating with external stakeholders.

For a board to lead by example in this regard, it should be a high performance board across all four pillars of effectiveness – dedicated people, effective information architecture, efficient structures and processes, and positive group dynamics. This usually starts with the selection of board members, and the hiring and firing of the CEO. Fraud at the hiring stage is not uncommon if the process is hastily conducted: Yahoo CEO Scott Thompson was fired after only four months due to resumé fraud, for example. Fraudsters often display character traits and styles that could indicate their intention to commit fraud – such as being extremely tough, political, ruthless, selfish, and greedy. It is crucial, therefore, that boards observe and listen to candidates for the C-suite and boardroom (and to their former employers) to determine if they are morally sound. Board members should be able to read human nature well and weed out those whose characters might lead them to commit fraud.

In addition to hiring morally sound senior executives and directors, companies should set realistic performance goals. These are targets that can be met without unethical behaviour such as linking flawed compensation schemes to aggressive sales goals, as described in the Wells Fargo case.

A company can cultivate a positive culture by rewarding employees for other things than just meeting financial goals. In particular, an organisation could reward an employee who has underperformed targets for the right reasons. Meeting the target would then not be the sole measure of success. Ethical behaviour and integrity should be rewarded and formalised into incentive programmes, while unethical actions should be punished and not tolerated. This will reinforce a strongly positive, anti-fraud culture.

Companies are more likely to maintain such a culture if all employees are aware of different types of fraud and their consequences. Anti-fraud training can raise awareness of this risk throughout the company. Good employees will be aware of possible signs, acts, and omissions of fraud, and know their responsibility to report questionable activity. Bad employees who plan to commit fraud would know that they were being watched, with a high chance of being caught should they transgress. A positive culture will reduce the opportunity for fraud, and make it more likely that such activity will be either deterred or detected early.

A positive work environment is part of a healthy corporate culture. An open-door policy, candid conversations, and easy access to high-level management all help to prevent fraud by making communication easier. Fraud occurs less frequently when employees have positive feelings about an organisation than when they feel unequal, exploited, ignored, abused, unrecognised, or threatened. Excessive pressure and expectations, ruthlessness, and office bullying do not make for a positive work environment and should be avoided at all cost. These are toxic behaviours that spread quickly and create room for fraud.

Strengthen Board Oversight Expertise with Special Focus on Legal, Compliance, Risk, Fraud, and Financial Reporting

Boardroom failures and scandals involving fraud often lead to the conclusion that the directors did not have the expertise to oversee the complexities of the business. The quick solution is to hire experts to sit on the board. Certified Public Accountants (CPAs), CPAs certified in Financial Forensics (CFFs), Certified Fraud Examiners (CFEs), and Certified Internal Auditors (CIAs) can all add oversight expertise as directors. These professionals can oversee and consult on internal control audits, risk management, compliance, and forensic analysis.

Another critical step is to increase fraud awareness at board level. Directors must have a solid understanding of fraud risk in general, fraud risks facing the company and their underlying drivers, and anti-fraud strategies. This includes being aware of the four factors contributing to fraud that we have discussed in this chapter. During board discussions on fraud risk, directors should consider the presence and weight of these factors and act accordingly to prevent fraud.

Board members also need to gain insights on regulatory and governance requirements regarding fraud, compliance, and other issues. For global companies, boards need greater expertise on national laws, global stock market regulations, international law enforcement, institutional investors, NGOs, and communication.

Tools for Anti-fraud Activities: Assessment, Prevention, Detection, and Investigation

In today's fast-changing environment, fraud is increasingly complex and sophisticated. What's more, a company might be judged by public opinion long before any fraud case comes to court. Directors must therefore move with the times and adjust their attitude and mentality regarding anti-fraud activities, as Figure 14.6 provided by Diane de St Victor, outlines.

Effective anti-fraud activities should concentrate on assessment, prevention, detection, and investigation.

In April 2019, Nissan Motor Co severed its two-decade connection with former saviour Carlos Ghosn. Shareholders removed the former chair and CEO from the company's board following his arrest for numerous alleged financial crimes. In the spring of 2019, the company had received a report from an external panel that said Ghosn's long tenure at Nissan led to power being 'concentrated in his hands'. The report also called for measures to improve the carmaker's governance. Nissan's new CEO Hiroto Saikawa, Ghosn's protege-turned-accuser, said the company may claim damages against its former chair. 'Today is a key turning point for Nissan', Saikawa said on 8 April 2019 on NHK, Japan's broadcaster. Ghosn denied the legitimacy of the charges.

Since his dramatic escape to Lebanon at the end of the year, achieved by hiding in a box for audio equipment on a plane, Ghosn has been embroiled in accusations of financial misconduct. In 2022, France issued an arrest warrant against him, accusing him of misusing company funds and engaging in money laundering related to a Renault-Nissan subsidiary.

Yesterday	Today
Is this something we can do legally?	Is this something we can live with?
Is it permitted?	Is it acceptable?
Compliance	Integrity / conduct
No one will know	It will come up
Don't get caught	You will be caught
Being judged based on standards of conduct applicable at the time	Yesterday's conduct being judged on today's standards
Local impact	Global impact
Slow impact	Immediate impact
You knew	You should have known
One thing at a time	It's all commingled

Figure 14.6   Compliance and Integrity – Yesterday and Today

Source: Adapted from Diane de St Victor.

Assessment

The board of directors or the board of supervisors should regularly assess the organisation's fraud risk. This includes reviewing the status of the four main factors that might lead to high-level fraud (Figure 14.7). Boards should assess the likelihood and significance of fraud along each dimension, and the effectiveness of the organisation's anti-fraud controls. Such a process will allow the company to build on its strengths and address areas of weakness on a continuous basis.

Prevention

The board of directors or supervisors should focus on prevention to reduce fraud opportunities in the organisation. Figure 14.8 identifies some priority actions for directors in this regard, understand what management is doing, and identify red flags at an early stage (Figure 14.9).

Detection

A board member must have a healthy level of scepticism and ask lots of questions. The educated director should think like an investigator.

Investigation

It is the board's job to assess, prevent, and detect high-level fraudulent activity. When bad things happen, boards need to get actively involved in the investigation and ensure that the process is thorough and effective. This should

Fraud Factor Assessment

	INJUSTICE	LAX OVERSIGHT	FINANCIAL ILLITERACY	PROBLEMATIC CULTURE
LIKELIHOOD				
SIGNIFICANCE				
PREVENTIVE ACTIVITY				
DETECTIVE ACTIVITY				
INVESTIGATIVE ACTIVITY				

Figure 14.7   Fraud Factor Assessment

JUSTICE AND FAIRNESS	SOUND OVERSIGHT	FINANCIAL LITERACY	POSITIVE CULTURE
Broaden the concept of conflict of interest	Organisational design	Hire experts	Tone at the top
Be aware of the consequences of board decisions under influence	Reporting structure	Conduct training	Lead by example
Know the cases when one stakeholder takes advantage of the others or the company	Code of conduct/ethics	Understand the deep consequences of financial crime	Effective communication
	Ethics hotline	Identifying and measuring financial fraud	Hire right board members and C-suite executives
	Audit committee oversight		Careful background check
	Oversight on management's practice on fraud risk		Weed out executives that are extremely 'tough' on others but not themselves
	Investigative process		Fire those that are political, ruthless, selfish, and greedy
	Adequate remediation		Realistic performance goals
	Controls on approvals, authorisations, verifications, reconciliations, or segregation of duties		Open-door policy
			Positive work environment

Figure 14.8   Preventive Activity

	BOARD	BOARD COMMITTEES	C-SUITE	OTHER SENIOR MGT	LOWER MGT
ATTITUDES					
INCENTIVES					
PRESSURE					
OPPORTUNITY					
INVESTIGATIVE ACTIVITY					
POTENTIAL SCHEME					
FINANCIAL REPORTING FRAUD					
MISAPPROPRIATION OF ASSETS					
EXPENDITURE & LIABILITIES MANIPULATION					
FRAUDULENT REVENUE AND ASSETS RECOGNITION					
OTHER MISCONDUCT					

Figure 14.9   High-level Fraud Detection

include appointing a competent, independent internal or external legal counsel charged with carrying out the investigation, access to confidential information, timelines for regular reports, process of resolution, communication, disclosure, and protocols to follow legal and regulatory requirements.

When things start 'going south' as unethical behaviour or financial crime are discovered, the company's reputation will most probably be severely damaged. Boards need to face reality, act swiftly, take responsibility, and mitigate fraud risk to reintegrate integrity, and reduce exposure and further damage. Mitigation strategies need to take into account whether this was a systemic issue.

The case of Wells Fargo serves as a reminder that fraud happens frequently and can occur in any organisation, country, or industry. High-level fraud is especially damaging as it can result in huge financial losses for the company and its stakeholders, legal costs, and ruined reputations that can ultimately lead to the organisation's demise. If the board turns a blind eye to such fraud, directors may themselves face litigation by shareholders.

Directors have a legal and moral responsibility to implement a proactive oversight framework, to lead by example, communicate constantly, and follow through on anti-fraud policies. The costs of preventing fraud are far lower than the potential losses when it happens. By taking the lead on this issue, boards can help to provide essential safeguards and secure an ethically and financially sound future for their organisation.

Throughout Part II, we have seen how boards are constantly challenged and sometimes fail. In Part III, we examine board best practices with the aim of providing guidance and inspiration for directors around the world.

Recent move in addressing Greenwashing

A study conducted by the European Commission in 2020 scrutinised 150 environmental assertions in advertising and product labelling across the EU. Alarmingly, it revealed that 53.3% of these claims were either vague, deceptive, or unfounded, and that 40% of them were unsubstantiated.[18] Such deceptive practices, known as greenwashing, pose significant risks to businesses. Consequences may include erosion of consumer and investor trust, legal liabilities, and damage to reputation.

In response, there has been a movement towards combating greenwashing in Europe. For instance, in 2022, the United Kingdom introduced the Green Claims Code, offering guidelines to businesses for crafting precise and transparent environmental claims.[19] Similarly, in 2024, the European Commission adopted new legislation, the Directive on Green Claims, prohibiting generic environmental claims and misleading product information.[20]

(continued)

---

[18] European Commission (2020). Environmental Claims in the EU.

[19] GOV.UK. (2021). Green claims code. 20 September. https://www.gov.uk/government/publications/green-claims-code-making-environmental-claims

[20] European Parliament. (2024). Press Release, 17 January.

(continued)

In March 2023, the oil company Shell faced more than 20 court cases filed by environmental advocacy groups. In response, Shell stated in their report, 'Litigation does not enable the global cooperation required to change both supply and demand for energy.'[21] Among these legal disputes was a case filed in the United Kingdom by ClientEarth, an environmental law organisation, targeting Shell's Board of Directors. 'Our central allegation was that by adopting and pursuing an inadequate energy transition strategy, the Board was mismanaging the material and foreseeable risks that climate change presents to the company, in breach of its legal duties.'[22] Notably, ClientEarth gained support from large institutional investors including AP3 (Swedish national pension fund), Nest (UK pension fund), and AP Pension (Danish pension fund). Despite these actions, in May 2023, the UK High Court dismissed ClientEarth's case, with their subsequent appeal application meeting rejection.

---

[21] Shell. (2023). Shell plc Energy Transition Progress Report 2022.

[22] ClientEarth. (2024). ClientEarth v Board of Directors of Shell plc, Legal Briefing. January.

PART III
Board Leadership

Joanne Marker and Board Values at Comfre

*T*horsten was pushing his food around his plate at Joanne Marker's dinner table. He had taken one bite since the plate had arrived twenty minutes earlier.

'OK, spill it Thor', Joanne said.

The young man looked up at his aunt, startled.

'You said you wanted some advice?' she said.

Thorsten sighed and put down his fork. He had recently joined the board of Kloetzel & Brothers, a global financial services company, but he already had some concerns.

'How did you know when something wasn't right? Or was really wrong? On the boards you were on, I mean', he asked.

'Well Thorsten, it's like this.' Joanne put her elbows on the table and clasped her hands for emphasis. 'Board directors, they're held to the same standards as everyone else – except they're not.' Thorsten raised his eyebrows. 'They're held to even higher standards. So, whatever's going on, you need to speak up now and fight for what is right.'

'But what if they don't listen to me?' Thorsten said. 'I mean, I'm the new, young guy.'

Joanne reached across the table to her nephew and patted his hand.

'Ah. Have you tried talking to James? I mean, over coffee or lunch?' James Caspar was Kloetzel's chair.

Thorsten nodded miserably. 'Then, my dear, you might need to rethink your service to this board', she said.

'Is that what happened to you? I mean, at Comfre?' Thorsten asked.

It had been a while since Joanne had thought about the Argentinian food company where she had held a seven-month board directorship almost 20 years earlier. She had accepted the position due to her eagerness to work in emerging markets – a wish she came to realise was perhaps overeager.

'That was a case of failed due diligence, I'm afraid', she said.

'You? Not doing your due diligence? I find that hard to believe', Thorsten said.

In Joanne's second board meeting at Buenos Aires-based Comfre, she had learned that the publicly listed company was asking the board to approve two major investments: one in a big dairy company and another in a beef farm. It was the first she had heard of the deals, and they were reaching the end of the meeting. Joanne frantically flipped through the briefing papers, wondering if she had missed something, but there was no background information on the proposed deals. She asked many questions to try to understand the strategic logic of vertically integrating, but the answers from Comfre CEO Rodrigo Martinez were too vague for her liking.

During the last coffee break of the day, another independent director, Julio Diaz, sidled up to Joanne. Away from the others, he told her that the two companies were owned by two of Martinez's brothers-in-law. Alarm bells rang in Joanne's head.

In the final discussion at that meeting, she raised the conflict of interest issue, doing her best to remain polite yet firmly voicing her concerns. The chair, Antonio Alvarez, thanked Joanne, and reassured her that the deals fully complied with Argentinian legal requirements. The board voted to approve the investments, although she abstained.

Joanne felt sick for the duration of the 13-hour return flight. A week later, after going through Comfre's numbers in more detail, her discomfort was turning to alarm. She called Diaz to ask him what he thought about her emerging hypothesis. They looked at the figures together and discussed their concerns, both of them increasingly convinced that something was really wrong.

For days, Joanne tried reaching Alvarez, but his secretary kept informing her that he was unavailable. With a heavy heart, she prepared her resignation letter and printed it off. She called Diaz to inform him of her decision, and he confirmed that he would be doing the same the following day. They decided they would each make a final attempt to reach Alvarez to discuss their concerns.

The next day, Joanne turned on the news to see that investors had responded negatively to Comfre's proposed deals, and that the company's stock price had taken a dive. She again dialled Alvarez's number but there was no reply. Then the phone rang. It was Diaz. He told her that Comfre was being investigated for accounting fraud.

After dinner, Joanne tried to catch up on other work. But she found herself wondering over and over why she hadn't enquired earlier about the ownership of the Comfre group – and wondering whom she could have asked to better understand the context. Finally, she gave up trying to work and turned on the TV, to catch the end of the late-night news. She caught her breath when she saw the images of Alvarez being arrested in Buenos Aires for alleged accounting fraud.

***

'You'd better know what kind of board you're on sooner rather than later, Thorsten dear', Joanne said.

The young man nodded, and pushed his plate away.

'I think I need to schedule a call with James', he mumbled, wiping his mouth.

CHAPTER

15

Board Leadership and Values

Corporate governance does not exist in a vacuum, but in a social context, and that alone demands that governance systems not be divorced from a sense of purpose and values. In addition, governance builds on a number of disciplines – law, regulatory policy, control, economics, management, and leadership – all of which are influenced in one way or another by moral philosophy. Today, the intensifying calls for good governance have once again underlined the fundamental importance of values, ethics, and morality in social and public action.

As boards continue to reel from spates of corporate scandals in all contexts and economies, and increasingly make the front pages of newspapers for the wrong reasons, a painful realisation has dawned on them. Yes, the metrics, documents, and other instruments of board activity and power may appear formidable and well-structured. Yet these may prove to be powerless and wholly ineffective when ethical breaches lead to corruption and the destruction of shareholder and social value on an unprecedented scale.

When the media later dissect the boards of collapsed companies, the most distressing part of the story was often the apparent normality, even banality, of their pre-scandal activity. There were nomination and governance committees distributing reports and updates, and in many cases a large proportion of the directors were independent, including luminaries from other industries, apparently unconflicted, and even from academia.

Quality Boards Live and Breathe Integrity

The cumulative effect of recent corporate scandals has been to place integrity at the front and centre of a board's mandate. Whereas a company's management needs to comply with rules and guidelines, including ethical guidelines,

In February 2017, the board of Unilever, the Anglo-Dutch household goods and food manu-facturer, rejected a US$143 billion takeover offer from Kraft Heinz. The proposed heavily leveraged bid would have been one of the largest deals in corporate history. In withdrawing its bid, Kraft cited a lack of strategic merit. Yet what derailed it within less than 48 hours was the clash of corporate values the two companies represented.

With a history spanning 130 years and roots in the health crises of Victorian England, Unilever has come to be recognised as a leader in sustainable business. It has been com-mitted to reducing its environmental footprint and acting as a force for social good. Its Sustainable Living Plan, introduced in 2010, now informs every aspect of Unilever's global operations. So do the company's corporate social responsibility programmes: instead of co-alescing around a CSR label, they have been embedded in all of Unilever's business targets.

Kraft Heinz is run by private equity firm 3G Capital, famous for growing its business through acquisitions followed by aggressive cost-cutting and heavy job losses. Unilever shareholders, 70% of whom are long-term investors, were also sceptical about the bid. Meanwhile, the UK's largest trade union, Unite, described Kraft as 'predatory' and said that any deal would lead to job losses among the two companies' combined UK workforces of nearly 9,000.

In the first quarter of 2019, Kraft Heinz wrote down the value of some of its brands by US$15.4 billion. It also posted a US$12.6 billion loss for the fourth quarter of 2018 and confirmed that the US SEC was investigating its accounting practices. By contrast, Unilever, like its European peers Nestlé and Danone, is increasingly focusing on new niche brands and healthier products.

a board of directors is expected to aim higher. A board is in a good position to be the natural guardian of a consistent set of values that emanate from deep-seated and strongly internalised beliefs. And safeguarding these values goes hand in hand with embracing integrity.

The appeal to integrity is not merely an abstract moral exhortation. Smaller or larger conflicts of interest abound in board work. Dealing with them with awareness and integrity becomes essential. In an increasingly uncertain busi-ness environment, the old, practical 'give and take', with a tangible sense of reciprocity between parties, may not be enough to win the trust and loyalty of employees, investors, and customers. This also requires honesty, a sense of openness, and a willingness to listen to and accommodate the other party's needs. And it requires compassion, rather than just rules, policy, and clear precedents. Reinforcing an organisation's relationships takes a lot of trust, and more often than not a heart.

Integrity is often seen as a strong driver of a board's success. The under-standing of the term, and what it means in practice, will vary from organisa-tion to organisation. But most will agree that having integrity means doing the right thing regardless of whether or not it is popular, attracts publicity, or results in immediate gains. When divorced from integrity, individuals' and organisations' intellect, resourcefulness, and action may quickly become self-serving, devoid of meaning, and even toxic for their relationships with the outside world.

Which and Whose Values?

More than any other part of an organisation, the board understands that values morally underpin every action and initiative the firm undertakes. The board must be clear that values are not paperwork to be sorted out or boxes to be ticked in a questionnaire. Rather, they make us human and connect to our deeply felt need to do good and contribute.

This may sound very lofty and hard to grasp. But we should remember that values lie at the heart of corporate culture – itself a blueprint of values, beliefs, rules, and patterns of behaviour that provides the organisation with a coherent way of looking at the world. Progressive boards have upheld the notion that business is, and must be, ultimately about people. From this vantage point, organisations are recast as deeply value-laden spaces where humans learn together and share their successes as well as failures.

Encouragingly, the discussion of values in business is not nearly as distant from the real world of contracts and performance targets as one might assume. At a time when business competition and service delivery are being pervasively disrupted, organisations can no longer rely on the output of top-down, bureaucratic, impersonal operation centres to delight customers and fire their imaginations. For this, they need employees who give the best of themselves and of their talent, creativity, and dedication. This rarely happens when companies rely solely on the old tools of hierarchy, obedience, or monetary compensation. Rather, it is a sense of shared values that inspires employees' most collaborative and imaginative efforts.

People are not drawn to innovate and create, and to break down silos in their company, simply because they receive a pay cheque every month. They do so because they feel recognised and respected for who they are and what they believe in. The best organisations recognise the potential value of their culture as a potent asset, a consistent boost to their brand equity, and a magnet for talented individuals with integrity. In the long term, a vibrant company culture rooted in clearly defined and publicly upheld values is possibly the most powerful instrument for attracting and retaining talent.

Other stakeholders also increasingly demand that organisations demonstrate honesty, openness, loyalty, and a passion for contributing to society. Although this may of course play out differently depending on the company's

In the wake of the #MeToo movement that started in the United States against the sexual abuse of women (and sometimes of men), and quickly gained traction across the globe, several large corporations and their boards have had to grapple with the fact that bad behaviour by their top management or directors can negatively impact the business. Leslie Moonves, who ran CBS for more than 20 years as CEO and chair, was forced to resign by the company's board in September 2018 for alleged past sexual misconduct. As part of the settlement agreement that ousted him, Moonves was forced to give up US$34.5 million of stock awards. The CBS board reacted quickly once the scandal broke in summer 2018 and launched an independent investigation into the allegations. But it was also strongly criticised for not having addressed the problem sooner.

All too often, however, today's organisations thrive on stability, predictability, and control, and are committed to a bureaucratic model according to which companies and their employees perform their tasks in a machine-like way. This view has become entrenched to the point where it is rarely challenged, despite the obvious limits it imposes on the richness of organisational life. Viewed through this lens, people become easily replaceable and in some contexts very nearly obsolete.

Unsurprisingly, therefore, statements of a company's values, including its vision and mission, were often drafted by a few representatives of senior management with support from the PR or marketing communications departments. A neat one-page document listing these values was then placed behind glass, framed, and hung on the wall.

Strong boards today know that this won't do. More importantly, they understand that values can never be dictated by 'someone at the top'. A firm is a live, dynamic organism, teeming with rich and complex discussions, conversations, and narratives. Often, the best place to learn what makes the people in the firm tick is in the informal spaces by the office water cooler or its social media equivalent, where employees exchange information, speculate about future outcomes, voice their hopes and grievances, and jointly try to make sense of the reality around them. Yet for decades, this 'bottom-up' narrative remained completely hidden from the organisation's official views and perspectives, which were dominated by management and its 'black-and-white' structures and processes.

Modern boards have grasped that the intersection of values prioritised by employees, management, and customers should serve as the basis for developing a shared vision of 'who we are' and 'what we stand for'. This vision then informs the company's mission, strategy, and policies, right down to everyday work practices.

Boards are expected to have a vision for their organisations – one that recognises the company's purpose, inspires pride in its employees and confidence among customers, and sounds genuine and accessible to investors. Vision and mission are still relevant in articulating shared purpose and direction. They are also useful for making abstract ideas practically relevant, tangible, and action oriented.

Most importantly, the values that have been captured as part of a shared vision need to be practised, lived, and celebrated. It is not enough to write them down. To quote a modern-day management thinker, Henry Mintzberg, 'We cannot take for granted that the production of rules and regulations, organisational charts, roles and responsibilities, held together by chains of command and lines of authority will allow human values and judgment to flourish.'[1]

---

[1] Mintzberg, H. (1979). *The Structuring of Organizations*. Pearson.

purpose and DNA, the underlying consistency of expression and integrity of action will not go unnoticed. In the present economic, political, and social environment of a 'trust deficit', relentless uncertainty and change, these externally facing values are crucial to a company's reputation.

An effective board helps to define the company's guiding values and aspirations and ensures that these circulate throughout the organisation – including at the day-to-day operational level. In recent years, the emergence of new approaches such as the core values method has offered practical ways to build and renew culture in an organisation. This puts boards in a stronger position than ever to examine the company and raise questions such as:

- What is the ultimate purpose of our collective effort?
- What aspirations are we pursuing?
- What is the impact of our undertaking on society?

Board Values vs Organisational Values

Of course, boards will struggle to safeguard and oversee the 'values' conversation within their organisations if they have never taken the time before to reflect on the culture and values of the board itself. Here, the directors' personal values – which we already discussed in Chapter 9 – can serve as a simple yet productive starting point.

A passionate, committed board understands that it cannot simply find values in literature or copy them from a PowerPoint presentation. Instead, it will reflect and actively draw on values that its members have developed and honed over their many years in corporate leadership and public service. The board's values will then resonate with those of the individual directors, which are shaped by unique sets of individual accomplishments, visions for the industry and organisation, ethical outlooks, and moral beliefs.

Describing the board's collective values in a succinct manner will not always be easy. But the main contours of the ethos – of what is permissible and what is not, what the board believes in, and why these beliefs are non-negotiable – should be discernible to everyone, if not for how they are defined then certainly in the way they are projected and practised.

The board is responsible for articulating its culture and promoting values as benchmarks of the beliefs and behaviours inside an organisation. When a company has determined its vision, mission, and values, it is essential that the board demonstrates leadership to communicate, endorse, and implement them.

Reflecting this new board remit, the role of the chair has expanded in a similar direction. In addition to conducting board meetings in a focused and organised manner, the chair is now looked upon as a source of moral authority, particularly in times of crisis. His or her visible public stance on ethics in the context of corporate vision and values statements can contribute to dispelling the widely held perception that business is at best ethics neutral or even devoid of ethics.

Effective boards understand the importance of values, communication, and vision in building a successful company. They also recognise their own role in striving toward this goal. Put simply, boards are designed and equipped to build credibility and trust in ways that executive teams cannot. The best boards also set positive precedents and contribute to defining new standards and practices of global governance.

Family Values in Business

In general, family-owned companies have consistently shown a heightened sensitivity to defining and promoting their values. Many have actively negotiated a creative tension between family and business values, aiming to put forward a third category of 'family business values'. Some family companies have chosen to subsume their business organisation within an overarching, family-centric structure, recognising that the family needs to prosper before the business can grow as well.

Taking a far-sighted position on an ethical question, even though it may hurt short-term profitability, is an important aspect of a board member's responsibility. And it is crucial for instilling values throughout an organisation. Through daily practice and use, such values can visibly link the priorities of the leadership team with the day-to-day activities of the organisation. And the board and the company will have a solid foundation of integrity as a result.

'Without social justice, the economy is dead.' These were the words of Emmanuel Faber, Danone CEO, during a 2016 speech to graduates at the Hautes Etudes Commerciales (HEC). Faber, a champion of environmental, social, and governance (ESG) and responsible capitalism, is the former chairman and CEO of Danone, who was ousted in 2021 by the company's board following pressure from activist shareholders. Artisan Partners and Bluebell Capital Partners, which together own less than 6% of the Paris-based food giant called for his removal. They blame Faber for 'a combination of poor operational record and questionable capital allocation choices'. Danone was perceived to have cared more about people, the planet, and social responsibility than its shareholders, and its CEO paid the price.

A New Board Arena for Joanne Marker: Chairing the Board

*J*oanne Marker sat in the back of the car and again reviewed her notes. From the top of
her documents, she picked up the biography of her lunch host George Drakos, Chairman
of the board of Nordic PharmaSolutions (an innovative large cap pharma company,
based in Denmark).

George is widely esteemed for his remarkable success as one of Europe's longest-serving
CEOs. Over a span of 32 years with Olympus TechCrafters, he served as Chief Executive
for 12 years. Before that, George held various high-ranking positions across Asia and
Europe. George has been the Chairman of PharmaSolutions (150 billion market cap) for
eight years. He is also the Chairman of CartoVision Technologies and a non-executive
board member of TelePass Communications AG.

Joanne had met George only once before, when they were both on a panel on 'Tech for
Good' in Davos a few years back. She had found him a calm presence, who had made
thoughtful, deeply informed, and measured contributions, and obviously highly experienced. When she received his email a few weeks back, inviting her to lunch while he was
in London, her curiosity was piqued. She guessed George must be approaching his late
60s by now. As the car passed the Royal Academy of the Arts, the intuition that George
might be looking for a successor as Chair of PharmaSolutions again crossed her mind.
George was not the kind to outstay himself.

The company mission was certainly compelling: 'To revolutionize pharmaceutical
discovery through cutting-edge AI technology, delivering innovative and life-saving med-
icines to improve global health outcomes.' Her questions were grouped into four buckets:

1. **People:** Did PharmaSolutions have the right competences and depth of experience
   among its members to be able to both support the tremendous opportunities that

AI offered in the area of molecule discovery, as well as to oversee it? She wondered about any succession plans or board education to address this. When she had reviewed the board composition, she noted that there were none younger than 50.

2. **Information architecture**: She had scanned GlassDoor reviews of PharmaSolutions. While there were many positive comments about opportunities to develop and attend conferences, as well as compensation packages, she found this comment disturbing:

Despite soliciting feedback, senior managers fail to take action on received feedback and instead become defensive and dismissive of employee concerns.

Unrealistic expectations are placed on team members to complete numerous 'urgent' tasks within tight deadlines, prioritising quantity over quality and leading to a punitive atmosphere if mistakes occur.

Conflicting instructions from senior managers cause confusion and inconsistency regarding task prioritisation, deadlines, and review procedures.

What was the board doing to oversee organisational culture? Were the right KPIs in place to ensure that risk-taking was encouraged, and were these consistent and well aligned with strategic objectives?

3. **Structures and Processes:** Joanne had noted that there were six board committees: Audit, Risk, Science, Nominations & Governance, Remuneration, and Sustainability. Were all these committees really necessary? Fewer, more focused committees help to keep the discussions at the right level, in her experience. And she wondered how the board professionalism would show on the chair succession process.

4. **Board Culture:** With 13 board members, this was one of the larger boards Joanne had come across. Were all board members really speaking up and voicing their concerns in the boardroom? Or were the real decisions happening at the Committee level?

The car pulled to the curb and Joanne was swept into the restaurant to her table, where George was waiting for her. After they exchanged pleasantries and ordered, George spread his napkin in his lap and smiled.

'Joanne, let me get straight to the point. I will be stepping down as Chairman of the Board in the spring. Age limit, you see. After discussion with the nomination committee, we believe that you would be a great candidate to succeed me. You have tremendous experience, and a great deal of respect as a board member, known for your strategic acumen and dedication – and of course your commitment to integrity. Also, we really value your independence, and external experience.'

Joanne felt a rush of mixed emotions flood through her. She was honoured to be considered for such a prestigious position, but she also knew the weight of responsibility that came with it. She listened intently as George outlined the nomination process and the expectations that came with the role. As they ate, George explained his philosophy to Chairmanship at PharmaSolutions, and what he had accomplished during his tenure.

Joanne asked some of the questions she had prepared, but decided to leave the more technical points for the time being.

When she returned home, Joanne read through all the governance documents and financial reports that the Board Secretary sent to her. She then requested that the Board Secretary set up a series of meetings with the board members and the CEO, each discussion delving deeper into the company's vision, challenges, and opportunities.

'What are the key strategic priorities for the company over the next five years?' Joanne inquired during one of the meetings with the CEO. 'How do you envision the role of the Chairman in fostering challenge, collaboration and alignment among the board members and executive team?' She also articulated her own vision for the role of Chair, emphasising the importance of transparency, accountability, and inclusivity. Caring but daring as well.

After careful deliberation, Joanne made her decision. She would love to do it. And she felt she could make a true difference. PharmaSolutions had all it took to become the first European mega cap and she would be proud to help it get there. She was also convinced that the company had the potential to make a positive impact in the world, to solving a number of debilitating illness using its capabilities and resources. She had the experience and energy to make real impact at PharmaSolutions – and also had a personal mission to be a positive role model for women board members and executives who one day aspired to be chairs of boards of directors. The timing was good too, with several of her board mandates coming to an end. She imagined that the role would take easily 50% of her time, especially initially as she onboarded.

She called George to tell him that she accepted his invitation.

***

The following Monday, Joanne received an invitation to a Zoom call from Eleanor Pelletier, PharmaSolution's Lead Independent Director and Chair of the Nominations Committee. From her study, Joanne logged into the call five minutes early, to check that the lighting and audio settings were optimal.

'Thanks for making the time, Joanne.' For the next 15 minutes, Eleanor gave a detailed description of each of the steps of the selection process. Joanne was impressed by how well-thought-out and structured it was, as well as the level of discipline and diligence that it entailed. In addition to Joanne, the nominations committee was considering three other candidates.

Eleanor asked for Joanne's consent to collect feedback from relevant stakeholders – including the Chairs of her current boards and former team members. The purpose was to gather evaluations of past leadership performance. The Nominations Committee would then meet to deliberate the list of candidates to the board for deliberation and discussion, against an established set of criteria – including alignment with the company's strategic objectives, and leadership experience (including non-executive board committees and senior executives).

Selected candidates would be invited to an in-person interview with the Nominations Committee members, to delve deep into the different dimensions of her experience (notably risk and crisis management, but also her experience with regulators, overseeing culture, and other areas they deemed pertinent).

The final two shortlisted candidates would meet the full board. Their input would be included in the final selection decision.

16

Becoming the Chair

The Role of the Chair

The chair is responsible for the leadership of the board. This entails ensuring the effective operation of the board and its committees, in conformity with the highest standards of corporate governance. He or she sets the board agenda, which should be primarily focused on strategy, performance, value creation, and accountability, and ensures that issues relevant to those areas are considered by the board. The chair must make sure that the board determines the nature and extent of any significant risks that the organisation is willing to embrace in implementing its strategy, and also that directors review the effectiveness of the company's risk management and internal control systems on an ongoing basis.

Facilitating constructive debate and decision-making, and generating productive board dynamics, is another of the chair's key roles. This includes building in adequate time for discussion of all-important agenda items (and strategic issues in particular). And it involves devoting attention to complex or contentious issues, making sure that non-executive directors in particular have sufficient time to consider them. Part of the chair's role in promoting meaningful boardroom exchanges is to secure accurate, timely, and clear information for directors, especially regarding the organisation's performance.

Building links between the board and management, including through appropriate delegation of authority, constitutes an important component of the chair's role. (We will discuss board–management relations in more detail in the next chapter.) Promoting effective relationships and communications between non-executive directors and members of the executive committee is critical in order to enable a productive exchange. Here, the chair needs to secure access to senior management without intruding on the CEO's responsibilities.

It is vital that the chair continually monitors the board's composition, balance, and diversity (in terms of competencies, perspectives, and gender), and plans the succession for board and senior management appointments. When new directors and committee chairs join, the chair needs to arrange comprehensive, tailored on-boarding programmes and induction processes for them. Ensuring the effective establishment, composition, and operation of committees is critical, as is making sure that committee chairs are held accountable.

The chair is responsible for proper disclosure in the annual report of information regarding the organisation's governance perspectives and the board appointment process – including a description of the board's policy on diversity and gender, any measurable objectives it has set, and progress on achieving these. The disclosure should also include a description of the search and nomination process.

Board education is also within the chair's sphere of responsibilities. He or she must ensure that directors continually update their skills, knowledge, and familiarity with the organisation, in order to contribute fully on both the board and its committees. This includes regularly reviewing and agreeing individual training and development needs with each director, as well as addressing the needs of the board as a whole.

The chair has the task of monitoring board performance and effectiveness, via a formal annual evaluation of its main committees and individual directors, as well as an externally facilitated evaluation, perhaps every two years. These evaluations should consider the balance of skills, experience, independence, and knowledge among the directors, how well the board operates as a unit, and any other factors relevant to its effectiveness. More importantly, the chair acts on his or her views, as well as on the results of the performance evaluations, by recognising the board's strengths and addressing its weaknesses. Where appropriate, he or she proposes new board members or seeks the resignation of existing directors.

The chair also has a role in ensuring effective communication with shareholders, host governments, and other relevant stakeholders, and in making sure that the views of these groups are understood by the board. When proposing the re-election of directors, the chair confirms to shareholders that, following a formal evaluation, these individuals continue to perform effectively and demonstrate clear commitment. In addition, the chair needs to check that the organisation is maintaining a dialogue with its principal shareholders about the remuneration, governance, and strategy of directors and senior managers.

An effective chair maintains a harmonious and open relationship with all executive directors, providing advice and support while respecting their executive responsibility. As we will see later in the chapter, supporting and advising the CEO in strategy development and other matters is an important element of the chair's role.

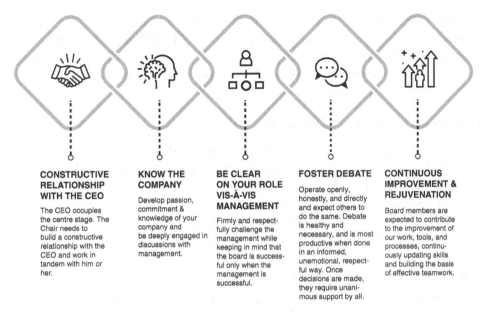

CONSTRUCTIVE RELATIONSHIP WITH THE CEO

The CEO occupies the centre stage. The Chair needs to build a constructive relationship with the CEO and work in tandem with him or her.

KNOW THE COMPANY

Develop passion, commitment & knowledge of your company and be deeply engaged in discussions with management.

BE CLEAR ON YOUR ROLE VIS-À-VIS MANAGEMENT

Firmly and respectfully challenge the management while keeping in mind that the board is successful only when the management is successful.

FOSTER DEBATE

Operate openly, honestly, and directly and expect others to do the same. Debate is healthy and necessary, and is most productive when done in an informed, unemotional, respectful way. Once decisions are made, they require unanimous support by all.

CONTINUOUS IMPROVEMENT & REJUVENATION

Board members are expected to contribute to the improvement of our work, tools, and processes, continuously updating skills and building the basis of effective teamwork.

Figure 16.1   Five Golden Rules Inspired by Great Chairs (such as Risto Siilasmaa, Hsieh Fu Hua, Beat Hess, Rolf Soiron, Christoph Franz, Michel Demaré, and Others)

Great chairship uses many dimensions, summarised in in Figure 16.1, which captures golden rules inspired by great chairpeople.

Effective Chairs are Active

It is increasingly common for chairs to play a more active role in the organisation, while not overlapping with the CEO's executive style. The active chair is a key player in driving boardroom culture and setting the direction of the organisation together with the board. The chair ensures that the board not only understands the business and its customers, but also impacts the organisational culture. Visibly present, the active chair sets a tone of integrity and clearly defines what this means in practice.

By regularly working in the business (at least one or two days a week, and more often three or more), the chair participates in the supervision of the firm's operations. An active chair challenges strategic thinking, co-creates the organisation's strategy with the board and management, and closely monitors the execution of business plans. In-depth oversight and review of the CEO, as well as an in-depth oversight of management and the talent pool, is key for the active chair. The chair spends a great deal of time and energy coaching and advising the CEO and senior executives, and serves as an active liaison between the board and management.

The active chair is a dedicated leader of the board who takes its performance extremely seriously and works tirelessly to discipline and energise it. By constantly scanning the external world, they develop the board's stakeholder knowledge. The chair also serves as the company's representative in key stakeholder relationships, as well as when crisis strikes.

Transitioning into the Role of the Chair

Becoming a chair requires a set of leadership skills needed to foster a constructive board culture and lead high-quality discussions and decision-making, which is distinct from the role of an executive. Great chairs exert influence without jostling for power, trying to run the show, or stealing the C-suite's thunder. Despite the understatement, they have a disproportionate impact on board dynamics, board culture, and board agenda.

Recognising the qualities of great chairs

Based on our research and experience of working with many boards, there a number of dimensions which characterise great chairs.

Graceful in the exercise of power. Effective chairs take up their authority with great care and nuance. They realise that legitimate authority comes from the board as a body – and their role therein – rather than from them as an individual. Effective chairs do not exercise authoritarian leadership, rather they act as agenda-setters, promotors of constructive dissent, builders of authentic consensus, and as a conduit for the Board's voice.

Able to subordinate their egos. Effective chairs accept that the CEO is the company's public face. As such they are willing to cede the limelight and operate behind the scenes. They see themselves as first-among-equals rather than leader-in-charge. They know that boards tend to work better when their members feel that their standing is on the same level and that their contributions are genuinely heard and valued.

Able to work in tandem with the CEO. Essential to the chair's role is their relationship with the CEO, which needs to be a nuanced balance of both support and challenge. (We will be looking at that more in the next chapter.)

Stewards of their companies. Effective chairs embody, defend, and actively promote the purpose and core values of their organisations. They set the tone on the board, steer the development of the vision and strategic framework in alignment with its values, shape the culture, and set the constraints within which the CEO can work. To ensure adaptability, they strive for continuous improvement and rejuvenation of skills on the board and beyond. Dedicated to their organisation's long-term survival and success, they supervise management's effectiveness across shorter time horizons. Thus they maintain the board's focus on the longer-term time frame while keeping the management team focused on the short- and medium-term time frame. When chairing entities such as family businesses and sovereign wealth funds, the board focus may be cross-generational, stretching up to 25 years or even 75 years (in the case of state-owned funds for example). Stewardship also implies working towards leaving the board in better shape than it was when you joined it.

According to André Hoffmann, Vice-Chair of Roche Holdings:

> What's most important is that the long-term substance of the company, its mission, its relevance, its impact on multiple stakeholders continues to grow with time . . . I'd like to talk about 100 years; I know 100 years sounds incredibly long, but I think that's the sort of time scale that we need.[1]

Rising Expectations of Chairs

The scope of chairs' responsibilities has continued to expand steadily in recent years, to the extent that it has been described as 'all-encompassing'.[2] In the not-so-distant past, a chair's role was primarily about providing the board with basic guard rails – procedural and ethical. Duties included facilitating an agreed number of board meetings every year, overseeing the agenda, and keeping the board – and the organisation – on track. Running the board meetings smoothly was considered their key competence.

Today, this is clearly not enough. As the source of the highest supervisory authority in the corporation, the role of the chair is to provide the organisation with a clear steer on navigating the growing turbulence that organisations face. Central to this is making sure the business is embracing and confronting uncertainty and constant change – not hiding from it. In this more active function, their activities encompass a much wider scope – as demonstrated by the choices they tend to make, as shown in Figure 16.2.

Chairs are increasingly grappling with crises and black swan events, on top of digital transformation, climate change, heightened regulation, and investor scrutiny.[3] The almost perpetual state of crisis management has intensified the need for speed in chairs' decision-making, action, and communication. In addition, organisational and cultural transformations are occurring on an ongoing basis.

---

[1] Oxford Conversations on Ownership: André Hoffman. (n.d.) Saïd Business School. https://www.sbs.ox.ac.uk/research/centres-and-initiatives/responsible-business/oxford-ownership/oxford-conversations

[2] Deloitte. (2022). Board effectiveness and the chair of the future. 5 September. https://www.deloitte.com/gh/en/our-thinking/insights/topics/leadership/board-effectiveness-chair-of-the-future.html

[3] Deloitte. (2022). Board effectiveness and the chair of the future. 5 September. https://www.deloitte.com/gh/en/our-thinking/insights/topics/leadership/board-effectiveness-chair-of-the-future.html

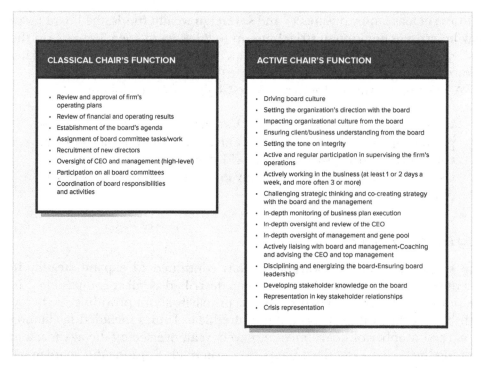

CLASSICAL CHAIR'S FUNCTION

- Review and approval of firm's operating plans
- Review of financial and operating results
- Establishment of the board's agenda
- Assignment of board committee tasks/work
- Recruitment of new directors
- Oversight of CEO and management (high-level)
- Participation on all board committees
- Coordination of board responsibilities and activities

ACTIVE CHAIR'S FUNCTION

- Driving board culture
- Setting the organization's direction with the board
- Impacting organizational culture from the board
- Ensuring client/business understanding from the board
- Setting the tone on integrity
- Active and regular participation in supervising the firm's operations
- Actively working in the business (at least 1 or 2 days a week, and more often 3 or more)
- Challenging strategic thinking and co-creating strategy with the board and the management
- In-depth monitoring of business plan execution
- In-depth oversight and review of the CEO
- In-depth oversight of management and gene pool
- Actively liaising with board and management•Coaching and advising the CEO and top management
- Disciplining and energizing the board•Ensuring board leadership
- Developing stakeholder knowledge on the board
- Representation in key stakeholder relationships
- Crisis representation

Figure 16.2   The Choices Made by Active Chairs

As a direct result, chairs need to engage with a broader range of stakeholders than just shareholders, including regulators, suppliers, employees, customers, and activists. As such the chair acts as a liaison between broader societal developments and the board – helping to inform its strategy process. This is a key function, as boards are increasingly taking their responsibility to society seriously – as demonstrated by the fact that 55 FTSE 150 boards had a committee in 2023 to oversee environmental and social topics, nine more than in 2022.[4]

Embedding strategy and stakeholder engagement into the board's role is no easy task. It demands more active, more forward-looking and decisive chairmanship. A strong chair exerts influence within the board by knowing when to broaden the discussion versus when to rein it in toward greater alignment and convergence. To do so, the chair needs to be skilled at playing different roles and able to judge when best to play each of these:

- Stimulating discussion and equal participation within time limits.
- Keeping discussions focused.
- Fostering true engagement and trust within the board.
- Allowing space for all related questions to be entertained.

---

[4] SpencerStuart (2023) 2023 UK Spencer Stuart Board Index: Sustainability and ESG Committees. https://www.spencerstuart.com/research-and-insight/uk-board-index/sustainability

- Encouraging persistence and mutual respect.
- Encouraging constructive dissent.
- Building real consensus.
- Driving clarity of board conclusions.

This tension between opening toward growth (and encouraging the required divergence), while retaining discipline and moving toward alignment (convergence) is well summed up by Lotte Marschall, Chair of GAME (an NGO working for lasting social change for children and youth through youth-led street sports and culture).

> In my opinion, a board is responsible for leading and developing the business, while keeping it under prudent control. The board needs to find the right balance between the various opportunities and challenges for the Company and ensure responsibility towards its employees, business partners and society as a whole. Diverse perspectives are needed in the boardroom to pursue its key purpose – creating value.[5]
>
> Lotte Marschall, Chair, Board member,
> Independent non-executive director

Chairs as Transformational Leaders

Chairmanship is a high-stakes arena. Chairs are held accountable as never before – by the public, the media, investors, customers, suppliers, employee, and regulators. Board chairs have to accommodate a growing number of often competing demands, requiring them to act as transformational leaders encompassing a broad set of capabilities (see Figure 16.3).

- Commitment to the organisation's vision and mission.
- Helping articulate the ambition.
- Articulating and reflecting a sense of purpose.
- Anchoring governance, ethics, and values and defining the board culture.
- Working tirelessly to broaden the board's perspective.
- Defining sustainable business models.
- Leveraging the board members' talent to help the organisation achieve its mission.
- Becoming more impactful.
- Putting all the strategic topics on the table.
- Bringing together and connecting a diversity of perspectives.

Figure 16.3 Transformational Chair Leadership Dimensions

---

[5] Lotte Marschall (2024). About. LinkedIn. https://www.linkedin.com/in/lottemarschall/?originalSubdomain=dk

Chairs are tasked with providing the big picture as well as helping the board zoom in and out of different contexts; they are able to adjust the altitude of the discussion focus as needed. They lead the board to questions that have not been raised but should have been raised – and know when to dive deep. As such the role of the chair is really to facilitate the discussion, to tune it to the right level – as expressed by the chair quoted below:

> I quickly learned I hadn't actually assumed 'command' of anything! The chair of this Board is most definitely NOT a commander. The chair is the chief communicator, the chief collaborator, the chief cooperator. That's the role I assumed.
>
> Doug Tisdale, Past Chairman (2018–2020) of the Board of
> Directors at Regional Transportation District – Denver

This often requires prompting the board to have the conversations they might be avoiding – initiating tough conversations – what some call extraordinary conversations – on long-term, open-ended issues, such as those listed in Figure 16.4.

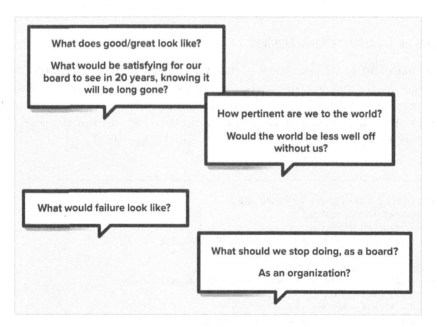

Figure 16.4   Extraordinary Conversation Topics Initiated by Board Chairs

Vigilance toward Continuous Board Evolution

The quality of board discussions relies on the breadth of knowledge of its members and their ability to draw on this knowledge when needed. Chairs nurture board members' curiosity as a core value that underpins the company's innovation and connects today's challenges with future solutions. They actively seek out ways of adding new understanding of emerging fields, trends and practices to the board and the organisation. There is a trend toward more depth in specific areas of expertise. For example, a growing number of boards have a standalone science and technology committee, and are considering recruiting directors with experience in cybersecurity.[6]

Chairs also need to keep on top of the demographic shifts that boards need to countenance: Millennials and members of Gen Z are increasingly entering the workforce and sitting on boards. As this cohort seeks greater autonomy and flexibility than previous generations, the chair needs to consider how to balance that autonomy with accountability. Since part of the chair's role is board renewal and building a board culture that is inclusive and adapted to the future, they must ensure diverse perspectives and be on the lookout for biases which may be excluding voices.

Making the Right Decisions about Chairmanship Roles and Styles

Becoming a chair requires the ability to let go while remaining ultimately responsible. This requires thoughtful decisions about how to play their role – which is largely based on knowing how to balance three dualities:

> *Supervise or support.* A key chair responsibility is to keep a close eye on the CEO's performance through appropriate reporting, auditing, and supervision. But they also need to explicitly decide whether, to what extent, and how they will provide support in the form of coaching and/or mentoring. They will fine tune this approach in keeping with the organisation's context and the CEO's maturity and readiness. Even in times of stability and working with a well-established CEO, a strong chair will be involved enough to coach and support as necessary.

---

[6] Spencer Stuart. (2023). Spencer Stuart U.S. Board Index finds S&P 500 boardrooms prioritizing CEO experience and financial expertise. 20 September.
https://www.prnewswire.com/news-releases/spencer-stuart-us-board-index-finds-sp-500-boardrooms-prioritizing-ceo-experience-and-financial-expertise-301933447.html

Passive or active. Being 'active' can mean representing the company in dealings with external stakeholders in ways that the CEO cannot, connecting with the parts of society that are less on the radar screen of the management team, or simply less reachable. As non-executive chair of Singapore Airlines from 2006 to 2016, Stephen Lee Ching Yen engaged with unions on a personal basis, regularly averting difficult situations. In doing so, he drew on his prior experience as Chair of the Singapore National Employers Federation (1988–2014) and member of the National Wages Council (1978–2016). Crucially, he did not interact with the unions in a capacity as an immediate decision-maker.

Inside or outside focus. Given the time constraints, where should the chair focus their attention? If a restructuring is required, or a culture transformation is getting underway, the chair will focus more on internal issues. The archetype of this will be a private equity board driving an initiative in operational excellence. In a well-aligned organisation, on the other hand, dealing with technology, regulation, political instability, and social transformation will lead the Chair to set his or her sights on external issues.

Knowing when to take charge, partner, or stay out of the way

When it comes to matching chairmanship style with specific scenarios in organisational life, an effective chair needs to be able to gauge accurately and rapidly whether to take charge, partner, or stay out of the way (Figure 16.4).[7] As shown, there is a growing expectation for chairs to be more decisive, particularly when the company's purpose and values need to be asserted. This includes situations such as selection of the CEO but also addressing high-level ethical issues, remuneration, and the board's structure and inner workings. Intervening at the very onset of a crisis, a chair is likely to achieve competitive simplification which in turn improves the firm's financial performance during the crisis.[8] Equally important is the ability to determine where they should be engaging management to co-create or oversee – for example, strategy, setting risk appetite, overseeing resource allocation, and overseeing the talent pipeline. Equally important is knowing when to steer clear of the executive to allow them their own room for manoeuvre (see Figure 16.5). This also requires that they adapt their style depending on the strategic context and focus (see Figure 16.6).

---

[7] Charan, R., Carey, D. and Useem, M. (2013). *Boards that lead: When to take charge, when to partner, and when to stay out of the way*. Harvard Business Review Press.

[8] Krause, R., Withers, M.C. and Waller, M.J. (2022). Leading the board in a crisis: strategy and performance implications of board chair directive leadership. *Journal of Management* 50(2): online.

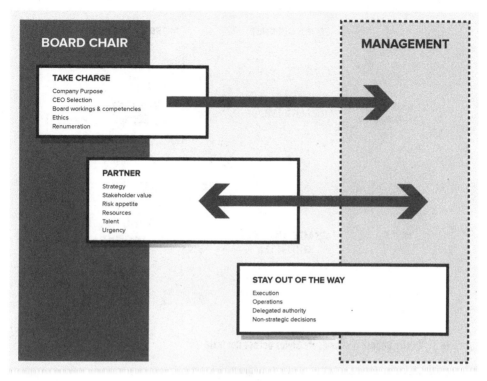

Figure 16.5   Tuning How You Work with Management as a Chair

Source: Adapted from Charan et al., 2013.

In May 2023, PwC global chairman Bob Moritz demanded change at PwC Australia over unauthorised sharing of confidential information about the government's tax plans with other partners and staff. PwC Australia chief executive Tom Seymour subsequently stepped down.[9]

Expressing dismay at the decision in 2021 of Norway-based mobile carrier Telenor to sell its stake in Myanmar to the M1 Group – seen as close to the military junta – 47 global and Myanmar-based human rights organisations wrote to the company's board chair Gun Waersted to intervene and reconsider the decision.[10]

---

[9] Tadros, E. and N. Chenoweth. (2023). PwC global intervenes in Australian tax leaks scandal. 12 May. https://www.afr.com/companies/professional-services/pwc-global-intervenes-in-australian-tax-leaks-scandal-20230512-p5d812

[10] The Wire Staff. (2021). Rights groups dismayed as Norwegian telecom giant sells Myanmar stake to Junta-linked company. 14 August. https://thewire.in/world/rights-groups-dismayed-as-norwegian-telecom-giant-sells-myanmar-stake-to-junta-linked-company

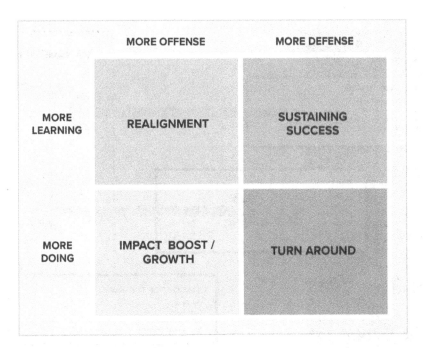

Figure 16.6   Chairs Choose and Navigate Styles across Contexts

In the aftermath of the Covid pandemic, Australian courts upheld rulings that found Qantas airline's outsourcing of baggage handlers, cleaners, and ground staff – a total of 1,700 workers in total – to be unlawful. This led to calls for the company's chair and board members to step aside.[11]

Managing the Transition

Like all challenging transitions, it is essential to get off to a strong start. Here are some things new chairs can do that help:

Elicit strong support to aid the transition. To make the process of shifting roles as efficient and effective as possible, both the new chair and the CEO must have an excellent transition support process. This includes dedicating time to building their relationship, sometimes one-on-one, gaining alignment on roles, ground rules (do's and don'ts), and operating principles (for example, regarding escalation and communication).

---

[11] Ilkonomou, T. (2023). Qantas chairman, board under pressure after outsourcing of almost 1700 jobs ruled illegal. 13 September. https://www.9news.com.au/national/qantas-judgment-from-high-court-over-outsourcing-during-pandemic/dd7870f3-13c4-44e7-b9d6-cb3959847c42

Find a mentor or non-competing peers to engage with. Because of the nature of the role, the chair cannot develop trusted-advisor relationships with members of the executive team or with key external advisors who work with the company. As such, advice from experienced chairs is invaluable in helping to avoid common traps, make sound decisions, and navigate board politics through the transition and beyond. Mentors need not come from the same context – in fact it may be an advantage if they don't. The chair of a leading German retailer, for instance, was successfully mentored by a leading Swiss industrial chair, despite national and industry differences.

Cultivate a network of advisors. The successful chair relies on expert advice when it comes to board renewal, strategic reviews, M&A, and more. They are keenly aware of advisors' potential conflicts of interest and finds ways to manage them to serve the firm better. Great chairs keep an eye on rejuvenating their board to ensure skills are fresh and focused. The chair of a 200 billion+ company told us he was rotating the HR consultant for board search every two to three years, as 'the advisor starts playing his own game in board nominations very soon'. Another chair recruited a renowned investment bank solely to help with the mechanics of a successful US$70 billion transaction but still used extensively the advice of a niche firm (of fewer than 20 employees) with whom he had enjoyed a trusted relationship.

Be a learning chair that leads a learning board. Board work is evolving rapidly and new best practices are developed on an almost daily basis. Confronted with many unknowns, chairs must be comfortable asking for help and continuing to learn and lead a learning board.

Ensure there is a best-in-class support system. Despite their relative isolation, chairs should leverage their staff and notably the board secretary who can provide an excellent anchor. The secretary has become a discreet but essential asset for large organisations. Rigorous, efficient board processes (such as strategy process, risk process, nomination process, nonfinancial audit process) are similarly critical to organisational resilience.

Chair rotations are central to governance renewal: As of 2020, more than half of the UK's FTSE 100 boards were led by individuals who were chairing a listed company board for the first time. Of the 46 chair appointments in the FTSE 100 in the four years to the end of 2019, 24 had never chaired a quoted company before.[12]

---

[12] Spencer Stuart. (2023). Are you ready to become a board chair? Leadership Matters 6 August. https://www.spencerstuart.com/leadership-matters/2020/august/are-you-ready-to-become-a-board-chair

Dr Doug Gurr stepped down after seven years as Chair of the British Heart Foundation on 20 October 2022. In his time as Chair, Dr Gurr shaped the Foundation' strategy to 2030, helped it to navigate the COVID-19 pandemic, and supported the initiation of significant scientific initiatives including the Big Beat Challenge and our Data Science Centre.

Dr Charmaine Griffiths thanked the chair: 'I want to thank Doug for his immense contribution to the British Heart Foundation and our mission to save and improve lives. Doug's leadership has been instrumental in overcoming some of the biggest challenges in our 61-year history, while his advocacy for making significant investments in cutting-edge areas of science has ensured we remain at the forefront of research to save and improve lives.'

https://www.bhf.org.uk/what-we-do/news-from-the-bhf/news-archive/2022/october/we-pay-tribute-to-departing-chair-dr-doug-gurr

---

In March 2024, veteran broadcaster and magazine editor Ita Buttrose stepped down as chair of the Australian Broadcasting Corporation (ABC) after five years in the role. Communications Minister Michelle Rowland said Buttrose had shown outstanding leadership at the broadcaster during her tenure.

'Ms. Buttrose was the right chair for the right time. Ms. Buttrose is a giant of Australia's media industry and the government thanks her for her exemplary service', the minister said. 'Ms. Buttrose is a formidable corporate leader who has served with distinction, speaking truth to power and upholding governance standards to protect independent public broadcasting', she said.

'She navigated the public broadcaster through a challenging period that included strident political criticism, the COVID-19 pandemic and the ongoing transformation of the ABC so it can remain an essential part of Australian life in the digital age.'

https://www.crikey.com.au/2023/08/22/ita-buttrose-abc-chair-term-end/

May 2023: Eugene A Gargaro, Jr to Retire as Board Chair of Detroit Institute of Arts (DIA).

Elected Board Chair in 2003, Gargaro guided the DIA through periods of significant growth and transformation, effectively shaping the institution into one of the country's premier art museums. In addition to its extensive and continually expanding original programmes and exceptional resources, the DIA's diverse collection of more than 65,000 art works puts it among the top five in the nation.

'Throughout the past two decades, the DIA has grown into a national superstar due to the hard work and commitment of our Board of Directors, our exceptional senior leadership and curatorial teams, our dedicated museum staff and volunteers, and many other partners. I am immensely proud of what we have accomplished together. I believe the DIA will continue to enjoy the worldwide reputation, stature, and respect it deserves, and I look forward to witnessing its ongoing growth and impact.'

Gargaro leaves a remarkable leadership legacy that includes the DIA's US$158 million renovation, expansion, and grand reopening in 2007, maintaining the museum's fiscal health during the 2008–2009 global financial crisis, and spearheading a strategic initiative in 2013–2014 to guide the museum through Detroit's bankruptcy, achieving the DIA's US$100 million commitment to the Grand Bargain in 10 months and securing its art collection and independent status for generations to come.

https://dia.org/about/media-room/news/eugene-gargaro-jr-retire-board-chair-detroit-institute-arts-prominent-civic

Leaving a Lasting Organisational Impact as Board Chair

The single most important differentiator for effective board work is the contribution made by its the chair.[13] This key and unique role requires a unique blend of knowledge, leadership and maturity, as well as firm conviction anchored in values. The great board chairs have been able to use their knowledge, skills and judgement to have significant impact not only on their organisations – but also on the broader social context. Key to this is a productive relationship with management, which we will address in the next chapter.

---

[13] Cossin, D. and M. Watkins (2018). Becoming the chairman. [online] *The European Business Review*. https://www.europeanbusinessreview.com/becoming-the-chairman/; Shekshnia, S. (2018). How to be a good board chair. [online] *Harvard Business Review*. https://hbr.org/2018/03/how-to-be-a-good-board-chair; Banerjee, A., M. Nordqvist, and K. Hellerstedt (2020). The role of the board chair – a literature review and suggestions for future research. *Corporate Governance: An International Review* 28(6): 372–405.

Appendix 16A – Checklist: Board Chairs as Stewards

CHECKLIST FOR BOARD CHAIRS AS STEWARDS

☐ Ensure effective operation of the board and its committees with the highest standards of corporate governance

☐ Ensure effective communication with key stakeholders, host governments, and that the views of these groups are understood by the board

☐ Set an agenda that is primarily focused on strategy, performance, impact and accountability, and ensure that issues relevant to those areas are considered by the board.

☐ Ensure that the board determines the nature and extent of the significant risks the organisation is willing to embrace in the implementation of its strategy, and that the board reviews the effectiveness of risk management and internal control systems on an ongoing basis.

☐ Set the agenda, style and tone of board dynamics aiming at the promotion of constructive debate and effective decision making.

☐ Manage the board to ensure that adequate time is allowed for discussion of all agenda items (in particular strategic issues) and to ensure that complex or contentious issues are dealt with effectively, making sure in particular that non-executive directors have sufficient time to consider them.

☐ Ensure that board members receive accurate, timely and clear information, in particular about the organisation's performance.

☐ Ensure appropriate delegation of authority from the board to the executive management.

☐ Ensure that all board committees are properly established, composed, and operated.

☐ Build an effective and complementary board, regularly consider its composition and balance, diversity and succession planning for board and senior management appointments.

☐ Ensure that directors continually update their skills and the knowledge and familiarity with the organisation required to fulfil their role both on the board and on board committees.

☐ Regularly review and agree with each director their training and development needs, and addressing the needs of the board as a whole.

☐ Support and advise the CEO, for example, in the development of strategy.

☐ Maintain access to senior management as necessary and useful, but avoid intruding on the CEO's responsibilities.

☐ Promote effective relationships and communications between non-executive directors and members of the executive committee.

☐ Ensure that the performance and effectiveness of the board, its main committees and individual directors is formally evaluated.

☐ Act on the results of the performance evaluation by recognising the strengths and addressing the weaknesses of the board and, where appropriate, proposing new members to be appointed to the board or seeking the resignation of directors.

☐ Establish a harmonious and open relationship with all executive directors and the CEO, in particular providing advice and support while respecting executive responsibility

Joanne Marker Enters the Chair Arena

*T*hree months later, Joanne reflected on the process in its entirety, which had been instructive. She learned a great deal from the different personalities she met, and from her own deep dive into the science and the technologies involved.

When she received George's call informing her that she had been selected, Joanne was ready to discuss next steps. Together they spoke about planning the transition. This included several meetings to discuss key responsibilities, ongoing projects, relationships with stakeholders, and evolving regulation. Joanne would shadow meetings, as well as separately discuss past decisions and challenges. By March, George would formally step down from the position, and Joanne would assume the role of Chair at the second board meeting of the year. George assured her that he would remain available for the remainder of the year to provide her with guidance on any matters. Also, the CEO had a plan to ensure a smooth integration into the leadership team. Joanne mentioned that she wanted the Board Secretary to collect feedback from stakeholders, including board members, executives, and others, at the end of the first six months of her Chair tenure, to identify areas for improvement and ensure ongoing success.

Joanne knew that the journey ahead would be challenging, but she was ready to embrace the responsibilities of chairmanship and leave her mark on the organisation she would grow to love.

CHAPTER

17

The Chair–CEO Relationship

The partnership between the chair and CEO is the critical catalyst to ensure that the four pillars interact to promote board effectiveness. A healthy relationship between the two may differ in form depending on the company, its situation, and the personality of the individuals – but the essential preconditions are trust and role clarity. It is vital that both the chair and CEO clearly understand their respective roles, which need to be both distinct and additive. In practice, this means that the chair and CEO do not overlap in the work they do. Rather, each performs a unique function, building upon the efforts of the other, to jointly enhance the quality of the board's work.

The chair and CEO must meet regularly to communicate and review issues, opportunities, and problems. Furthermore, their relationship needs to be one of openness and integrity, and be underlined by a clear division of responsibilities. We've explored the chair's role and responsibilities in the previous chapter. Let's now take a look at the role of the CEO, and what is essential for success in this key executive leadership function

The Role of the CEO

The CEO is the leader of the organisation, managing it within the authorities delegated by the board and implementing the strategy. In most cases, the CEO develops the key content of the strategy process, such as competitive analysis and proposals, and ensures effective co-creation of key strategic recommendations with the board. He or she ensures that previously agreed corporate strategy actions are well reflected in the business.

In conjunction with the chief financial officer, the CEO develops an annual budget and funding plan consistent with agreed corporate strategies, and presents it to the board for approval. This should include developing processes and structures to ensure that capital investment proposals are thoroughly reviewed, associated risks are identified, and appropriate steps taken to manage these risks.

The CEO drives the culture of the organisation through role modelling, principles, incentives, and other means. As such, a key function of the chief executive is to ensure business is conducted in accordance with sound principles. Furthermore, he or she is responsible to the board for the organisation's performance in line with agreed business plans, corporate strategies, and policies, and keeps it updated on progress in this regard.

In addition, the chief executive plans human resourcing to ensure that the company has the people and capabilities it needs to achieve its plans. This includes overseeing a healthy talent pipeline and ensuring that robust management succession and development plans are in place. This HR strategy should be presented to the board from time to time. It entails developing a structure and establishing processes and systems to ensure the efficient organisation of resources. The CEO also leads the top management team, including through the development of performance targets and appraisals.

Communication is also important, because the CEO is the public face of the company. Part of his or her job is to develop and promote effective communication with shareholders and other relevant stakeholders. For example, financial results, business strategies, and, where appropriate, targets and milestones need to be communicated to investors.

Chair–CEO Dynamics – the Hallmarks of a Productive Relationship

As we saw at the start of this chapter, a healthy relationship between a CEO and chair is characterised by significant trust, frequent and open communication, and yet not too much closeness or dependence. The chair is a visible actor and is deeply familiar with management's operations, though is not actively involved in their execution. In addition, the chair clearly communicates the boundaries of what constitutes acceptable ethical behaviour and intervenes when these are crossed. During a crisis, the chair steps up and takes a leadership role by supporting the CEO (or firing him or her and managing the succession if needed) and communicating externally.

In a healthy relationship, the CEO respects the chair's input and seeks his or her guidance on key strategic and risk-related matters. The chief executive proactively supplies the chair with necessary information, and demonstrates accountability by reporting against the agreed strategy, as well as flagging key risks as they arise.

There are several simple indicators of a healthy relationship between the chair and CEO.

- **A clear and well-planned board agenda**, with timely and relevant information supplied by management, which does not place an undue burden on the organisation. Meeting minutes document actions and who is responsible for them.
- **Consistent and respectful messages** from the chair and CEO to management with regard to strategy and risks.
- **Mutual respect of boundaries and roles.** The chair does not consult with senior executives without first asking the CEO's permission; similarly, the CEO doesn't talk to individual directors without first aligning with the chair.
- **Regular communication** between the CEO and chair. This gives the chair access to relevant management information and systematic updates on key events and pipeline issues. And the CEO is able to execute strategy with a free rein.
- **Clear trust** between the chair and CEO, as demonstrated by mutual support for strategic decisions made in the boardroom and in the organisation. Trust is easily revealed by each assuming good intentions from the other on all interactions.

Warning signs for possible dysfunction in the chair–CEO relationship include:

- **Unreasonable requests:** A chair who demands extensive, detailed financial analysis or in-depth reports on operational issues may lack trust in the CEO. This results in a considerable cost to the CEO and management in terms of the energy required to supply the information, and generates stress and ill will. As the CEO senses the lack of trust, he or she becomes more defensive and may begin to suspect the chair's motives. The overall effect is to undermine trust between the two.
- **Operational interventions:** A chair who starts intervening directly in the organisation's operations and issues directives to management often signals a lack of trust in the CEO's leadership. Alternatively, the chair may just be used to being in a leadership role, and may feel that he or she is more competent than the CEO. A lack of discipline in maintaining this important boundary undermines the CEO's authority in the organisation.
- **Lack of consistency on strategic direction:** If the chair and CEO express different visions of the organisation's strategic direction and key risks,

this spells trouble in their relationship. A lack of alignment will necessarily lead to disagreement about how to mobilise organisational resources, not to mention differing expectations with regard to CEO accountability and reporting.

- **Indecision by the board:** If the board cannot come to a decision, this may signify that it is receiving inadequate information from management, or that the chair is not productively facilitating the conversation. If information is the problem, this could indicate a breakdown in communication between the chair and CEO.
- **Board members directly approaching management:** When communication between the chair and CEO breaks down, directors may be frustrated and approach senior or even junior managers to try to find out what is going on. This can make the CEO defensive and undermines his or her trust in the chair's ability to restrict board members to their proper role.
- **Lack of respect for the CEO from the board:** If directors fail to listen to the CEO, or make comments that show a lack of respect for his or her opinions or competence, this can signify a key disconnect in the CEO–chair relationship. The chair needs to defend the CEO and ensure that he or she is properly supported; failing to do so quickly kills trust and goodwill.
- **Lack of respect for the chair from senior executives:** The chair is the boardroom leader and the lead governance actor of the organisation, and as such merits respect from executives, as well as senior and junior staff. If senior executives make jokes in the boardroom at the chair's expense, and the CEO does nothing to stop it, this denigrates the importance of the chair's role. Ultimately, this undermines the authority of both the chair and the board.
- **Boards that are overly impressed by their CEOs:** Boards who are enamoured with their CEO are at risk of becoming complacent, and may not exercise sufficient scrutiny of the chief executive's actions. A dynamic of dependence on the CEO may result, resulting in a sense of reduced responsibility and suppressed dissent. This dynamic can translate into reduced accountability and a culture of CEO impunity.

In 2018, Tesla's compensation committee approved CEO Elon Musk's US$55.8 billion pay package. The compensation committee failed to observe commonly accepted norms, such as negotiating with the CEO or benchmarking with the CEOs of comparable companies. At the time, many of Tesla's board members, including his brother Kimbal Musk, had close financial and social ties to Elon Musk. In the 2024 ruling against Musk, Judge McCormick found that the directors allowed Musk to dictate the terms of the compensation plan amount and timing. Ira Ehrenpreis, a prominent venture capitalist and longtime friend of Musk chaired Tesla's compensation committee at the time. Antonio Gracias, a Tesla director from 2007 to 2021, referred to the package 'a great deal for shareholders'.

Tests of the Chair–CEO Relationship

In 1993, Maersk Mc-Kinney Moller stepped down as CEO of Maersk after 28 years, and was succeeded by Jess Soderberg. Moller handed over the chairship to Michael Pram Rasmussen in 2003 but remained active in the group's decision-making and activities, frequently going to its Copenhagen headquarters and travelling around the world to represent Denmark's largest privately owned enterprise. Soderberg was fired in 2007 due to mistakes made after Maersk's €2.3 billion takeover of P&O Nedloyd, the world's third-largest container line at the time. Nils Smedegaard Andersen was then hired to replace him.

A crisis situation involving an integrity breach can also strain the relationship. The chair may be tempted to blame the CEO, suspecting him or her of improper conduct – or of not maintaining sufficiently firm boundaries in this respect. Or a director may have a (real or perceived) conflict of interest. In this case, the CEO may suspect the chair of cronyism or not being sufficiently diligent in screening the board members.

When the relationship between chair and CEO is put to the test, both need to remember their roles and their duty to serve the best interest of the company. In such situations, it helps if both are personally resilient, do not succumb to stress as a result of external pressures, and do not overreact emotionally. One way to reduce the tension, and to re-establish productive exchanges, is to have a pre-agreed protocol according to which the CEO and chair agree to abide by certain principles before reacting. For example, they could agree that in times of crisis, they should be immediately available to speak to one another – in person if possible – and that their first exchange will be devoted only to asking questions and not expressing judgements. In this way, they will seek to understand the situation before evaluating the events and potential outcome.

Maintaining integrity, and not succumbing to psychological needs or indulging in self-deception, is critical in such situations. Mature, self-aware individuals with integrity will reflect on their own role in contributing to the healthy functioning of the chair–CEO relationship. And even if they are dissatisfied with the consequences for them personally, they will fulfil their duty toward the board and the organisation at all times.

Even in the best chair–CEO relationship, there are situations that put the pair to the test. Succession, for example, is often a sensitive topic. The CEO's succession is the responsibility of the chair or the relevant board committee. However, when the chair raises this issue with the CEO and asks for information regarding the leadership bench strength among the senior executive team, it can create tension in the relationship. Such discussions may provoke resistance from the CEO, who may consciously or subconsciously feel that the chair is seeking to replace them. Likewise, when the CEO discusses the chair's retirement and succession, the chair may feel a similar deep sense of rejection – especially if he or she (usually an experienced and powerful individual with a track record of success) is coming to the end of his or her career.

Case: Boardroom Tension with Employee

At a major global investment bank in London, during the first boardroom meeting of the year, the Chief Talent Officer was invited to present the results of the latest employee engagement survey. She reported that there was a disconnect between the culture espoused by the company versus the behaviour that was being rewarded and practised by its senior leaders. The bank had been going through a growth period during which there were many programmes focused on culture and work–life balance, but increasingly senior staff were being pressured to deliver financial results. Thanks to their extraordinary achievements, staff had legitimate pride. And jokes were circulating about the 'amateurishness' of the non-executive board members who were not investment bankers. In concluding, she addressed the chair, whose name was Peter Lyre, saying: 'Employees are starting to wonder if the information we have is the truth. No pun intended', she laughed. Silence fell in the boardroom, all eyes of the directors going first to the chair and then to the CEO. How should the chair react? Was this a play on his name? Should the CEO intervene? Or minimise his involvement?

The Ideal Attributes of a Chair to be a Secure Base to the CEO

Increasing regulatory pressures, demands for effectiveness, expanded accountability, and higher social expectations tend to overstretch CEOs and require chairs to be far more involved than they traditionally have been in the past. The chair can no longer be a distant individual, but instead needs to be fully committed to understanding the organisation's issues and devoted to its success. Chairs who possess the following 'ideal' attributes will be more likely to be a secure base to the CEO and be critical to her or his success:

- **Character and courage:** The chair must be seen to be an honest broker, a straight-talking, open-minded leader focused on doing what is right for the long-term health of the organisation. He or she should be forthright and not hesitate to speak his or her mind, but also should not rush to judgement.
- **Consensus-building:** The chair must keep all sides productively engaged and focused on the important issues. This means having a good sense of what needs to be done and, at the same time, not being easily sidetracked by others' attempts to dilute negative results, exaggerate good outcomes, or engage in debates over unimportant matters. The chair encourages constructive dissent in order to build a true consensus.
- **Relevant experience:** Effective chairs understand the CEO's job of building and managing a strong and cohesive team. Having had experience of running an organisation, chairs can establish effective processes for the oversight and support of the CEO and top management team.

- **The ability to be an external spokesperson:** There are times when the chair has to be a credible spokesperson for the organisation – such as in a crisis. He or she needs to be well-versed in such a role and remain focused on the relevant message in order to avoid portraying the organisation in a bad light in the media and/or with regulators.
- **Dedication and commitment to board work:** An effective chair is willing to do the homework by going through the details as well as understanding the broad concepts, and prepares thoroughly for board meetings. These activities may require additional time; for example, to understand what is not in the meeting materials.

These attributes will enable the chair to cultivate and foster respect and trust from the CEO, which is necessary to build a positive and constructive relationship. This is in turn essential for ensuring best-practice governance of the organisation. The CEO is also key to ensuring this partnership works effectively. The two need to recognise the importance of this relationship, understand their respective roles and responsibilities, and do their part in making it work.

A healthy relationship between the board and management is also crucial for effective governance. It is this issue to which we turn in the next chapter.

Joanne Marker Confronts Failing Board Culture

*J*oanne Marker was attending her first board meeting at JenJolt, a software services company providing outsourcing services to major corporations. She had become increasingly interested in the dynamic nature of the competitive landscape, and was keen to explore how IT could be a strategic lever in her industries of expertise.

With her knowledge of the markets, and with her global network in some of JenJolt's potential spheres of interest, Joanne was excited to explore ideas for different alliances that she felt were promising for growth. Her meeting documents were highlighted, and she had detailed notes questioning some of the assumptions behind the scenarios presented in the board briefing.

Joanne had arrived at JenJolt HQ at 7:40 am, after flying into San Francisco the previous night. She had talked to a few other early arrivers over a cup of coffee. At 8:00, she sat down and waited. The others continued to stand, eating pastries and making jokes that sounded like they might be golf-related. All the other seven directors were 40- to 50-year-old white men, many of whom had gone to the same Ivy League business school.

She re-read her notes while she waited. The chair, Stephen McElvoy, entered the room at 8:10, together with CEO Jerry Morgan. The two were laughing as they sat down in the two vacant seats. Joanne looked around, but all around her were smiling faces. She seemed to be the only one irritated by this ten-minute delay.

Just after the mid-morning break, Joanne raised her hand. McElvoy nodded at her.

'A question: Will Jerry be staying for the whole meeting?' she asked. There was silence for a moment.

'Well, that's what we usually do – no secrets here!' McElvoy clapped Morgan on the shoulder. 'We're just trying to help Jerry, who's doing a fine job. It's not easy, we know. And we all appreciate what he's doing here'.

Joanne looked around the table, but no one would meet her gaze.

'OK then', she said.

She then asked Morgan some pointed questions about the markets he had entered, the strategic alliances he had created, and why he wasn't targeting different geographies. In her view, his answers were unsatisfactory. But when she looked at the other directors, they didn't make eye contact.

Six months and two JenJolt board meetings later, Joanne forced herself to speak up. McElvoy nodded at her, unsmiling. He had already come to dread her questions.

'I would like to request that the board have a discussion without Jerry present', Joanne said. 'It's nothing personal', she said to Morgan. 'In my experience it's good practice to have a conversation without the chief executive present'.

Morgan flushed and stood, despite the protests of the other directors that this wasn't necessary.

'Sure, Joanne. No problem', Morgan said, winking as he exited the room. 'I've got tons to catch up on before lunch'.

McElvoy stared across the table at her.

'So, what is it you wanted to say, Joanne?'

She explained her concerns about Morgan: that he had failed to identify a number of competitive threats and was racking up dangerous levels of debt with his acquisition plans.

The other directors defended him. 'Give him some time, Joanne. He's just ramping up', said Alex Lincoln, another independent director.

'And just how much time do you want to give him, Alex?' Joanne asked. 'When is the cut-off, would you say? I think JenJolt is in a critical situation, and we need to act now'.

'What about 12 months – this time next year?'

'Too long', Joanne said. 'Six, max. He'll have run the company into the ground in a year'.

'That's a bit harsh on Jerry', said Will Jones, another director. 'Give him a chance!' Others came to the CEO's defence too.

'Gentlemen', she said, 'I can see I am the only one who thinks that a change in leadership is a priority for this company's survival'.

After returning home late that evening, Joanne pressed the send button, emailing McElvoy her letter of resignation from JenJolt's board. He replied immediately: 'I am sorry to lose you Joanne. But don't you think you are over-reacting?' he wrote.

Five months later, Joanne opened The Wall Street Journal *to the Business News section for her morning update. The headline jumped out at her: 'Departure of Morgan from the helm of JenJolt'. The article detailed how the board had closed ranks and was refusing to confirm or deny if Morgan had been fired. But the journalist reported that an unnamed source had attributed Morgan's departure to being the result of 'a rampant acquisition spree and spiralling costs, combined with little ability to deliver on promised growth'.*

The article also questioned the forthcoming announcement of annual results by the company.

CHAPTER
18

The Board–Management Relationship

Observing boards' decision-making is an exciting and relatively new undertaking. In the past, researchers found it difficult to study directly the mechanics of board activities. This precipitated the growing interest we see today in considering and analysing the board on the strength of its decision-making capacity and characteristics.

Of major importance in this context is the issue of the board's relationship with management. Today's active boards seek to play a distinctive and additive role in the organisation. What's more, the nature and quality of their communication with management is critical in defining and achieving a sustainable business culture. There are two main aspects of the board–management relationship: supervision and support.

Supervision

In its supervisory role, a board works to ensure that management is making sufficient effort in critical strategic areas, such as managing risks and responding to competitive threats. The focus on compliance that was typical in the past has proved insufficient in a competitive globalised environment. As a result, boards have become more directly and deliberately involved in charting their companies' strategy. They have emerged as a source of extended vision, helping to contextualise and interpret many of the opportunities and challenges facing the organisation.

In maintaining a clear view of the company's strategic differentiators, the board has an important role to play in drawing out relevant and necessary information from management, and in the process challenging and testing it. How far the board can go in 'interrogating' the management is a gauge of the trust and goodwill that has been established between the board and the executive team, and also depends on the quality of the questions that the board asks.

With more directors having become involved in strategic decisions in recent years, boards increasingly want to have a say in how management goes about complex new initiatives, including change processes. In this context, it is no longer rare to see the board put forward its own sets of metrics and incentives. Just as a strong board needs a regular dose of internal dissent to remain healthy, boards are embracing the need to challenge management views and proposals in areas that have long-term repercussions for the organisation's well-being.

The board's supervision of management initiatives also implies follow-up, and in particular monitoring implementation progress. This may take various forms. For example, the board may task management with preparing an implementation plan for specific recommendations that the board has endorsed. Listing and circulating action items has become a key board process that starts immediately after the board meeting itself (usually within 48 hours). Minutes, on the other hand, are prepared at more length as they have legal weight, and are presented a few weeks before the following meeting for adjustment. Periodic monitoring reports, annual or otherwise, will then provide details on action points included in previous implementation plans, especially if these actions are still outstanding.

The board should be able to review and comment on the design and results of specific programmes, but also to conduct thematic reviews of management issues and initiatives on a regular basis. Technology can facilitate many of these processes, particularly if it combines self-evaluation features

---

Peter Cuneo became CEO of Marvel Entertainment in July 1999 with the company in dire financial straits and its corporate culture depressed. He turned the company around, and 10 years later it was sold to Walt Disney for more than US$4 billion. Cuneo credited Marvel's active board for helping to make the turnaround possible.

'In order to execute this turnaround we knew we had to be supported and surrounded by the brightest, most aggressive minds we could attract', Cuneo said. 'The individual members of Marvel's board were encouraged . . . to be much more involved in the business than merely attending quarterly meetings.'[1] He noted that the board played the role of a trusted advisor for Marvel's senior executives on current and future business developments, but never made decisions for them.

Marvel Cinematic Universe became one of the biggest movie franchises in history, with over a dozen box-office hits. In 2019, the Marvel movie 'Avengers Endgame' earned an astonishing US$1.2 billion in its opening weekend. Despite Disney's decision to dismiss the chairman of Marvel in 2023 as part of a cost-cutting campaign aimed at eliminating 7,000 jobs to save US$5.5 billion, Marvel remains steadfast in its operations.

---

[1] Reiss, R. (2010). How Marvel became a business superhero. Forbes, 1 February. https://www.forbes.com/2010/02/01/peter-cuneo-marvel-leadership-managing-turnaround.html#387e1e a76fa1

with project management and also collaborative and work-sharing software capabilities. When tackling complex, multistakeholder undertakings, the board may choose to be creative in fulfilling its supervisory role by devising custom timetables, roadmaps, dashboards, and other tools that help visualise and measure progress as well as follow-up.

Support

In addition to their role as auditors of company performance, boards also have an advisory role to play. Directors' expertise should help management in making important strategic decisions. In particular, setting organisational strategy has emerged as an area where effective boards have performed an advisory, collaborative role.

It has also become commonplace for board members to search outside the organisation for relevant trends and data (see also Chapter 5). Directors are conscious of the dynamics of disruptive change, which inspires them to examine how familiar issues play out in different industries, segments, and markets.

Working out and recognising their own role and use of authority has been a continuous challenge for board members around the world. To begin with, the dual roles of supervision and support come with different time horizons. Boards therefore need to balance them carefully.

The tension between supervision and support has sometimes been recast as a tension between accountability and organisational development. Directors who settle fully into an accountability role may become unlikely to play a robust developmental role. Nonetheless, much of this tension can be defused when the board is energised by the organisation's mission. Such boards are in a good position to exercise adequate controls while providing independent viewpoints – a powerful combination that can mitigate many types of management behaviour, including overconfidence and excessive risk-taking.

Blurring the Board–Management Relationship

Board members have a responsibility to know, and understand in detail, the backgrounds of key executives in the firm. High performing boards tend to nurture and invest in each director's relationship with top executives, often using tools such as *dual coaching*. Similarly, a key priority for the CEO should be to build a strong relationship with the board – formal, informal, professional, human, and social. The CEO would be well advised to know about the board members' occupations, businesses, and families. He or she needs to listen and ask questions consistently and be seen to attach real value to the board's opinions.

So far, so good. As long as boards and management teams embrace the relationship in all its facets and social complexity, they will have a healthy, robust foundation to build on, right? Not always. In reality, there are many ways in which the difference between the roles of the board and the management team can become blurred.

For instance, company founders, family members, and alliances with board members that are based on these relationships, may exert a strong positive or negative influence on the culture of the organisation. Through his or her sheer knowledge of the company, a CEO may have overwhelming influence on board decisions. This immediately creates an imbalance of power.

In addition, there is a powerful 'birds of a feather' phenomenon in business that chips away at the distinction between board and management roles. Many directors are themselves current or former CEOs. Consciously or otherwise, the fraternising instinct may be tough to resist. This can lead to a sense of misplaced solidarity and patience, even with a CEO who has clearly long outlived their usefulness.

Similarly, ex-CEOs on the board often accept dated solutions and strategies that are oblivious to the realities of today's marketplace, let alone that of the future. This is because their judgement and acumen have been compromised by an overwhelming sense of familiarity, past achievements, and the feeling of what it was like to be the top executive in their old organisation. When mixed together, these perceptions can give rise to an unyielding, even if not openly articulated, need to protect the CEO.

Conversely, in some organisations, CEOs wield considerable power over the board, and can greatly influence the process of selecting directors. In many cases, dominant CEOs will prefer board members similar to themselves – not just in terms of demographic characteristics such as ethnicity, social background, and gender, but also in terms of personality type – and may exercise this bias in the director recruitment process.

Research has shown that the longer the CEO's tenure, the more likely he or she is to have allies installed on the board. And some of them will support the chief executive's decisions no matter what. This trend has been further amplified by the arrival of the 'celebrity CEO'. For many years, there has been a tendency among corporations to recruit larger-than-life, charismatic chief executives, typically from outside the company, and to bring them in amid frenzied media attention that shouts if not 'saviour' then certainly 'superhero'.

The trouble with overbearing, overconfident, and narcissistic CEOs is that they sincerely believe they are creating shareholder value even as they are destroying it. Many of them are enthusiastic risk-takers, pushing through dramatic ramp-ups in spending on M&A, capital investment, and R&D. In the long run, these behaviours will interfere with management's ability to stay in touch with organisational reality, thus preventing real learning and change.

For example, Fiat Chrysler Automobiles in 2014 initiated a civil lawsuit against its former Australia CEO whom it accused of breaching the law and his contract by giving cars to celebrities and inflating contracts to benefit his financial interests. For his part, the former local CEO denied breaching his legal duties and said the Chrysler Asia Pacific CEO and other senior company officials had approved his actions. It is then hard to decipher what is healthy and what not.

Writing Governance Codes is Easier than Changing Behaviours

Boards that do address the issues of learning and change are often particularly hopeful that revising governance codes will produce meaningful shifts in the way their directors interact with top management teams. What many boards fail to realise, however, is that for all their good intentions, writing something down is not the same as implementing it in daily communication and action.

Through the write-up of hundreds of pages of codes and manuals, a board may aim to change an organisation by conducting an in-depth internal survey, mapping out the roles and responsibilities of the board and management, and rating different areas for effectiveness and importance. The changes may be first drafted by one director and then sent to all the other board members for amendments, with the final text then discussed and agreed – word by word – by the board as a group.

But this does not guarantee real progress, nor that the quality of the relationship between the board and management will ascend to a new level. All too frequently, despite greater lucidity on paper, only minor changes may be observed in practice. Tellingly, strong top executives tend to resist and resent even soft challenging and questioning of self-edited performance targets, strategic thrusts, results, or succession plans.

This is not to say that all exercises and initiatives aimed at specifying more clearly the roles and domains of the board and management are doomed from the start. On the contrary, there is great value to be derived from tasks such as detailing existing areas of responsibility, outlining perceived 'missing' areas, clarifying decision authority in specific scenarios, defining the respective roles of the chair and CEO in setting agendas, and documenting perceived road-blocks. But this value will only present itself when the board recognises these exercises for what they are – departure points in a long and demanding process of individual and group adaptation, change, and commitment.

On high-performing boards, a big part of that commitment comes from understanding that creating sustained business value requires a strong CEO. Such a chief executive needs to be matched with an equally strong board that is ready and willing to engage with them dynamically. This is a very different power equation from the one we described earlier in this chapter, where a weak board protects an underperforming CEO out of a false sense of solidarity and identification.

To balance the CEO's influence, directors should re-examine the board's composition with the objective of bringing in knowledgeable, independent, and skilled members who can act as counterweights to the chief executive and provide oversight of the corporation. Directors can also help to restore the board's influence by using their own human capital – such as their status as a former CEO, or their experience on a board compensation or auditing committee. All these undergird the social nature of the decision-making process that takes place in the boardroom.

In theory, independent directors should enjoy more decision-making influence and power than dependent board members. However, empirical research has uncovered little evidence that the dependent/independent distinction is significant in relation to influencing the board's decisions and its relationship with the CEO.

Crucially, and regardless of the organisation's performance, the board should under no circumstances waver in its ability to observe and judge management's behaviour objectively. Once the board finds itself seduced by the company's perceived power and success, its capacity for discharging its duties will likely become compromised. Boards of directors are important monitors of corporate behaviour, and can rein in opportunistic action on the part of top management by providing incentives for it to pursue appropriate goals. Overbearing executives are increasingly seen as a *result* of the corporate system, in addition to performance systems and structures, power allocation, and managerial beliefs. In many organisations, the absence of challenge or resistance from shareholders and other stakeholders, including the broader financial community, may have encouraged management's illusion of grandeur and vast control.

Finally, today's boards have a tangible and growing role to play in managing the organisation's relationship with stakeholders such as governments and the broader public – a topic we will cover in greater detail in Chapter 32. Successful companies run by overconfident leaders may be exciting to watch – but at some point, stakeholders are likely to demand mechanisms that will mitigate the downside risk of narcissistic CEOs. Those checks are expected to come from the board, particularly as twenty-first-century boards become more diverse and independent. And effective diversity is the theme of the next chapter.

CHAPTER 19

Effective Diversity

Diversity is Good . . . But Why; and When?

The assertion that diversity is good has become a mantra in business. Many studies demonstrate the advantages of diversity for companies in search of new ideas, observations, strategic directions, and competitive advantage. Organisations may derive tangible *task-related benefits* from diversity, because having a variety of expertise enables a firm to assign each part of a task to people with the relevant knowledge. Diversity also has *innovation-driving benefits,* because people with different perspectives see things differently. This can lead to creativity and a questioning of assumptions, and ultimately to new synergies.

However, diversity also comes with downsides, because it raises barriers to alignment. These include *communication-related barriers.* People's different frames of reference mean that words and actions can have very different significance: this makes communication less efficient and can lead to conflict that may be difficult to resolve. Other barriers arising from greater diversity are related to *identity and trust:* we find it harder to identify with and deeply trust people who are different to us.

When there is a strong need for innovation, and shareholders represent divergent views, diversity is a key strategic advantage. But the situation is different when there is a single shareholder with a clear view of what needs to be accomplished, and when the need for innovation is limited – for example, where a private-equity firm has taken ownership of a company and is seeking to turn it around. In that case, board diversity can lead to time being wasted on conflict and difficult communication, detracting from the discipline required.

In order to tap fully into the benefits of diversity, boards need to manage this process well. That itself calls for a significant investment of energy and time and requires a dedicated and skilled chair. Ultimately, diversity is a choice (see Figure 19.1).

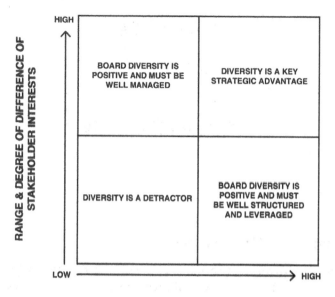

Figure 19.1   Diversity at the Board Level

Diversity as a Considered Choice

In previous decades, when corporations did choose to become more diverse, it was as a result of a powerful external push – and in many cases, a jolt delivered by momentous, structural changes in the marketplace. One such milestone came about in the 1990s, when a number of US multinationals started generating more than 50% of their revenue from international markets. Suddenly, the user of their products in the US Midwest was no longer their typical customer. Predictably, this gave rise to widespread interest in understanding, communicating with, and marketing to other countries.

It has become mainstream to say that a board's composition should more closely resemble the make-up of the company's stakeholders. This entails having directors with diverse objectives, social and economic agendas, communication channels, and preferred technologies. In this chapter, we focus on five dimensions of diversity – gender, culture, personality, age, and social background – and look at how a strong chair can manage these to make a board more effective.

Gender

The debates regarding gender balance in the boardroom have zoomed in on many of the obstacles to understanding and practising diversity, and have brought several questions to the fore. Should boards of directors as well as

Since the early 2010s, Malaysia has been actively striving to enhance gender diversity in boardrooms. This endeavour commenced with the recommendation of boardroom diversity by the Malaysian Code on Corporate Governance in 2012, followed by the enforcement of board diversity disclosures by the Bursa Malaysia Berhad stock exchange in 2015. In the early 2020s, significant updates were made to these requirements: the Code on Corporate Governance advocated for a minimum of 30% women directors on boards in 2021, and Bursa Malaysia mandated the inclusion of at least one female director on boards in 2022.

Moreover, the Institutional Investors Council Malaysia introduced similar expectations in 2022, aiming for a 30% representation of women on boards within three years. This initiative reflects the global trend where major institutional investors have begun to vote against all-male boards.[1]

In 2023, female board members had achieved a significant milestone, representing 30.6% among Malaysia's top 100 public listed companies, and nearly 25% across all listed companies, as reported by the 30% Club Malaysia.

C-suites strive to fulfil self-imposed gender quotas? And are certain types of societies better predisposed to opening the boardroom to greater numbers of female directors?

In many societies around the world, women are still in the process of entering the workforce in more substantial numbers – a key long-term prerequisite for their assuming corporate leadership positions. In addition, research

In 2019, Amazon appointed a black woman to its all-white board of directors amid increasing pressure on the company to diversify its leadership team. Rosalind Brewer, Starbucks' chief operating officer, became the fourth woman and the only person of colour on Amazon's 10-person board. Firms face growing demands from shareholders and activist groups to add more women and people of colour to their board. In 2018, BlackRock, the world's biggest asset manager, asked companies in its portfolio with fewer than two female board members to disclose their attempts to increase board diversity. This trend is evident not only in the United States but also worldwide. For instance, Norway's sovereign wealth fund, the largest sovereign wealth fund in the world, has been taking a stand to vote against companies in Europe and the United States for their insufficient representation of women on boards. In 2023, it decided to extend this stance to Japan, announcing its decision to vote against all-male boards, impacting 300 listed companies.

---

[1] Bursa Malaysia. (2023). Bursa Malaysia applauds progressive PLCs for embracing board gender diversity and censures PLCs with all male boards. 2 June. https://www.bursamalaysia.com/bm/about_bursa/media_centre/bursa-malaysia-applauds-progressive-plcs-for-embracing-board-gender-diversity-and-censures-plcs-with-all-male-boards

has suggested that diversity, including gender diversity, has been shown to produce more pronounced positive effects in countries with stronger shareholder protection[2] – because this motivates the board to draw on the diverse knowledge, experience, and values of each director.

Much effort has been made in academia, the media, and elsewhere to correlate female representation on boards with companies' financial, operational, or strategic performance. This constitutes a laudable attempt to identify a 'selling point' for advocating more female directors, although the findings so far have been mixed.

In a 2015 MSCI study, companies with at least three female board members outperformed others in overall returns on equity by an average of 36%. A similar study in 2022 by MSCI showed that companies that have a greater percentage of women on their boards exhibit superior performance in environmental, social, and governance (ESG) dimensions.[3]

Such findings have led more institutions to view gender diversity as a yardstick for making investment decisions. For instance, a number of asset management firms have launched funds which invest specifically in companies showing high levels of gender diversity on boards and in senior leadership. One such investment fund is the Street Global Advisors' Gender Diversity Index ETF, which was launched in 2016 and seeded with an initial US$250 million from the California State Teachers' Retirement System (CalSTRS).[4]

More fundamentally, however, boards should challenge the validity of the underlying research question. It is truly necessary to place a burden of proof on female executives and proponents of greater gender diversity? Is a greater female presence on boards only desirable if it comes with a guarantee of demonstrable and consistent improvements in a company's quantitative indicators? Do women need to be 'better than men' before they gain more equitable representation in the boardroom?

The business community must revisit these simple yet deep-seated issues with more clarity and integrity if it is committed to long-term improvements in corporate governance. It is also possible that gender diversity creates different *distributions* of performance (for example, by truncating downside risks on large transactions or integrity issues) rather than levels of performance.

---

[2] Post, C. and K. Byron (2014). Women on boards and firm financial performance: a meta-analysis. *Academy of Management Journal* 58(5): 1546–1571.

[3] MSCI. (2022). Women on boards progress report 2022 https://www.msci.com/documents/10199/36771346/Women_on_Boards_Progress_Report_2022.pdf

[4] BusinessWire. (2016). State Street global advisors launches gender diversity EFT to help investors seek a return on gender diversity. 7 March. www.businesswire.com/news/home/20160307005890/en/State-Street-Global-Advisors-Launches-Gender-Diversity

Culture

The growing diversity of nationalities represented on corporate boards has likewise posed complex questions and raised practical obstacles to boards' long-term performance, as well as to day-to-day operations. What is obvious is that for all the incessant talk of globalisation, a truly global culture remains conspicuous by its absence.

To develop an understanding of other cultures, we need to be able to examine our own. The tricky thing about culture is that it is very much the software running through the human brain – and, much like real software, it is invisible (see Figure 19.2). At an individual level, culture is about mental programming and conditioning, the bulk of which takes place in childhood and school. This early-life process leaves every individual with a set of fundamental assumptions about themselves, others, and the world. According to cross-cultural communication studies pioneer Edward Hall:

> Culture hides much more than it reveals, and strangely enough what it hides, it hides most effectively from its own participants. Years of study have convinced me that the real job is not to understand foreign culture but to understand our own. I am also convinced that all that one ever gets from studying foreign culture is a token understanding. [To study another culture] is to learn more about how one's own system works.[5]

At a minimum, the opportunity to learn about one's own cultural profile, habits, and emotional triggers will strengthen one's confidence and boost self-acceptance. Crucially, this teaches us that others may be very different in terms of their cultural backgrounds – and that is okay.

Personality

Personality is an important aspect of diversity. While there are many ways to differentiate between personalities, one increasingly popular theory is the Big 5, according to which there are five different dimensions of personality. The NEO PI-R, for example, is gaining acceptance as a personality tool. It defines the five big dimensions as being emotionality, extroversion vs introversion, openness, agreeableness, and conscientiousness; each of these five dimensions has six subdimensions or facets. (For a more detailed description of the NEO PI-R, see Chapter 7.)

---

[5] Hall, E. (1959). *The Silent Language*. DoubleDay.

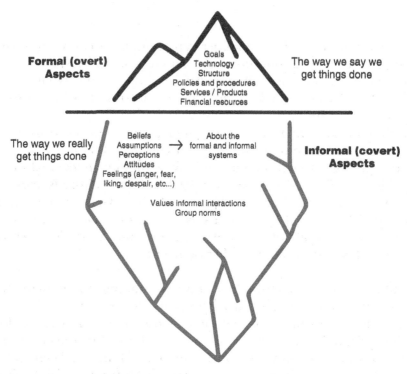

Figure 19.2   Cultural Iceberg
Source: Adapted from Stanley N. Herman.[6]

Diverse personalities can bring great benefit to the boardroom by stimulating debate and challenging perspectives. However, because this is a less obvious element of group diversity, it can sometimes be poorly managed and become dysfunctional. Often, too, diversity of personality is uncomfortable and therefore unconsciously resisted. Some personality dimensions might even result in the emergence of an in-group. For example, if the chair is fast-paced in meetings, he or she might become highly impatient with directors who are more methodical. And at lunch, the chair may unconsciously choose to sit next to someone who resembles them on this dimension, thereby becoming closer to that person and building up trust. It is therefore particularly important that the chair is aware of personality differences and the challenges these may present in boardroom discussion.

Figure 19.3 shows a board mapping of personalities. The CEO (an Italian from Sicily) had a high score on the emotionality dimension, while the British

[6] In French, W.L. and C.H Bell, Jr. (1978). *Organization Development: Behavioral Science Interventions for Organization Improvement*, 2e, p. 16. Prentice-Hall..

EMOTIONALITY	Resilient		Responsive		Reactive	
N1 Worry	0 Unworried; calm; unconcerned	33	43 Usually calm, sometimes worrying	58	68 Worrying, tense, apprehensive	100
N2 Anger	0 Even-tempered; slow to anger	33	Seldom angry, but can be provoked	58	Quick to anger, hot-blooded	100
N3 Moodiness	0 Optimistic; contented; no blues	33	43 Sensitive to losing, but recover well	68	Self-blaming; pessimist; blues	100
N4 Social concerns	0 Socially confident, self-assured	33	Gets embarrassed, then get over it	58	Sensitive to embarrassment, shy	100
N5 Self indulgence	0 Resists temptation; stoic	33	Sometimes yield to temptation	58	68 Easily tempted; self-indulgent	100
N6 Sensitivity to stress	0 Resilient to stress and crises	33	43 Experiences stress, but can cope	58	68 Sensitive to stress & pressure	100
EXTRAVERSION	Introvert		Ambivert		Extravert	
E1 Warmth	0 Reserved; distant; cool	33	43 Moderate engagement	58	68 Attached; affectionate; warm	100
E2 Outgoingness	0 Loner; prefer privacy	33	Mix well, but enjoy privacy	58	68 Sociable; prefer company	100
E3 Assertiveness	0 Non-assertive; passive	33	43 Comfortable in foreground	58	68 Dominant; speak up; leading	100
E4 Activity level	0 Slow-paced; inactive; laid-back	33	43 Ordinary pace and energy level	58	68 Active; energetic; fast-paced	100
E5 Excitement seeking	0 Conventional; avoid risks	33	Enjoy moderate stimulation	68	Seeking pleasure, thrills, adventure	100
E6 Positive emotions	0 Serious, sober, lacking enthusiasm	33	43 Neither serious nor cheery	58	68 Cheerful; light-hearted; joyful	100
OPENNESS	Preserver		Adaptor		Explorer	
O1 Imagination	0 Down to earth; focused; realistic	33	Occasional daydreamer	58	68 Imaginative; abstract, creative	100
O2 Aesthetic sense	0 Prosaic, unmoved or bored by art	33	43 Moderate interest in art	58	68 Artistic, aesthetic, stylish	100
O3 Depth of emotions	0 Discount own and others' feelings	33	Accounting of feelings	68	Interested in own and others feeling	100
O4 Willingness to experiment	0 Habitual, like routine & familiar	33	43 Try new things incrementally	58	Experimental; seeking novelty	100
O5 Intellectual curiosity	0 Practical; here and now	33	43 Moderate interest in abstraction	58	Inquisitive; theoretical; curious	100
O6 Tolerance for diversity	0 Conservative; dogmatic	33	43 Middle of the road	58	68 Liberal; unconventional; tolerant	100
AGREEABLENESS	Challenger		Negotiator		Conciliator	
A1 Trust in others	0 Cynical; sceptical; suspicious	33	43 Cautiously trusting	58	68 Trusting; forgiving; accepting	100
A2 Candour	0 Guarded; cautious; political	33	Tactful, not open	58	Frank; open; straight-forward	100
A3 Consideration for others	0 Self-absorbed; high self-interest	33	43 Giving if asked	68	Considerate; helpful; nurturing	100
A4 Compliance	0 Competitive; head-strong; fighter	33	Can compete if necessary	68	Cooperative; compliant; peaceful	100
A5 Modesty	0 Self-promoting; seen as arrogant	33	Feel equal to others	58	Self-effacing; humble; modest	100
A6 Sympathy	0 Hard-hearted; rational; justice rules	33	43 Caring for others selectively	58	68 Soft-hearted; merciful; sympathetic	100
CONSCIENTIOUSNESS	Flexible		Balanced		Focused	
C1 Sense of competence	0 Unprepared; inefficient; unsure	33	43 Quite well prepared and confident	68	Self-confident; planned; resourceful	100
C2 Orderliness	0 Disorganised; unmethodical	33	43 Sometimes disorganised & untidy	58	Neat; tidy; organised; meticulous	100
C3 Sense of responsibility	0 Unreliable; bending the rules	33	43 Follows the rules most of the time	58	68 Stick strictly to the rules; reliable	100
C4 Need to achieve	0 Easy-going; unambitious	33	43 Relaxed about success	58	Driven; ambitious; enterprising	100
C5 Self discipline	0 Distractable; procrastinating		43 Quite focused, but can waste time		Finisher; workaholic; self-pacing	100
C6 Deliberateness	0 Hasty; snap decisions	33	43 Makes considered decisions	58	68 Cautious; deliberate; thorough	100

Figure 19.3   Individual NEO Profiles of a Board

chair was at the other end of the spectrum. While both were high-performing individuals, this difference created difficulties in communication that had become excruciating. When well-managed, the combination of a resilient chair and a sensitive CEO can be wonderful: the heightened sensitivity of the CEO helps the organisation tackle challenges and threats, while the chair offers a safe psychological base. But when poorly managed, that combination becomes a threat to the organisation.

Age

Age diversity has become increasingly important for boards in the context of innovation. The demands put forward by innovation – particularly the need to think about and anticipate trends in the market – require boards to display diversity of thinking and have the right mix of directors who will make innovation part of every board discussion.

The business risk of not understanding innovation has become more acute than ever. Toyota, for example, made changes to its organisational structure, including its boardroom, in both 2016 and 2017. It cited the need for quick judgement, decisions, and action through *genchi genbutsu* (onsite learning and problem-solving), because 'the changes the company faces require a different way to think and act'.

As boards recognise the need to accelerate innovation, they have also been more receptive to appointments of young members whose background may greatly expand the board's collective experience and expertise. One of the board members at private Swiss bank Vontobel, Björn Wettergren (born 1981) is an engineer MBA and founding family member whose previous roles spanned banking, venture capital, and human resources. This illustrates the bank's commitment to adjusting its board structure as digital technologies – the cloud, robotics, advanced analytics, cognitive computing, and artificial intelligence – reshape its service delivery.

Social Background

Social background is another critical dimension of diversity. The 2016 Brexit referendum in the United Kingdom highlighted long-standing tensions and distrust between 'big business' and employees. As part of her campaign to become Prime Minister, Theresa May revisited the theme of workers playing a larger role in the boardroom, as a way of overcoming the legacy of boards reproducing the same elite, narrowly defined social and professional circles. May suggested it was time for employees to have more input into the way businesses are run.[7]

---

[7] e4s. (2016). Should employees be part of the boardroom? 1 August. http://recruiter.e4s.co .uk/2016/08/01/employees-boardroom/

The experience of northern European, particularly Scandinavian, economies that placed employee representatives on boards as far back as the 1970s shows that this is a long-term project that requires a cultural change to be successful. Shifts in the power balance – and the ensuing power struggles – are inevitable. So are issues of confidentiality, because sensitive information may easily be channelled to the workforce. And like in the early days of any diversity initiative, there is always the risk of going through the motions by appointing token representatives whose voices may or may not be heard.

Having directors with diverse social backgrounds is helpful for ensuring a wide range of viewpoints (and therefore for preventing blind spots). But if this diversity is not well managed, it may result in tensions that can lead to governance failures – as in the case of Hull House.

We Have Embraced Diversity . . . Now What?

At a practical level, board members will develop a deep appreciation of how to capitalise on their team's diversity. In particular, they will learn to understand the strengths that reside in individual directors' competencies, and how these can transfer, multiply, and inform new areas of the organisation's activities and competitiveness. For example, many companies that expanded into central and eastern Europe during the 1990s later built on this experience and their newly acquired skillsets by formulating an expansion strategy for the Asia-Pacific region in the 2000s. In doing so, they drew on their executives' knowledge and expertise gained in emerging markets, and internalised it as a powerful differentiating factor in the company's future strategy.

In the long run, pursuing diversity becomes a journey and a learning process. As on all journeys, companies and organisations that are overseen by inspired, visionary boards will not hesitate to take risks, adopt contrarian approaches, and push the envelope. They will challenge and redefine existing narratives of diversity by creating new role models; nurturing diverse talent through mentoring programmes; and pursuing alternative paths to excellence in diversity. Much of this will entail deep thinking about what the source of the company's competitive advantage will be in 10 years' time.

Well-defined objectives and outcomes are a crucial element of any organisational effort aimed at strengthening commitment to diversity and then managing that diversity effectively. Board members must be able to show, rather than just feel, their new outlook on diversity – whether it relates to gender, culture, or other attributes. Their knowledge must translate into a skillset, and the behaviour that this drives should become automatic and take the form of a habit. From there on, board members and executives should be able to measure their progress and growth toward excellence.

They say a little knowledge is a dangerous thing, and the same is true of diversity. Many boards have succumbed to the temptation of approaching diversity in a mechanical way – by ticking boxes, or filling stated as well as unstated quotas. True, even going through the motions like this may be better than doing nothing, as it may at least produce modest results. But as copious research has shown, diversity can only be a powerful predictor of a company's performance when it is understood and managed well. Boards that are superficially diverse but have failed to address, reflect on, and mobilise that quality will soon face issues of miscommunication and resentment as directors report overwhelming feelings of being 'thrown together'. In this scenario, diversity turns into a liability as the board underperforms 'normal' homogeneous teams by a wide margin (see Figure 19.4).

The Chair's Role in Building and Nurturing Diversity

It is a recurring theme in this book that the chair has an important role to play – and the task of integrating diverse board members into a high performing team is no exception. The board chair leads the way in embracing

---

ESG Measures for Investment

Diversity is just one aspect of 'responsible investing', guided by measurable sets of ESG principles. These considerations include environmentally friendly products, effective use of technology, and building equitable workplaces.

Indicators such as the executive/employee pay ratio, the level of transparency in reporting balance-sheet data, or the absence of tax-avoidance schemes are no longer 'nice-to-know' nuggets of information. Rather, they provide a substantial gauge of a company's health, sustainability, and long-term growth prospects.

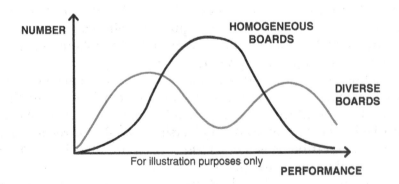

For illustration purposes only

Figure 19.4   The Impact of Diversity on Board Performance
Source: Adapted from DiStefano et al.

inclusiveness and diversity. He or she is conscious of the need to do more than just respond to demographic trends in the outside world.

To start with, models of building consensus are largely determined by culture. According to Lewis,[8] the US style of arriving at a consensus can be characterised as structured individualism, as senior and middle managers make individual decisions. UK directors are likely to be more comfortable with casual leadership, while Scandinavian executives will fall back on the principle of *primus inter pares* – in other words, 'the boss is in the circle'. Depending on their cultural make-up, boards in other countries may lean toward autocratic, top-down styles or a combination of hierarchy with group agreement. Once consensus has been built, the question of who is accountable arises. In some cultures, it is the individual manager; in others, it is the boss. In Asia, one could argue that the entire team is collectively accountable.

Leadership styles are strongly defined by culture too. Depending on the particular cultural context, leaders may demonstrate and look for technical competence; place facts before sentiments, and logic before emotion; and be deal oriented, with a view to immediate achievements and results. Alternatively, they may choose to rely on their eloquence and ability to persuade; inspire through force of personality; and complete human transactions emotionally. Or they will dominate with knowledge, patience, and quiet control; display modesty and courtesy; and create a harmonious if paternalistic atmosphere for teamwork.

Boards can only bridge differences if they understand what these are. Building diversity is an ongoing process whereby collectives create their own world of meaning, and where directors integrate new meanings and add new dimensions to themselves. Ultimately, they learn about themselves and about the need to understand others, recognise the inherent contradictions, and learn to embrace other people's realities.

Chairs can do a lot of good work in this area – not only in educating the board, but also in setting the tone for management and the entire organisation. The company should visibly advance from aspiring to diversity awareness to achieving and disseminating sensitivity, understanding, and knowledge. Once these become widespread, the organisation and the board may be truly able to celebrate diversity as a key part of their identity and achievement.

A board chair who is committed to growing diversity in the organisation will encourage others to understand very clearly who they are; to recognise the 'spectacles' or filters that colour their perceptions; and to seek common ground in all situations. Board members will learn to switch their cultural gear in order to improve interaction. And as they invest time and patience into

---

[8] Lewis, R.D. (1996). *When Cultures Collide*. Nicholas Brealey Publishing.

building trust across a diverse board, they will take differences in decision-making into account.

Many types of exercises help bring a board with a diversity of perspectives towards more shared views. This helps build constructive dissent, which is itself at the heart of good governance. For example, one we use is the board history exercise (see Table 19.1). Board members are encouraged to share (and draw!) their experience of the most significant moments in their tenure at the company. This allows the building of a common view of the past based on diversity of understandings, which by itself helps reconcile views to the future.

Diversity brings specific expertise to a board, as well as increased potential for innovation. Poorly managed diversity, however, can be disruptive by hindering communication and eroding mutual trust. A strong board will thus develop processes to manage diversity well. Even well-established boards should have a systematic board composition oversight, with regular assessment of required capabilities (from expertise to familiarity) and a current composition matrix. And as we will see in the next chapter, boards also need to have a detailed overview of the organisation's executive talent pipeline.

Table 19.1 The Board History Exercise

The exercise starts with short individual talks, in which board members identify their personal views, before engaging smaller groups (say three or four) into a group task which brings these views together.

Individual Task

Identify the three most significant events that happened in your company for *your time period*.

Restrict your choice of events to those events that hold significance for your company today and continue to influence the company:

- Something that happened externally: changes to industry, markets, political shifts, new regulations.
- Changes in company boundaries: mergers, acquisitions, sell-offs, new product markets.
- New management philosophy or introduction of a new process, technology, or IT system.
- Change in leadership (hiring, retirement, etc.).
- Event 1: _____
- Significance: _____
- Event 2: _____
- Significance: _____
- Event 3: _____
- Significance: _____

Group Task

- Group members share their individual list with others.
- Select one significant event per group member.
- Finalise your list.
- Make sure the group has a balance of EXTERNAL and INTERNAL events.
- For each event, draw a picture or icon.
- Each group member should get prepared to give a brief description of their event

The exercise closes with a presentation of the different posters/pictures. These can become part of board folklore . . .

CHAPTER 20

Stewardship from the Board

More than ever, boards need to act as a counter-balance to the short-term thinking that pervades much of the corporate world. To avoid succumbing to the pressures that drive the behaviour of many business leaders, boards must remain vigilant and define clear boundaries to guide decision-making for the long term. As such, they act as stewards, enabling the organisation to thrive and sustain growth while enhancing the wealth of its stakeholders and the well-being of the societies in which it operates. This is what we call stewardship.

Stewardship draws on notions of accountability, long-term orientation, and responsibility for protecting assets over time. With the clear objective of benefiting society with its aligned values, structures, and processes, steward-ship provides a firm's leaders and employees with the clarity of purpose to generate value in the broader sense. The essential idea is that those who are entrusted with wealth of any kind have an obligation to hand those assets on in better shape than they inherited them. And the board has a key role to play as a steward of the organisation. I have explored this topic in depth with Ong Boon Hwee, then CEO of the Stewardship Asia Centre, in a separate book.[1]

Society increasingly expects business to contribute to creating lasting and more inclusive value. At the same time, firm ownership is ever more complex and varied – including state-owned enterprises, family businesses, sovereign wealth funds, publicly traded companies in which institutional investors hold large stakes, and so on. Stewardship offers a way to meaningfully address both legitimate societal expectations and the complexity of ownership structures.

Stewardship encourages business leaders to shift mindsets, and to crea-tively engage their organisations and other societal actors to enhance wealth creation for all over time. Until recently, the dominant view was that business

---

[1] Cossin, D. and B.H. Ong (2016). *Inspiring Stewardship*. Wiley

should focus on creating value for a firm's owners and shareholders. But along with expanding their global footprint, today's companies are being compelled to redefine their view of corporate achievement and success.

My own work on stewardship rests on a belief that the language of stewardship is critical and reflects deep values embedded in organisations' personalities. Researcher Abraham Lu and I conducted an empirical study of the narratives that companies construct and use to communicate their purpose and activities. Their choice of terms – both conscious and unconscious – reflects their view of the world and their underlying values, beliefs, and culture. Using word content analysis, our quantitative study of word incidences by potentially well-stewarded companies and those less well-stewarded helps to build a picture of the major differences in narrative between them.

What we found was striking: there are indeed clear differences in the way companies refer to their stakeholders and employees, as well as in the word usage related to appetite for debt or innovation and time horizon. Words are used differently by different companies, and the choices of words align well with material differences between firms. We then examined words used in more than 2,500 annual reports from 872 companies with sales of US$10 billion or more over several years, a study that we have now expanded to 16,000 firms across 15 years. From this, we constructed an Implied Stewardship Index, based on the relative difference between sets of words, to compare material metrics such as investment in R&D, trends in labour, and use of financial leverage and check word use versus actual company choices. Words are strongly related to the values truly displayed by companies in regard to material choices (such as capex or R&D spending) as well as cultural attributes (such as agility or conservativeness). And the link between narratives and actual performance is important. To the point that the methodology has been used to consistently perform in the financial markets since 2019.

Supported by our quantitative study, we identified three key dimensions of stewardship, as illustrated in Figure 20.1.

| LEADING WITH IMPACT TO DELIVER RESULTS | LONG-TERM VIEW OF VALUE CREATION | CONNECTION WITH COMMUNITIES & SOCIETY |

Response Options & Combinations

Transparency	Sourcing	Timeliness	Tone	Influence
Disclose information and any affiliation to organisation	Provide citations, links etc. to credible source for accuracy	Take time to create good responses from a good point of view	Respond in a tone that reflects on the high standards / quality	Focus on the most influential sites related to the industry

Figure 20.1   Stewardship's Three Dimensions

Building Upon a Rich Cross-disciplinary Legacy of Thought

Stewardship has its theoretical origins in several different traditions. The notion of treating people with respect is implicit in many streams of ethics and philosophy. There is often a sense of service and duty that characterises the spiritual concept of stewardship. In a business sense, the focus is more on the sense of oneself as being responsible for something greater than simply the individual or company, and over a longer time horizon extending beyond one's lifetime. In economics, agency theory states that individuals will act in their own self-interest, and need to be incentivised or constrained to act for the benefit of the organisation. Stewardship theory, which grew out of organisational psychology and sociology, says that individuals will act to protect the assets they control on behalf of their owners and society at large, and are motivated by autonomy.

Psychological, Organisational, and Cultural Influences on Stewardship

A number of factors – social, organisational, and individual – interact to affect the likelihood of stewardship emerging in a given context. Individuals who are intrinsically motivated and are driven by higher-order needs are more likely to act as stewards than those who rely on external rewards. But stewardship is not just a matter of getting the right people – context matters too. For example, individuals may be more likely to act as stewards in cultures that place greater relative value on institutional collectivism (that is, a sense of connection to society as a whole, rather than an affiliation with an in-group such as a family unit). However, it is important to avoid generalisations, given the complex intersection of different factors.

Countries such as Singapore and Switzerland provide examples of organisational stewardship. By securing the foundations and building conducive and supportive structural conditions, they enable stewardship to flourish.

Steward Leaders Build on their Unique Strengths to Drive Stewardship

There are many business and national leaders whose personalities and legacies have come to exemplify stewardship. These leaders come from very different organisational contexts, including financial and institutional investors, family foundations, transgenerational family businesses, public agencies, and state-owned enterprises. In searching for what stewardship looks like, my co-author and I studied steward leaders at work in a variety of organisations and environments – notably in volatile and uncertain contexts requiring clear and bold direction, at inflection points, and during crises. We found a range of compelling examples from whom we can learn.

Ratan Tata's clear focus on business success combined with social and national economic impact helped to provide India with a solid domestic industrial base over the course of his tenure (1991–2012), illustrating how impactful steward-ship can be in an emerging-market context. Family business Maersk had a clear long-term focus from the start, and this continues today. Founded by Arnold Peder Moller, the business grew from a shipping company into a global trade conglomerate, whose legacy was secured through its structure as well as its deeply held values.

There are many more examples of stewardship, which vary in context and form, in state-owned firms as well as in family companies or widely held publicly traded corporations. Zhang Ruimin took Haier from being a low-quality manufacturer in 1980s China and transformed it into the world's lead-ing white goods producer. Eiji Toyoda's unique lean management philosophy (the Toyota Way) was disruptive and paradigm shifting. Warren Buffett's unique and far-sighted investment strategy is built on a holistic and innovative method of asset selection. And when Chung Juy-yung founded Hyundai in 1946, his efforts not only led to the creation of a highly successful conglomer-ate, but also made a key contribution to the foundation of post-war Korea's industrial base.

Steward Leaders Deliver Long-lasting, Meaningful, and Inclusive Impact

Stewardship requires leaders who have strong drive and a passion for the organ-isations they lead and the societies they live in, and who are conscious of the trade-offs required to ensure their meaningful contribution over time. Many of the steward leaders we studied had critical turning points in their upbring-ing, developed key values that drove them, and had people who inspired them. Whether through their internal value set or personality, they have a unique ability to create meaning through stories, build trust, and foster organisational knowledge sharing. Driven by a compelling sense of purpose, steward leaders are able to engage employees with the vision of the contribution they are making.

Well-stewarded organisations focus on delivering current performance without compromising future impact in terms of earnings. They also ensure the continuity of the capabilities and relationships that form the basis of their ability to create future value. Success for these organisations can be measured as the net positive impact on future generations in terms of economic, social, and environmental performance. They are willing to sacrifice short-term prof-its in the interest of securing longer-term benefits for the organisation.

Conservative financing is one way to ensure continuity of operations and resilience in the face of crisis. Our study findings reinforce this: companies scoring highly on our Implied Stewardship Index use 50% less long-term debt than firms scoring at the lower end. Safeguarding the future requires having a vision of where the company is going and making the trajectory possible by investing in capabilities such as R&D, marketing, and branding. Well-stewarded organisations are able to operate effectively over longer time horizons, enabled by a culture based on trust, and by structures that are well aligned with the company's strategy and purpose. And crucially, these organisations are supported by boards that think strategically toward the medium and long term, feeding and nurturing the succession pipeline to secure the leadership legacy over time.

Firms need to play their part in building a healthy ecosystem in which stewardship can flourish. They can do this internally, by stimulating intrinsic motivation in employees, and externally, through clear links to stakeholders and the surrounding communities, which cultivates a landscape of greater transparency and trust. Organisations that are well stewarded have a clear sense of where they are going and why, are strongly committed to creating wealth in both the medium and long term, and build governance systems that foster effective exchange and supervision among the relevant actors.

As such, stewardship is built on a virtuous spiral (shown in Figure 20.2). Steward leaders build on their own vision and purpose for the organisation to inspire their people, both through the strategy and the culture. This then contributes to societal well-being and the company's integration into society. These societal connections then help the steward leaders to scan the environment and adjust course if required, realigning the organisation to deliver on its promise. In the process, its employees and other stakeholders are inspired by its integrity. And so on.

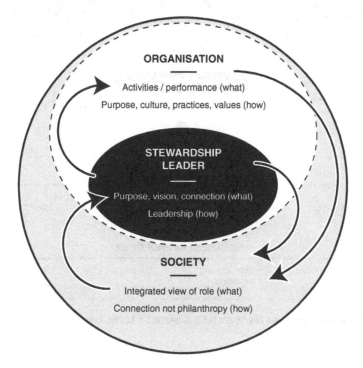

Figure 20.2   The Stewardship Landscape

The Stewardship Landscape

While stewardship relies on strong leaders to drive it, several other important actors ensure that management balances issues of short- and long-term strategic relevance. These actors also consciously scan for and manage risk. Effective oversight helps to keep the organisation on track, so that people perform their roles with a high degree of conscientiousness, competence, and integrity. As well as an enlightened and responsible CEO, therefore, company owners, boards, and management have their respective roles to play in ensuring that the right governance is in place.

The important relationships between the owners, the board, and the management are depicted in Figure 20.3. Together, all three steward the firm – safeguarding and growing values, and benefiting its stakeholders and the wider community over the longer term. As trusted and responsible stewards, they seek to hand over a thriving business and organisation, which is in better shape, to the next generation or to their successors.

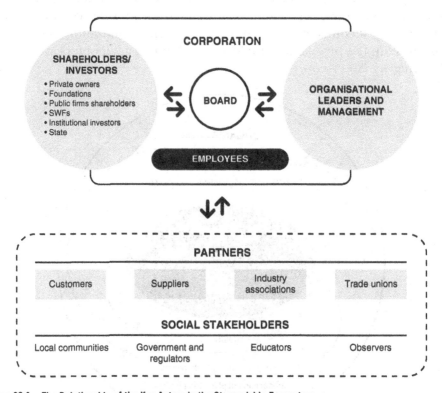

Figure 20.3   The Relationship of the Key Actors in the Stewardship Ecosystem

Becoming a Steward Leader: What it Takes

Although there is no template for steward leadership, the steward leaders we studied share three key characteristics. Firstly, they are transformational individuals who inspire their followers to excel and achieve superior performance through their charisma, inspiration, intellectual stimulation, and individualised consideration. We call this leading with impact.

Secondly, through a combination of prudence and care, steward leaders safeguard the future and ensure that the organisation and its stakeholders thrive over the long term. They exercise the judgement and discipline to sacrifice short-term profits for long-term gain. This enables the organisation to regenerate over time. Finally, by being transparent, accountable, and responsible, steward leaders demonstrate a deep understanding of the organisation's broader social impact to bring about positive social change.

Individual steward leaders have very different personalities and ways of behaving. What they share is their ability to use their strong personal conviction to drive and sustain organisational purpose and culture, to enable decision-making and activity that is consistent and aligned, and to invest in nurturing high-quality connections both internally and externally, demonstrating their understanding of the firm's integral role in society.

Through deep self-awareness and knowledge of their gaps, steward leaders pursue a journey of lifelong learning. Building on our research, we have developed an assessment tool to help board members assess their own strengths and any areas that need to be addressed as they work to secure their own stewardship legacy. This questionnaire is intended to identify development gaps and is most helpful when used in the context of a coaching conversation; it is included in our book *Inspiring Stewardship*.

Stewardship Risks

Leaders are human and vulnerable to hubris. Dizzying rates of change mean that our ever more connected world is vulnerable to shocks, currency fluctuations, and other forms of volatility. For steward leaders and their organisations, reinvention, flexibility, and adaptability are essential. Failing to identify threats can jeopardise the very survival of the organisation and the future of all those involved with it.

Many leaders fall victim to their own success, and stay fixed in their ways. Others become enamoured with their own views, overconfident and increasingly isolated in their thinking. Henry Ford, one of the business stewards of the world, fell into anti-Semitism, buying a paper (*The Dearborn Independent*) and promoting his values aggressively, hence threatening the reputation and survival of his business. Great steward leaders acknowledge that they are vulnerable to risks – including those related to reputation, cognitive and behavioural biases (which distort leaders' perception of reality), leadership transitions, leadership feuds, and political risks. Great stewards enhance their self-awareness and manage their own weak points, by pursuing lifelong learning and by building diverse teams to challenge them and promote a healthy counterpoint to their own views.

Boards are Key to Fostering Stewardship

Our notion of stewardship advocates committed co-creation between owners and managers working together to build a company's future. Although some have argued that such engagement creates an excessive burden, we would counter that it is the quality of connection that needs to improve, rather than the quantity. Co-creation does not necessarily imply an additional reporting burden. In some contexts, stewardship might translate into a greater focus on the quality of interaction between management, boards, owners, and shareholders. In other contexts, it might mean taking ownership and initiative to fill in institutional gaps, and to reinforce capabilities where they are lacking.

By acknowledging and building on the organisational connections that do exist, stewardship helps to build a firm's wealth over time, lifting societal players along with it. There are clear long-term financial, economic, social, and other benefits to be gained as a result. Boards have an important role to play in fostering stewardship at the firm level. I therefore encourage you to consider what impact you can make as a steward leader – individually and collectively – so that we can work together to make stewardship a reality.

PART IV
Board Best Practices

CHAPTER 21

The Board as a Strategic Asset[*]

Boards are responsible for the long-term success of their organisations. This means that strategy must be one of the central elements of board work. Unfortunately, directors are often highly confused as to what they should and shouldn't do regarding strategy. Boards commonly place strategic responsibility on the shoulders of the organisation's executives, believing that strategic thinking is what CEOs and their teams should do. But a board taking this view often ends up acting as a mere rubber stamp of the CEO. And other boards that try to get substantively involved in strategic decision-making often find themselves clashing with the executive team. Neither approach makes sense or allows a board to add real value.

This chapter aims to clarify how boards can better assess their strategic responsibilities in order to make a truly effective and value-adding contribution to the organisation. Although national differences do matter, all boards today have some aspiration to be more engaged in strategy. The real question is how they can use their skills to do that effectively while keeping the executive team fully engaged.

A board's strategic responsibilities cannot be defined in a one-size-fits-all manner. Instead, three dimensions help to determine its impact on strategy. These are:

- **The meaning of strategy** – strategy can be defined in different ways and have different time frames, and board members must reach a common view on these.
- **The role of the board** – a board can play a supervisory and monitoring role, support management in engaging with external and internal

---

[*] This work stems from my work with Estelle Métayer. For more on this topic, see Cossin, D. and E. Métayer (2014). The board and strategy. *MIT Sloan Management Review.*

stakeholders, or take on a meaningful co-creation role. Each represents a different way for boards to participate in the strategy process.

- **The context of the firm** – the board's involvement in strategy will also depend on the context in which the company operates. In a chaotic context, a board may need to have a hands-on approach to strategy development that would clearly be unproductive in a simple context.

Five Definitions of Strategy

There is not enough debate about what strategy really means for boards and top executives, and what it can achieve when done well. Boards first need to discuss the time frame for their strategic reflection. Whereas executives typically look at a three- to five-year horizon in considering strategy, boards may take a longer view over five to ten years. Anchor shareholders of quality, such as families or states, may look even further ahead, perhaps 25 years (to the next generation) or even a transgenerational 50-year view. I tend to see an evolution toward longer time frames, despite the incredible uncertainty of today's world. This produces a clear division of tasks that helps the relationship between the board and management.

Having clarified the timeframe, the board should address what individual directors understand strategy to be. The lack of a universally accepted, up-to-date definition of strategy often results in boards and management sticking to the most traditional concepts – vision, mission, and actions – rather than reflecting on what they might be able to achieve if they took time to explore what strategic thinking means to them.

Here, boards might consider at least five definitions to refine their notion of strategy:

Strategy as planning. From this perspective, strategy serves to establish the organisation's vision, mission, values, and purpose. It helps to define the firm's long-term objectives, programme of action, and resource-allocation priorities. This is what most of us know as the traditional approach to strategy. It is defined by a structured, step-by-step process that Jack Welch of GE championed in the 1980s to implement total quality management and improve productivity, efficiency, and profit. This view of strategy gave rise to the notion of 'strategic planning', which has become a cherished practice in most corporations, although it has been heavily criticised by management thought leaders such as Henry Mintzberg.[1]

Strategy as redefining one's competitive domain. Here, an organisation uses strategy to address its industry boundaries, the key players, where the company stands, and how the industry might be changing.

---

[1] Mintzberg, H. (1994). *The Rise and Fall of Strategic Planning.* The Free Press.

Amazon, for example, is now entering the health-care sector following its acquisitions of PillPack and Whole Foods, and its joint venture with Berkshire Hathaway and JPMorgan in this area. Samsung redefined its industry from electronics to 'lifeware', producing a wide range of stylishly designed digital products including cell phones, televisions, and cameras to rival those of Apple, Sony, and Motorola. And Fujifilm – unlike Kodak – survived and thrived during the transition from film to digital because the company took numerous steps to alter its strategic view of the competitive domain. For instance, Fujifilm jumped out of its traditional industry by using its knowledge of chemicals to diversify into a new line of antioxidant cosmetics and make optical films for LCD flat-panel televisions.

Strategy as a focused response to overcome a key challenge. On this view, well-illustrated by Richard Rumelt in his book *Good Strategy, Bad Strategy*,[2] strategy consists of diagnosing the nature of the key challenges, developing an overall approach to overcome obstacles, and designing a set of coordinated actions to accomplish this. A company's main challenge may come from risks and opportunities in the economic and business environment (such as fluctuating oil prices), or from the competitive landscape in the form of a rival with a new business model. It can even stem from internal issues, such as an organisational structure that does not allow for full value creation. Corporations that are often exposed to large risks, such as natural resource or commodity firms, are used to operating with a close eye on risks and opportunities and thus implicitly use this type of strategic thinking. They are well aware of break-even prices and the dynamics of capital expenditures amid market upswings and downswings, and tailor their strategies accordingly. Another example is the automotive industry: in early 2019, BMW and Daimler announced a new €1 billion joint venture aimed at countering the disruption caused by 'Uberisation' and autonomous cars.

Strategy as identifying and reinforcing core competencies. In this case, strategy is a vehicle for achieving long-term, sustainable competitive advantage and profitability. IBM's Research Division, for example, repeatedly reinvented itself successfully, each time reconfiguring its core strategy to find and transform research ideas into businesses with new products. From the 1940s to the 1970s, the division relied mostly on corporate funding to produce long-term research. In the 1970s and 1980s, it emphasised collaborative teams and shorter-term projects funded by the business units. By the 1990s, the research division

---

[2] Rumelt, R. (2011). *Good Strategy Bad Strategy: The Difference and Why It Matters*. Crown Business.

was looking to its customers and their research arms to jointly develop innovative new projects. More recently, it has been imitating a venture-capital model to fund promising new ventures.

Strategy as optimising value contribution to key stakeholders. This definition of strategy sees the primary role of business as serving customers, or supporting employees and contributing to society in general. Monitoring and optimising how the company maximises benefits for its major stakeholders lies at the heart of such a strategy. In early 2019, for example, outdoor clothing company Patagonia announced that it would donate the US$10 million it had saved as a result of US President Donald Trump's corporate-tax cuts to environmental-protection groups.

Given these different meanings, board members should align themselves before addressing executives in strategy sessions. Most management teams are less sensitive to the five definitions than directors are; for executives, strategy is whatever the CEO considers it to be. Boards, on the other hand, need to clarify what they see as primary to the organisation and thus which of the five possible interpretations of strategy they want to focus on – or, if several matter, then which one should dominate. This is not a static decision: one view of strategy may be more essential in the medium term and another in the long term.

Boards are fully justified in doing this: in today's complex environment, such strategic thinking, along with a debate on the appropriate time horizon, can lead to deep shifts in an organisation's orientation. Directors can assess the strategic timeframe and decide which of the five options matters most to them, versus where they see their executive teams focusing. For example, board members can individually assign points to each of the five definitions of strategy, and then tally the results in order to have productive discussions on differences of views among themselves and, later, with management.

By bringing clarity on these issues before engaging with executives, boards can alleviate much of the tension in strategy discussions and retreats, for example. This in turn leads to deeper, richer interactions with management – including in executives' own work on strategy through more classical lenses such as competitive analysis, threats, and opportunities.

Clarifying the Board's Role

Nonetheless, some argue that strategy is a CEO-only role. They say the best strategy resides in a synthetic, actionable view that can only be developed by a hands-on individual with deep knowledge of the company – in other words, the chief executive. But this view nonetheless recognises that the board selects the CEO and can challenge his or her strategic thinking, even if only to convince itself of the chief executive's ability. So even the most remote boards still have a role to fulfil in choosing the right CEO to match the board's view of the organisation's future (and thus its strategy).

Boards also have to balance the different possible roles they might play, which affects how they will engage their strategic muscle. A board's culture, rules, and practices will of course help to determine which roles dominate. A German board, for example, will most likely favour a supervisory perspective, while a Canadian board may see direct involvement as more essential. Three roles in particular tend to dominate board work on strategy:

Supervision and monitoring. A board with a supervisory role focuses on monitoring corporate performance and executive team behaviour against the key performance indicators (KPIs) of the defined strategy. The board is there to ensure the performance of the organisation and its executives in selecting and implementing a course of action. This supervision therefore covers everything: strategy development, design, and implementation. But this role requires the board to have specific supervisory skills including a systematic view, attention to detail, and an understanding of consistency and control. All of these can be adapted to supervising strategy as well as results. The board must engage in a process of probing and sensing using appropriate hard and soft metrics, while paying attention to risks, strategic inconsistencies, and flaws that could threaten the business. Developing these processes and skills is thus a prerequisite for board supervision of strategy.

Co-creation. Board members typically have vast experience to complement that of the organisation's management. Directors' networks with key stakeholders – regulators, governments, customers, and even employees – can give them an edge in understanding key signals within and outside the organisation and thus help them to co-create strategy with management. Co-creative boards can help to open executives' minds to previously unseen realities and steer the strategy debate beyond any blind spots management may have. Blind spots typically arise because of executive myopia. True co-creation most probably requires regular, highly structured strategic board sessions (perhaps at every other board meeting), complemented by a one- or two-day retreat with management. Successful co-creation will typically leverage both management's internal information and the board's external intelligence and experience to produce a long-term strategic perspective with more options and flexibility than executives' views alone would normally offer.

Support. In this role, the board helps management by coaching and advising executives, and by engaging external stakeholders, including key customers, to ensure the success of the management's strategy. The board thus lends management credibility and authority. In times of crisis, a supportive board can be the key to success, while too much distance can be a recipe for disaster.

In May 2018, the Australian Prudential Regulation Authority (APRA) issued the final report of its inquiry into problems at the Commonwealth Bank of Australia (CBA). The authority highlighted 'inadequate oversight and challenge by the board and its gatekeeper committees of emerging non-financial risks; an overconfidence in the operation of the board and its committees, and a lack of benchmarking to assess effectiveness; unclear accountabilities starting with a lack of ownership of key risks at the Executive Committee level'.[3] In 2013, 2015, and 2016, CBA audit committee reports suggested that the bank was having repeated issues in its compliance with anti-money-laundering regulations. But the APRA report said members of the board audit committee were not routinely given, and did not ask for, copies of these audit reports, instead relying on summaries.

Another seeming example of a board failing to provide adequate support was at BP after the Macondo field blowout crisis in 2010. Given that BP had a prior catastrophe in 2005 in Texas, which killed 15 workers, some doubt whether the board did all it should have done to monitor the company's safety management procedures and its overall safety culture. Many also viewed CEO Tony Hayward as being quite isolated during these difficult times, and questioned whether deeper involvement from the board and its chair might have helped BP better manage the situation. Although the board removed Hayward as CEO, its own failings to lead the organisation's culture were arguably equally at fault in the catastrophe. Having a board more focused on a supervisory role may have been fine during the simpler context of normal BP operations. But a quicker switch to strong support during the chaotic aftermath of the explosion might have enhanced the firm's reputation and long-term prospects.

A strong board can thus weigh and map the roles it seeks to play – whether supervisory, co-creative, or supportive, or a combination of these. This will provide greater clarity about directors' involvement in the organisation's strategy debate, so that they can truly add value. What's more, executives will have useful and reassuring clarity regarding the separation of strategic roles, especially when the board might be perceived as micromanaging. The quality of board

[3] Kaker, D., J. Broadbent, and G. Samuel. (2018). Prudential inquiry into the Commonwealth Bank of Australia. Final Report. 30 April. https://www.apra.gov.au/sites/default/files/CBA-Prudential-Inquiry_Final-Report_30042018.pdf

work improves too. A board that may lack the necessary skills to take on a co-creative role, for example, could design a board education and workshop process to address areas of weakness. What counts is that the board understands its role and how that impacts its involvement in strategy. Once it has clarity on this, the board can better address execution of its strategic responsibilities.

Taking Context into the Mapping Process

When a board maps the five meanings of strategy and its potential roles, direct-ors should take into account the context in which they believe the organisation operates. Boards should ask themselves if that context is stable, or whether it might change sometime in the future. In today's fast-moving world, context can quickly shift from simple to complicated, and from complicated to com-plex – or even all the way to chaotic.

In general, boards spend far too much time on issues that can be considered simple or at most complicated, such as financials and operations. My view is that boards can add most value in complex or chaotic contexts, where executive teams are typically overwhelmed and lack the diversity of views to fully under-stand the situation and make optimal strategic decisions. When the dominant context becomes complex or chaotic, boards become essential to the long-term success of the business. Organisational resilience and survival require early detection of threats, along with the ability to interpret these and engage confi-dently, and then to recover and exploit opportunities quickly. It is a time when experience, judgement, and a willingness to make a strong shift – such as remov-ing rather than steering a CEO – become key to organisational success.

All boards must be prepared to adapt swiftly to changes in context. They must be ready and able to alter, quickly, their interpretation of the meaning of strategy and adjust their role. Focusing on customers in a stable environ-ment cannot remain a board's priority when a context change puts employee safety or the organisation's entire reputation at stake (as illustrated by Tesla's confrontation with US regulatory authorities in 2018, for example). It may become essential to rebalance not only strategic priorities but also what strat-egy itself entails. As a result, the board may need to change its role quickly.

The Impact of Context on Strategic Views and Roles of the Board

Figure 21.1 summarises boards' strategies, roles, and views in different con-texts, mapped from simple to chaotic following Snowden and Boone's meth-odology.[4] The context mapping depends on the number of dimensions to

---

[4] D.J. Snowden and M.E. Boone elaborate on this framework. See Snowden, D.J. and M.E. Boone (2007). A leader's framework for decision making. *Harvard Business Review* 85(11): 68–76.

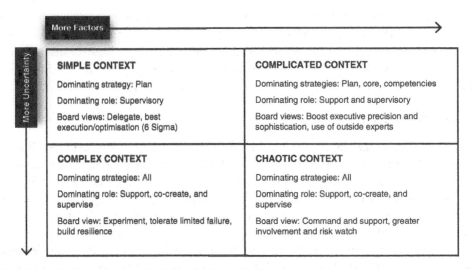

Figure 21.1   The Role of the Board in Strategy is Affected by Context

consider (more factors make the context more complicated), and the level of uncertainty or risks within each. For example, Swiss watch manufacturing could be considered complicated, with many dimensions and much sophistication, but less risky than oil drilling. Refineries, meanwhile, could be seen in a chaotic context, because the uncertainty of oil prices and climate change combine with many dimensions and processes.

The Board's Ultimate Strategic Significance

Organisational leaders are confronted with an incredible rise in complexity: from society, technology, governments, alternative business models, global changes, and environmental factors, as well as shifting economic conditions. Even the most experienced and fine-tuned leaders cannot be expected to respond consistently well to all these challenges, especially in a chaotic environment.

Boards are now essential to strategic success. Unfortunately, however, most are failing to add strategic value. Past crises have increasingly strengthened boards' fiduciary role toward the company, sometimes at the expense of the strategic value they can add.

More than ever, organisations need strong boards of high-quality individuals who are focused and dedicated. In addition, directors must have access to accurate and well-designed information, be able to establish meaningful structures and processes, and implement board dynamics that foster effective debates and result in good decisions and actions. But even high-quality boards of this type can fail if they do not address the spectrum of responsibilities they have on strategy. Following the mapping process in this chapter can help boards greatly improve their strategic performance and transform themselves into a life-saving, competition-beating, opportunity-enhancing asset for their organisation.

In helping to shape an organisation's strategic direction, boards increasingly need to have a strong command of financial matters. The next chapter therefore offers a director-level briefing on key finance and accounting concepts.

CHAPTER 22

Is the Board a Team?

Fundamentally, the Board is *Not* a Team

The chair of one of the largest European financial institutions approached us for guidance on how to make her board work as a team. To her surprise, we suggested that a credible, high-performing board is in fact not a team in the traditional sense of a group of executives or managers. This sparked a discussion on what factors best define a board's competence and where a board's dynamics and workings differed substantially from those of a team (Figure 22.1). Historically, boards of directors have operated as groups of individuals rather than as teams.

Where they did act as a team, it was typically in an ad hoc manner, by convening on a regular basis to hear updates and make decisions. To a large extent, this syncopated rhythm reflected the board's physical makeup – of members who were not sharing a permanent office, had board positions or other affiliations in different companies, and gathered for the purpose of addressing issues and problems. Rather than a classic project team, their meetings resembled a hackathon – working within defined blocks of time and focusing on scoping and defining specific collaborative tasks.

Under competent chairmanship – one that provided high-quality background materials, presentations, Q&A and discussions, and allocated time fairly to each director – the ad hoc team that was the board could indeed become effective and produce inspired solutions. Nonetheless, standard team-building and trust-building measures and exercises were rarely applicable to boards' modus operandi. A football team may be a good metaphor for project teamwork, with team members who are acutely aware of each other's position on the pitch pulling together tirelessly in order to score goals. By contrast, a board's operation is defined much more loosely; its mandate is to determine what and where the goal is. This does entail a degree of cohesion on values

	TEAM	BOARD
Socialization and familiarity	Fit in with the team's processes and rituals	Understand expectations Mitigate friction and stress
Interaction and time	Daily shared experiences	Limited time to build relationships
Information	A wealth of shared information sources Constant feedback, formal and informal	Prioritise access to pertinent knowledge and developmental tasks related to board members' roles
Leadership	Safe environment Implicit trust	Focus on solving problems Committed to developing adaptability and agility
Role	Execute strategy Solve operational problems Short-term focus	A nexus of contracts that make up the corporation Source of social capital Informed decision makingAvoid making short-term decisions
Accountability	Relying on authority and hierarchy Defined by reporting lines Rooted in managerial discourse	Primacy in governance Role-model ethics and integrity Discretion in discharging authority Provide wisdom and proportion Rooted in prevalent professional, political, personal discourse
Structure	Well defined and understood Governed by formal rules	Relatively loose A mix of statutory rules and unwritten rules

Figure 22.1   Teams vs Boards

and direction. So while a board is not a closely knit team like a football side or a project team, there are certain team-like qualities that are beneficial, which this chapter discusses.

Boards Must Allow for Controlled Instability and Dissent

Many governance situations require that board members act as sources of constructive dissent and well-thought-out criticism rather than stand together as a team. Indeed, a dialectic process is at the very heart of a board's work. Effective directors help the board foster open, honest, direct debate and expect the same from their peers. They understand that debate is healthy and necessary, particularly when conducted in an informed, dispassionate, and respectful manner.

Boards need to know when to act as a secure base to the organisation, providing stability in the face of disruption and fragmentation, and when to challenge more aggressively In other words, there are areas in which divergence of thinking is key to the board mandate and others where it is potentially highly damaging.

A good Board of Directors team is one where ideas are flowing – and where each idea is met with an initial welcome, an intellectual challenge, an expression of gratitude, a rigorous scrutiny and a readiness for action.[1]

Hendrith Vanlon Smith Jr. Managing Partner at
Mayflower-Plymouth

Convictions can be the Fuel in a Board's Teamwork

Through discussion with the aforementioned chair of the European financial services firm, we realised that she felt the board was missing a stronger sense of inner cohesion. We agreed that in general terms, a strong board is likely to evolve toward eventually acting more like a team. The question was, where should the chair apply her personal latitude? Should she aim to direct, reinforce, and possibly accelerate that process? Within executive teams, nurturing behaviours of collaboration and trust has become a hot topic. Should the board then invest in team-building and trust-building exercises? Should its members start shadowing each other as a way of 'walking a mile in a colleague's shoes'?

The trend has been for boards to meet more and more frequently, and has been one of the factors in nudging boards to take on more team-like qualities. On top of this, there are other, even more powerful forces at play whose cumulative effect is to strengthen a board's teamwork. We refer to these as **board convictions**.

Until the early 2000s, it might have been enough for board directors to subscribe to a set of values. However, values have since become more ambiguous, fraught and conflicted. A case in point: our client, the financial services provider, was keen to bill itself as a leader in sustainable business. At the same time, the bulk of its financing activity had to do with sectors like oil and gas, and shipping. To face these complex issues with integrity is one of the areas where a board can fundamentally add value. Rather than simply poking holes in the management's strategy, it can speak and act with a collective conviction to lend the board's decisions unanimous support.

The landscape is very disorientating right now, but boards need to guide the management team, get them to be honest about the company's ability to deliver against its net-zero plans, and do that in a way that serves multiple stakeholders.[2]

Goh Swee Chen, former chairwoman,
Shell Companies in Singapore

---

[1] https://www.linkedin.com/in/hendrith-vanlon-smith-jr/
[2] Eco Business. (2023). Shareholder activism puts board directors of energy majors in difficult positions. 19 October. https://www.eco-business.com/news/shareholder-activism-puts-board-directors-of-energy-majors-in-difficult-positions/

This is particularly relevant in companies which have a portfolio approach to their activities. I have learned a lot from the governance of investment committees. In an investment firm, the key decision body (board or investment committee) can shift assets sharply. It is thus important to have strong convictions from the board. In classical corporates with fixed assets, there is less flexibility and thus more natural resilience from the organisation to board decisions. Dissent is easier to live with, and decisions (or absence of decisions) less impactful. So, when companies have businesses that resemble a portfolio of investments, the board or investment committee must make significant decisions backed by a strong conviction coupled with a team-like process. My personal view is that with the conflicts and disruptions we are going into, the corporate as a portfolio of activities will become a more widespread model. And thus boards will need stronger conviction processes at large around forward views. Boards strive to be agile but also forward-looking. They pursue data- and evidence-based long-term trends, no matter how disruptive or painful those may be. And in so doing, they will need more team-like abilities (Figure 22.2).

An effective board will discern which areas in the board's decision-making are underpinned by members' shared convictions and therefore non-negotiable – and will then apply team-like behaviours to those areas. On other topics, the board understands that smooth sailing from one agreement

A team-like board is capable of

- Mobilising collective strengths and capabilities.
- Making sure directors know the chair's role and their own role.
- Recognising that the board's mandate goes beyond observing the company's activities and reviewing the data they have received. It encompasses actively weighing the implications and ultimately making decisions in order to solve problems.
- Providing an environment of psychological safety.
- Working as a constructive group, maintaining a group dynamic that enables directors to operate in an effective and high-functioning manner.
- Acting as a learning board that regards learning not only as digesting information but as an inherently, deeply social activity: Board members meet, work together, make sense of different contexts and situations, and seek to absorb them on a personal level as well as in the company's own 'world.'
- Similarly fostering a learning environment in the organisation.

Figure 22.2   What are a Board's Team-like Qualities?

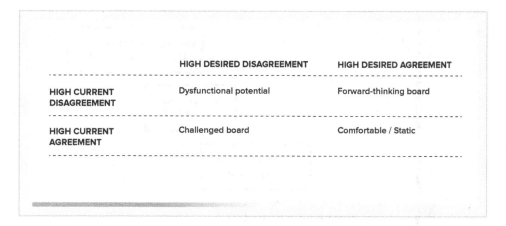

Figure 22.3   Navigating between Agreement and Disagreement

to another poses risk. It is unlikely that a 'team approach' will encourage board discussions and decisions that are required to safeguard value creation in the long-term.

Figure 22.3 outlines several scenarios where progress hinges on the board's ability to navigate between agreement and disagreement. For example, stronger teamwork is preferable in governing an investment committee where assets can be moved quickly and sharply, there is a lot of flexibility, and forward views have a dramatic impact on strategy. Typically, this is not the case in a classic corporate organisation that manages large-size fixed assets.

As boards adopt the qualities of a team, there are many challenges to overcome: 90% of board members rate their individual performance as very effective. Yet only 30% rate their board performance at the same level. This suggests that some reinforcement of the connective tissue that holds the board members and the board's workings together is needed.

The Overarching Objective is to Make Boards Cohesive and Potent

Teamwork that spells success in the boardroom is one that builds cohesion and potency. We understand potency as efficacy, through the ability to wield authority or influence and have effect. A board's potency is often a function of its maturity – and of the members' clear understanding of where on the maturity curve the board is currently positioned (Figure 22.4).

Boards begin as collectives of individuals who are learning to pick up on the group's social norms and interaction nuances (board culture), and who may on occasion push back on executive decisions. As boards mature, they will become more comfortable with giving space to exchanges of divergent views and dissent. In the next phase, there will be discussion areas in which they

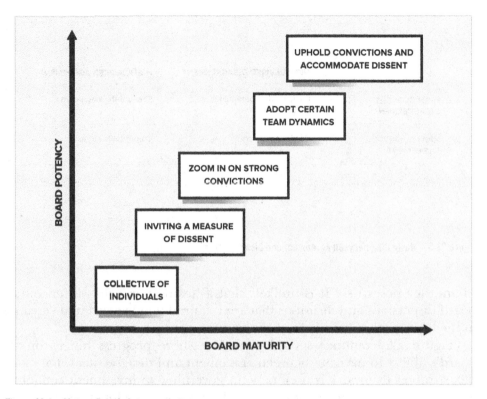

Figure 22.4   Mature Boards Increase in Potency

share strong convictions – which in turn will feed a teamwork ethos within the board. A highly sophisticated and mature board will have members who are aligned with its convictions and sense of purpose with belief and confidence, and can also accommodate smart dissent. At this stage of maturity, disruption and dissent do not substantially lessen a mature board's cohesiveness and potency.

Ways to Nudge a Board up the Maturity and Potency Curve

Do not pursue consensus blindly. Effective boards are highly aware that in a disruptive business environment, maintaining board harmony at all costs may hamper bold and imaginative decisions. Worse, a board that regards consensus on all matters as essential often flounders in a state of paralysis or avoids discussions where divergence is latent. It becomes ineffective at best and harmful at worst.

> Board members don't want to critique their peers. This is why courage, combined with respect, is something I find so important. It's

about taking a stand – while at the same time respecting other points of view.[3]

> Anne Mulcahy, former chairperson and CEO of
> Xerox Corporation

Dissent, when well engaged, increases trust. When members can freely express their differences of opinion and why, they come to trust one another's authenticity and intentions. Productive dissent dissipates suspicion of political motives, and allows assumptions to be openly challenged.

> One core rule: Always assume the best of intentions from others. When someone says something you don't want to hear, delivers news you'd rather not receive, or makes a suggestion you think is insane, rather than lash out, stop and ask a clarifying question.[4]
>
> Risto Siilasmaa, former chairman of Nokia

Continually boost the board's diversity intelligence quotient (DQ). One way of nurturing this diversity of views that can help boards act effectively at critical junctures in the company's development and growth is by recruiting board members whose backgrounds and mindsets will diverge from dominant thought patterns on the board. True diversity should encompass geopolit-ical views, ESG issues, social background and, importantly, age. Although the merits of diversity have been richly documented, when exposed to financial pressure many boards tend to fall back on what they deem familiar – as if their effort in boosting diversity had been simply an exercise in ticking boxes.[5]

> We have an obligation to choose the right profile of candidates, representing all of the various capabilities and skills we need to make a great contribution to our boards.
>
> We have to be tough-minded about our accountability for getting really well-qualified, capable and different candidates to be part of our teams.[6]
>
> Anne Mulcahy

---

[3] EgonZehnder. (2017). Interview with multidirector Anne M. Mulcahy. January. https://www.egonzehnder.com/insight/interview-with-multidirector-anne-m-mulcahy

[4] Siilasmaa, R. (2019). Entrepreneurial leadership: a new approach to strategy when you can't plan for predictability. *Leader to Leader, 2019*(92): 32–36.

[5] Maclellan, L. (2022). Board diversity declines when companies face financial pressure. 11 August. https://fortune.com/2022/08/11/board-diversity-declines-when-companies-face-financial-pressure/

[6] EgonZehnder. (2017). Interview with multidirector Anne M. Mulcahy. January. https://www.egonzehnder.com/insight/interview-with-multidirector-anne-m-mulcahy

Diversity of backgrounds and views needs to be well managed on the board. The formative stages of diverse teams can be uncomfortable when compared with homogeneous teams. However, with effective norms, diverse teams do report better decision-making (Figure 22.5).[7] In poorly managed diverse teams, mistrust and suspicion will lead to conflict and stereotyping, as well as guarding of information.[8] Managing diversity requires not only monitoring board composition and regular assessment of capabilities, but also acknowledging differences and the unique value that each member brings to the discussion as a result (Figure 22.6). In aggregate, this will raise the board's and the directors' DQ – which measures the ability to distinguish behaviours produced by the diversity in question from behaviours that are specific to individuals.

Aim for steady improvement and rejuvenation. A potent board cultivates intellectual strength. It recruits members for their skillsets but also their willingness

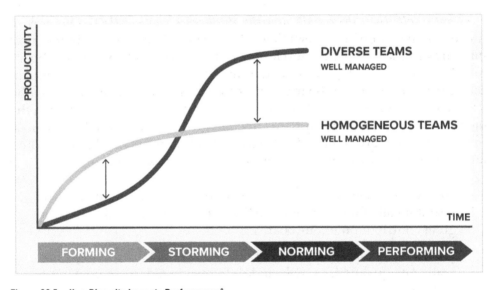

Figure 22.5   How Diversity Impacts Performance[9]

[7] Rock, D. and H. Grant (2016). Why diverse teams are smarter. *Harvard Business Review*, 4 November. https://hbr.org/2016/11/why-diverse-teams-are-smarter

[8] DiStefano, J.J. and M.L. Maznevski (2000). Creating value with diverse teams in global management. *Organizational Dynamics* 29(1): 45–63.

[9] Korn Ferry Institute (2019). The Inclusive Leader: Optimizing diversity by leveraging the power of inclusion. https://www.kornferry.com/content/dam/kornferry/docs/article-migration/Korn-Ferry-The-Inclusive-Leader_2019_06.pdf

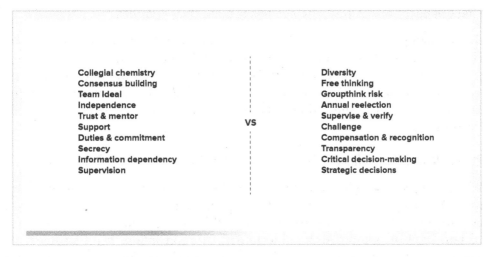

Collegial chemistry		Diversity
Consensus building		Free thinking
Team ideal		Groupthink risk
Independence		Annual reelection
Trust & mentor	VS	Supervise & verify
Support		Challenge
Duties & commitment		Compensation & recognition
Secrecy		Transparency
Information dependency		Critical decision-making
Supervision		Strategic decisions

Figure 22.6   Board Team Dynamics Paradoxes

to table topics of substance and relevance. It aims to build a reservoir of cognitive power that is vastly greater and more inspiring than the sum of its parts. As part of this commitment, board members continually improve the board's teamwork by enhancing the quality of the board team's ways of working, skills and processes, and tools and techniques.

Nurture an effective culture of governance on the board. This culture is anchored in personal, collective, and professional values such as openness, creativity, criticality, and generosity. Often, it takes an external shock – a change of management, an incident that affects the company's reputation, or a grave breach of ethics – to alert the board that the existing board and company cultures may be out of sync with the organisation's operating context.

The Australian Institute of Company Directors, in collaboration with a team of organisational psychologists, has identified four main archetypes of boardroom culture – and how each is liable to tipping over into dysfunction:

1. A board that is overly collaborative and hence 'too close to see'.
2. A board that is sceptical and allows suspicion to override trust.
3. Expounding an advisory culture that eschews responsibility.
4. A personality-led board that marginalises other members.[10]

---

[10] Petschler, L. (2019). How would your board respond to a psychologist in the board room? Australian Institute of Company Directors, 1 August. https://www.aicd.com.au/regulatory-compliance/regulations/reporting/psychologist-in-the-boardroom.html

Effective Board Teams are Adept at Juggling Competing Priorities

Boards acting as teams need to balance competing tensions in their dynamics. However, rather than pulling members into different directions, these built-in paradoxes can be a source of energy board work, as board members constantly assess what best suits the work at hand (Figure 22.6). Increasingly, a board needs to internalise these dual sets of attributes if it is to be considered fit for purpose.

Potent Boards Know When to Converge and When to Diverge – and Value Both

While boards are not teams per se, the ability of a board to act as a team along certain convictions is becoming a key capability in an increasingly conflicted and uncertain context. We have seen in this chapter that a board needs a certain level of potency to be able to act with conviction. With strong trust and cohesion, potent boards value dissent which contributes to scrutinising decisions through different lenses. Sensitive to their own unconscious bias, potent boards value and leverage the unique contributions of their diverse members to elevate their collective decision-making. With members who collectively hold a sense of purpose and commitment to the best outcome for their organisation, the board as a team coalesces compellingly around decisions that have impact on the organisation's performance.

Appendix 22A: Characteristics of a potent board checklist

BOARD POTENCY CHECKLIST

A potent board typically displays the following characteristics:

- ☐ There is a common sense of **purpose** for directors
- ☐ Directors are clear about their **roles** on the board
- ☐ There is effective **communication** among directors
- ☐ Individuals are **valued** as board directors
- ☐ The board is highly **valued** by other parts of the organisation
- ☐ Directors feel **proud** to be a member of the board
- ☐ **Morale** among directors is high
- ☐ There is effective and appropriate **leadership** on the board
- ☐ All directors **perform** to the best of their ability on the board
- ☐ Directors have a high level of **stakeholder awareness**
- ☐ The board has clearly **defined** their **stakeholders**
- ☐ There are clearly defined **standards** for working practices for the directors
- ☐ Board working standards are **monitored** and **feedback** given on a regular basis
- ☐ Director **training and development needs** are systematically identified
- ☐ Directors are adequately trained and are **competent** to perform the professional aspects of their jobs
- ☐ **Resources** are identified and made available for training needs
- ☐ Directors are encouraged to try **new work methods** or introduce new ideas
- ☐ **Innovation** is rewarded on the board
- ☐ **Problems** related to the company's business are quickly identified
- ☐ Once identified, the board is quick to address the problems
- ☐ Problem solving is seen as an opportunity for learning and growth
- ☐ We feel we can solve any problem the board encounters
- ☐ The board believes it can become unusually good at producing high-quality work
- ☐ The board expects to be known as a **high-performing** team
- ☐ The board has **confidence** in itself
- ☐ The board believes it will get a lot done when it works hard
- ☐ The board expects to have a lot of **influence**.

Appendix 22B: Board members' cultural and cross-cultural competences checklist

CULTURAL & CROSS-CULTURAL COMPETENCE CHECKLIST

Board members' cultural and cross-cultural competences:

☐ I am conscious of the cultural knowledge I use when interacting with people of different cultural backgrounds

☐ I adjust my cultural knowledge as I interact with people from a culture that is unfamiliar to me

☐ I am conscious of the cultural knowledge I apply to cross-cultural interactions

☐ I check the accuracy of my cultural knowledge as I interact with people from different cultures

☐ I enjoy interacting with people from different cultures

☐ I am confident that I can socialise with locals in a culture that is new to me

☐ I vary the rate of my speech when a cross-cultural situation requires it

☐ I am sure I can deal with the stresses of adjusting to a culture that is new to me

☐ I enjoy living in cultures that are unfamiliar to me

☐ I am confident that I can grow accustomed to the shopping conditions in a different culture

☐ I change my verbal behavior (for example, accent, tone) when a cross-cultural interaction requires it

☐ I change my non-verbal behavior when a cross-cultural interaction requires it

☐ I use pauses and silence differently to suit different cross-cultural situations

☐ I alter my facial expressions when a cross-cultural interaction requires it.

23

A Primer on Finance Essentials for Directors

Companies around the world have been working to create high-performance boards, usually with directors coming from diverse backgrounds. Nevertheless, accounting and finance drive a significant proportion of board decisions. Directors are therefore expected to have a strong grip in these areas – but as we saw in Chapter 14, financial illiteracy on corporate boards remains widespread.

This chapter provides an essential foundation in finance and accounting from a board-level perspective. It is intended for directors who are not financial specialists. It aims to show board members the fundamentals of how to read financial reports, interpret between the lines of financial statements, implement a desired capital structure, apply valuation techniques, make better M&A decisions, and oversee risk.

Directors who are well-versed in finance can have a great impact on a board's effectiveness. They can understand what drives a company's performance and foresee the likely strategic outcomes of board decisions. It becomes easier for them to resist management fads such as financial and accounting engineering and excessive borrowing. And they are better placed to detect fraud, or avoid M&A pitfalls that can destroy value. Financially literate boards and directors don't suffer from misconceptions, but instead make wise decisions about what creates long-term value.

Reading Financial Reports

Board members do not produce accounting documents, but approving them is part of their responsibility. In short, financial statements show us the money: where it came from, where it went, and where it is now.

The conceptual underpinnings of corporate reporting:

A **balance sheet** shows what a company owns and owes at a specific point in time. It provides detailed information about a firm's assets, liabilities, and shareholders' equity at the end of the reporting period. It does not directly show the flows into and out of the accounts during the period.

   The following formula is the most fundamental principle of accounting: ASSETS = LIABILITIES + EQUITY. In other words, the left-hand side of the balance sheet reflects what the organisation invests in (the assets), and the right-hand side shows how it finances itself to fund these assets (the liabilities, notably debt and equity). Overvaluation of assets and undervaluation of liabilities are classic elements of financial fraud that board members should watch out for.

An **income statement** shows how much money a company earned and spent over a specific time period. To understand how income statements work, we start at the top with the sales made. This is also referred to as the 'top line'. Then we go down, and at each step, we deduct certain costs or operating expenses associated with earning the sales. At the bottom, after deducting all of the expenses, we learn how much the company actually earned or lost during the accounting period. This is the literal 'bottom line' of the statement.

   Note that profit does not necessarily correspond to money made. Indeed, some elements of the income statement, such as depreciation, are notional amounts ('non-cash items') and thus do not affect the cash position. Also, some balance-sheet items are not reflected in the income statement even though they affect cash positions. These include working capital elements such as inventories, accounts payable owed to suppliers, and accounts receivable that are due and still unpaid by customers.

A **cash flow statement** reports a company's inflows and outflows of cash. It shows whether the business stayed positive or negative based on the cash flow exchanges with other companies over a specific period. This is very important because a company needs cash on hand to pay its expenses. It is vital to understand that profits do not correspond to cash. Depreciation affects profits but not cash. And working capital or capital expenditures affect cash but not profits directly. Thus, a good approximation of cash flow is to reinstate the depreciation taken out from profits and to subtract changes in working capital and capital expenditures.

   While an income statement can tell us whether a company made a profit, a cash flow statement shows whether it generated cash.

Profits can be notional, but cash is a more substantial economic reality. The cash flow statement shows changes over time rather than absolute amounts at a point in time, and is thus a strong indicator of the health of an organisation. The bottom line of the cash flow statement shows the net increase or decrease in cash for the period. Board members should pay close attention to cash flow statements, because they correct the accounting distortions of income statements and provide a more realistic picture of whether an organisation makes money.

Understanding Ratios to Analyse Operating Strategies

Ratios are calculated from financial statements. They turn accounting data into valuable information, helping directors to understand operating details, measure progress toward goals, and benchmark with competitors in the same industry. From the perspective of shareholders, bankers, regulators, and analysts, ratios also measure a company's successes or failures. Directors need to receive regular reports and monitor the company through financial ratios.

Growth ratios. Organic or internal growth stems from a strategy, the natural growth of the market, or the creation of a new market through new product development. External growth occurs entirely through acquisitions.

Sales Growth = the percentage growth in sales from period one to the next CAGR

$$\left(\text{Compound Annual Growth Rates}\right) = \left(\frac{ending\ value}{beginning\ value}\right)\frac{1}{Number\ of\ years} - 1$$

Profitability ratios are among the most used and the most important accounting ratios. They are measures of performance in generating profits. Of course, profits are more meaningful when they require fewer assets to generate them (and thus cost less capital). They are also more meaningful when they require fewer sales. Thus, profits are typically related to other financial-statement items. Note also that profits (also called net income or earnings) can sometimes be simplified into items higher up the income statement, such as EBIT or EBITDA which ignore taxes or depreciation.

EBIT $\left(\text{Earnings before Interest and Tax}\right)$

EBITDA $\left(\text{Earnings before interest, taxes, depreciation, and amortisation}\right)$

ROIC $\left(\text{Return on Invested Capital}\right) = \left(\text{EBIT}^* \left(1 - \text{Tax Rate}\right)\right) / \text{Invested Capital}$

ROE $\left(\text{Return on Equity}\right) = \text{Net Income} / \text{Shareholder Equity}$

ROA $\left(\text{Return on Assets}\right) = \text{Net Income} / \text{Total Assets}$

- Note that if we consider the relationship Assets = Debt + Equity, then ROE and ROA can be inferred from each other once we know the leverage of the company (its debt level).

Profit Margin = Net Income / Sales

Gross Profit Margin = (Sales − Cost of Goods Sold) / Sales

EPS (Earnings per Share) = Net Income / Number of Shares

Operating efficiency is as strong a driver of profitability as margin is. A good measure of efficiency is the asset turnover, that is, how much sales are produced by US$1 of assets.

Asset Turnover = Sales / Assets

Note that these ratios typically relate to each other. One well-known relation is the so-called DuPont decomposition: ROA = Margin × Asset Turnover. In other words, the Return on Assets is driven as much by margin (here Net Income/Sales) as it is by efficiency. Thus a 1% efficiency gain is equivalent to a 1% margin gain.

Leverage ratios look at the extent to which a company has relied on borrowing to finance its operations. A high leverage ratio may increase a firm's exposure to solvency risk and business downturns, but may also lead to higher returns for equity holders.

Debt Ratio = Total Debt / Total Assets

Debt-to-Equity ratio = Total Debt / Equity

Interest Coverage Ratio = EBIT / Financing Costs

Liquidity ratios indicate a company's ability to pay its current obligations. In other words, they show the availability of cash and other assets to pay all its bills on time.

Current Ratio = Current Assets / Current Liabilities

Quick Ratio = (Current Assets − Inventory) / Current Liabilities

Many other ratios can be calculated, notably for operations, client engagement, and employee retention. Manufacturing defects, for example, is an indicator of whether a company should anticipate increasing customer complaints and returns that can ultimately hurt business. Directors need to know what the company's customer churn and retention rates are, because firms lose their advertising and marketing investment when customer dissatisfaction rises and customers leave. Board members should also be aware of the company's employee churn rates, because constantly hiring and training new employees is expensive and can negatively impact a company's image.

Interpreting between the Lines of Financial Statements

What might management hide? What do auditors look for?

Management often has an incentive to manipulate the company's financial statements. Directors should know what auditors look for, and also be aware that auditors do not always catch manipulation. There are several basic types of financial statement fraud:

Sales manipulation. Sales are vulnerable to misrepresentation. Common ways to manipulate sales include recording them before they are actually earned, or making up sales that do not exist. The timing of recognition of sales (and expenses) is also a key issue. A classic manipulation is to push sales into the business system (for example, to storage owners, dealers, or independent representatives), thereby accounting for them internally.

Expenses manipulation. This can include capitalising normal operating expenses. Other methods include shifting current expenses to a future period to boost current earnings, or moving future expenses to the current period in order to create a 'bottom' and then increase future earnings.

Incorrect asset valuation. Overstating inventory, fixed assets, and accounts receivable inflates company assets. This can include not recording the full expense of raw materials, not writing off unsellable inventory, or misreporting current inventory. Failing to record depreciation expenses of fixed assets is also fraudulent.

Hidden liabilities. Manipulating liabilities can include not recording accounts payable or keeping certain liabilities off the balance sheet. Complex related-party or third-party transactions do not usually add value, but can be used to conceal debt off the balance sheet. Omission of warranty and product liability could also be a way to hide liabilities.

Improper disclosures. These can include misrepresenting the company and making false representations in press releases and other company filings. Some disclosures might be intentionally confusing and not understandable. Other improper disclosures include hiding significant events, management fraud, or changes in accounting policy or auditors.

Globally, the four most common financial-statement frauds are revenue/ accounts receivable frauds, inventory/cost of goods sold frauds, understatement of liabilities or expenses, and overstatement of assets.

How to Identify Red Flags in Financial Statements

A director should be vigilant about anything in a company's financial statements that raises a red flag. For example, if the firm's leverage ratios are too high, this indicates that it is taking on too much debt. If this is accompanied by falling sales and margins, the company may not be in a sound financial situation. For very cyclical businesses, a combination of these red flags could be a significant concern.

If a company has years of declining sales, it is losing momentum for long-term growth. Cost-cutting could help with profitability, but a company with consecutive years of declining sales needs to revisit its growth strategy. On the other hand, rapid sales increases are also a red flag. Between 1996 and 2000, for example, Enron's sales increased by more than 750%, from US$13.3 billion to US$100.8 billion. Sudden and unexplained changes in sales could be a red flag, as could sales to unknown entities and sales through complex transactions.

A trend of declining profit margins could mean that management is sacrificing profitability for growth. Be aware that an economic downturn could lead to lower margins naturally. Companies need to maintain healthy profit margins to cover operating expenses and the costs of delivering products and services.

Another red flag could be raised if management proposes to extend the depreciable lives of assets. Reducing depreciation expenses could overstate income. In the 1990s, for example, Waste Management Inc. avoided depreciation expenses by assigning and inflating salvage values and extending the useful lives of the garbage trucks that the company owned. A management team that overestimates the lives of assets may well be using other accounting tricks too.

Directors should be aware of 'other' items on the financial statements. These could come under 'other expenses', 'other assets', or 'other liabilities'. It raises a red flag if these 'other' items are large relative to the overall business. Board members need to find out what they are. How often do they occur? Why doesn't management specify them clearly? Are managers hiding secrets? Apart from the 'other' categories, companies also hide problems with 'restructuring', 'asset impairment', and 'goodwill impairment'. Inconsistent expenses trends could signify manipulation, so directors need to investigate any anomalies.

It is a red flag if sales increase together with customer returns, because management could be resorting to manipulation through 'bill-and-hold' sales.

Here, the company creates the impression of a sale by billing the customer, but it never ships the goods. In the following accounting period, the company could report that there was a customer return. Doing this allows management to report higher sales in the current period. Directors need to dig deeper if this happens.

Increasing sales without a corresponding growth in cash flows could be another accounting anomaly. A shortage of cash could indicate rising accounts receivable or inventory, meaning that cash is tied up with customers or inventories. This red flag indicates poor management: an inability to forecast demand, or poor supply chain management.

Cash flow is difficult to manipulate and is a good sign of a healthy company. Unsteady cash flow could indicate accounting tricks, such as capitalising purchases instead of expensing them. When costs are capitalised, the resulting expense is spread over several years rather than reporting all of it in the current year. This will lead to overstated assets and income. This scheme was used in the WorldCom fraud.

Implementing Desired Capital Structure

A key board responsibility is to ensure that the company is well funded to achieve its business objectives. Its capital structure often depends on the availability of internal funds and the organisation's risk appetite. A company can choose from many different possible capital structures. Once a company has decided to seek external capital, it can decide the instruments. The two main sources of financing are equity and debt.

Equity. A company is generally formed by investors subscribing for shares in return for a claim on the firm's profits. When the company generates a profit, the directors may decide to pay a dividend to shareholders. Profits retained can be used to fund future growth or future dividend payments. From the company's perspective, equity funding is relatively low risk, because there is no obligation for the firm to return the funds invested, or to pay dividends.

Stock markets allow investors to buy and sell shares in publicly traded companies. These firms gain access to capital, while investors have an opportunity to own a slice of the company and potentially gain depending on its future performance. This market can be split into two main sections. The primary market is where new issues are first offered (in an initial public offering, or IPO), while any subsequent trading takes place in the secondary market.

Debt results from borrowing money from others. It is repaid over time or at maturity, usually with interest on the loan. When a company uses debt financing, in many jurisdictions it will pay less taxes. In addition, debt appears less expensive than equity financing (although it may not be so once adjusted for risk), and does not dilute the interests of existing shareholders. Debt financing usually has covenants attached, which require the company to agree to certain conditions. Large quantities of debt could impose financial burdens on the company, and potentially put it in financial distress. Debt is thus at the root of credit risk. This is substantial for many organisations, and needs to be watched for suppliers, clients, and partners.

Some debt instruments, such as corporate bonds, can be bought and sold by investors on credit markets around the world. These debt, credit, or fixed-income markets are much larger than the world's stock markets.

Understanding Valuation Fundamentals

The discounted cash flows (DCF) method is a way of assessing, in present-value terms, a sequence of net cash flows over time, taking into account the cost of financing (or any given discount rate).

Estimating Cash Flows

The most common valuation technique is the free cash flow to the firm method. By discounting all the cash flows over the life of the project or company, we determine the value of the project or company.

$$\text{FCFF (Free Cash Flows to the Firm)}$$
$$= \text{EBITDA} - \text{the annual change in working capital} - \text{taxes}$$
$$- \text{capital expenditure required by the project each year}$$

or, expressed equivalently:

$$\text{FCFF} = \textit{Net} \text{ Income} + \text{Depreciation} - \text{the annual change in working capital}$$
$$- \text{capital expenditure}$$

Cost of capital, or weighted average cost of capital (WACC)

The cost of capital is the weighted average cost of equity plus the cost of net indebtedness after tax, weighted relatively according to the debt/equity ratio of the capital employed.

Example

If 75% of capital employed in a company is equity and 25% is debt, gearing is 0.33. If the cost of equity is 13.33% and the tax-adjusted cost of debt is 6%, then the cost of capital is $\{(13.33 \times 0.75) + (6 \times 0.25)\}\% = 11.5\%$.

NPV, the Net Present Value

How can a business figure out whether a new project is financially viable? Net present value (NPV) is the most used method for valuing a project or company:

$$NPV = -Investment + \sum_{t=1}^{T} \frac{FCFF_t}{(1+WACC)^t}$$

where T represents the time period (e.g. number of years considered) and t is the year considered.

NPV compares the initial costs of a project with the total value of future cash flows from that project. Because these future cash flows are worth a different amount than if that cash were earned today, a discount rate is applied to the future revenue, allowing the business to compare the future revenue to alternative investments today. The discount rate is the average cost of capital for the company (the WACC described above).

Real Options

The real options method is a way to value flexibility, future opportunities, rights, and abandonment options in investments. It is based on mathematical option-pricing methodologies and does not rely directly on discounted cash flow methods. This approach can bring valuable insights when contingencies make DCF methods difficult to use, and when decisions in the future depend on the evolution of values across time.

Market Multiples

A comparable company analysis is a process used to evaluate the value of a company using the metrics of other similar-sized firms in the same industry. The assumption is that similar companies will have similar valuation multiples.

The most widely used multiples include the following:

- P/E ratio (Price of shares/Earnings per Share)
- EV/EBITDA (Enterprise Value or Market Capitalisation + Debt over EBITDA)
- P/EBITDA
- P/Sales (the so-called sales multiple).

Many other ratios can easily be calculated to cater for specific situations.

Making Better M&A Decisions

What is synergy in an M&A deal?

Synergy is defined as a state in which two or more things work together to produce an effect greater than the sum of their individual effects. This can also be expressed as 'the whole is greater than the sum of its parts'.

Good reasons for M&A synergies include reducing costs and increasing capabilities, market pricing power, or product offerings. But although M&As can be successful, they may sometimes occur just because managers want to build empires or boost individual egos, regardless of whether synergies exist. Directors thus need to have a rational analysis to see the justifications for such deals.

What are the key decisions in M&As?

First, successful M&As need a **strategic rationale**. A merger or acquisition should be designed for growing scale and scope, redefining a business or industry, and achieving long-term competitive advantage. The rationale must be clearly communicated to stakeholders. And please remember that strategy works only if integration works: integration preparation should thus go hand in hand with early analysis.

Second, **risk analysis**. There is no doubt that acquisitions can offer growth opportunities, but they are by nature complex and prone to risk. When considering an M&A strategy, opportunity often comes with risk and uncertainty. The pricing structure should take into account the risks considered, even those as fundamental as culture risk.

Third, **due diligence** is crucial. Pre-merger planning needs to include a formal review of the targets, and an evaluation of culture, organisational fit, and other non-financial elements. The price and financing ought to be appropriate and beneficial. Pre-merger planning could also include key integration processes, coordinated decisions, efficient communication, a marketing plan, and targeted milestones. Successful M&As require active management to achieve these milestones.

Fourth, **deal negotiation**, **pricing**, and **structuring** are key. There is no acquisition that is good whatever the price, and a strong discipline in not overpaying is at the heart of a good acquisition programme.

Fifth, **merger integration** should include the new company's design, and the integration of human resources, technical operations, and customer relationships. Integration needs to be completed quickly, and should be prepared and priced in before the deal. Arguably, dedicated integration managers should ideally be involved during the deal negotiation.

Finally, boards need to conduct a **post-integration analysis**. How well did the acquisition go? Have we achieved the strategic goals? What did we learn in the process to help make the next deal more successful? Ideally, such a step will already have been planned from early in the deal negotiation.

What do we know about M&As through empirical studies?

Larger companies and cash-rich firms typically make bad deals. Private companies make better deals than public ones.

Size matters. Acquirer announcements are negatively related to company size. The returns are more negative the larger the deal is relative to the size of the acquirer. This usually leads to integration issues later.

Mergers that focus on the core activity increase shareholder value, whereas diversification acquisitions have a bigger share of value-destructive deals.

Payment methods make a difference, revealing the discipline required in the process. Cash payments are positive for the acquirer, whereas stock-for-stock exchanges have lower returns for the acquirer. This stems from the discipline required in cash deals that use the balance sheet of the acquirer and are thus more strenuous than stock deals.

M&As involving companies with greater cultural differences perform worse. Cultural conflicts lead to managerial issues in the combined company. Culture is the number one driver of integration failure.

This topic is also covered in Chapter 26.

Overseeing Risk

Regulators and other stakeholders have pushed boards to be more active in risk oversight. As we saw in Part II, failing to manage risk properly can threaten the board's reputation. Through their risk oversight role, directors can decide the risk appetite of the company, design risk policies and procedures, and monitor management's implementation of these. Grasping the language of risk helps board members to communicate better.

Although risk is a complex topic, familiarity with the following terms is a good starting point:

- **Arbitrage:** the purchase of one security and simultaneous sale of another to give a risk-free profit. Some finance professionals also call arbitrage the purchase and sale of two securities that are similar but whose risks do not cancel.
- **Basis risk:** the residual risk that results when the two sides of a hedge do not move exactly together. Basis risk is central to optimal hedging theories, such as minimum variance hedge. This risk is at the heart of the failure of hedges, and it is thus important for board members to supervise when an explicit hedging programme is in place. Any hedge presents a basis risk and directors should be aware of what the basis risk and of the principles behind this.
- **Break-even analysis:** an analysis of the level of sales at which a project would just break even.
- **Call option:** an option to buy an asset at a specified exercise price on or before a specified exercise date (cf. put option). Call options exist on financial instruments such as stocks and currencies, as well as on commodities.

- **Correlation coefficient:** a measure of the closeness of the relationship between two variables. It consists of the ratio of the covariance to the product of the standard deviation of the variables.
- **Decision tree:** a method of representing alternative sequential decisions and the possible outcomes from them.
- **Derivative:** an asset whose value derives from that of some other asset. Major derivatives include futures (traded on exchanges), forwards (traded over the counter), swaps, options, and credit derivatives.
- **Hedging:** buying (or owning) one asset and selling another in order to reduce risk. A perfect hedge produces a riskless portfolio. However, differences between the asset to hedge and the hedging instruments, as well as changes in time horizon, make perfect hedges extremely rare.
- **Future:** a contract to buy a commodity or security on a future date at a price that is fixed today. Unlike forward contracts, futures are traded on organised exchanges and are marked to market daily.
- **Market risk (systematic risk):** risk that cannot be diversified away. The CAPM (Capital Asset Pricing Model) measures an asset's exposure to systematic risk via the beta coefficient.
- **Monte-Carlo simulation:** a method for calculating the probability distribution of possible outcomes, for example from a project. It combines a large number of mathematically generated scenarios (for example, across a distribution of an input price such as an oil price) to produce a distribution of an output, such as the NPV of a project. This method can thus provide probabilities of the NPV being above a certain number depending on the oil price.
- **Moral hazard:** the risk that the existence of a contract will change the behaviour of one or both parties to it. For example, an insured firm may take fewer fire precautions.
- **Normal or Gaussian distribution:** a symmetric bell-shaped distribution that can be completely defined by its mean and standard deviation.
- **Risk appetite:** the level of risk an organisation is willing to take. It often reflects management's attitude towards risks and is thus useful for board members to supervise and (often) help define. It can be defined across the different KPIs considered for the organisation; for example, by giving acceptable bands.
- **Sensitivity analysis:** an analysis of the effect on a project's profitability of possible changes in one dimension, such as sales or costs. No project analysis today should come without it.
- **Spot exchange rate:** the exchange rate of a currency for immediate delivery (cf. forward exchange rate).
- **Spot interest rate:** the interest rate fixed today on a loan that is made today (cf. forward interest rate).

- **Spot price:** the price of an asset for immediate delivery (in contrast to the forward or futures price).
- **Standard deviation:** a classic measure of risk that consists of the square root of the variance – a measure of variability or volatility. Like all mathematical measures, it is well-defined for rather liquid assets (such as traded stocks, commodities, or currencies), and is less useful for less coherent environments. The latter include situations affected very directly by people, such as M&A integration.

Financial literacy is crucial for efficient and effective board oversight. In this chapter, we discussed six financial topics:

- reading financial reports;
- interpreting between the lines of financial statements;
- implementing desired capital structure;
- understanding valuation fundamentals;
- making better M&A decisions; and
- overseeing risk.

Boards are responsible for the integrity of the company's financial reports, so directors need to analyse and interpret between the lines of financial statements. When a company decides on financing, directors need to ensure that shareholder expectations for return on investment and bondholder expectations for repayment are both carefully managed. Desired capital structure is a balance of the pros and cons of different financing alternatives.

Understanding valuation fundamentals helps directors to make better M&A decisions. Although boards should not be involved in day-to-day risk management, directors need to communicate in risk language in order to send a message that risk management is an integral component of governance.

24

The Intricacies of Subsidiary/Holding Governance

Larger organisations in particular may have tens or even hundreds of wholly or partly owned subsidiaries, which raises the question of how to govern them. Simply put, should they be governed at subsidiary level or at group level? And how does the role of the director change as a result? Interestingly, these questions arise in 100%-owned subsidiaries, as well as in those where the group has a majority stake or even a large minority holding. This chapter reflects on the diversity of best practices from different environments in the hope of inspiring further governance evolution in this area.

The issue of subsidiary/holding governance is becoming even more important for three reasons:

- the rise of national interests;
- increasingly engaged financial actors; and
- the dynamics of business transformation.

As countries around the world increasingly seek to assert their national interests, their regulators and governments are asking for governance decisions to take place in their country and not at international headquarters. They have thus started imposing decision powers at national governance level, including in banks and insurance companies. National interests must now be protected in many areas, such as financial stability, health, and food safety. Regulators are asking for national subsidiaries to have effective boards, not just boards on paper.

As a result, subsidiaries of international groups must often go beyond complying with national laws. They must also ensure that governance, strategic decisions, and the management of any failures all protect that country's national interest. These issues therefore need to be considered at national or local level as part of a decision process. Group governance can no longer simply be imposed at national level. National boards of international groups are thus becoming more significant.

Second, previously passive financial actors, including sovereign wealth funds, increasingly regard governance as a key driver of risk and performance. They are therefore becoming more engaged in nominating or influencing board members, leading to what can effectively become a subsidiary–holding relationship, albeit at the other end of the spectrum to the fully owned subsidiaries of many groups. These financial actors are so proactive, creative, and resourceful that they are helping to redefine subsidiary/holding governance.

Finally, and most importantly, business transformation has shaken traditional organisational structures. Companies confronted with the reality of natural selection need to evolve and innovate. Often, this entails self-cannibalisation or diversification, which are best achieved in external but controlled entities. One classic example of this is Nestlé and Nespresso. Ant Financial and Alibaba are another good example. Sometimes, innovation requires separation and creation of a fully new entity, even if it comes to reintegrating later. Firms may also need to separate previously joint activities in order to be able to sell or restructure that business more easily.

The art of subsidiary governance is to balance alignment with the holding company or group with the independence of a subsidiary's decision-making. This balance will vary depending on context. For example, the oil majors keep a tight rein on their subsidiaries, joint ventures, and production-sharing agreements. The boards of these entities have strict rules to follow, directors are direct employees of the owner, and decisions are clearly brought back to group level whenever something critical happens. The group tightly controls structures (including the shareholder agreement, board organisation, and committees) and also culture (as reflected in board practices, the notion of independence, and the style of board discussions).

At the other end of the spectrum, many financial actors, including sovereign wealth funds, tend to take a slightly looser approach. For example, the International Finance Corporation (IFC), the investment arm of the World Bank group, nominates independent external directors to be board members of its investee companies, sometimes even when the IFC holds a large stake. Similarly, Temasek, the sovereign wealth fund of Singapore, mostly uses independent directors and allows quite a bit of freedom of structure in its subsidiaries, even the fully owned ones. In the latter case, shared culture will typically ensure a certain level of consistency between the fund's overarching objectives and the decisions of its subsidiaries.

In subsidiary governance, the two main levers for adjusting the intensity of control or independence are structures and culture.

Structures

Some groups have embedded strong structures in their subsidiary governance. These can emanate from the original shareholder agreement. For example, board representation, or structures such as committee choices and chair nominations, can be clearly set out in the structuring of the organisation. In some family businesses, the representation of different family members across the group's various subsidiaries provides a basic structure. My team and I work with a family where the siblings and their children hold board positions in different subsidiaries according to their own skillsets. In addition, the siblings sit on the group board along with independent directors.

Some of the most sophisticated structures for subsidiary governance are found in the oil and gas industry. For example, I work with a national oil company that has more than 100 subsidiaries. The group proceeded by mapping these subsidiaries in terms of their strategic importance and the governance influence that the group has (some are joint ventures with strong foreign partners). The group then mapped board decisions across three dimensions:

- Long term value, typically including strategy and capital expenditure decisions.
- Short-term performance, including the annual budget, operational organisational matters, and individual performance.
- Organisational health, including HSE (Health, Safety and Environment) responses, risk reviews, and board effectiveness.

Within these categories, about 25 typical decisions are mapped. A decision is then taken as to whether the owner representatives on the board should be proactive in representing the group, or whether the directors should have the responsibility to choose. A director who proactively represents the owner might engage in mandatory consultation with the group at the appropriate level – such as an asset manager within the group or an individual responsible for governance (Figure 24.1).

The structure thus allows for a complete mapping of the group's engagement at subsidiary level, depending on the nature of the subsidiary, the group's willingness to engage, and the type of decision considered. It also illustrates the duality of ownership representation on these boards, as some decisions are taken fully independently while others require direct group representation. The clarity brought by the system is valuable.

	KEY DECISIONS	DIRECTOR'S POSITION TOWARDS OWNER: REPRESENTATION	DIRECTOR'S POSITION TOWARDS OWNER: INDEPENDENCE	OWNER CONSULTATION CONTACT: GROUP CEO	OWNER CONSULTATION CONTACT: ASSET MANAGER	OWNER CONSULTATION CONTACT: OTHER RELEVANT CORPORATE
LONG-TERM DIMENSIONS	Business Plan (& changes)	▒		✓	✕	
	Major CAPEX (above X threshold)		█	✓	✕	
	Dividend and/or changes to related policies		█	✓	✕	
	Capital Structure	▒		✓		✕
	M&A and divestures at Subsidiary level	▒		✓	✕	
	Changes in by-laws		█			✕
	Changes in key policies (e.g., HSE)		░			●
YEARLY CONSIDERATIONS	Annual Budget	▒		✓	✕	
	Major client supply/pricing agreements		░		●	
	Business and Financial KPIs		░		●	
	Budget deviations (threshold specific)		░		●	
	Capex deviations (threshold specific)		░		●	
	Changes in Organisational Structure		░		✕	
	Major restructurings/layoffs		█		✕	●
	N-1 executive change		█	✓		
BUSINESS HYGIENE	Approval of Audit and Risk Reports		░			
	Disclosure reports (Financial, Audit, HSE)		░			●
	CEO appointment, removal or change; CEO succession plan	▒		✓		
	CEO review and compensation		█			✕
	Changes in Governance (e.g., new sub-committee)		░			●
	Company HR policy (e.g., compensation policy)		░			●
	Changes in director's role		█			✕
	Subsidiary board member nominations			✓		✕

POSITION

░ BOARD MEMBER DECISION WITH OPTIONAL CONSULTATION

▒ SHAREHOLDER DECISION WITH BOARD MEMBER INPUT

█ BOARD MEMBER DECISION WITH MANDATORY CONSULTATION

CONSULTATION PROTOCOL

✓ APPROVAL

✕ RECOMMENDATION

● INPUT

Figure 24.1 Holdings Governance Map

Source: Adapted from several subsidiary governance frameworks of publicly listed companies in Europe, Asia and Africa.

Culture

Another way to tune subsidiary governance is through the culture embedded within boards and within directors themselves. This is a strong driver of success, as organisations such as Temasek have shown. Indeed, culture may appear to be the best driver of successful subsidiary governance, or even investee governance. This happens when truly independent directors share the same fundamental values – notably integrity, a sense of purpose, and responsibility – and the same overarching national or organisational objectives, and then decide freely what is right for the organisation.

The challenge for the group is thus to drive a well-aligned culture across subsidiaries while preserving the spirit of independence that is fundamental to good governance. This is often quite difficult. More tightly controlling groups risk having a small number of like-minded directors who lack the diversity and competitiveness of their peers in a more open group. Best practices thus include fostering a natural selection process among board members themselves, with those most able to combine alignment and independence rising further faster.

To help develop alignment, a group should organise regular sessions that bring together directors from different subsidiaries. These gatherings should focus on key dimensions such as essentials of governance effectiveness, as well as other timely issues such as cybersecurity or geopolitics, for example. Ideally, the sessions will use multiple formats and shapes (lecturers, speakers, panels, and brainstorming groups), and take place throughout the year to ensure engagement and continuous education.

There is a risk of driving the subsidiary governance process too much through culture and not enough through structures. The risk is that the homogeneity of board members will make governance less effective, especially when creativity and innovativeness matter. It is thus important to welcome some disruption and encourage a true diversity of perspectives when governing subsidiaries. This can be done within the framework of common values that are well appreciated by all involved.

By establishing the right structures and culture, groups and organisations can fine-tune subsidiary governance to their purpose. The key is to balance independence and alignment. The most engaged groups determine the level of alignment they want at each subsidiary and then create it through these two levers. In the next chapter, we discuss how boards can enhance entrepreneurial leadership.

CHAPTER 25

Fostering Entrepreneurship from the Board*

The legacy of Apple co-founder Steve Jobs is that of a genius, an innovator of the most creative and visionary kind. But in 1985, the company's board let Jobs go after he got caught up in a fight with then CEO John Sculley. Sales of the second-generation Mac, the Macintosh Office, had been disastrous. Jobs argued for a discounting strategy, but Sculley was firmly opposed, convinced that this would result in an unacceptable loss. The board sided with the CEO and said that Jobs was too disruptive to the company.

Thirty years later, Sculley spoke of his regret. 'I came from corporate America. There it was kind of secular, there wasn't the passion that entrepreneurs have', he said. 'I have so much respect now decades later for founders, for the belief and passion and vision that they have. So to remove a founder, even if he wasn't fired, was a terrible mistake.'[1] Sculley added: 'I really blame the board. Because I think the board understood Apple before I came, they understood Steve. They knew what my experience was and what it wasn't. And I really believe there could have been a solution to keep me and Steve working together, because we were really good friends up until that point.'[2]

The conflict between Jobs and Sculley exemplifies the tension at the centre of many boards. With the proliferation of regulation across sectors and an

* Parts of this chapter were developed in an unpublished article with Sophie Coughlan and Peter Wuffli

[1] Edwards, J. (2105). Former Apple CEO John Sculley admits Steve Jobs never forgave him, and he never repaired their friendship, before Jobs died. *Business Insider*. 27 May. http://uk.businessinsider.com/john-sculley-admits-steve-jobs-never-forgave-him-before-jobs-died-2015-5
[2] Lane, R. (2013). John Sculley just gave hos most detailed account ever of how Steve Jobs got fired from Apple. Forbes. 9 September. http://www.forbes.com/sites/randalllane/2013/09/09/john-sculley-just-gave-his-most-detailed-account-ever-of-how-steve-jobs-got-fired-from-apple/

increased focus on compliance, directors dedicate considerable attention to overseeing risks. But in effectively managing short-term downside risk, boards may be stifling innovation and entrepreneurial leadership. Good corporate governance helps to ensure high-quality decisions that enhance a firm's performance over the long term. And in many industries today, entrepreneurship is central to the corporate renewal needed for long-term success.

By undermining entrepreneurship, therefore, boards may be failing in their real responsibility. Would a new Jobs avoid being fired today? Maybe not. In the hope of charting a more harmonious way forward, this chapter explores where the tensions are, how good governance can enhance entrepreneurial leadership, and the main levers for practical implementation.

'Best Practice' Governance vs Entrepreneurship

Have regulatory and governance standards stifled entrepreneurial leadership? Danish inventor Thomas Lund thinks so. In the early 1980s, Lund founded Dansk Teknologi at the age of 32. His mission was to stimulate innovation in product development, manufacturing, and production systems, in areas such as nitrogen oxides (NO_x) reduction, offshore drilling technology, flight catering, hospital products, analysis instruments, and digital dosing pumps. Dansk Teknologi has worked with the boards of many leading Danish multinationals and other global companies, and several of its products have received international awards and have worldwide patents. Lund himself has served on the boards of several leading organisations, including the Grundfos group, the Poul Due Jensen Foundation, and the central board of Danish Industry. And he has suffered the isolation of being entrepreneurial on a large company board. 'At many companies, boards kill innovation', Lund says.

In deterring innovation, boards are threatening what is often the lifeblood of business value creation. Although today's widespread public scepticism toward business leaders, and especially those in the financial industry, is understandable, we should avoid damaging entrepreneurship and long-term value creation in the process.

The trend toward more detailed and formalistic regulation reflects a belief that risks can be 'organised away' with appropriate rules. Yet this approach ignores the fact that failure is an inherent and necessary part of capitalism – which is itself based on a natural selection process – and of real long-term business value creation. Directors must therefore seek to strengthen entrepreneurship at board level and develop a greater and smarter appetite for measured risks.

Boards Should Actively Encourage Entrepreneurship

What are the distinguishing features of a company's culture, strategy, or behaviour that make it entrepreneurial in nature? And how can boards best support the development of such attributes – or at least prevent them being suppressed – in the organisations they govern?

To address this, scholars have developed the concept of an organisation's entrepreneurial orientation (EO).[3] This consists of five components: risk-taking, or the firm's willingness to commit resources to ventures whose outcome is uncertain; proactiveness, or the ability to anticipate future opportunities in terms of both product development and industry disruption as well as customer insights and markets; innovativeness, as reflected in the types of products and services the organisation introduces to the market; competitive aggressiveness, or how directly a company attacks its competitors and pursues target markets; and autonomy, or how independently an individual or team initiates an idea and follows it through.

Much has been written about the correlation between entrepreneurial orientation and company performance,[4] and about how firms can enhance their EO. But there is far less literature on the role of boards in encouraging entrepreneurship in well-established firms.

This is a pity, because boards can support management in several ways to give companies a more entrepreneurial mindset. First, directors can help to build a culture of innovation and autonomy; for example, by role-modelling constructive dissent and asking the right questions regarding cross-department initiatives. Second, boards can help management to build incentive structures that encourage ownership and collaboration; for example, by sharing accountability across departments for success. In addition, by demonstrating real passion for the business and investing their own resources, directors can help to foster a culture of calculated and committed risk-taking. Finally, board members' experiences from other industries can be vital in identifying potential disruptions to the competitive space (Figure 25.1).

Innovativeness and Autonomy

Large organisations must cross typical corporate boundaries in order to innovate. Companies that encourage interaction across departments, for example, help their employees to understand more fully how different parts of the business work together to deliver to the customer. Such exchanges also allow

---

[3] See for example Miller, D. (1983). The correlates of entrepreneurship in three types of firms. *Management Science* 29(7): 770–791; Lumpkin, G.T. and G.G. Dess (1996). Clarifying the entrepreneurial orientation construct and linking it to performance. *The Academy of Management Review* 21(1): 135–172; and Covin, J.G. and D.P. Slevin (1991). A conceptual model of entrepreneurship as firm behavior. *Entrepreneurship Theory and Practice* Fall: 7–25.

[4] See also Urban, B. and J. Barreira (2010). Empirical investigations into firm technology orientation and entrepreneurial orientation. *International Journal of Innovation and Technology Management* 7: 329–351.

Dimension	Characteristics	Implications for the Board
Innovations & Autonomy	Time & space for experimentation	Define dashboard of innovation KPIs, shared across departments
	Cross-functional, diverse teams spanning boundaries	Role model a culture of constructive dissent and boundary-spanning
	Openness to discussion and opposing views	Balance of independent and executive directors
Ownership & Proactiveness	Sufficient resourcing / space allowed	Incentive structures which encourage collaboration among the leadership team (shared accountability for success, e.g. R&D Marketing)
	Shared accountability / recognition for success	
	Engagement and initiative	
Passion & Risk-taking	Energy and fun	Some resources allocation for uncertain reward
	Lack of orthodoxy	Role modelling passion
		Directors having 'skin in the game'
		Supporting culture-building initiatives
Competitive Aggressiveness	Identifying competitive space to occupy	Offering perspectives from other industries
		Identifying potential disruptions
	Targeting competitors' consumers	

Figure 25.1   Entrepreneurial Orientation from the Board
Source: Cossin (2020).[5]

people to collaborate and build on one another's ideas. In addition to providing forums for interaction, entrepreneurial firms realise that giving employees some degree of autonomy, in the form of time to explore and pursue innovative ideas, can lead to value-creating initiatives.

Founded in 2002, Australian software company Atlassian is a leading provider of collaboration, development, and issues-tracking products for teams. The firm had its IPO in 2015 and was valued at US$30 billion in the spring of 2019, following years of strong sales growth.[6]

---

[5] Cossin, D. (2020). *Fostering Entrepreneurship from the Board.* IMD Board Center. DOI:10.1002/9781119615705.ch19.

[6] Novet, J. (2019). Atlassian shares hit a record after Goldman analysts recommend buying the stock. 9 May. https://www.cnbc.com/2019/05/09/atlassian-shares-hit-record-after-goldman-recommends-buying-the-stock.html

Atlassian gives its employees space to experiment: 'You have to give people the time and latitude to think creatively', says its co-CEO Mike Cannon-Brookes. Twice a year, the company runs 'Shipit' days, during which teams form and agree on what they think is the most important problem to fix. Each team then has 24 hours to come up with a possible solution. Projects are voted upon in successive rounds until a select few remain. If a solution seems worth developing further, then there is a cross-silo team that has already worked together and is ready to go. One of the benefits of the process is that it allows for creative disagreement, because different teams may think of different ways to fix problems. What's more, the best idea wins, not the one that is owned by the best-connected individual or favoured for other political reasons. Previous Shipit days produced JIRA Service Desk (an enterprise helpdesk software) and Confluence (an enterprise team collaboration software), which now account for a large proportion of the company's sales.

Another approach, often used by larger companies, is to use external sources of innovation to reduce organisational risk in developing new ideas and products. For example, Connect+Develop, introduced by Procter & Gamble (P&G) in 2001, is considered as one of the first crowdsourcing platforms that has since led to many new products. One of them is P&G's US$1 billion brand Febreze, which began as a product to refresh household textiles. As the business developed, P&G saw the potential to grow the brand by broadening into air care more generally, and collaborated with external companies to develop additional Febreze products.

Passion and Risk Taking

To inspire and capture the best ideas from people, companies need to create an environment that stirs their employees' passions. Boards can play a useful role in this process. Directors who demonstrate real commitment and take personal risks for the company – not least in a financial sense, so that they have 'skin in the game' – help to build a company culture in which a sense of ownership can flourish. Board members also need to support management to build this kind of ownership culture.

Boards have an important role to play in bringing passion to a company, but can only perform it if the boardroom culture encourages open exchanges between directors. As we have seen in this chapter, board members may be overly sceptical and inject excessive doubt, suffocating new ideas as they emerge. Building trust at board level is therefore essential if directors are to bring 'crazy' ideas and creativity, and help fan emerging entrepreneurial fires within the company.

Mergers and acquisitions are another area where boards need to balance entrepreneurial instincts with prudent risk assessments. We will look more closely at this in the next chapter.

Consider the case of Zappos CEO Tony Hsieh, who rescued the online shoe and clothing company from certain disaster in 1999. He revived the firm, building annual sales from virtually nothing to US$1 billion. And by pledging to create a culture that empowered employees and made customer service a central priority, Hsieh built Zappos into a unique brand, resulting in the firm's inclusion in Fortune's 'Best Companies to Work for' list. 'Positive office culture assures you of passionate employees, outstanding performance and the ability to attract the best talent,' Hsieh said.[7]

Innovations included a yearly Culture Book (available to anyone interested in its content), a Face Game (in which users score points based on their ability to correctly identify fellow employees), nap rooms, a petting zoo, a bowling alley, karaoke, and other events. Each employee was also challenged to make at least one improvement every week to help Zappos better reflect its core values – including 'be humble', 'do more with less', 'be passionate and determined', and 'create fun and a little weirdness'.

But a growing conflict between Hsieh and the Zappos board ultimately forced the sale of the company to Amazon in 2009 for more than US$1.2 billion. The board viewed what it called 'Tony's social experiments' as PR stunts that were distractions for the business, and pressured Hsieh to focus less on employee happiness and more on selling shoes. Worried that the board might fire him and destroy the company culture, Hsieh approached Amazon, which he believed better understood Zappos' culture.[8]

Over the years, he dedicated himself to rejuvenating downtown Las Vegas, pledging US$350 million in 2013 towards redevelopment. Until his retirement in August 2020, Hsieh stayed with the company as a CEO. Tragically, just three months post-retirement, his vibrant legacy was cut short at the age of 46, succumbing to a house fire.[9]

[7] Hollender, J. (2013). Lessons we can all learn from Zappos CEO Tony Hsieh. *The Guardian*, 13 March. http://www.theguardian.com/sustainable-business/zappos-ceo-tony-hsieh
[8] Hsieh, T. (2010). Why I sold Zappos. *Inc Magazine*. 1 June. http://www.inc.com/magazine/20100601/why-i-sold-zappos.html.
[9] Obituaries. (2020). Tony Hsieh, retired Zappos CEO, dies at 46 after house fire. *Los Angeles Times*, 27 November. https://www.latimes.com/world-nation/story/2020-11-27/tony-hsieh-retired-zappos-ceo-dies-at-46

CHAPTER

26

The Board's Oversight Framework for M&As

Companies are looking beyond industry boundaries and national borders for external growth opportunities. While merger and acquisition (M&A) activity is cyclical, deals themselves have become increasingly complex and sophisticated. This is stretching the abilities of boards, and is compelling directors to devote more time, focus, and dedication to M&A oversight. M&A decisions are among the most important that a board must make. And for many directors, the M&A process is one of the most challenging, frustrating, and dangerous.

Decisions to approve or reject offers are closely watched and criticised by investors, public authorities, and other stakeholders. The directors of the acquiring company may face disapproval for paying too much and leaving money on the table, and must weigh concerns about empire building or egos. They also face mounting pressure from employees, suppliers, customers, the media, and regulators, all of which could be affected by an M&A deal.

In a fast-moving situation, directors are supposed to make all the most important decisions in a very short period of time. Their personal interests are also at stake, because directors of both the acquirer and target companies will often lose their board seats as a result of a deal. The M&A process is a stress test for boards – if anything goes wrong, the directors may be liable for damages for breaches of duty or other alleged transgressions in making the deals. Even when legal liability is less of an issue, the reputational stakes are high. In short, directors are vulnerable when overseeing M&A deals.

This chapter presents an M&A oversight framework for board members. Given the high-stakes role that directors play, deals have to be well conceived and structured, and implemented with discipline. When boards fail in their M&A oversight and succumb to deal mania, the process becomes even more stressful. But the four-stage approach outlined in Figure 26.1 can help directors make better M&A decisions.

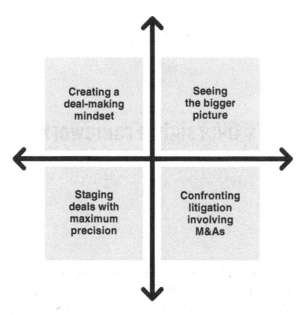

Figure 26.1   M&A Board Orientation

Creating a Deal-making Mindset

M&A deals can start with a simple phone call. In April 2015, Royal Dutch Shell's CEO Ben van Beurden explained how the company's acquisition of BG Group came about. 'I called [BG Group Chair] Andrew [Gould] up and we had a very good and constructive discussion about the idea and it very quickly seemed to make sense to both of us', van Beurden said. In under a month, the two companies arranged a US$70 billion oil megamerger.[1]

Such a phone call may appear to be a sudden event with too much information and urgency. But it may not seem so sudden to experienced directors – they conceive deals all the time, including preparing to buy or sell the business the next day if the price is right. A board with a deal-making mindset will not struggle to make the case for how a certain transaction will fit with the company's strategy.

Boards with strong M&A DNA have institutionalised the merger and acquisition process, possibly with an M&A committee. The task of this committee is to supervise the company's M&A strategy, challenge management's thinking on potential transactions, and analyse potential mergers, acquisitions, investments, or disposals.

---

[1] Zhdannikov, D. and K. Schaps (2015). Sunday telephone call sparked $70 billion Shell-BG deal. 8 April. Reuters.

Such a board is always prepared for transactions, and has current knowledge of how specific deals can create value. Stakeholders, including shareholders, are encouraged to propose deals that might be beneficial. Dry runs are typically organised, with investment bankers presenting a proposal. The deal flow is structured and analysed by looking at the type of acquisitions or buyers that the organisation could target, and possibly mapping them into a matrix. Simulated discussions, outside real transactions, are encouraged.

A quick consensus on the board regarding a deal typically reveals a lack of preparation. Discussions need to be rich and tense, or else the board will certainly fail. Acquisitions are complex, and directors should challenge them. 'Boards must have the diversity of knowledge necessary to grasp the full implications of management's recommendations and to remain independent judges of them', Gould says. 'I am a firm believer that all boards should have their own body of industry specialists amongst the other skills that boards require.'[2]

Contrary opinions can typically be levered into a better deal. To have such opinions, a board needs to have the means and structures to collect adequate information. For example, one director may stress regulatory risk. This led Syngenta to negotiate a large breakup fee with both Monsanto and ChemChina, its potential buyers, in the case of regulatory problems – something that enhanced the overall value of the deal. Good board work on acquisitions will be structured, will require much information and specialisation, and will lever constructive dissent.

Seeing the Bigger Picture

When considering a merger or acquisition, executives and deal advisors are often caught up in the idea of the deal itself, and come close to being enamoured with the transaction (or sometimes hating it!). An active board should be willing to focus on the big picture and investigate the deal's assumptions more deeply in order to reassess all the challenges, risks, and opportunities.

This big picture could be a corporate strategic shift, a stream of similar transactions to support one strategy, or simply an industry trend. Deals driven by a bigger strategy often succeed.

The board's big picture could also relate to the geographic, macro, economic, governance, technological, regulatory, or societal environment.

Staging Deals with Maximum Precision

The board's comprehensive and objective oversight can help management to follow a disciplined process at every stage of a transaction. Figure 26.2 illustrates the six phases of an M&A deal.

---

[2] Andrew Gould HPB presentation at IMD, May 2016.

China's largest business property developer, Dalian Wanda Commercial Properties, a US$40 billion company, signalled a major shift in strategy in the 2010s. Knowing that China's real estate market could have an uncertain future, Dalian Wanda decided to reduce its reliance on property sales and make forays into 'alternative, income-generating businesses away from the property market'.

The CEO of the company, Wang Jianlin, was once the richest man in Asia, known for becoming an aggressive acquirer in pursuing this strategy. Dalian Wanda bought the US cinema chain AMC Theatres in 2012; British yacht maker Sunseeker International in 2013; Infront Sports & Media and the World Triathlon Corporation in 2015; and Legendary Entertainment for US$3.5 billion in 2016. From a strategic shift perspective, the company successfully expanded overseas to diversify away from China's property market, even though it then faced pressures to scale back this foreign expansion.

Despite the success, the financial strain induced by the COVID-19 pandemic significantly impacted Dalian Wanda. By 2023, reports emerged that the company was exploring the sale of its sports marketing division to bolster its financial position.[3]

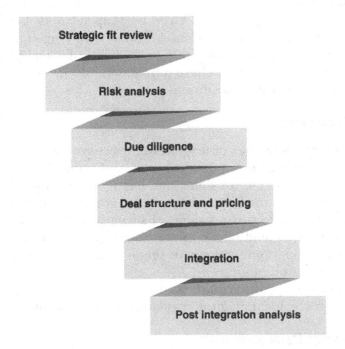

Figure 26.2 A Board M&A Process

---

[3] Crowley, A.-J., E.-V. Farr, and M. Vinn (2023). Exclusive: Dalian Wanda weighs sale of Olympics rights manager Infront – sources. 18 August, Reuters. https://www.reuters.com/markets/deals/dalian-wanda-weighs-sale-olympics-media-rights-manager-infront-sources-2023-08-17/

Strategy Fit Review

The board needs to understand clearly why the deal is being proposed. With a majority of M&A deals well demonstrated to be destroying value, directors need to be convinced that this particular deal is different. They should ask questions such as:

- How was the deal sourced and what alternative deals are being considered?
- What are the potential and unique benefits?
- What is the key driver of the deal: to strengthen core business, acquire a technology, establish market presence, or gain market share from competitors?
- How realistic are the underlying assumptions about synergies? (Synergies are typically highly overvalued by executives and advisors alike. Integration needs to be thought through from the start.)
- Does the culture of the target align with that of the acquirer? (Culture clashes are the number one cause of integration failure.)

The board has a responsibility to be independent, create an open discussion environment, encourage debate, and keep dominant individuals in check (such as the CEO or a particular board member). In this way, everyone can contribute openly to the strategic fit analysis. This is particularly important when a CEO puts his or her job on the line if a deal is not approved – raising the question of why they are so motivated to transact.

Some deals have been ripe with conflicts of interest. These include Glencore's 2013 acquisition of mining company Xstrata, when Xstrata management was financially incentivised to sell, and the Glencore CEO sat on the Xstrata board. Glencore had begun investing in Xstrata in the 1990s, to leverage the benefits of controlling production in addition to trade.

Risk Analysis

No matter how diligently the board works, there are always information gaps and uncertainty. M&As can create tremendous value, but most of it is never captured by acquirers. And although there is no doubt that acquisitions can offer growth opportunities, such deals are by their nature complex and risky. In any M&A strategy, opportunity is accompanied by risk and uncertainty.

Deals often have financial risks. Boards therefore need to assess the sensitivities of net present values to growth rates, input prices, and discount rates. But directors' risk analysis must go well beyond this and cover human dynamics too. Egos and office politics typically prevent objective debate within the leadership team, advisors make deals for fees and are not accountable for the results, and leadership differences may exist between the acquirer and the target. Human factors could also lead to other risks, such as a flawed strategic rationale, pricing discrepancies, financing flaws, and poor post-acquisition execution.

'My observation from both near and far is that the human failing is by far the most critical element in badly judged large M&A transactions. The ability to retain the power of the CEO role and the degree of intellectual humility necessary to execute it properly is not given to many people', Gould writes. 'Hubris is an occupational hazard for leaders, it feeds on isolation, and business leaders can deceive themselves and distance themselves from reality. . . It is important to point out that hubris syndrome can be acquired during the exercise of power and may disappear once the individual has left the position of influence.'[4]

Regulatory barriers are considered to be one of the biggest threats to global M&As, with 71% of executives in a survey in 2016 blaming competition regulators for their failed deals.[5] A record number of deals are being blocked or abandoned as a result of antitrust hurdles – including Comcast's US$45 billion offer for Time Warner Cable, which was abandoned after regulators raised concerns that the deal would create a monopoly. In addition, the US authorities have blocked some M&A deals on national security grounds. In March 2018, for example, US President Donald Trump blocked a proposed US$117 billion buyout of US chipmaker Qualcomm by Singapore-incorporated BroadCom.

Regulatory concerns vary by sector, according to the above survey. In the energy, mining, and natural resources industry, executives cited environmental regulations as their biggest concern when considering future deals. In the telecommunications, media, and technology sector, meanwhile, data protection and cybersecurity regulations are the top concerns. During deal structuring, it has become commonplace to include heavy penalties – often on the bidder – if the transaction is not subsequently approved.

In general, the risk of integration failure is the top M&A concern for boards, as capturing synergy is one of the biggest risks. To make integration work, boards have to communicate constantly with stakeholders, stabilise the morale of their respective companies, supervise the integration of structures and processes, and approve specific initiatives to achieve the strategic objectives. Some boards shed the decision responsibility and opt instead for co-CEOs, co-Chairs, or two headquarters. A good example of this was the Lafarge Holcim merger of two proud competitors, which involved a delicate balance of power. But such a practice usually does not work in the long term.

---

[4] Andrew Gould, Chair BG, in IMD High Performance Boards presentation.
[5] Smith Freehills, H., FT Remark, and MergerMarket (2016). Beyond borders: the future of dealmaking. 18 April. https://www.herbertsmithfreehills.com/insights/2016-04/beyond-borders-the-future-of-dealmaking

Either one company comes to dominate the other, or the two firms work separately rather than as one unified entity.

Due Diligence

Due diligence is a critical process to validate accounting and technical information and the acquisition rationale, in order to obtain a true understanding of the target company and how the transaction might advance the buyer's intended strategy. For larger transactions, management should present the board with a report describing the scope, timeline, and resources for each due diligence phase, along with the due diligence results of each phase.

A thorough due diligence process could include commercial and operational matters; legal, financial accounting, and tax issues; employee benefits and human resources; the US Foreign Corrupt Practices Act; reputation, integration and synergy, and insurance; and environmental and engineering factors. Boards should oversee the entire process.[6]

Due diligence should address not only the financial side of the deal, but also non-financial aspects related to its technological, operational, and reputational dimensions. Regarding the tangibles, boards need to devote sufficient time to any possible issues related to intellectual property and technology before these cause damage. But directors also need to do their non-financial due diligence and look at the intangibles – including the compatibility of culture, the reaction from stakeholders, and the morale of employees.

In driving non-financial due diligence, a board can ask various questions. What if stakeholders do not like the deal? What will happen to the morale of the employees of both companies? What if the highly specialised people and top talents do not believe in the deal? How can all the intangibles be managed? The board must undertake a thorough, well-documented investigation before acting.

Deal Structure and Pricing

Boards should be especially vigilant when evaluating the financial aspects of a deal. How much value will truly be created, and is the premium paid worth it? And who is pricing the deal? Investment bankers are typically conflicted, but internal teams may have their own motivations as well. Sometimes many elements are hidden in a complex structure, using partial share and options deals, or a staggered payment scheme such as earnouts. Although these can reveal a smart risk management strategy that alleviates overpricing risk, they can also hide a certain complacency: it is always easier to pay in shares than in cash!

---

[6] Deloitte. (2016). M&A: The intersection of due diligence and governance. May.

In addition, boards should consider all the alternatives to acquisitions – such as joint ventures, organic growth, alliances, and partnerships – as well as the reason why the acquisition is more promising, and not only more stimulating emotionally.

While Monsanto's offer set a benchmark for valuing Syngenta, pricing could become a secondary consideration for ChemChina. The company's investment in Syngenta was widely seen as a way to secure food supplies for China's huge population and have access to Syngenta's intellectual property and crop care technology. Unlike Monsanto, ChemChina had no incentive to dismantle, reintegrate, and sell parts of Syngenta to extract synergies, thus making it a more credible partner for the company's employees and society at large.

Integration

Before approving a deal, directors need to review the integration plan and assess its realism. What is the timeline? How fast can the target company be integrated? What are the expected problems? Who will lead the integration? Ideally this person will already be involved in the pre-deal and deal process. Company culture is a particularly sensitive integration issue, and thus differences and compatibilities are high on the board's deal risk map. People, and which key positions to retain, are also an important consideration. Both culture and people should therefore be part of the integration KPIs. And the board should be updated regularly on the progress of the integration against these and other indicators.

Companies often underestimate the timing and cost involved in completing an overseas integration. In some jurisdictions there are significant employment entitlements, requiring a complex consultation with the affected

Companies need to have strong in-house structuring and pricing skills. Otherwise, they will put themselves in the hands of others and risk overpaying directly or indirectly (through a poor structure, for example). Vodafone's US$183 billion takeover of Mannesmann in 2000 was the biggest cross-border bid in history. In total, Vodafone paid 56 times earnings, a 72% premium to Mannesmann's closing share price. Five years later, Vodafone announced that it was taking a goodwill charge of US$40 billion. The company admitted that the record post-acquisition write-down was due to overpayment. This deal destroyed significant value, largely because the flawed valuation was done by outsiders.

Boards should be aware that, regardless of the sophisticated financial models used in pricing, valuation is always relative. Value is measured in the eyes of the beholder. What may provide value to one acquirer or target may not provide the same value for others. At the same time, there is no deal that is good enough regardless of the price. Overpricing often causes the acquirer to fail, because it reveals a lack of discipline – and not only financial.

employees. Such factors could become obstacles to successful integration. Thus, those responsible for leading the integration will ideally already be involved at the pre-deal negotiation stage.

Post-integration Analysis

Finally, boards need to review regularly the integration after acquisition along a series of questions:

Do we have a strong process for tracking deal success?

Are we achieving the strategic goals?

Have we focused on the right issues?

Ideally, such a step will already have been planned from an early stage of the deal negotiation.

Confronting Litigation Involving M&As

In the M&A process, board directors are vulnerable to litigation in many legal environments – not least in the United States, where 9 out of 10 M&A transactions are legally contested by investors.[7] A board's failure to complete all the required homework on a deal, including obtaining adequate insurance coverage, could result in significant damage to the deal and the company. The following five examples illustrate how litigation typically arises when boards fail to handle deals properly.

Conflicts of Interest

Conflicts of interest continue to dominate the discussions in M&A litigation. Typical conflicts include the involvement of a large shareholder in the deal, management negotiating employment and compensation packages during the deal, and advisors' dealings on all sides. Boards that fail in their oversight here could be sued for breaching their duty of care.

In 2011, Barclays Capital and Del Monte Corp agreed to pay the food company's shareholders to settle a case that raised a conflict of interest. The Delaware Court of Chancery found that the advisor, Barclays, helped with the buy-side financing and failed to disclose its relationship with the target. It also found that Del Monte's board failed to provide the oversight that would have checked Barclays' misconduct. Del Monte paid US$65.7 million of the

---

[7] Cornerstone Research. (2015). Shareholder litigation involving acquisitions of public companies. February.

settlement, while Barclays Capital paid the remaining US$23.7 million, according to the court filings.

Lack of Disclosure

In M&A deals, class-action lawsuits are often filed, alleging that boards have failed in disclosure – for example, concerning the existence of the M&A negotiations, the deal terms, or other material information about the transaction. This could cause a dilemma for the boards of target companies. If the disclosure is too early, shareholders could allege that they were injured by the premature announcement; but if the disclosure is too late, shareholders could claim that they were injured because they sold their shares before the merger announcement and the subsequent large price increase.

Lawsuits can also be brought against the acquiring company. These might allege that the board failed to disclose the M&A negotiations, or the deal's future prospects and effect on the acquiring company, in a full and timely manner. These suits can involve huge potential damages for companies on both sides of M&A deals.

Hostile and Friendly Takeover

The directors of a target company who resist a hostile takeover could be sued. Shareholders could allege that the board members breached their fiduciary duty and denied them the opportunity to profit from the high offer price.

The directors of a target company who approve a friendly takeover could also be sued. Disgruntled shareholders could allege that the company was being sold for too little, and that the directors made a bad decision.

Pre-acquisition Mismanagement

After an acquisition, the new company may sue the previous directors and executives of the target company, claiming that they mismanaged the business prior to the deal. This is problematic for the prior directors and board, since they no longer control the company and may have no insurance coverage.

Post-acquisition Mismanagement

After the acquisition, the board and directors of the acquiring company can be sued in connection with their management of the target firm. This might happen when the new management team has little experience of operating in a particular industry or market.

Boards need to take an increasingly sophisticated approach to the M&A process. Yet the main principles are simple:

- creating a deal-making mindset, with strong due diligence and risk analysis;
- seeing the bigger picture;
- staging deals with maximum precision, including structuring, pricing and integration;
- confronting litigation involving M&As.

Boards and directors are crucial in helping their companies capture value during the M&A process and reduce the risk of failure. I encourage every board and director to consider the four principles above when preparing for their company's next M&A transaction.

In this chapter we saw how corporate culture can often be crucial to the success or failure of an M&A deal. We now return to the issue of boardroom culture, and to the key relationship between the chair and CEO.

Acknowledgement

This chapter was initially written as an article with Abraham Lu.

Boards and Oversight of KPIs

KPIs are a Language – and are Indispensable for Boards

The term KPIs has been bandied about so extensively that in many executives' and directors' minds, it is largely synonymous with targets, metrics in general. In reality, good-quality KPIs are increasingly seen as both drivers of a company's strong performance and key outcomes of effective boards' discussions. In the context of governance, they allow boards to assess how likely the company's strategies are to succeed in the long term. As instruments of organisational learning, KPIs help boards and companies grapple with a constantly shifting competitive, technological, geopolitical, and societal landscape.

KPIs allow a board to ensure that the company is using resources appropriately and efficiently. To that end, KPIs capture financial and non-financial performance as well as the use of budget. In today's organisational and board environments, however, there is no hiding from the strategy conversation. Studies show that in the absence of coherent, data-driven vocabulary to aid directors' oversight, boards will often be forced to resort to proxies.[1]

When properly defined and tracked, KPIs can enable boards to enforce their expanding mandate in overseeing the strategy process and the company's ability to handle risk as well as future-proof the business. Well-crafted KPIs are a source of board members' shared understanding in their oversight of how the company is executing on its long-term strategy. But how unbiased can they truly be? There an elevated board can challenge the strategic thinking behind while preserving the tactical advantage of KPIs. Indeed, a robust body of KPIs will facilitate performance management, improve decision-making, and enhance accountability.

---

[1] Massicotte, S. and Henri, J.F. (2021). The use of management accounting information by boards of directors to oversee strategy implementation. *The British Accounting Review*, 53(3): 100953.

KPIs Need to be Credible to be Useful

From a governance standpoint, effective KPIs are those that are directly linked to strategy and risk, enable the board to raise timely and pertinent questions, and help identify where the underlying issue may be. These are some of their attributes:

Clearly connected to strategic objectives, as opposed to operational goals. The scope, form, time frame, and structure of specific KPIs are useful only to the extent that they align with the company strategy, industry, and organisational structure. As a measure of performance against a specific target, a KPI should be underpinned by a set of criteria that signal success in achieving a strategic objective. A simple question to ask is: '*How will we know when we have achieved the end goal?*' In a retail bank that has adopted agile ways of working, for instance, the KPI of '80% of squads delivering their tasks on time and on budget' works. It is a do-or-die indicator that the agile model and architecture are bearing fruit, have achieved scale, and are manifesting the company's long-term strategic vision of a competitive, innovative and predominantly digital player.

The measure is easy to understand. Existing benchmarks are available. The executive team is responsible for establishing the most relevant performance measures, while the board's responsibility is to ensure that these KPIs are appropriate to track progress against strategic goals. That means that KPIs need to be well scoped and backed by precise targets and metrics. Fundamentally, they are designed to measure variables that indicate progress towards achieving objectives – and to make the causal link with those objectives as unambiguous as possible.

A mix of leading and lagging indicators. KPIs should be both leading (forward-looking) and lagging (backward-looking) in nature. Leading indicators are introduced to predict other operational or financial outcomes. Examples include average cycle times, defect rate, or number of products a customer purchases. Lagging indicators, on the other hand, are typically used to confirm what has recently happened and to identify patterns. These tend to be financial metrics that track how well the organisation is doing. Examples include profits, revenue, expenses, renewal rate, or customer count.

They are a component in external reporting and/or are required to be presented at board level. Boards don't need to reinvent the wheel with every KPI. There is no dearth of industry association-defined measures of excellence the board can adapt for its own use. For a retail bank, those may include areas such as service innovation, digital innovation, digital wealth, and frictionless and omnichannel service delivery. Where absolute measures are not readily available or practicable, relative-to-peer indicators may be applicable.

Have a bearing on risks and other areas that are of concern to the board. KPIs could measure the quality of relationships with key stakeholders, and enable the board to anticipate and manage stakeholder pressures. They could also track regulatory changes, competitive shifts, geopolitical tensions and major tech developments – and as such serve as early warning signals.

Provide answers to pointed questions. Facilitate learning. A relevant KPI will help answer fundamental questions. In doing so, it will identify current as well as emerging gaps in strategising and knowledge. This is a crucial quality in a complex business landscape where strategic assumptions may be competing or even contradictory – for example, maximising shareholder returns in the short term balanced with achieving Net Zero commitments in the long term.

An effective board will strive to ensure that the KPIs it oversees are: **1. well-scoped** (relevant); **2. well-aligned** (with strategic objectives); **3. well-structured** (reflective of actual progress); **4. robust** (providing clarity on causal links between metrics and objectives); **5. comprehensive** (covering the full range of strategic objectives); and address the full array of **6. stakeholder relationships**.

Zooming in on the KPIs that Matter – and that Tell a Story of How the Company Creates Value

Once the board has a well-defined set of KPIs in place, is it assured of the ability to track and measure success? Not always. Sooner or later, many directors become concerned that pursuing KPI targets is not necessarily synonymous with managing the company's long-term health. Like all numbers, KPIs have a way of taking on a life and logic of their own. Disconnects and disincentives creep in, as do unintended consequences. A sense of arbitrariness may linger in the air. In a worst-case scenario, a company may find its KPIs working at cross-purposes with long-term strategy.

KPIs Should Measure What is Critical

In order to be meaningful, KPIs need to relate to the company's priorities if it is to deliver on its long-term strategic vision. When defining indicators, it is essential to go beyond revenue and profitability, to track the health of its strategic drivers (are they improving, worsening, stagnant?). Take employee satisfaction – once upon a time, it amounted to little more than the output of an internal survey. That was before companies realised what a powerful predictor it really was for customer satisfaction and retention. If innovation is the lifeblood of the enterprise, rather than measuring R&D spend, consider a metric that relates to cross-functional collaboration (increasingly important for the development of game-changing products and services) – for example the number of ideas or projects that result from cross-functional interactions.

The difficulty in wading into non-financial territory, however, should not be underestimated. Across different surveys, close to 100% of directors consider non-financial KPIs as critical. At the same time, 50–60% of directors typically agree that their boards do not receive good information on these KPIs. Interestingly, academic research tells us that monitoring non-financial KPIs and the related disclosure practices is influenced by the quality of the board.[2] In other words, it takes a good deal of creativity, openness, and strong divergent thinking on the part of board members to pick non-financial KPIs that will tell a coherent and relevant story.

To overcome the difficulty, directors may be tempted to cast the net wide and come up with a long list of KPIs. That will rarely work well. It is best to stay focused and indeed three to five critical measurements – if well selected, defined and traced across time – may be all that a company department needs to monitor. Having too many KPIs tends to dilute attention and result in a data dump rather than an inspired discussion. By the same token, in many contexts an effective KPI can be remarkably straightforward: 10 new app features per year. Zero passenger fatality rate. KPIs may even take the form of Yes/No. Done/Not done. (Some companies may end up wrestling with the 'definition of Done', but that is another topic.)

A Keen Focus on Value Creation

In a landscape of ecosystems thinking and blurred company (and industry) boundaries, boards will do well to gain a better understanding of their companies' value drivers (sometimes called performance drivers) and where and how specific KPIs track these. Value drivers are factors that increase the worth of the business or enhance the prospect of future growth. They represent parameters that the business can influence and that will have a material effect on the company's performance. They track what really defines success for an organisation.

Amid growing complexity, it is essential to map the different elements of the company's business system or value chain, to understand better which elements are dependent on other elements – in other words, what drives the

---

[2] Bini, L., Giunta, F., Miccini, R., and Simoni, L. (2023). Corporate governance quality and non-financial KPI disclosure comparability: UK evidence. *Journal of Management and Governance* 27: 43–74.

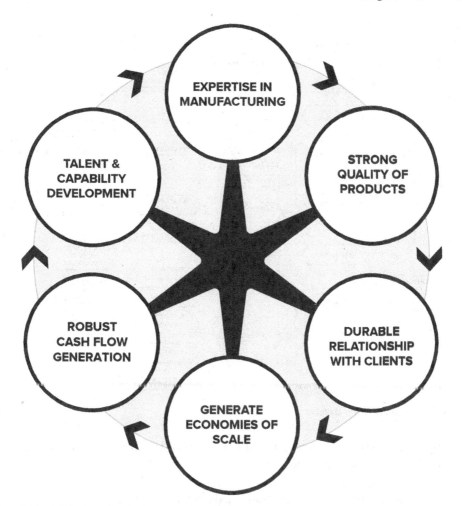

Figure 27.1   A Value Creation Flywheel for a Manufacturer

value of the business. A value chain or a flywheel concept may help map these. See a simple example in Figure 27.1 of a flywheel landed during a board discussion that will inspire KPI structure.

In Figure 27.2, a more advanced financial drivers mapping can help as well.

KPIs Help Diminish Substantial Business Risks Linked to ESG

To stay mitigate risk linked to growing ESG regulations and investor pressures, stakeholder, social and environmental metrics are increasingly important to track. There has been growing interest among boards and investors in operationalising ESG oversight. As such, boards need to ensure that management has put forward KPIs that track the material topics for the organisation.

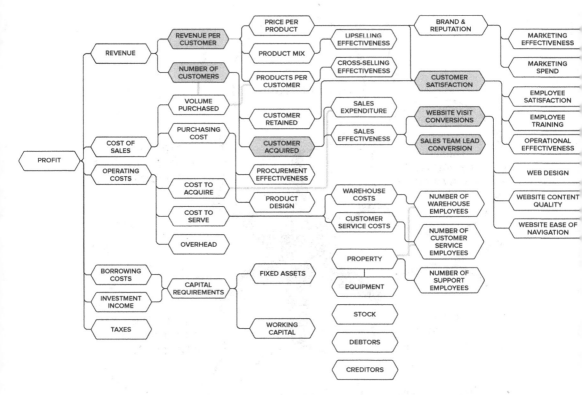

Figure 27.2   Financial Driver Mapping

Among other tasks, the board should be involved in the process of selecting standards frameworks such as:

- Sustainability Accounting Standards Board (SASB);
- Climate Disclosure Standards Board (CDSB);
- Task Force on Climate-related Financial Disclosures (TCFD);
- Greenhouse Gas (GHG) Protocol; and
- Global Reporting Initiative (GRI).[3]

Although standardising ESG performance measures has been a work in progress, market consensus has been solidifying on ESG performance and its relationship to company value. Market players recognise that companies with high ratings for ESG factors present an overall lower risk than their competitors[4]. In the meantime, supervisory boards at companies like ING have

[3] Sullivan, K., M. Bujno, and J. Raphael (2022). The role of the board in overseeing ESG. Deloitte. https://www2.deloitte.com/us/en/pages/center-for-board-effectiveness/articles/role-of-the-board-in-overseeing-esg.html

[4] Whelan, T., U. Atz, and C. Clark. (n.d). ESG and Financial Performance. https://sri360.com/wp-content/uploads/2022/10/NYU-RAM_ESG-Paper_2021-2.pdf

One example of an investment firm that was able to successfully challenge a company's KPIs, on the basis that it was not factoring in enough ESG factors that posed an 'existential threat' was US activist and impact investment firm Engine No. 1 (whose tagline is: A new way of seeing value). It successfully campaigned to replace four members of ExxonMobil's board of directors despite owning only 0.02% of the company's shares. In this way, it was able to challenge more traditional KPIs, in order convince Exxon's large shareholders, including BlackRock, The Vanguard Group and State Street, to back its plans, that Exxon's focus on fossil fuels threatened future returns. Since then, Engine No. 1 has launched two ESG funds. Instead of excluding companies based on ESG criteria, these funds seek to align companies that it invests in with its ESG goals, taking an active role in corporate governance. We find it useful to refer to Engine No. 1's ESG goals in considering KPIs (see Appendix 27A).

created special, *ad hoc* ESG Committees, composed of board members, that are responsible for supervising ESG performance and advising management on dilemmas to be addressed.

KPIs and Human Capital

Human capital has a major impact on an organisation's ability to create value and sustain growth.[5] Investors increasingly emphasise the link between human capital and firm performance, and the need for board oversight of human capital. COVID-19 has accelerated this trend. By 2019, asset managers such as Blackrock had called for greater board diversity, corporate strategy and allocation, compensation that promotes long-termism, counters environmental risks, and supports opportunities and human capital management. More regulatory, political, and other governing bodies are requiring human capital management reporting. Board members need to understand which human capital dimensions are strategic, and determine which indicators best track the health of these dimensions over time (refer to Chapter 29 for a more detailed discussion).[6]

A Dynamic Approach to KPIs

At board level, KPIs can work as a dashboard – one that is dynamic rather than static. The board's task is to review the dashboard on a regular basis to answer the following question: 'Given the company strategy, what performance data would be the strongest indication of a successful strategy implementation?'

---

[5] IntegratedReporting.(n.d.).Creatingvalue.https://www.integratedreporting.org/wp-content/uploads/2017/05/CreatingValueHumanCapitalK1.pdf

[6] Abel, A.L., R. Washington, R.L. Ray, and S. Charas. (2020). Brave new world creating long-term value through human capital management and disclosure. The Conference Board. https://www.conference-board.org/topics/human-capital-benchmarking/brave-new-world-creating-value-through-HCM

There may well be attractive indicators out there for which data is not yet available – and that is acceptable. The board may tag such an indicator as 'To Be Included' and outline future actions that are required to source the data in question.

A strong board will regard KPIs as an evolving subset of PIs. Although committee-level work may well involve a detailed review of PIs, only high-level PIs will be presented to the board for its deliberations. Similarly, the board may opt to make adjustments to the PIs and KPIs on a regular basis, highlighting some as new KPIs and relegating others to PIs as appropriate.

When taking a high-level view of whether KPIs are doing their job, board directors may wish to consider the following five essential questions when assessing if their KPIs are fit for purpose:

1. Are our KPIs in alignment with our values and with our purpose?
2. Do we have too superficial an approach to KPIs?
3. Do we use KPIs to transform the organisation? Are they forward-looking?
4. Do we use our KPIs to reflect the issues that are likely to make a strong difference to the organisation and key stakeholders?
5. Do we have too many irrelevant KPIs? Can we discard some of our KPIs?

In the same vein, according to a Data Warehousing Institute metrics report, effective KPIs will cascade from strategic dashboards to tactical and operational dashboards.[7] This trickle-down effect – from the boardroom to the day-to-day operations – is a powerful factor in fostering an organisation's culture of performance and feedback (Figure 27.3).

Recognising that KPIs are a means to an end – the end being intelligence, rapid adaptability, and learning, the board should allow for innovation in KPIs as well as in setting out parallel and alternative methods and procedures in constructing PIs and tracking improvements, particularly on the customer-facing frontline.

Hi-tech Display and Review of KPIs

In an environment of complexity and uncertainty, the issues and objectives that KPIs reflect become more three-dimensional. Presenting KPIs as rows on a spreadsheet may not cut it with today's business audiences. Agility goes hand in hand with prioritisation – often powered by dynamic tools like Kanban

[7] Sontag, M. (n.d.). tracking success: 7 characteristics of effective KPIs. https://www.repsly.com/blog/consumer-goods/tracking-progress-the-7-characteristics-of-an-effective-kpi#:~:text=Effective%20KPIs%20%E2%80%9Ccascade%20from..,staff%20that%20are%20effecting%20them

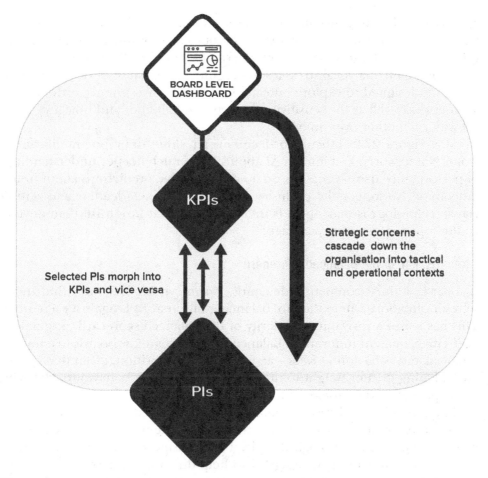

Figure 27.3   Board-level Oversight of KPIs

boards. Vibrant and clear visual displays such as priority maps and dedicated KPI boards can help board members to make sense of data quickly.

Digital and AI have likewise been a game changer in how companies go about setting and evaluating KPIs. With huge volumes of data at their fingertips, tracking and reviewing KPIs in real-time, and at individual, team, and company units of analysis has become a legitimate expectation. At the same time, companies are exploring ways of leveraging AI systems to design what they term smart KPIs. Smart KPIs can be descriptive – analysing historical and current data; predictive – anticipating future performance and potential outcomes; and prescriptive – making actionable recommendations.

This new generation of tools and techniques is invaluable as boards and board committees examine KPIs that resemble clusters of moving targets. Capital and finance committees, for instance, are taking a multidisciplinary approach to due diligence in order to review the use and allocation of capital and map it onto the company's strategic objectives, ratings aspirations, and other goals and targets. In reviewing risks, the board of Prudential Financial has adopted an analytical stress-testing regime that includes a variety of stress scenarios designed to explore outcomes across the investment portfolios and businesses, as well as the sensitivity of assets and liabilities and how they interact with each other over time.[8]

Was Figure 27.2 difficult to decipher, let alone draw out ramifications from? Not to worry: Fed into an AI application, much deeper understandings of performance drivers emerge. So do more reliable predictions about future outcomes.[9] No longer the exclusive domain of business leaders and statisticians, technology is making KPIs more dynamic and insightful than anyone could hope for just a few years ago.

A Renaissance of the Balanced Scorecard

As boards address competing demands, it is inevitable that they find themselves in situations where they are balancing different KPIs against each other. This has led to a revival in popularity of the balanced scorecard, originally a 1980s management innovation. Balanced scorecards allow boards to combine financial and behavioural KPIs – an appealing proposition, given that boards are assigning greater weight to metrics such as culture, behaviours, diversity, risk exposure, and customer outcomes.

For example, until recently boards rarely discussed cyber-security issues. In directors' minds, cyber-security was a budget item, a regulatory requirement, or a purely technological topic. Today business scorecards have come onstream that are specially designed to help directors achieve cyber-security resilience. These novel tools combine business context-based insights and metrics on the biggest cyber-security risks facing the company with data on the investments that management has made to mitigate the risks and their impact. The output enables board members to engage in meaningful discussions and evaluations of their organisation's cyber-security resilience.[10]

KPIs for Board Members

When designing their dashboard, board members need to ensure they don't simply accept the KPIs that management proposes. Instead, ensuring that board

---

[8] Prudential Financial, Inc. 2022 Annual Report.

[9] Kiron, D. et al. (2023). Governance for smarter KPIs. *MIT Sloane Management Review*, 6 November. https://sloanreview.mit.edu/article/governance-for-smarter-kpis/

[10] Pearlson, K. and M. Prakash (2024). Board level balanced scorecard for cyber resilience. Proceedings of the 57th Hawaii International Conference on System Science.

members understand the value drivers and key risks is fundamental to their design. When designed with precision and backed with accurate data, KPIs are valuable tools for board decision-making that is focused and grounded – to ensure the company stays on course and better anticipate risks ahead.

Appendix 27A

CHECKLIST

Robust and comprehensive KPIs   In cases where boards want to drill down further, for example in the case of suspected crisis or underperformance, the following may assist in helping the board to explore where metrics may be lacking:

1. **Strategy, Corporate Purpose, and ESG**
   - How is management ensuring that stakeholder considerations and ESG matters are integrated into strategic and business decisions, as well as enterprise risk management? Are there appropriate metrics to measure performance against goals, to ensure that disclosure controls and procedures support both voluntary and mandated ESG disclosure? Does management compensation include some element of ESG incentive-related compensation?
   - Does the company engage in ESG efforts, including support for education, health care, food security, supplier diversity, and social justice?
   - To what extent is the company engaging in ESG disclosure and related materiality considerations in the company's reporting efforts, and on the corporate website?
   - Are there standards and policies regarding sustainability and social responsibility, including environmental issues, lobbying and political contributions, and human rights?
   - How is management staying informed of developments and trends in ESG disclosure, regulatory statements and guidance, statements by significant institutional investors, shareholder proposal trends, activities of non-governmental standard setters, peer company benchmarking, and federal legislation?

2. **Financial**
   Capital access
   - How is the company currently leveraged?
   - How do bank covenant restrictions impact the business and its future plans?
   - Do shareholders have to provide equity or personally guarantee loans? Is bringing in an outside investor and issuing preferred stock a viable option?

Financial performance

- How does the company compare in terms of liquidity, activity, profitability, and solvency measures?
- Are financial controls in place?
- Are the financials audited or reviewed by an outside CPA?

3. Risk

- To what extent is the company's strategy consistent with the agreed-upon risk appetite and tolerance for the company?
- To what extent is the CEO accountable for building and maintaining an effective risk appetite framework and providing the board with regular, periodic reports on the company's residual risk status?
- Is the executive compensation structure appropriate in light of the company's articulated risk appetite and risk culture, and is it creating proper incentives in light of the risks the company faces?
- Is there sufficient independence in the risk management function and the processes for resolution and escalation of differences that might arise between risk management and business functions?
- What are the primary elements comprising the company's risk culture? Does the 'tone from the top' reflect the company's core values and the expectation that employees act with integrity and promptly escalate non-compliance in and outside the organisation?
- Are internal systems of formal and informal communication across divisions and control functions in place to encourage prompt flow of risk-related information within and across business units and (where needed) timely escalation of information to senior management (and to the board or board committees as appropriate)?
- Are reports from management, independent auditors, internal auditors, legal counsel, regulators, market analysts, and outside experts considered appropriate regarding risks the company faces and the company's risk management function?

Specifically, when it comes to cyber-security risk, the following elements are important factors to consider and measure performance:

- Have the company's mission-critical data and systems been identified?
- Is there an actionable cyber-incident response plan in place that designates responsibilities among critical employees, includes procedures for containment, mitigation, and continuity of operations, and identifies necessary notifications to be issued as part of an established notification plan?

- Has the company developed and deployed effective response technology and services (such as off-site data back-up mechanisms, intrusion detection technology, and data loss prevention technology)?
- Are prior authorisations in place to permit network monitoring?
- Is the company's legal counsel conversant with technology systems and cyber-incident management to reduce response time?
- Have relationships with cyber information-sharing organisations and law enforcement been established?

4. Human Capital

Metrics in this field are rapidly evolving and need to be tuned to the specificities of the human capital of the firm. They may include human resources, compensation and benefits, diversity and inclusion, but also risk management and governance:

- Does the talent strategy support the business strategy?
- How does the performance incentive structure reinforce equity (this could include for example metrics on minimum rates of pay, pay equity analysis, CEO Pay Ratio, % employees bonus eligible, level of pay competitiveness)?
- Diversity and inclusion (new hire, turnover and promotion rates for diverse employees, % diverse leadership, percentage of workforce completed unconscious bias training).
- How effective are production/service capabilities?
- What is the depth and breadth of management?
- Are there any key person dependencies in terms of technical knowledge, production skills, or customer contacts?
- Is there a management succession plan?

Some boards also look at HC Financial metrics, including revenue generated per FTE, Human Capital Return on Investment, Human Economic Value Added, and Human Capital Market Value.

5. Shareholder Activism and Engagement

- Does senior management actively oversee and participate as appropriate in engagement with key shareholders? Do they listen and learn about shareholder viewpoints and develop enduring relationships?
- How does management seek to understand key shareholders' views about corporate purpose, and how it relates to ESG issues, such as climate change, DEI, and corporate culture?
- How does senior management stay informed of proxy advisor perspectives?

- Does management actively seek to understand how shareholder activists view the company, including its strategies and governance practices? How is this information used to identify vulnerabilities?
- How actively is management monitoring changes in share ownership?
- Are defence preparation plans being updated and activated if needed? This many include identifying special proxy fight counsel, reviewing structural defences, putting a poison pill on the shelf, and developing a 'break-the-glass' communications plan.

6. Crisis Management

- Does the company have business continuity plans in place that are appropriate and adequate to the potential risks of disruption identified, and that account for relevant contingencies?
- Is there an up-to-date crisis management plan to assist the company in reacting appropriately, without either under- or overreacting?

CHAPTER 28

The Talent Pipeline

T alent has become a critical resource and an integral component of a company's overall business strategy. The governance discussion has therefore also shifted to focus on human capital, and on talent oversight as part of strategic planning. In particular, a company's ability to build its pipeline of effective leaders has become a strategic consideration. This is often referred to as leadership 'bench strength' – the capabilities and readiness of potential successors to move into key professional and leadership positions.

Although issues of human capital and capabilities are not new to board agendas, a board's oversight mandate has often been seen primarily in terms of risk governance, ethics, and corporate responsibility rather than talent. And when boards did play a part in issues related to talent, their involvement typically focused on appointing, mentoring, and monitoring the performance of the CEO, alongside board composition, tenure, and appointments.

The Board's Responsibility for Talent Management

Now that corporations have universally recognised talent as the key ingredient in their success, and acknowledged that the 'war for talent' rages on unabated, where does that leave the board? What is the board's responsibility in terms of the organisation's talent management?

Depending on the specific issue, boards get involved at different levels. At the basic operational level, many boards are doing more of what they have been doing for years: they are expanding their oversight of management's activities related to talent acquisition, development, retention, and employee engagement throughout the organisation. Directors may be expected to examine talent supply and demand data as part of capital investment and business strategy reviews on an annual basis, or even more frequently. This includes developing learning paths for high-potential individuals across the organisation. As in other areas of governance, the board acts to foster high productivity and performance.

However, in the new people- and talent-focused landscape, there is more to be done in the boardroom than supervising long-standing hiring procedures. Proactive boards will identify key positions within the organisation's leadership (it may be a handful of posts or a couple of hundred). They will actively learn about the talent pipeline that is in place to fill different types of positions, especially should a particular role need to be filled urgently in the future. With top jobs, such as that of CEO, the board will recognise that recruiting for the C-suite is commonly coordinated at a global level. Effective boards will have a succession plan in place, as well as a set of predefined metrics to gauge the new CEO's job performance and its effect on the company's results and reputation.

In addition to procedural considerations, the board should have an instinctive, almost visceral appreciation for the type of leader the company needs for the context, as well as a few years later. The ideal candidate's professional experience, industry background, leadership style, and track record, and to some extent even nationality and personality, must be a good fit with the current juncture in the company's growth, and also with the challenges ahead. Does the firm need someone who will tread lightly and respect the delicate consensus that has been established within the organisation over the years? Or has complacency set in, meaning that the company needs a leader who will shake things up and disturb the old order? Or will the new CEO's main task be to keep tabs on spending and restore financial discipline?

Whether the company is aiming for radical transformation, a return to profitability, aggressive expansion, or another scenario, the new CEO chosen by the board must be a solid fit for what lies ahead – even if the short-listed candidates come from different industries or countries.

In February 2017, luxury fashion retailer Barneys named Daniella Vitale, the company's chief operating officer, as its new CEO. Her predecessor as chief executive, Mark Lee, said that the company had put a succession plan in place in 2012 for Vitale to become the CEO in 2017.

Lee had himself mentored Vitale when they worked together at Gucci and then at Barneys. By the time Vitale became CEO, she had plenty of leadership experience in the company, and had worked in several different parts of the business. After her tenure at Barneys, Vitale served as Chief Brand Officer at Tiffany & Co, and later assumed the role of CEO at Salvatore Ferragamo of North America in 2021.

From succession plans to transitioning leaders, boards have a role to play

By the same token, today's global executives expect the transition process to be nurturing. In their minds, the most valuable personal development is challenging and experiential: it broadens skills, builds expertise, offers the opportunity to work in other countries and cultures, tests judgement, gives autonomy, and promotes visibility.

Companies can provide systematic support to help improve the success rate of leaders in transitions. According to Michael Watkins, 'Organizations can help transitioning leaders to leverage the time prior to switching jobs by providing them with information, access, and coaching support to diagnose the situation they are walking into, the relationships they need to build, the resources they need to secure and the expectations they need to set.'[1] This is a radical departure from the long-established practice in organisations of matching a person's evidence-based qualities with those of the job to be performed. This approach was built on an obsession with proof and written documentation, as if writing up an activity actually made it happen.

Transitions into new leadership roles typically test an executive's mettle from day one, with pressure to diagnose, strategise, delegate, and communicate effectively. Success or failure during the transition period is a strong predictor of how the executive will fare overall in the job. Promotions, by contrast, often challenge the new leader to learn to delegate and communicate differently.

Once the leader has obtained insight into the key learning goals, he or she can work towards speeding up every transition. Leaders then need to focus on identifying the best sources of intelligence. Obviously, they will consume the available documentation and analyses about the business. But this is usually far from being sufficient. Real insight comes from identifying the people who can provide more fine-grained insight into why things are as they are, enabling the leader to look at the business with the eyes of a historian.

It is critical to understand how the organisation got to the state it is in at the time of a leader's appointment. If serious problems were not addressed early enough to avoid a crisis, then why? What does this say about the culture and politics of the company, and about the competence and courage of its leadership? If bad decisions were made, how did that happen? What does this say about decision-making processes and team dynamics?

The New Talent Dynamic: Culture, Values, Community

As well as identifying key positions and the talent pipeline that is available to fill them, boards shape talent dynamics within their company at a much more

---

[1] Narasimhan, A. and J.L. Barsoux (2014). *Quest.* IMD Publishing, p. 88

fundamental level: that of overseeing and defining the organisation's culture. This reflects the trend of regarding talent as a key asset and therefore an intrinsic part of the risk culture of an organisation.

In Chapter 15, we examined organisational culture as a source of coherence and continuity that helps employees make sense of what goes on around them. We noted that in the twenty-first century, a company's culture – which stems directly from people's values and beliefs – can make or break the firm's fortunes in areas such as talent attraction and retention, brand recognition, and reputation with stakeholders. We also showed that the main forces driving a successful organisation forward – innovation, creativity, and imagination – tend to thrive in an environment where a sense of shared values trumps any organisational, bureaucratic, or even monetary considerations. In addition, the need to develop new products, enter new markets, or combat new competitors also dictates the demand for specific types, profiles, and cohorts of talent.

In many situations, organisations simply do not possess enough strategic knowledge regarding talent development. As such, the board has can play a clear role in providing leadership and guidance on the entire gamut of talent-related considerations. These include nurturing a talent-friendly corporate culture, establishing robust talent pipelines, developing sound and transparent recruiting and performance monitoring mechanisms, and having succession plans for filling the roles of top executives, especially in a crisis or following the sudden departure of top talent. Increasingly, boards expect to monitor strategic talent management areas such as HR strategy, organisational culture, employee engagement, succession planning, and development.

Much of the board's expanded sense of commitment to looking after the talent pipeline comes from the evolving view in the business community of leaders and leadership. In the past 50 years, the leadership debate has migrated from exceptional individuals having 'the right stuff' in terms of a scientifically determined leadership skillset, to a much more distributed and dispersed take on what constitutes leadership and where it resides. In consequence, many organisations and their boards have broadened their definition of talent in ways that allow them to target and capture the leadership potential throughout the workforce.

As a result, boards no longer see succession simply in terms of reporting the number of potential candidates within an organisation. Directors are looking for more visibility into executive management successors and asking for greater rigour regarding the professional development of succession candidates, including exposure to these individuals at board level. In addition, boards have been facilitating a broad-based shift in focus from individual to organisational learning. They have also sought out opportunities to meet with senior management personnel below the top level, thus getting a direct view of the talent pipeline.

As firms cast a wider net in building a diverse boardroom, a growing number of directors now come from professional accounting and legal firms, or build on previous roles as general counsels and HR specialists. That makes them more likely than their peers to understand issues related to executive talent (such as succession planning) and non-executive talent (such as employee engagement). In addition, and unlike in the past, a growing number of directors and chairs attend breakfast meetings with young staff. This gives them a better understanding of young employees' motivation for joining the company, as well as a glimpse of the firm's emerging talent 'DNA' that will shape its future identity, competitiveness, and innovation.

As well as conceiving the natural habitat of talent within the organisation infinitely more broadly than in the past, companies are also abandoning the deep-rooted top-down approach to talent management that allowed for very little employee engagement. Instead, with the aim of unleashing talent 'hidden in plain sight', employees are given more control of their personal and professional development. In particular, talent has come to be seen not only as a key competitive differentiator, but also as a magnet for new talent – because talent attracts talent, because talent can recognise other talent, and because talented people want to join winning, motivated, and high-performing teams. This is where boards need to exert influence throughout their organisation and nurture a mindset of 'we shall become whom we have hired'.

To avoid the intensifying pressures of product commoditisation, and to tackle disruptive change in its industry head on, a company must be able to deliver unique customer value. That can only be created by employees who bring a full measure of their initiative, imagination, and zeal to work every day. Unfortunately, there is not much room in strait-laced, bureaucratic, top-down organisations for higher-order, intrinsically human qualities such as passion, ingenuity, and self-direction. The machinery of bureaucracy was invented in an age when human beings were seen as dispensable – the weakest link in the production chain of command. Multiple layers of bureaucracy may have been designed to facilitate an organisation's processes and to keep things moving – but in reality, they inevitably take over and start to dictate. This puts a firm limit on which part of themselves individuals are allowed to bring to their jobs.

Meanwhile, many organisations have begun to pursue the opposite goal, of replacing hierarchy with community. It is within a community that humans are drawn to work together and share a sense of purpose, and where economic need is no longer the be all and end all. In a community, the opportunity to contribute is not bounded by narrow job descriptions. Control is peer-based rather than coming from a boss. Emotional satisfaction, rather than financial gain, drives commitment. In sum, workplaces that have self-organised as

> ### Board-like Roles as Preparation for Board Membership
>
> Steve Vamos, who joined the Telstra board, had been chief executive of two multinational subsidiaries operating in Australia (Apple and Microsoft) and was able to experience the board-like role of running regional operations for both companies, governing a number of Asia Pacific subsidiaries and others around the world. He learned 'the art of the boardroom' to make important points through careful and thoughtful questions, and to express views to management without being directly instructive.[2]

communities may act as genuine and powerful amplifiers of human talent and capability. The modern-day workforce seeks out organisational designs that are based on respect for the ability and wisdom of humans at work, without the daily battle against the isolating and alienating effects of rigid, hierarchical management.

A board should also be aware of its own potential talent issues, especially as demands on its organisational skills and overall abilities increase and as its composition changes. Boards need directors who are independent of management; who have more time to devote to board service; and who have expertise in risk, global trends, talent, technology, sustainability, and social media. In addition, boards may require improved communication, education and development, coaching, and mentoring skills, and, perhaps, more experience with regulatory agencies.

As managers move through transitions and develop into organisational leaders, they eventually become part of the talent pool for the board. Board-like roles (running business units or regions) are good preparation for executive directorships. Even for the most talented and experienced leaders, the role of executive board director is a very different function and responsibility.

In addition to talent management, boards must also pay increasing attention to the challenges and opportunities presented by social media. The next chapter assesses these and suggests ways for directors to increase their effectiveness in the digital age.

---

[2] Fraillon, D. (2015). How not to behave in the boardroom. *Financial Review*, 1 June. www.afr.com/leadership/how-not-to-behave-in-the-boardroom-20150601-ghe5va

CHAPTER 29

Human Capital Evolution for Boards

Human capital management is increasingly recognised as a key strategic lever for company performance, value creation, and stakeholder engagement. There is a growing expectation that as 'assets', a company's employees need to be managed like a firm's physical and capital assets. According to the Human Capital Management Coalition, a group of over 36 institutional investors representing over US$9 trillion in assets, skilful management of human capital is associated with better corporate performance, including better risk mitigation. Given its essential role in long-term value creation, it is considered material to evaluating a company's prospects.[1]

HCM relates to how a company manages the risks and opportunities related to its people.[2] It refers to how companies can deliver long-term value to people along dimensions of performance, safety, engagement, culture, diversity, equity and inclusion (DEI), compensation, retention, gender pay equity, among others.[3] Once the exclusive domain of Human Resources, HCM is now top of mind in many boardrooms. Much of this chapter is indebted to the insights and the work of Cathi Raffaeli, board member of Abrdn, one of the exceptionally talented board members that has inspired this book content.

---

[1] Elkeles, T. (2023). The value of human capital experts on boards. NACED, 13 November. https://www.directorsandboards.com/articles/board-composition-article/the-value-of-human-capital-experts-on-boards/

[2] CFI. (n.d.). Human capital management. https://corporatefinanceinstitute.com/course/human-capital-management/

[3] Georgiev, G.S. (2020). The human capital management movement in US corporate law. *Tuland Law Review 95*.

Board Responsibility for Human Capital

The board responsibility when it comes to HCM is linked to both its strategic and oversight roles. First, the board must understand where the strategy intersects with human capital, and to carefully map out the full range of implications. It needs to set the priorities over different time horizons, to ensure that HCM reinforces the different dimensions required to execute on the strategy. Finally, it needs to ensure it has the right data to gain a clear understanding of where it is now (baseline) and its roadmap to the future, and to establish responsibilities for getting there. At the same time, there is growing pressure from investors and regulatory bodies to disclose where HCM is creating risk for the organisation.

Some companies are choosing to address this responsibility by expanding the remit of their compensation committees to include HCM – for example by explicitly incorporating DEI and employee engagement into their charters, and in some cases renaming them to reflect this broader mandate. Fifty-four S&P 500 companies changed the name of their compensation committee between 2022 and 2021, and 24 of these added 'human capital'.[4] Indeed, the compensation committee can play an important role in setting the overall expectations, by translating strategic objectives into performance incentives and succession plans, ensuring a baseline is established and data is collected. In this way, it plays a key role in linking the HCM strategy to management.

While committees can be instrumental in this work, HCM as a whole is the responsibility of the full board. It needs to make sure it considers the following questions:

1. **Mapping where strategy intersects with human capital:** What are the human capital implications of our current strategy over different time horizons? This may lead to questions including upskilling to leverage AI effectively, the implications of the energy transition on remote and hybrid talent or how to retain GenZ. This is of course dependent on a number of specific factors, including the industry and regulatory context. For example, an energy company transitioning from oil to renewables will have a different set of priorities than a clothing retailer considering the impact of AI on how it analyses and uses consumer data when it comes stocking merchandise, determining pricing strategies, and creating customised advertising campaigns.

2. **Setting the ambition:** Where do we want to go? How does the company compare with its competitors? Are there unique capabilities or other

---

[4] Tover, T., R. Newbury, and D. Delves (2022). The compensation committee role in human capital management is growing. wtw, 17 November. https://www.wtwco.com/en-ca/insights/2022/11/compensation-committee-role-in-human-capital-management-is-growing

factors that the company can leverage to disrupt itself or the industry? Or to consider a new business model altogether? What are the key associated HCM risks?

3. **Setting the metrics and collecting the data:** What are the meaningful metrics that the board needs in order to understand where it is currently and where it wants to go? How can we measure this?

As the nature of work is reshaped through a convergence of physical, societal, and digital forces, applying insight and foresight to issues of talent, environment, and technology has emerged as an essential board skill. Conversations about the workforce, diversity, and social responsibility have found a home in most boardrooms. The workforce itself has evolved from an inclusive group of full-time employees to an ecosystem including full- and part-time staff, temporary workers, contractors, gig-economy participants, as well as suppliers and service providers embedded in the organisation, developers, and others.

Faced with shifts in ways of working and attitudes to work, companies are embracing approaches that facilitate speed, agility, and adaptability, and lead to a more fluid, digital, and human-centric workplace – adapt, pivot, reinvent, and reimagine. Once a domain of tech startups hungry for rapid growth, these attributes have become everyday reality for organisations around the world. Employers are also aiming to create all-round healthier workplaces that will motivate all who are engaged with the organisation.

Norges Bank Investment Management (NBIM), the sovereign wealth fund that manages Norway's US$1.2 trillion Government Pension Fund Global and owns on average 1.3% of all the world's listed companies, has set out its expectations across four themes, stating that companies should:

1. integrate HCM into policies and strategy;
2. integrate material HCM risks into risk management;
3. disclose material information related to HCM; and
4. engage responsibly and transparently.

In a document it released, 'Human capital management: expectations of companies', NBIM stated: 'As a financial, global and long-term investor, we expect companies to adopt robust human capital management policies and practices and to report publicly on their efforts.'[5]

---

[5] Roach, G. (2022). 'Effective management of human capital increasingly critical to company success,' says NBIM. *IR Magazine*, 18 August. https://www.irmagazine.com/reporting/effective-management-human-capital-increasingly-critical-company-success-says-nbim

Investors and regulators alike have been vocal in encouraging firms to disclose more about the value of their human capital assets in the interest of maximising firm performance and shareholder returns. They believe that HCM disclosure contributes to more accurate firm valuation. Shareholders want to receive more information about company leadership, talent, and company culture. Investors are doubling down on executive compensation and succession management, as well as recruitment, engagement, and retention of talent.

Growing Stakeholder Demands for HCM Disclosure

In 2019, BlackRock and State Street Global Advisors issued letters urging businesses to strengthen their focus on corporate purpose, workforce strategy, and culture.[6] As of 2023, the SEC recommends that companies provide 'a narrative, in the Management Discussion & Analysis, about how the firm's labor practices, compensation incentives and staffing fit within the broader firm strategy.' It also recommends that companies disclose:

- The number of employees as well as their employment status (full-time, part-time, or contingent workers).
- Employee turnover data.
- The total cost of employees, including compensation.
- Workforce demographic data, including effectiveness of recruiting and developing talent.[7]

Bodies such the Sustainability Accounting Standards Board (SASB) also include HCM dimensions in their reporting framework, including employee health and safety, as well as diversity, inclusion and engagement and labour practices.

Setting the right metrics

More comprehensive ESG disclosure requirements, coupled with the evolution of increasingly standardised ESG reporting frameworks such as SASB, GRI, and PRI, have made it easier to benchmark companies' HCM performance. HCM reporting mostly focuses on compensation and benefits, corporate culture and values, talent, DEI, and health and safety.

These measures are evolving. For instance, fair and effective compensation systems that are designed to retain top talent increasingly introduce executive

[6] Young, A. (n.d.). What happens when talent strategy has Board oversight? Accenture banking blog. https://bankingblog.accenture.com/talent-strategy-board-oversight

[7] Investor Advisory Committee. (2023). Recommendation of the SEC investor advisory committee's investor-as-owner subcommittee regarding human capital management disclosure. https://www.sec.gov/files/20230914-draft-recommendation-regarding-hcm.pdf

Table 29.1 HCM metrics are shifting from inputs to outputs and outcomes

INPUTS	OUTPUTS / OUTCOMES
Employee statistics	Revenue per headcount
Workforce composition	Productivity gains
Compensation	Employee motivation and engagement
Employee benefits	Workforce stability
Recruitment costs	Internal hires %
Spending on training and development	Absence rates
Training hours / number of courses	Accident rates or days lost to injury
Reward schemes to align employee behaviors with strategic goals	Industrial relations issues

Source: Adapted from The International Integrated Reporting Framework.

remuneration models to drive innovation and long-term value creation. These elements of remuneration may be tied to specific behaviours, activities, and outcomes of innovation initiatives. For a more strategic view of HCM, board members can reconceptualise reporting from a focus on inputs to a focus on outputs and outcomes (see Table 29.1).

More concretely, some examples of emerging HCM financial metrics that are helpful for board members to track include:

- Human capital return on investment
  - Gross profit per dollar of direct costs of HC
- Human economic value added
  - Economic value created per employee
- Human capital value added
  - Operating profit per full-time employee equivalent
- Human capital market value
  - Contribution of one full-time employee equivalent to economic value creation
- Revenue generated per full-time employee.[8]

---

[8] The Conference Board. (2020). Brave new world. 23 December. https://www.conference-board.org/publications/brave-new-world-creating-value-through-HCM

There is also growing pressure from influential investors such as NBIM for companies to integrate material HCM risks into risk management. Companies are not only expected to report on their HCM strategies and processes, but also to integrate DEI and health and safety considerations systematically into risk management frameworks. This applies to the full workforce, including employees and also those contracted throughout the supply chain as well as seasonal, part-time, and temporary workers.

Beyond disclosure and reporting, boards are responsible for oversight of broader talent management issues and connecting these to the company's strategy, culture, purpose, and values. NBIM, for example, is pushing boards to encourage the development of a culture of investing in people and the creation of a safe and positive working environment.

Culture as the Safeguard of Long-term Value Creation

By taking a view of where the organisation is going and the different opportunities it wishes to seize, the board has a unique role to play in shaping value-creating human resources practices, including culture. In addition to setting the right tone at the top, board members can take an active view in probing key dimensions culture, to assess the degree to which it is reinforcing or detracting from the strategic execution – or conversely creating risk. The Denison Culture survey, for example, can give board a clear picture of how organisations rate (compared with a benchmark of over 1,000 organisations – along four key drivers of high performance – mission, adaptability, involvement, and consistency. The survey can provide board members with insights into question such as:

- Does your team understand your mission and where you're heading?
- Do they believe the firm can stay competitive and adapt to changes in the market?
- Are your people involved, and do they feel they have the training they need?
- Are your values clear and being lived out through consistent processes?[9]

Board members can supplement these insights with direct interaction with employees, provided these are well-structured and coordinated with management. Some board members request lunches with younger employees, as they may be more direct in expressing their views and sharing their experiences.

---

[9] Denison Consulting. (n.d.). Change your culture to improve your performance. https://denisonconsulting.com/culture-surveys/

Staying Current with Emerging Expectations of the World of Work

From championing inclusive hiring practices to nurturing a culture of continuous learning and development, the board can play an important role in steering the company towards a future where human capital is not just an asset but a lever for innovation and sustainable success. To do requires questioning individual assumptions beyond the capabilities that the organisation needs (now and in the future). It requires rethinking the manner in which individuals will contribute their physical, cognitive, and emotional resources to organisations, and what this means for organisations. Board members need to ensure they are in touch with these evolving expectations and that practices evolve to stay relevant in an increasingly disrupted and competitive employer landscape.

Boards and Social Media

While I am certainly not a specialist of social media myself, I have discovered how much board members can learn from stepping out of their usual and sometimes dated ways. The extra effort to understand the evolution of the social and business environment through the social media lens is immensely rewarding and the tools available are truly productive. More learned individuals such as Estelle Métayer,[1] whose lectures and insights have inspired this chapter, can guide us towards better mastery of content.

In general, boards spend little time thinking about social media, and many directors are still accustomed to more formal and structured sources of news and information. But social media is increasingly a way of life and is fundamentally changing the way people interact and communicate – including by democratising the world's information and revolutionising the way we do business. In 2023, Facebook had 3 billion monthly active users. In 2023, X (formerly Twitter) had over 200 million users daily, and YouTube viewers collectively consume over 1 billion hours of content on average worldwide.

Social media are not only a way to share information, but also a forum for conversations between consumers and activists that can derail and destroy company reputations. Social media are transforming the context the business works in, such as employee-to-management relations. For the astute board member, social media present a fantastic source of information on the company, its context, the competitors, and the landscape at large. Board members should use social media to listen to what customers, employees, and other stakeholders are saying about the organisation – but they should probably not be creators of social media content themselves.

---

[1] President of Competia and serial board member of talent, with a tech and social media slant towards stewardship principles. One of the many truly exceptional board members full of passion and integrity who have inspired this book.

JP Morgan's Failed Foray into Twitter Q&A

In late 2013, JP Morgan announced a Twitter Q&A with its vice-chair, creating a hashtag #AskJPM. Having received a barrage of negative and sarcastic comments, the bank cancelled the event before the Q&A could go live. This has since become an oft-quoted example not only of misguided social media strategy but also of a major corporation supposedly unaware of and disconnected from its current public image.[2]

Although some industries are more affected by social media than others, most organisations are impacted in some way. CEOs still tend to be afraid of social media, often feeling that they do not have the time, or that it is somehow not relevant to them. Companies can be rather unsophisticated when it comes to formally gathering data from social media and using these for corporate strategy, operational plans, and risk management. Directors and executives don't always ask for this information – nor do they rely on it for decision-making. But board members and senior management can no longer overlook the effect that social media can have on a company's reputation, or the speed at which isolated digital rumblings can turn into a tidal wave of discontent.

In March 2010, Greenpeace posted a graphic video on YouTube claiming that Nestlé used palm oil in KitKats, and was thus contributing to the destruction of orangutans' habitats. Nestlé asked YouTube to remove the clip, citing copyright infringement; environmental campaigners told CNN the copyright infringement claim was 'a pretext for stopping the word being spread and an apparent attempt to silence us'. Greenpeace reposted the video on Vimeo, and many other users reposted it. On 20 May 2010, only 10 weeks later, Nestlé announced it would stop sourcing the unsustainable palm oil. This was a victory at minimal cost for Greenpeace and social networking.

At present, most companies are slowly coming to grips with the task of finding optimum tools and systems for scanning, analysing, and evaluating relevant social media content. Directors are learning how to ask the right questions, acquire the necessary capabilities for the organisation, and attract suitable talent for making sense of its digital footprint.

Why Boards Should Understand Social Media

Boards need to understand social media for several reasons:

- **To manage reputation risk**. In April 2017, United Airlines stumbled with its social media response following the forcible removal of a passenger

---

[2] Moth, D. (2013). Seven Twitter Q&As and the lessons that can be learned. Ecoconsultancy, 28 November. https://econsultancy.com/seven-twitter-q-as-and-the-lessons-that-can-be-learned/

The #MeToo movement against sexual harassment and sexual assault started to go viral as a social media hashtag in October 2017, following sexual abuse allegations against Hollywood film producer Harvey Weinstein. The movement has not only implicated individuals, but also cost several businesses substantially.

Streaming service Netflix reportedly lost US$39 million for severing ties with actor Kevin Spacey,[3] who played the lead character in the famous Netflix production *House of Cards*. In January 2018, hotel and casino company Wynn Resorts lost US$3.5 billion in market value after the emergence of sexual harassment allegations concerning CEO Steve Wynn.[4] And in the following month, shares in fashion retailer Guess tumbled almost 18%, and the company's market value fell by more than US$250 million in a day, after model Kate Upton accused the firm's co-founder Paul Marciano via Twitter of using his power to 'sexually and emotionally harass women'.[5]

from one of its flights. The airline initially would not admit it had made a mistake. Its CEO later had to apologise, losing face and some credibility in the process. United Airline's share price tumbled. The airline later settled the lawsuit that the passenger had filed.

- **To avoid blind spots**. Social media can help boards to pick up early signals. Different businesses have different cycles. A number of tools allow companies to scan social media and detect where rumours are coming from, enabling them to quantify the level of urgency.
- **To increase knowledge in ethical ways**. How intimately do you want to know your employees or your customers? Glassdoor is giving access to employee perspectives often differentiated from corporate surveys. It may offer intriguing insights revealing moods and sometimes facts. Target, the US supermarket chain, was able to identify when its customers were pregnant, often before the customers had made it public, through an analysis of their purchases. But should the firm have used this information for marketing purposes? Boards should be having ethical discussions about the use of private data.

---

[3] Fiegerman, S. (2018). Kevin Spacey cost Netflix $39 million. CNN Business, 22 January. https://money.cnn.com/2018/01/22/media/netflix-kevin-spacey-cost/index.html

[4] Shen, L. (2018). Wynn resorts loses $3.5 billion after sexual harassment allegations surface about Steve Wynn. Fortune, 29 January. http://fortune.com/2018/01/29/steve-wynn-stock-net-worth-sexual-misconduct/

[5] Reuters. (2018). Guess shares slump after model Kate Upron tweets about executive. 1 February. https://www.reuters.com/article/us-guess-stocks/guess-shares-slump-after-model-kate-upton-tweets-about-exec-idUSKBN1FL6BK

> ## Mozilla's Failure to Engage
>
> In March 2014, OkCupid.com, a popular online dating site, called for a boycott of Mozilla Firefox to protest against the world's second biggest web browser naming a gay marriage opponent as chief executive.
>
> Brendan Eich, a founder of Mozilla and creator of its technology, had made a $1,000 donation to opponents of gay marriage in 2008. OkCupid sent a message to visitors who accessed its website through Firefox, suggesting they use browsers such as Microsoft's Internet Explorer or Google's Chrome. Mozilla was slow to react.
>
> 'We didn't act like you'd expect Mozilla to act', wrote Mozilla Executive Chair Mitchell Baker in a blog post. 'We didn't move fast enough to engage with people once the controversy started. We're sorry.' A few days later, Eich stepped down.

- **As a source of independent intelligence**, by using sites such as socialmention.com and other social mentions sites. When BlackBerry announced that it was pulling out of the consumer market, it may have avoided the backlash had it used Sysomos to conduct a generational analysis. This would have demonstrated the differences in the product's reputation between age groups and the potential liability of simply taking it away. Many companies, including Nestlé, have set up social media command centres to get a better sense of what employees or other key stakeholders are saying about the firm and its products.

Board members increasingly understand that social media may serve as a digital red flag, pinpointing trouble before it acquires serious magnitude and ramifications. With continued advances in data analysis, social media may also be harnessed for its predictive power, highlighting problems and dissatisfactions that are bubbling under the surface and can be dispelled through simple, timely, and effective interventions.

The key thing to note is the speed at which information is shared on social media, which means that situations can escalate quickly. Under stress, it is difficult to think clearly and react appropriately. Companies therefore need to have a clear checklist of what to do in a social media crisis.

Besides crisis prevention and management, a good sense of what is brewing on social media can yield powerful insights into customer needs, perceptions, and satisfaction. In addition, smart organisations can cultivate a loyal digital audience by engaging with customers via social media and responding to their concerns. Effective social media engagement can also give a great boost to the company's brand visibility and credibility, both online and offline.

What Boards Should Do

While many boards today are still largely cut off from social media, this is rapidly changing. Boards need to take three steps in particular to get up to speed.

Social media can exacerbate the loss of confidence among clients and investors, as can be seen in the case of Credit Suisse, which collapsed in 2023. Online discussions, notably on platforms such as Reddit, heightened the scrutiny over the bank's operational and financial hurdles. This digital discourse triggered widespread apprehensions among clients and investors. This case showcases how digital platforms can hasten the downfall of financial institutions by disseminating information, whether accurate or speculative, at unprecedented speeds.

In 2024, the European Central Bank has requested certain banks to carefully monitor social media activity in order to identify any deterioration in sentiment that might trigger a bank run.[6]

Getting it right: directors don't post, they listen!

Social media is now a primary source of information. It is better for directors to refrain from proactive communication unless a solid protocol has been established by the board. Nonetheless, tools such as Hootsuite allow board members to easily track the organisation and its competitors or substitutes. Also, many tools allow a better understanding of rising trends. Thus, social media has become a source of independent intelligence. For example, www socialmention.com or meltwater social can help boards understand the landscape, notably in consumer goods markets. A debate on which tools are used by the different board members (and seeing holes and complementarities), and possibly a short session by a digital specialist from the firm on the most interesting opportunities, is worth engaging with.

Goldman Sachs' CEO, David Solomon, caused unease among some board members due to his DJ activities, reported in the *Financial Times*. It was particularly evident after a DJ music event in 2020 that violated COVID-19 social distancing guidelines.[7] Moreover, his DJ-related presence on social media platforms like Instagram raised concerns for the board, aligning with the bank's concurrent challenges, including laying off 3,200 employees and announcing financial losses totalling US$ 3 billion in 2023.[8]

[6] Spezzati, S. (2024). ECB asks some lenders to monitor social media for early signs on bank runs – sources say. Reuters, 24 January. https://www.reuters.com/markets/europe/ecb-asks-some-lenders-monitor-social-media-early-signs-bank-runs-sources-2024-01-24/

[7] *Financial Times*. (2016). Goldman chief David Solomon calls time on high-profile DJ. 16 October. https://www.ft.com/content/d11601b5-fba1-4603-acad-eb2ee587a8e3

[8] Maxwell, S. (2023). The blurred lines between Goldman's CEO's day job and his DJ gig. *The New York Times*, 6 February. https://www.nytimes.com/2023/02/05/business/david-solomon-dj-goldman-sachs.html

Ask Questions

The board should ask hygiene questions covering issues such as:

Social media policy
- Do we have a social media policy for employees?[9]
- Is this policy part of the employment contract?
- Does it define how the employee engages in social media, whether in his or her own name or that of the company?
- Is it clear who owns the intellectual property (see the article 'Lawyers, guns and Twitter: Who owns your Twitter account')?[10]
- Are employees receiving coaching and training?
- Is there a budget to support these initiatives?

Information gathering
- Which sources are we listening to? Does the list include review sites, blogs, Twitter and Facebook, as well as consumers' forums? Does it include LinkedIn and Google+?
- Is the company systematically gathering and analysing social media information to assess reputational risks?

Crisis management
- Do we have a response plan in case of digital crisis? And who is managing it?

Figure 30.1 provides an illustration of a social media early crisis protocol.

> In April 2022, a tweet from the account using the name and logo of pharmaceutical company Eli Lilly and Co (and bearing the blue verification checkmark) suddenly went viral, stating 'We are excited to announce insulin is free now.' Soon after, a number of fake Lily accounts were set up and continued to escalate the hoax. The result was a drop in stock price and a loss of US$15 billion in market cap. This points to the reputational risk that social media poses to companies – which boards are increasingly monitoring.

---

[9] Examples of social media policies can be found at http://socialmedia.biz/social-media-policies/.
[10] Gabe, G. (2009). Lawyers, guns, and Twitter – who owns your twitter account. *Search Engine Journal*, 27 May. http://www.searchenginejournal.com/lawyers-guns-and-twitter-who-owns-your-twitter-account/10612/

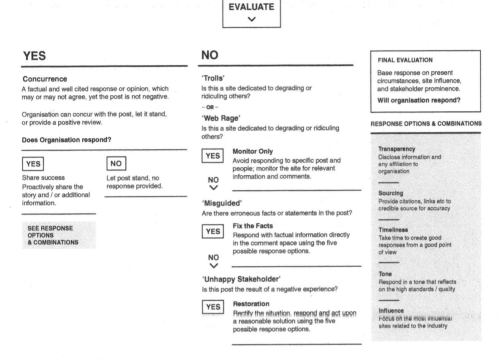

COMMENT OR POSTING

An organisation's own website/network or a post on another site. Is it a positive posting?

EVALUATE

YES

Concurrence
A factual and well cited response or opinion, which may or may not agree, yet the post is not negative.

Organisation can concur with the post, let it stand, or provide a positive review.

Does Organisation respond?

YES	NO
Share success Proactively share the story and / or additional information.	Let post stand, no response provided.

SEE RESPONSE OPTIONS & COMBINATIONS

NO

'Trolls'
Is this a site dedicated to degrading or ridiculing others?
– OR –
'Web Rage'
Is this a site dedicated to degrading or ridiculing others?

YES	**Monitor Only** Avoid responding to specific post and people; monitor the site for relevant
NO	information and comments.

'Misguided'
Are there erroneous facts or statements in the post?

YES	**Fix the Facts** Respond with factual information directly in the comment space using the five
NO	possible response options.

'Unhappy Stakeholder'
Is this post the result of a negative experience?

YES	**Restoration** Rectify the situation, respond and act upon a reasonable solution using the five possible response options.

FINAL EVALUATION

Base response on present circumstances, site influence, and stakeholder prominence.

Will organisation respond?

RESPONSE OPTIONS & COMBINATIONS

Transparency
Disclose information and any affiliation to organisation

Sourcing
Provide citations, links etc to credible source for accuracy

Timeliness
Take time to create good responses from a good point of view

Tone
Respond in a tone that reflects on the high standards / quality

Influence
Focus on the most influential sites related to the industry

Figure 30.1   Social Media Comment and Response Protocol
Source: Adapted from Shaun Holloway.

Occupy the space

The cost of ignoring the digital world during a crisis can be seen in BP's failure to address the Deepwater Horizon oil spill on social media. The space was soon occupied instead by an imitator posting false news. Thus, a key question for any organisation in the social media world is: are we occupying the space? The ability to occupy the space may well depend on engaging employees well beyond their usual responsibilities. This in turn will require the organisation to have a culture of engagement on social media through strong and proactive policies. While the well-documented Nestlé example of proactive management requires resources of large scale, a simple social media policy and a culture of social media engagement, fine-tuned by a daily practice in the organisation, can foster a transparent and engaged culture that will be resilient to external shocks. And in the next two chapters, we focus on the board's engagement with investors and stakeholders.

Acknowledgement

Many of the ideas in this chapter are based on the work of Estelle Métayer, and I would like to acknowledge my intellectual debt to her perspectives and thinking.

CHAPTER 31

Boards and Investors

There is a trend toward increasing engagement and advocacy by shareholders who expect to have greater access to boards. This has been accentuated by greater technology-enabled exchanges of information between boards and shareholders.

The impact of the transforming shareholder role has been felt on many fronts, including in the form of institutional shareholder-led initiatives regarding the composition of boards. There have also been regulatory changes in response to shareholder demands. These include 'say-on-pay' rules, where investors vote on executive compensation, as well as a requirement that shareholders approve dilutive transactions. Demands for shareholder engagement are likely to continue to intensify.

Information Design and Capital Raising: Crowdfunding

The proliferation of new approaches to raising capital has resulted in higher quality and transparency of information available to investors. From private equity to crowdfunding, the 'closed-shop' way of interacting on investment decisions is becoming a thing of the past. Instead, accurate and timely – often real-time – information is made available, thus delivering on the promise of digital technology. It has had a powerful effect on levelling the playing field between institutional and private investors, as well as between active and potential investors.

The Oculus VR is a virtual-reality headset that puts players into their favourite games. With over US$2 million raised in 30 days through crowdfunding in 2012, the Oculus team went on to raise additional investment capital and was acquired by Facebook two years later. The US$2 billion acquisition was controversial and many crowdfunding backers that contributed to the Oculus campaign expressed their desire to benefit from the company's success since they were the first supporters of the company.

Types of investors

- activist investors;
- institutional investors – required by US Securities and Exchange Commission regulations to vote all items on the proxy and to disclose their votes to investors;
- blockholders; and
- pension funds.

Investors differ by

- objectives;
- time horizon;
- size; and
- activity level.

Investors vary from institutional shareholders and pension funds, which often use asset management firms to manage their portfolios, to activist investors, who are more directly involved. Boards can actively frame the dialogue with major shareholders through ongoing, high-quality communication, and by engaging with them on key issues such as strategy, succession planning, and emerging risks.

One prominent board member, who also owns a sizeable stake in a large-cap pharmaceutical company, told me privately that he feels more powerful in shaping a firm's direction as an investor than as a board member. Investors exert strong influence by directly communicating their concerns, withholding votes from directors, waging a proxy contest to elect an alternative board, voting against company proxy items, or sponsoring proxy items of their own. These generally relate to compensation, board structure, anti-takeover protections, and bylaw changes. Or, of course, shareholders can simply start selling their shares.

The Move Toward Increasing Shareholder Engagement

Shareholder engagement serves as a constructive method for investors. This approach involves various forms of communication, including written correspondence such as emails and letters, as well as direct voice or video calls. Investors may request confidential face-to-face meetings with the company's representatives, often facilitated by the investor relations (IR) department. These engagements are typically conducted behind the scenes, and are maintained over the long term, allowing for the continuous monitoring of progress and improvements regarding the issues raised by the investors. As such, shareholder engagement is characterised by its non-confrontational nature, and a high level of confidentiality with restricted information disclosure.

On the other hand, shareholder proposals provide other means that allow investors to influence a company's decisions, by submitting resolutions for a vote during annual meetings. Even though the outcomes may not be binding, they can be a means to pressure the company to address their concerns. The trend of shareholder proposals is generally escalating, and in the United States recorded its highest number in 2023.[1]

In the United States, the main thrust of shareholder democracy is that directors should be more accountable to shareholder concerns; for example, regarding excessive compensation, risk management, and board accountability. Elements of shareholder democracy include majority voting in uncontested board elections, brokers being disallowed from voting in uncontested elections, the right of investors to nominate directors ('proxy access'), and 'say-on-pay' votes by investors concerning executive compensation.

Shareholder advocates believe that plurality voting lowers the quality of governance by insulating directors from investors. They advocate a stricter standard of majority voting, whereby directors must receive 50% of the votes to be elected. The impact of majority voting on governance is unclear. Dissenting votes are often issue-driven and not against the director personally – shareholders may vote against directors on the board's compensation committee in protest at the CEO's pay, for example. This might inadvertently result in the removal of directors with important strategic, operational, or risk qualifications.

In Europe, the European Shareholder Rights Directive (formally known as the Long-term Shareholder Engagement and Corporate Governance Statement) aims to contribute 'to a more long-term perspective of shareholders which ensures better operating conditions for listed companies', by:

- increasing the level and quality of engagement of asset owners and asset managers with their investee companies;
- creating a better link between pay and performance of company directors;
- enhancing transparency and shareholder oversight on related-party transactions;
- ensuring reliability and quality of advice of proxy advisors; and
- facilitating transmission of cross-border information (including voting) across the investment chain, in particular through shareholder identification.[2]

---

[1] ISS Corporate. (2023). US shareholder proposals jump to a new record in 2023. 24 May. https://www.iss-corporate.com/library/us-shareholder-proposals-jump-to-a-new-record-in-2023/
[2] Eur-Lex. (2014). Proposal for a Directive of the European Parliament and of the council amending Directive 2007/36/EC as regards the encouragement of long-term shareholder engagement and Directive 2013/34/EU as regards certain elements of the corporate governance statement. http://eur-lex.europa.eu/legal-content/EN/TXT/?uri=COM%3A2014%3A213%3AFIN

The Surge in Shareholder Activism on Boards

Shareholder activism is on the rise, exerting mounting pressure on corporate boards (Figure 31.1). In advancing the objectives in pursuit of their interest, among the various methods shareholders utilise to appeal to corporate boards, proxy fights stand out as the most assertive, at times aggressive, form of shareholder activism. Activists directly challenge the status quo by seeking to replace board members with individuals who can better align with the activist's views, often representing the interests of the hedge fund or investor group.

The global trend in shareholder activism showed a significant increase in 2023, reaching the highest number of activist campaigns.[3] Even more notable

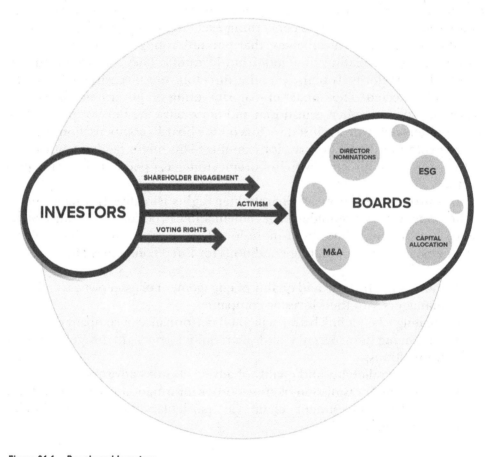

Figure 31.1   Boards and Investors

[3] Shimokawa, K. (2023). Evolution of investor activism. S&P Global, 15 December. https://www.spglobal.com/marketintelligence/en/news-insights/blog/evolution-of-investor-activism-breaking-down-2023-campaign-activity-and-assessing-future-trends

is the rise in the number of board seats secured by activists during this period, reflecting some successful board change campaigns.[4]

For effective preparation for a forthcoming proxy season, a thorough review of the board composition is crucial. This entails evaluating board members' skills and experience, the diversity of the board, and the alignment with the company's strategic direction, ensuring that the board composition reflects a balance of expertise and perspectives to demonstrate strong governance to shareholders.[5]

Employing the 'four pillars' approach can be advantageous when preparing for proxy seasons. Pillar 3 – Structures and processes – offers a concept for evaluating and enhancing the effectiveness of governance structures and processes. Simultaneously, Pillar 2 – Information architecture – plays a role in ensuring readiness for clear and effective communication, which is crucial when dealing with inquiries from shareholders, activists, and other stakeholders.

Staying informed about emerging trends and shareholder concerns is important for board members because it helps them anticipate potential challenges and adapt the company's strategy. As such, companies can be better prepared for the proxy season and in dealing with activist shareholders.

Trend of anti-ESG agendas in the United States

By 2024, a number of states in the United States have enacted anti-ESG laws, influencing the investment guidelines for public funds. These laws specifically discourage the integration of ESG criteria, particularly in the management of public retirement systems. The primary justification for these laws is the concern that ESG-focused investment strategies might compromise financial returns.

In addition, several states have passed anti-boycott laws that prohibit boycotts targeting certain industries, such as fossil fuels and firearms, which are often the focus of ESG agendas. These laws aim to safeguard these industries from ESG influenced divestment or exclusion.

In the trend of shareholder proposals, there has also been a noticeable increase in the number of anti-ESG proposals. However, these proposals have generally received minimal backing, with an average support rate of 2.4% in 2023.[6]

---

[4] Lazard. (2023). Annual review of shareholder activism 2023. 8 January. https://www.lazard.com/research-insights/annual-review-of-shareholder-activism-2023/
[5] MarketInsite. (2023). Preparing for proxy season. 24 April. https://www.nasdaq.com/articles/preparing-for-proxy-season%3A-how-boards-should-manage-activism
[6] Walsh, H. (2023). Assessing Anti-ESG Efforts in the 2023 Proxy Season. Sustainable Investments Institute. 28 September. https://siinstitute.org/special_report.cgi?id=95

During the 2010s and 2020s, Asia has undergone significant regulatory changes, fostering a more shareholder-friendly environment. This shift has sparked the emergence of activism in the region, leading Asia to witness a high number of companies targeted by activist demands. Following are two cases from Japan.

- Fujitec, a 75-year-old Japanese elevator manufacturer valued at US$1.9 billion, became the focal point of a prolonged activist campaign led by a Hong Kong-based activist fund in 2022. The following year, the campaign resulted in the removal of three board members and the subsequent replacement of the chairman, who was the founder's son. The emergence of the activist fund led to an upheaval in the conventional company's management and board composition.
- In January 2019, Olympus took steps to speed up reform of its much-criticised governance by welcoming a foreign activist investor to its board. As part of a shake-up of its leadership team, the Japanese company announced that it was inviting Robert Hale, a partner at leading shareholder ValueAct Capital Management, to become a director. The unusual move may be a belated reaction to foreign investors' criticism of how Olympus dealt with accounting improprieties earlier in the decade.

More boards are pursuing fuller and more effective engagement with shareholders. Online voting and participation is increasingly common: Intel typically collects hundreds of shareholder questions throughout the year via a message board, for example. Online-based practice has now been expanded to other companies around the world, especially following the challenges and restrictions introduced by the pandemic.

Overall, however, real shareholder involvement in publicly traded companies remains light. There is still a long process for investors to go through to understand the real intricacies of governance described in this book, and for them to become truly active players in this regard. At the same time, boards need to remain engaged with many other stakeholder groups besides investors. This is the theme of the next chapter.

CHAPTER

32

Managing Stakeholders

The economic and social upheavals of recent years have revived the old debate over the extent to which companies serve the interests of shareholders as opposed to stakeholders. Maximising shareholder value has been the prime focus of business ever since the birth of the corporation. Those who uphold this view may argue that the different groups that have a stake in the performance of a business often present conflicting agendas, and that these agendas will in any event be best served by keeping a close eye on the company's bottom line.

Many company directors share this outlook. They consider the firm's interactions with stakeholders such as governments, regulators, media, and the wider public as primarily a distraction from the business activities that the organisation was set up to perform. In extreme cases, boards may have an outright negative perception of some stakeholders, such as non-governmental organisations (NGOs). Directors may view NGOs as at best not having a direct relationship with the company; and at worst, as representatives of groups that are innately anti-business and typically a source of nuisance and opposition to a company's operations, as well as to its broader interests and general well-being.

Shareholders vs Stakeholders: A Definition

Whereas the definition of a shareholder has remained virtually unchanged for centuries, the concept of stakeholders has gone through many shifts over the past few decades. This has been largely in tandem with changes in the dominant discourses on business and management. Today's discussions of the roles, mandates, and expectations attached to corporations are firmly rooted in the paradigm of 'business in society'. In this perspective, a company's goals

In November 2023, OpenAI's board had dismissed CEO Sam Altman after allegedly receiving a letter written by several staff researchers warning of a powerful artificial intelligence discovery that they said could threaten humanity. The board had received previous grievances, including concerns over commercialising advances before understanding the consequences. However, after 700 employees threatened to quit and join backer Microsoft (MSFT.O), in solidarity with their fired leader, three board members resigned (Ilya Sutskever, Tasha McCauley, and Helen Toner) and Altman was back as CEO.

OpenAI's governance structure granted formal power over its corporate affairs to the directors of its not-for-profit. These directors' only goal was to ensure the fulfilment of OpenAI's mission. They had no fiduciary duty to OpenAI Global, LLC.

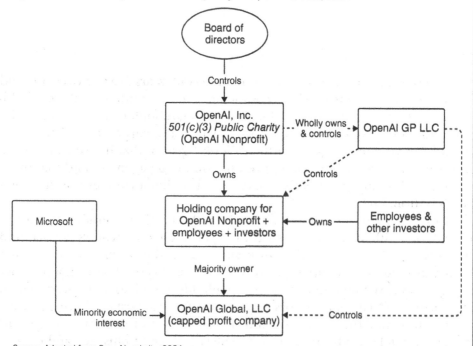

Source: Adapted from OpenAI website, 2024.

From the outset, the combination of the ethos of the original non-profit and the goals of the capped-profit arm gave rise to conflicts that were tough to resolve. In addition, the CEO's larger-than-life seemed to override the board's authority.[1] The board's *de facto* position thus weakened, becoming somewhat rubberstamping rather than a source of oversight. It may well have lacked the experience, seniority, and resilience it needed. Neither was it receiving sufficient information from management to fulfil its role in monitoring and anticipating mission-critical risk.

(continued)

---

[1] Peregrine, M. (2023). Leadership lessons from OpenAI's Wild Week. Forbes, 27 November. https://www.forbes.com/sites/michaelperegrine/2023/11/27/leadership-lessons-from-openais-wild-week/

> *(continued)*
>
> Throughout 2023, OpenAI's self-perpetuating board had lost five members, leaving it with four. In hindsight, that alone was a source of great vulnerability, particularly when dealing with cutting-edge technology and having reached a valuation of close to US$90 billion.[2]
>
> In the aftermath of the imbroglio, the company embarked on a process of rebuilding the board, presumably with a view to making it more diverse. Microsoft has secured a non-voting board seat. This was after Microsoft CEO Satya Nadella stated his wish to see governance changes at the company. According to reports, although technically not an owner, Microsoft has been entitled to up to 49% of the for-profit arm of OpenAI's profits.

and activities cannot be divorced from the impact they have – not only on stakeholder groups such as customers and employees, but also on local communities and society at large.

The stakeholder conversation is therefore increasingly relevant in the boardroom. Managing stakeholders is a complex undertaking that at times may feel like navigating a minefield of disparate perceptions and expectations. But as the spate of corporate and boardroom dramas this century has illustrated, how stakeholders see an organisation is a strong indicator of its health – particularly at critical junctures in the company's existence – and of its potential to create long-term value. Stakeholders also act as a company's moral compass, challenging it to do the right thing – on a day-to-day basis as well as in situations that are crucial to its survival.

How to Identify a Company's Key Stakeholders

Stakeholders that are critical to a company's long-term success are those that cannot be disregarded, ignored, or replaced without damaging the firm's reputation and long-term growth prospects. Typically, they include a government's law-making bodies and regulatory agencies, as well as public utilities; unions and other employee representatives; consumer associations and consumer rights advocacy groups; and influential NGOs that often set the tone and topic of debates on issues such as the environmental impact of a particular industry's or corporation's current projects.

Today, social expectations and corporate governance standards dictate that companies and boards continually elicit their main stakeholders' support, and engage them in active dialogue. Analysing different growth and risk scenarios will cast new light on which stakeholders act as gatekeepers on various frontlines and whose buy-in will be critical in executing new growth, innovation, and integration initiatives.

---

[2] Needleman, S.E. (2023). Everything you need to know about OpenAI's board. WSJ, 21 November. https://www.wsj.com/tech/ai/openai-board-members-directors-dea51459

MTN Nigeria was hit with a US$5.2 billion fine for failing to disconnect unregistered SIMs from the network in 2015. After a drawn-out process that involved engaging former US attorney general Eric Holder as a negotiator, the fine was reduced. Among other concessions to the government, MTN also agreed to list on the stock exchange. The listing was approved in May 2019. More generally, some have wondered whether heavy, politically motivated fines are being imposed, sometimes on the pretext of tax evasion or illegal money transfers abroad. This shows how stakeholder management can become sensitive and complex.

The Board can be Instrumental in Shaping the CEO–Stakeholders Conversation

Board members can exert strong influence in moulding the CEO's view of stakeholders, including NGOs. Directors can also offer considerable guidance and support as the chief executive goes about engaging with the company's stakeholders. To begin with, board members tend to have a broader range of access through their network and more open perspectives than CEOs, as well as a wider sense of the organisation's purpose. The board therefore has a critical role to play in backing and inspiring the CEO's interactions with stakeholders.

Importantly, even if the organisation is entering uncharted territory in reaching out to specific types of stakeholders, the board cannot limit its involvement to just ticking boxes and complying with regulations. Instead, listening to key stakeholders gives directors a good opportunity to understand the real concerns of the company's customers, suppliers, and employees, and the broader public. Many corporate disasters happened because the board was removed from what was happening on the ground. A sudden event whose repercussions may upset a firm's stakeholders – internal or external – is very likely to produce a crisis that the company will be hard pressed to defuse.

In that context, making the stakeholders' voices heard in the boardroom can be crucial in narrowing the gap between the board's perception and reality. As we saw in Chapter 17, the chair in particular is in a strong position to represent the company in building relationships with major stakeholders, and to bring the knowledge gained back to the boardroom.

The Process of Stakeholder Engagement

A survey conducted by the World Business Council for Sustainable Development (WBCSD) has revealed several challenges and barriers to effective stakeholder engagement. These obstacles are predominantly related to board-level issues, such as the board's limited understanding of stakeholder perspectives, a lack of sufficient skills or capacity for engagement at the board level, and an overall under prioritisation of stakeholder engagement in board activities.[3]

[3] wbcsd. (n.d.). Boards and their stakeholders. https://www.wbcsd.org/contentwbc/download/12423/185307/1

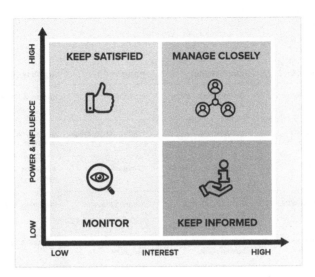

Figure 32.1   Stakeholder Mapping

The role of board oversight in management's engagement with stakeholders is a crucial aspect of corporate governance. To comprehend and manage relationships with stakeholders effectively, the process of identifying and prioritising stakeholders contributes to the effective stakeholder engagement strategies.

In initiating the engagement process, stakeholder mapping contributes to identifying and categorising all potential stakeholders based on their level of influence and interest in the firm's business operations. They include employees, customers, suppliers, investors, civil societies, government agencies, and local communities. Once stakeholders are identified, they can be placed based on their level of influence and interest, then categorised into four groups, as shown in Figure 32.1.

After stakeholders are mapped out, considering the concerns and interests of each stakeholder group helps determine the materiality for the company. Figure 32.2 displays examples of top materialities by stakeholder groups.

Developing a materiality matrix contributes to highlighting important issues that impact both the business and the stakeholders. The matrix assesses the factors based on their importance to business and stakeholders, across environmental, social, and governance (ESG) issues. The issues that fall into the upper-right quadrant require more attention (Figure 32.3).

These analyses play a crucial role in developing stakeholder engagement strategies, helping identify and prioritise key issues and stakeholders, allocate resources efficiently, and communicate effectively. They also support informed decision-making and enhance risk management by fostering understanding of the interests of essential stakeholders.

	CUSTOMERS	EMPLOYEES	INVESTORS	SUPPLIERS
1.	Climate & Energy	Occupational health & safety	Innovation	Climate & Energy
2.	Business ethics & transparency	Leadership & development	Product stewardship	Geopolitical shifts & dynamics
3.	Innovation	Digital transformation	Climate & energy	Advocacy, engagement & partnering
4.	Nutrition & health	Business ethics & transparency	Nutrition & health	Resources & circularity
5.	Labor practices & human rights	Labor practices & human rights	Resources & circularity	Nutrition & health

Source: Extracted from DSM Annual Report 2019

Figure 32.2   Stakeholder Key Concerns and Interests
Source: Extracted from DSM Annual Report 2019.[4]

By identifying material issues, companies gain a clearer perspective on which information should be disclosed. Key reporting initiatives, such as the Global Reporting Initiative (GRI), the Sustainability Accounting Standards Board (SASB), and International Financial Reporting Standards (IFRS) further enhance disclosures. Even though reporting requirements may vary by region and country, certain initiatives not only improve management's transparency but also provide the board with essential information to guide strategic decision-making and governance oversight.

Stakeholder mapping and the materiality matrix offer valuable insights into stakeholder engagement, however, they do not constitute comprehensive solutions for board involvement. Boards should proactively engage with stakeholders by facilitating direct interactions that enhance their comprehension of the broader business environment in which the company operates.

[4] DSM. (2019). Annual Report. https://annualreport.dsm.com/ar2019/xmlpages/resources/TXP/dsm/ar_2019/files/DSM-Annual-Report-2019.pdf

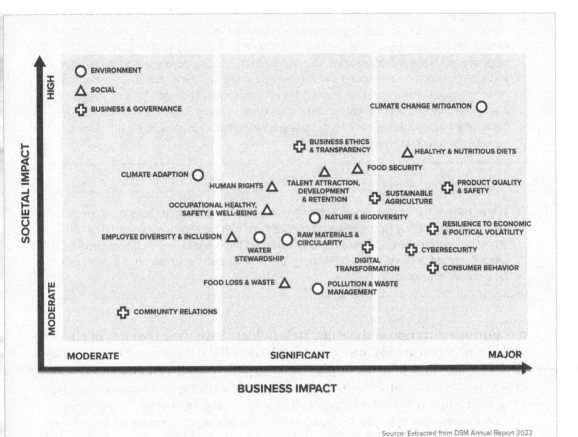

Figure 32.3 Materiality Matrix Example

Source: Extracted from DSM Annual Report 2022.[5]

Furthermore, boards should thoroughly analyse and respond to stakeholder feedback, exploring ways to integrate it into business operations, strategies, and public disclosures.

Anticipating Stakeholders' Influence and Impact

A company's strategic planning process must ensure that all stakeholder relationships are managed properly. This is particularly important for anticipating, assessing, and measuring the impact that these different groups can have on

---

[5] DSM. (2022). Annual Report. https://annualreport.dsm.com/ar2022/_assets/downloads/entire-dsm-ar22.pdf

Patagonia, a US outdoor clothing company, is known for its long-term commitment to the environment. Since 1985, it has pledged to donate 1% of sales to environmental causes, totalling over US$89 million. In 2022, the founder Yvon Chouinard, renowned rock climber and environmentalist, announced the transfer of Patagonia's ownership to a trust and a non-profit organisation, aiming to address the environmental challenges.[6] Recognising the clear materiality of environmental concerns within their industry, Patagonia has strategically framed itself around this commitment, making environmental responsibility a fundamental aspect of its corporate identity.

In March 2015, the board of South African Nuclear Energy Corporation (Necsa) suspended the CEO for disciplinary lapses, following consultations with the Ministry of Energy. The Ministry subsequently changed its position and instructed the board to reverse the suspension, which the board declined to do. The Ministry then announced the formation of a task team to investigate the board.

a company's direction and results. Stakeholders have their own sets of checks and balances that are likely to sound an alarm bell if the company tries to exaggerate its accomplishments or play down negative results. In many corporate crises, it is the stakeholders that provide early-warning mechanisms by flagging the company's shortcomings and its impending or recent transgressions.

This particular role played by stakeholders becomes even more important to an organisation's sustainability and success when it concerns international operations, especially those in developing countries. In these environments, stakeholders such as NGOs often compensate for underdeveloped legal, regulatory, and ethical frameworks. On the downside, cultural, historical, linguistic, and other barriers tend to be firmly entrenched. This means that situations can become fraught and dramatic scenarios can flare up quite unexpectedly, more so than in the company's domestic market.

Many companies have learned from experience that maintaining the local status quo is enough of an uphill battle in itself, and are therefore reluctant to discuss how their business affects local communities. There are even more constraints to negotiate in fast-growth markets run by authoritarian governments, where national and local regulations can change on a whim.

For today's companies, properly managing relationships with their stakeholders are no longer an afterthought subsumed to a larger project of maximising

[6] Chouinard, Y. (2022). A letter from Yvon Chouinard. Patagonia, 14 September. https://www.patagonia.ca/stories/a-letter-from-yvon-chouinard/story-127258.html

Disney English: A Game-Changing Approach to Chinese Stakeholders

In the early 2000s, The Walt Disney Company encountered repeated delays and obstacles in obtaining government approvals for construction of a theme park in Shanghai, China. Executives soon realised that the key to overcoming these problems were: listening, understanding, and accommodating the local authorities' and partners' aspirations for their country, their hometown, their families, and their own professional and career development.

The company discovered that one of the most prized commodities it could offer to its partners and their communities was the opportunity to learn English. That is how Disney English was born – a learning programme built around the company's own recognised curriculum, innovative technology, and involvement of popular Disney characters and stories.

Following the programme's success and rapid growth across a number of Chinese cities, Disney representatives said they were also pleased with the exposure the programme facilitated within the broader Chinese media market, which is traditionally restricted by government controls and quotas.[7]

Meanwhile, the US$3.7 billion Shanghai Disney Resort, run by a joint venture between The Walt Disney Company and three firms owned by the city's municipal government, opened in June 2016.

returns to shareholders. External stakeholders in particular are no longer relegated to the fringes of activity and influence. Governance imperatives, growing regulatory pressures, and the public's newly articulated expectations of accountability and social responsibility, have placed stakeholder engagement squarely on the boardroom radar. The availability of new communication platforms such as social media has brought an extra level of volatility into these relationships. But it has also allowed chairs and directors to be proactive, analytical, and empathetic when addressing stakeholder needs and requirements.

By paying increasing attention to stakeholders and societies, and taking a broader long-term view of the organisation's activities while at the same time delivering results, boards are embracing the concept of stewardship. In the concluding chapter, we discuss the importance of stewardship and the role that boards can play in promoting it.

[7] *Financial Times.* (n.d.). Disney to expand language schools in China. http://www.ft.com/cms/s/0/4d6cfd1a-8932-11df-8ecd-00144feab49a.html#axzz4JPoQq100

33

Board Oversight of Geopolitical Risks and Opportunities

A new, more contentious geopolitical era appears to be unfolding, with the possibility that a once stable and cooperative order is being replaced by a more turbulent and fragmented global landscape.

WEF's Global Future Councils[1]

Geopolitical and Geoeconomic Resilience has Moved to the Forefront of the Board's Agenda

In 2023 and early 2024, Bab al-Mandab hit the headlines all over the world when it became the target of drone attacks by Yemen-based Houthi rebel forces. The 20-mile-wide strait became the critical bottleneck in shipping lanes linking the Indian Ocean and the Mediterranean Sea via the Suez Canal, with a quarter of the world's shipping passing along this route.[2] Many shipping carriers opted for the longer and costlier route around Africa's Cape of Good Hope. Retailers from Tesco to Primark and Maisons du Monde, and automakers including Tesla and Volvo Cars, faced rising freight costs on top of running out of stock and product parts.[3]

---

[1] World Economic Forum. (n.d.). Global Future Council on the Future of Geopolitics. https://www.weforum.org/communities/gfc-on-geopolitics/

[2] National Geographic. (n.d.). This small strait is essential to global shipping. https://www.nationalgeographic.com/history/article/bab-al-mandan-red-sea-suez-shipping-crisis-houthis-gaza

[3] Elbahrawy, F., J. Ponthus, and M. Msika. (2024). Chaos in the Red Sea is starting to bite into companies' profits. 23 January. https://www.bloomberg.com/news/articles/2024-01-23/shipping-chaos-tesla-tesco-others-warn-of-impact?embedded-checkout=true

In a global survey in 2023, 93% of multinationals were reporting losses linked to political instability. A ramp-up in deglobalisation and decoupling from China is on the minds of growing numbers of business leaders.[4] GE, Boeing, GM, and Ford Motor (among others) have been disclosing the risk that US–China frictions add to their business.[5] In extricating itself from the Russian market and divesting its stake in Russian state-owned oil and gas company Rosneft after the invasion of Ukraine, BP accepted losses of up to US$25 billion.[6] As BP Chair Helge Lund pointed out, Russia's military action represented 'a fundamental change'.[7]

Geopolitical instability has become a deep source of complexity and uncertainty – as well as a material risk – for businesses (see Appendix 33A). While geopolitical shifts are not new, their frequency and magnitude are continuing to intensify in a way that few anticipated. The repercussions have been far-reaching – leading to an erosion of the legitimacy of the Western-led post-WWII political, economic, and social institutions in the eyes of growing numbers.

There is a blurring of lines between military, economic, and financial spheres, as well as between hard power and soft power. With terms such as blended tactics and hybrid wars, it has even become difficult to distinguish between war and peace. Influence has become the most coveted currency of all. As geopolitical factors converge with trends in technology adoption, data proliferation, economic trends, the biosphere, and demographics, the world is increasingly at risk of polycrises – where the effect of this interplay of crises exceeds the individual impact of any one crisis.

Sectors deemed to be of critical importance to global economy, such as semiconductors (and increasingly, artificial intelligence), have witnessed a reversal in an earlier trend towards globalisation. These sectors have been characterised by a high level of global integration and cooperation in the past. But they are confronted with a growing trend toward 'techno-nationalism', an economic ideology that links a nation's technological capabilities and self-sufficiency to its state security. This trend puts tech giants like Meta and Tesla

---

[4] How are global businesses managing today's political risks? 2023 Survey and Report. Produced for WTW.

[5] Hudson, C. (2023). Boeing, Nike wrestle with supply chain pressures over China risk. Bloomberg Law, 16 May. https://news.bloomberglaw.com/esg/boeing-nike-wrestle-with-supply-chain-pressures-over-china-risk

[6] Bousso, R. and D. Zhdannikov. (2024). BP quits Russia in up to $25 billion hit after Ukraine invasion. Reuters. 28 February. https://www.reuters.com/business/energy/britains-bp-says-exit-stake-russian-oil-giant-rosneft-2022-02-27/

[7] Associated Press. (2022).BP exiting stake in Russian oil and gas company Rosneft. 27 February. https://www.voanews.com/a/bp-exiting-stake-in-russian-oil-and-gas-company-rosneft-/6462526.html

HSBC was caught in a geopolitical storm when its largest shareholder, China's biggest insurer Ping An, initiated calls in 2022 for HSBC to be broken up. At the time, the global financial services group served 40 million customers in more than 60 countries and employed a workforce of 200,000. Founded in Hong Kong in 1865, HSBC moved its headquarters to London in 1992. As such, it was overseen by UK regulators, despite generating the bulk of its profits in Hong Kong and other parts of the Chinese market. The bank also announced plans to pivot to Asia and to generate more income from asset management activities in China.[8] In tandem, it accelerated plans to exit retail banking in underperforming Western markets.[9]

For more than a year, Ping An mounted a public, vocal campaign, maintaining that a standalone Asia business listed in Hong Kong would enjoy higher profitability, lower capital requirements, and greater decision-making autonomy. In addition, the shareholder was concerned that HSBC's balancing act of satisfying China's as well as Western interests would only become more difficult in the future.[10] Perhaps crucially, Ping An representatives argued that 'The HK-listed business would be able to focus on investing resources in Asia and be more attuned to local Asia market dynamics'.[11] Some analysts pointed out that as an entity partly owned by the Chinese state, Ping An's unusual assertiveness likely reflected a mix of political as well as financial goals: The Chinese government was no longer comfortable with the idea of leaving Hong Kong's most valuable asset in Western hands.[12]

HSBC Chairman Mark Tucker and the board repeatedly rejected proposals to restructure the bank, arguing that the costs and risks would be too great and thus would not deliver increased value for shareholders.[13] Eventually, Ping An's failure to win the backing from other major shareholders put what seemed to be an end to the debate about the bank's structure.

at risk of dropping off list of the world's top 10 largest companies by market capitalisation.[14]

The geopolitical tensions and shifts have revealed the extent of interdependencies created during the heyday of globalisation, including European

[8] Makortoff, K. (2020). How HSBC got caught in a geopolitical storm over Hong Kong security law. *The Guardian*, 30 September. https://www.theguardian.com/world/2020/sep/30/how-hsbc-got-caught-in-a-geopolitical-storm-over-hong-kong-security-law

[9] Cruise, S., L. White. and S. Li. (2023). HSBC management blasted by top investor Ping An. Reuters, 18 April. https://www.reuters.com/markets/deals/shareholder-advisor-glass-lewis-tells-hsbc-investors-vote-against-break-up-2023-04-18/

[10] Morris, S. and O. Walker. (2022). HSBC chief denies Beijing is behind Ping An push to split bank. *Financial Times*, 1 December. https://www.ft.com/content/d2176d7e-5013-4da0-9b85-3629c6c3206c

[11] Ziady, H. (2023). HBSC's top shareholder calls for breakup, expressing ,deep concern'. CNN, 19 April. https://edition.cnn.com/2023/04/18/investing/hsbc-ping-an-breakup-statement/index.html

[12] Marsh, N. (2023). HSBC foils plan by major investor to break up bank. BBC News, 5 May. https://www.bbc.com/news/business-65478826

[13] Dunkley, E. and S. Morris. (2023). HSBC accused by top investor of "exaggerating" break-up risks. *Financial Times*, 18 April. https://www.ft.com/content/adf7ac0a-48f8-40f5-a4c4-aa1a74a6d7aa

[14] Tucker, P. (2023). Geopolitical tension with China would hit US critical technology sectors hard, new study shows. Defense One, 31 August. https://www.defenseone.com/policy/2023/08/geopolitical-tension-china-would-hit-us-critical-technology-sectors-hard-new-study-shows/389931/

> For Apple Inc, China has been both its biggest international market and its largest manufacturing hub. In 2023, news that China's various government agencies had imposed bans on the use of Apple products in government departments and state-owned enterprises prompted investors to sell nearly US$200 billion-worth of the company's shares. Apple had played its cards in China exceedingly well, cultivating relationships with government bodies at central, provincial, and municipal levels; directly and indirectly creating hundreds of thousands of jobs; and abiding by local regulations to the point of removing politically sensitive apps.[15]
>
> Nevertheless, the company inevitably found itself in the middle of US–China geopolitical tensions, trying to maintain close ties with China's political leadership while diversifying its worldwide manufacturing bases. In its 2023 annual report, the company stated: 'If disputes and conflicts further escalate in the future, actions by governments in response could be significantly more severe and restrictive and could materially adversely affect the Company's business.'[16]

manufacturing's reliance on Russian energy, the wholesale outsourcing of sensitive medical and technological activities to China among other nations, as well as the sourcing of critical minerals and other materials from conflict zones scattered around the world. Jamie Dimon, Chairman and CEO of JPMorgan Chase, described geopolitics as the world's single biggest risk: 'We have dealt with inflation before, we dealt with deficits before, we have dealt with recessions before, and we haven't really seen something like this pretty much since World War II.'[17]

Geopolitical Competence is Now a Muscle that Boards Must Develop

There should be no board in the world who takes this very lightly at this stage.
Peter Voser, Chairman, ABB[18]

---

[15] *Financial Times* (2023). 'A shot across the bow': how geopolitics threatens Apple's dependence on China. *Financial Times*, 16 September. https://www.ft.com/content/558a1196-15ba-4869-9d69-6f5405e0a758

[16] United States Securities and Exchange Commission (2023). Form 10-K. https://s2.q4cdn.com/470004039/files/doc_earnings/2023/q4/filing/_10-K-Q4-2023-As-Filed.pdf

[17] Smith, E. (2023). 'We have dealt with recessions before': Jamie Dimon says geopolitics is the world's biggest risk. CNBC, 26 September. https://www.cnbc.com/2023/09/26/jamie-dimon-says-geopolitics-is-the-worlds-biggest-risk.html

[18] *World Economy News.* (2024). CEOs leave Davos to game out 2024 geopolitical scenarios. 31 January. https://www.hellenicshippingnews.com/ceos-leave-davos-to-game-out-2024-geopolitical-scenarios-2/

When there is so much uncertainty, CEOs and boards ask, 'What can I do to be better prepared?'

Rich Lesser, Global Chair, BCG[19]

As companies navigate the fraught geopolitical terrain, boards have a strategic role to play. Before integrating geopolitical considerations in organisational strategy, the onus is on boards to engage management in a conversation on topics that include:

- Is the business likely to be exposed to an unexpected geopolitical event?
- How can geopolitical factors affect our objectives?
- How well have geopolitical risks been factored into the risk management framework in the company?
- What role will the board play vs management in terms of geopolitical risks?
- How should a board set the tone for active geopolitical risk management?

Proactive board oversight will ensure that geopolitical risk management is included in its strategy, investment decisions, and broader risk processes. The board is instrumental in anticipating specific points of future geopolitical tension and how they intersect with the business. For instance, an escalation of the Russia–Ukraine military conflict was on the cards since the events of 2014 when Russian forces seized Crimea, following which the armed forces of Ukraine confronted Russian-backed separatists across a front line in eastern Ukraine. Yet how many corporations anticipated the ramifications that escalation of this conflict – which finally occurred in February 2022 to be followed by sweeping sanctions by the West against Russia – would have for the global electronics industry? The range of contingencies facing Western businesses in Russia was virtually impossible to predict.[20] They included Russia's position as the world's third-largest producer of nickel, which is used in lithium-ion and electric vehicle batteries. Ukraine, for its part, provides 70% of the world's supply of neon, the bulk of which is bought by the US microchip sector.[21]

[19] *World Economy News*. (2024). CEOs leave Davos to game out 2024 geopolitical scenarios. 31 January. https://www.hellenicshippingnews.com/ceos-leave-davos-to-game-out-2024-geopolitical-scenarios-2/

[20] Braw, E. (2022). Insurance and geopolitics. AEI, 28 June. https://www.aei.org/research-products/report/insurance-and-geopolitics-is-geopolitical-confrontation-making-international-business-uninsurable/

[21] KPMG. (n.d.). Immediate and long-term impacts of the Russia–Ukraine war on supply chains. https://kpmg.com/us/en/articles/2022/impacts-russia-ukraine-war-supply-chains.html#:~:text=Supply%20chain%20snarls%20and%20rising%20prices&text=Hundreds%20of%20ships%20laden%20with,and%20inflation%20around%20the%20world

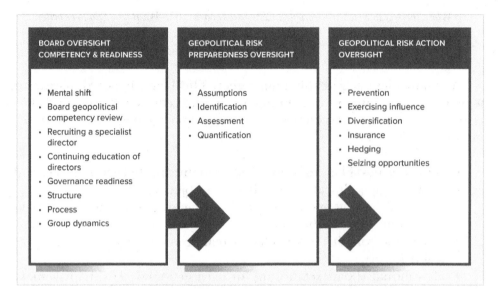

Figure 33.1   Three Stages of Overseeing Geopolitical Risks

There are three primary areas of board influence and action when it comes to overseeing geopolitical issues (see Figure 33.1).

For the board, it is critical to be clear about the strengths it can draw on – and the deficiencies it faces – in engaging management on the topics and implications of geopolitical risks. This requires that the board (1) adopt a geopolitical outlook, (2) assess its in-house expertise, (3) recruit for geopolitical knowledge and insight, (4) engage in continuing education and learning, and (5) ensure that it is equipped with the right structures, processes, and group dynamics to weigh in on geopolitical issues. Let's look at each of these in turn.

Adopting a geopolitical outlook

The trends and discourses of peak globalisation of the late twentieth and early twenty-first centuries have left many decision-makers in a comfort zone of 'higher, better, more'. Thought leaders such as the BlackRock Investment Institute actively challenge this classic business cycle view of today's economy. They argue that to hope for a soft landing as opposed to a recession is to miss the point entirely: The aggregate effect of structural realities – geopolitical fragmentation, coming out of the COVID-19 pandemic 2020–2222, low-carbon transition, and shrinking workforces – has been to disconnect from the cyclical narrative, thus stoking further volatility.[22]

---

[22] Fink, L. (n.d.). Annual Chairman's letter to investors. BlackRock. https://www.blackrock.com/corporate/insights/blackrock-investment-institute/publications/outlook

This is the long-term outlook the board and directors must take on to avoid complacency. Rarely in history has the paradigm of 'What has worked in the past is unlikely to work in future' been more pertinent. Building a lasting and resilient business requires that boards internalise geopolitical tensions as a driving force of the strategic planning process.

Assess in-house pool of expertise in geopolitics

Do we know what it is we don't know? Does the board have an idea of where its blind spots might lie when it comes to the language and knowledge of geopolitics? An internal competence assessment is an important first step. In the 1990s, US corporations found themselves generating upwards of 50% of their revenue in international markets. That spurred a wave of interest in international assignments, overseas study programmes and foreign languages – as well as market research, localisation strategies, and local content generation. Today, the magnitude of boards' response to what is unfolding in the world around them should be no less ambitious.

Recruiting for geopolitical knowledge and insight

Rising geopolitical risks dictate that companies place the right people in the boardroom in order to oversee geopolitical risks and opportunities effectively. Geopolitical expertise will go a long way in complementing a modern-day board's pool of knowledge in areas such as technology, digitalisation, cybersecurity, and regulatory frameworks. Many boards have recruited former diplomats, politicians, and senior civil servants as directors.

Providing directors with continuing education

To help directors improve their discernment of issues, it is necessary to fortify their overall geopolitical exposure through continual education. This may

In November 2023, former US Deputy National Security Advisor Dina Powell McCormick joined the board of ExxonMobil. In a press statement, ExxonMobil Chairman and CEO Darren Woods said: Dina is a distinguished executive with a rare level of geopolitical, national security, and economic experience. She has served two US presidents in diplomatic and national security roles and, more recently, led Goldman Sachs' sustainability efforts . . . ExxonMobil will greatly benefit from her global leadership and distinguished reputation as a leader who understands a challenging and changing global marketplace.[23]

[23] World Oil. (2023). Former US Deputy National Security Advisor joins ExxonMobil's board of directors. 12 November. https://www.worldoil.com/news/2023/11/12/former-u-s-deputy-national-security-advisor-joins-exxonmobil-s-board-of-directors/

come in the form of active coaching, formal training, tabletop exercises, or seminars conducted by leading experts, consultants, and specialists in the field. The training should be forward looking – how geopolitical tension is evolving and what kind of impact it will have on business in the future. In a world where misinformation and fake news are constantly available, an insightful geopolitical perspective is critical for boards. Continuing education will help directors connect geopolitical events with corporate strategy and come up with creative solutions.

The board's structure, processes, and group dynamics to address geopolitics

Wading into geopolitical questions cannot be a free-for-all or a string of spontaneous acts. Boards need to be able to answer questions such as:

- Who has responsibility for geopolitical risk management?
- What is the process that underpins the flow of information on geopolitical issues? and
- How are geopolitical issues discussed?

To provide thoughtful and informed answers, boards need to ensure that the guidance they provide on corporate decisions is supported by an efficient structure, strong processes, and effective group dynamics (see Figure 33.2).

For a checklist of questions directors may raise when evaluating the board's geopolitical competence, knowledge capital, and readiness to oversee management's performance, see Appendix 33B.

A Toolkit for Addressing Geopolitics

As organisations encounter new instalments in the ongoing permacrisis, forward-looking boards will ensure that some geopolitical tensions are factored into corporate decision-making. At the same time, unanticipated risks will test the resilience of the company's business models.[24] In developing an oversight framework for better anticipation and preparedness, boards need to focus on four areas: (1) assumptions, (2) identification, (3) assessment, and (4) quantification.

Underlying every piece of strategy and decision-making are **assumptions** – whether made explicit or otherwise – regarding the business environment and global markets. As paradigms shift, they exert a knock-on effect on previous sets of assumptions and expectations. Instead of a macro picture, the company

---

[24] World Economic Forum. (2023). The global risks report 2023. https://www3.weforum.org/docs/WEF_Global_Risks_Report_2023.pdf

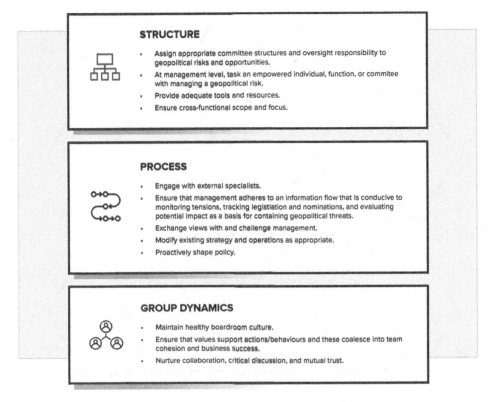

STRUCTURE

- Assign appropriate committee structures and oversight responsibility to geopolitical risks and opportunities.
- At management level, task an empowered individual, function, or commitee with managing a geopolitical risk.
- Provide adequate tools and resources.
- Ensure cross-functional scope and focus.

PROCESS

- Engage with external specialists.
- Ensure that management adheres to an information flow that is conducive to monitoring tensions, tracking legislation and nominations, and evaluating potential impact as a basis for containing geopolitical threats.
- Exchange views with and challenge management.
- Modify existing strategy and operations as appropriate.
- Proactively shape policy.

GROUP DYNAMICS

- Maintain healthy boardroom culture.
- Ensure that values support actions/behaviours and these coalesce into team cohesion and business success.
- Nurture collaboration, critical discussion, and mutual trust.

Figure 33.2   A Board that is Governance-ready to Answer Geopolitical Questions

is now looking at tangible threats that can directly affect top lines, bottom lines, and valuations.

At the time of writing (2024), the Russia–Ukraine war is ongoing, and it is not possible to anticipate if it will end in 1 year, 5 years, 20 years or next week. Nonetheless, assumptions behind unpredictable events can be expressed in terms of varying degrees of probability and corresponding impacts on reputation, sales, supply chain, finance, operations, and stakeholders. Allowing paralysis to set in because ostensibly, 'nobody knows' is a slippery slope that leads executives to underestimating or ignoring geopolitical risks. It is the board's responsibility to challenge perceived helplessness in the face of unpredictable risks and events.

Identification – to prepare for dealing with geopolitical risks, management needs to identify what those risks are. On the board's part, it is valuable to have a deep understanding of how these risks interconnect and cluster into discrete frameworks, and what the driving forces behind them are. As part of the oversight mechanism, boards can review the risks, the drivers, and the extenuating and attenuating forces that are on the management's radar.

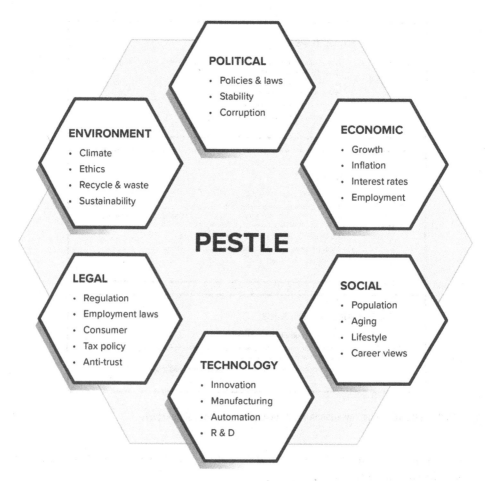

Figure 33.3   The PESTLE Framework of Macroeconomic Factors
Source: Adapted from PestleAnalysis.com.

PESTLE (sometimes spelled PESTEL) is one such framework, flagging specific political, economic, social, technological, legal, and environmental trends (see Figure 33.3) and the momentum they create in the geopolitical landscape, potentially affecting all aspects of the business.[25] Results of a PESTLE analysis can be linked with a SWOT analysis, painting a dynamic picture of an organisation's internal capabilities relative to external developments and threats.

Assessment – once geopolitical risks and opportunities have been identified, the board oversees management's development and stress-testing of

---

[25] Yüksel, I. (2012). Developing a multi-criteria decision-making model for PESTEL analysis. *International Journal of Business and Management* 7(24): 52.

geopolitical scenario plans. This assessment includes the likely and worst impacts, the time frame when the impacts will be felt, and the chain effects of corporate response, which might lead to changes in the company's strategy. To fulfil its duty of care and protect the company, boards should aim to look beyond the obvious and scrutinise all scenarios through different prisms:

- Geopolitical shifts can affect sales in markets that are vulnerable to geo-political shocks.
- Unstable geopolitical relationships can deter expansion in new and emerging markets.
- Unstable locations and policies may affect the company's ability to attract and retain talent.
- Insecure borders or military conflicts could impact supply chains and partnerships.
- Political and regulatory whims may create capital risk such as high cost of capital or loss of investment.
- Geopolitical turmoil may result in loss of assets due to confiscation or expropriation.

Time is an important dimension in conducting assessment of future risks. In terms of safeguarding business continuity and formulating response plans, a trend whose tipping point is projected to occur in 2050 is useful to iden-tity but will be assessed differently than an event that is looming on the 2030 horizon. Even then, some trends are sizable and obvious, yet they often fail to be assessed correctly. Cousins of both the black swan and the elephant in the room, they are what author and strategist Michele Wucker has termed 'gray rhino' risks.[26] This could be the expanding US budget deficit – or the growing political and business clout of evangelical groups in large parts of Africa, Asia, and Latin America.

Quantification – ss part of assessment, quantification is key to determining the optimal reaction. Quantifying geopolitical risks might be deemed difficult due to the complexity. If not done adequately, companies could misprice the potential negative impacts and choose less effective responses. Companies can use ad hoc methods to conduct internal analyses. For example, in a region that is suffering from geopolitical instability, a company may decide to quantify the impact on individual components of financial statements: assets, liabilities, equity, revenues, and expenses. Similar to a sum-of-the-parts analysis, tentative responses to the risks – avoid, mitigate, transfer, accept – can be integrated

---

[26] Wucker, M. (2016). *The gray rhino: How to recognize and act on the obvious dangers we ignore.* Macmillan.

into the financial forecasts. The company is then in a position to look at the cost/benefit of each response and make an informed decision.

Effective boards need to look closely at the quantitative models applied by management. Underpinning the market price of risk is the market participants' consensus at a given moment in time. This renders bond yield spreads and sovereign CDS premiums volatile. It is also advisable for directors to remain conversant with the latest analytical tools and techniques including systems powered by artificial intelligence (AI). On top of automating data collection, AI tools can rapidly and frequently draw out patterns in third-party risks and enrich decision-making with predictive analytics. The end result is a robust, dynamic, and scalable data model.

For a spot check on how well equipped the board is to oversee management preparedness to handle geopolitical risks, the questions listed in Appendix 33C can be helpful.

Overseeing Management's *Action* in Tackling Geopolitical Risk

Once a board has a good handle on management's preparedness, the board needs to exercise oversight over management's action in addressing geopolitical risk. In collaboration with management, boards are expected to develop strategic options for acting on geopolitical risks by making decisions and implementing them. Concurrently, geopolitical risks are to be integrated into the company's enterprise risk management (ERM) programme alongside and in relation to other risks such as economic, market, ESG, cyber, technological, and legal risks.

When geopolitical tensions evolve, a company needs to anticipate and assess the situation as early as possible. In some situations, geopolitical disruptions can be prevented or proactively influenced. In other circumstances, geopolitical risks can be mitigated well in advance through diversification. And in still other setups, geopolitical disruptions and costs could be minimised through insurance and hedging.

In overseeing action on the geopolitical risk front, a board may lean into a number of levers to exert influence (see Figure 33.4).

Prevention

Prevention is better – and less costly – than cure. This is doubly true of risky geopolitical and geoeconomic developments. Putting into place a system of early warning signs, getting a grip on disruption before it has materialised, and potentially avoiding high-risk locales completely. All of these go a long way in preventing negative outcomes.

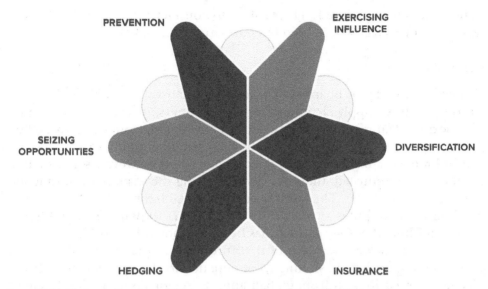

PREVENTION

EXERCISING
INFLUENCE

SEIZING
OPPORTUNITIES

DIVERSIFICATION

HEDGING

INSURANCE

Figure 33.4   The Levers Boards can Apply in Overseeing Action on Geopolitical Risks

In destabilised parts of the world, global companies may establish contingency measures. These will allow them to take swift action if necessary in order to protect people, assets, and reputation. For example, creating local subsidiaries with local boards that can easily be sold or let go in case of disruption.

Also, since the global pandemic, achieving supply chain resilience has been a hot topic for many corporations. Beyond strengthening partnerships with key suppliers (who should formulate their own business continuity plans), companies are well advised to join their partners in running scenario testing – revealing how the chain and its component parts are likely to behave in a crisis.

Exercising influence

The old maxim – the best way to predict the future is to create it – is very much at home in the world of geopolitical risk. Boards and C-suites are not just passive bystanders in the world's geopolitical theatre. Often their best bet is to put forward specific positions on political issues and then shape the geopolitical and regulatory landscape according to their values and by engaging with key stakeholders at local, national, and supranational levels. In the long run, these efforts may contribute to establishing a vibrant consultative process involving businesses and government agencies.

Smaller companies that lack the clout of their large peers may opt to enter into coalitions and alliances. Typically, boards are involved in overseeing the political influencing process. Their role is to consider reputational risks and make the process transparent and open to scrutiny by stakeholders.

Diversification

It is never too early for boards to consider alternatives to established manufacturing centres, supply chain and logistics partners, or even selected strategic priorities. Manufacturers across the ASEAN region, from the early 2000s, appeared to be facing impending doom as multinationals were lured to China's lower-cost base. On several occasions since, however, some of the operations have returned, their owners reassessing the wisdom of putting all their eggs in one basket. The latest wave in this tug-of-war had had to do with US–China trade disputes as well as with the COVID-19 pandemic. Suddenly, pursuing a China Plus One strategy has become eminently sensible.[27]

Christine Lagarde, President of the European Central Bank (ECB), has spoken about global trade shifting from dependence to diversification, from efficiency to security, and from globalisation to regionalisation. She has also pointed out that more and more economic activity between countries was directed by values.[28] Reflecting that trend, 'nearshoring' has ceded ground to 'friendshoring' as business partners seek out not just geographic proximity but similarity of geopolitical outlook.[29] As foreign direct investment flows prefer geopolitically aligned markets, Mexico has replaced China as the largest trading partner of the United States.[30]

Bocar Group, Mexico's global auto parts supplier specialising in light-metal castings and assembly, has been a champion in making the Mexican logistics industry more attractive and competitive. Embracing digitisation, continuous upskilling, and a vision of sustainable mobility including electric and hybrid vehicles, the company has been recognised for supplier excellence by partners including GM. Founded as a family business, the company has also invested in manufacturing plants in the United States and in technical and engineering centres in Germany, China, and Japan.[31]

---

[27] Hsu, S. (2021). Which Asian nations can benefit from the 'China plus one' strategy ? The Diplomat, 11 June. https://thediplomat.com/2021/06/which-asian-nations-can-benefit-from-the-china-plus-one-strategy/

[28] Lagarde, C. (2022). A new global map (speech). European central Bank, 22 April. https://www.ecb.europa.eu/press/key/date/2022/html/ecb.sp220422~c43af3db20.en.html

[29] *The Economist.* (2023). What is 'friendshoring'? 30 August. https://www.economist.com/the-economist-explains/2023/08/30/what-is-friendshoring

[30] Spinetto, J.P. (2023). Mexico's friend-shoring moment may have to wait until after elections. Bloomberg UK, 16 September. https://www.bloomberg.com/news/newsletters/2023-09-16/mexico-s-friend-shoring-moment-may-have-to-wait-until-after-elections

[31] Moreno, I. (n.d.). Bocar: Anticipating customer needs to sustain growth. Mexico Business News. https://mexicobusiness.news/automotive/news/bocar-anticipating-customer-needs-sustain-growth

Insurance

Cost-effective insurance (such as political risk insurance) is a key factor in risk mitigation. If a company operates in a country where geopolitical risks are intensifying, with the right insurance coverage, it can maintain business continuity or at least secure compensation for business disruptions. Political insurance instruments may cover a wide range of damages across the value chain. Specific insurance products have been designed to help clients build cross-border resilience plans, such as political risk or violence insurance, reputational risk insurance, and terrorism insurance.

Boards and directors ought to ensure that the geopolitical insurance programme proposed by management will measure up to the scale of the geopolitical events in question and cover damages from disruptions.

Hedging

Apart from insurance, geopolitical risk can be hedged in different ways. Geopolitical threats often result in ripple effects that have impact across financial markets. Adverse movements in currency, real-assets and financial assets can diminish the value of investments in countries that are affected. Hedging – if used properly – can minimise the negative impact. Boards and directors who oversee geopolitical risk management need to understand the principles and ways of hedging as a way of dealing with geopolitical threats.

Sovereign credit default swap (SCDS) spreads can be used as a proxy for country risk as they capture sovereign credit risk, political risk, and macroeconomic risks. Similarly, currency swaps can hedge against currency risk exposure by swapping cash flows in the foreign currency with domestic currency at a predetermined rate. In addition to SCDS and currency, the purchase of precious metals such as gold, silver, palladium, and platinum is also positively related to geopolitical threats and may be used to hedge against geopolitical risk. Directors need to understand the fine line between speculation and hedging using derivatives: whereas speculation generates risk, hedging through the right instruments will reduce risk.

Seizing the opportunity

The board's remit in supervising geopolitical risk is to ceaselessly evaluate different options, mitigate risk, and align capabilities into a competitive edge. Throughout the separate stages of developing a board's oversight of preparing for and taking action on geopolitical risks, effective boards understand the big-picture aspects of risk management:

- **Very few events – if any – spell end-of-the-world, catastrophic consequences**. In many ways, geopolitical shocks are just that: short-burst, short-lived occurrences. Average market response to unexpected geopolitical shocks has been quite modest historically. During the first week of trading that transpired in the aftermath of the 9/11 attacks in 2001, the S&P 500 Index fell sharply, by nearly 12%. Yet, the market went on to recoup the entirety of these losses within 25 business days.[32]

- **Boards should aim to win the war rather than every single battle**. For all the preparedness measures, instruments, and mechanisms that boards have installed, there will be times when a board and its directors will fail to anticipate or recognise certain geopolitical risks. The bigger prize is to be found in leveraging geopolitical risk preparedness and action to future-proof the organisation towards agility and resilience so that it can sustain growth and value creation for the long term.

- **Star performers among boards and their members not only tackle risk – they thrive on it**. When the going gets tough, the tough get creative. In the geopolitical risk arena, best-in-class companies explore risks from multiple perspectives, deal with them head-on and try to find a different angle. Far from getting overwhelmed, they probe the situation for hidden opportunity. On the face of it, the 2003 SARS outbreak in China was no walk in the park. Yet, in retrospect, that crisis paved the way for the rise of Alibaba and other homegrown ecommerce giants.

The questions in Appendix 33D will help board members gauge the board's relative strength in overseeing management actions vis-à-vis geopolitical risks.

Appendix 33A: Business dimensions affected by geopolitical risk

- Economic activity, growth, and profitability
- Business operations, business continuity, and value chains
- Supplies of energy and raw materials
- Capital controls, exchange controls, and currency devaluations
- Access to trade routes and transportation infrastructure
- Stock market returns
- M&A activity
- Discriminatory actions against a targeted company, including nationalisation, expropriation, or confiscation of assets
- Investment impairments due to violent political unrest or war
- Unforeseen changes in regulatory frameworks, taxation, price controls, import quotas, and tariffs

---

[32] BlackRock. (n.d.). A framework to assess and price geopolitical risk. https://www.blackrock.com/us/individual/insights/blackrock-investment-institute/geopolitical-risk-framework

- Rapid developments in the adoption and regulation of AI and quantum computing, and the attendant cyber-security threats
- Workforce disruptions and industrial action.

Appendix 33B: Evaluating the board's geopolitical competence

- Does your board have the capability to form its own perspectives on geopolitics?
- Does your board include members with geopolitical expertise?
- Does the board have the right people, structure, processes, and group dynamics to oversee key geopolitical risks and to challenge management?
- How often is the board briefed on geopolitical developments and their potential implications?
- Will your corporate structure need to change to manage geopolitical risk?
- Are your board's information systems responsive to geopolitical information and data?
- Does the board understand how geopolitical risks map onto the company's enterprise risk management policies and procedures?
- Who or which committee is responsible for monitoring, analysing, and interpreting geopolitical risks?

Appendix 33C: Gauging management's preparedness to handle geopolitical risks

- What corporate strategy assumptions could be derailed by geopolitics?
- If geopolitical risks challenge management's critical risk assumptions, is the board ready to push for a strategic shift?
- How can 'unknowable' geopolitics be planned for and understood?
- Which framework does the management team utilise to identify and assess geopolitical factors? Is the geopolitical framework robust? What are the critical factors identified?
- What suggestions does the board have for management to improve monitoring to identify shocks early or to have adequate visibility over the supply chain to identify threats?
- Does the board understand the process for managing geopolitical risk through scenario analysis and stress testing?
- Considering possible geopolitical trajectories and new economic scenarios, how might geopolitical uncertainties affect the company's valuation and financial statements?
- Is management addressing geopolitical risk in a comprehensive fashion (covering cultural, technological innovations, social, and legislative dimensions)?

Appendix 33D: Overseeing management's actions in dealing with geopolitical risks

- Do the board and management translate perspectives and preparedness on geopolitical risk into actions?
- Does your board work with management to prevent geopolitical risk in the first place?
- How can your company's voice be heard without risking adverse reactions from the government or the public? Will influencing strategy such as lobbying work in your industry?
- Does your board have robust processes and controls to protect against bribery and corruption while exercising political and legal influence?
- What is the nature and extent of corporate superpowers' intervention and influence on the governments of small countries?
- How quickly can your company reduce supply chain dependency on a market affected by geopolitical tensions?
- How does diversification offer resilience and stability in the company's growth and performance? Could diversification increase other risks?
- What inputs can the board give on geopolitical risk insurance?
- How does the board tell the difference between management's hedging practice and speculation?
- Is the company capable of using derivatives to hedge against risks?
- Are there opportunities for enhancing growth when geopolitical risks are minimised?
- Is the company willing to accept a certain level of geopolitical risk to harness opportunities?
- Are geopolitical opportunities and risks considered simultaneously as part of the strategy setting process?

CHAPTER 34

ESG Oversight in the Boardroom

Climate change, social justice, biodiversity, gender inequity – these are just some of the issues on the growing list of sustainability and social concerns that have dominated public discourse in recent years. This has been accompanied by increasingly vocal societal expectations of corporates to address these, and boards are taking notice. Of FTSE 100 boards 54% have now established some variation of an ESG committee[1] and more than 90% of S&P 500 companies publish ESG reports.[2]

While increasingly common on the board agenda, board oversight of ESG is complex for a number of reasons. Regulatory requirements are evolving rapidly, demanding considerable time and effort for organisations to remain conversant with, even for basic compliance. Clearly defining what is material can also be a challenge, as is the diversity and amplitude of stakeholder expectations. Identifying salient metrics to monitor ESG performance is not always straightforward. Finally, collecting and disclosing ESG performance is becoming a critical issue for both regulators – and investors. This chapter provides a framework for boards to come to grips with the key dimensions of ESG oversight (summarised in Figure 34.1) and the essential decisions it needs to make in order to thoughtfully exercise its responsibility and strategic acumen in this area – including a study we did which helps shed light on how to avoid the risk of greenwashing.

---

[1] KPMG. (2023). ESG oversight. KPMG Nigeria Board Governance Centre, May. https://assets .kpmg.com/content/dam/kpmg/ng/pdf/esg-oversight-the-boards-role-and-focus.pdf
[2] McKinsey Sustainability. (2022). Does ESG really matter – and why? 10 August. https://www .mckinsey.com/capabilities/sustainability/our-insights/does-esg-really-matter-and-why

Figure 34.1   ESG Compliance Oversight: Laying the Foundation for ESG Practices

Compliance with ESG Requirements

There is a growing amount and stringency of regulatory action around ESG reporting, notably in the United States and the European Union but also increasingly in other parts of the world. These relate to climate change, diversity and inclusion, supply chain transparency, and human rights, among others. The SEC announced rules in March 2022 to improve and standardise disclosures to identify more proactively ESG misconduct, to prevent mislabelling of funds as green, and has also introduced human capital reporting requirements. Nasdaq has put into place board diversity disclosure requirements. States are also taking action on this front: California's Climate Corporate Accountability Act requires companies with over US$1 billion in turnover to disclose GHG emissions annually.[3]

---

[3] Hsueh, L. (2023). Analysis: The potential global impact of California's new corporate climate disclosure laws. PBS News Hour. 15 October. https://www.pbs.org/newshour/nation/analysis-the-potential-global-impact-of-californias-new-corporate-climate-disclosure-laws#:~:text=California%20Gov.,starting%20in%202026%20and%202027

In 2021, a high court in The Hague ruled that Shell had to take immediate action to cut its carbon emissions by a significant 45% before 2030.

In February 2023, ClientEarth, an environmental law charity, filed a lawsuit against the board of directors of Shell plc, asserting that it had failed to adequately address and mitigate climate change. While ultimately unsuccessful, this approach demonstrates a significant shift in focus in climate-change-related litigation, toward breaches of fiduciary duty by boards of directors. Directors have a crucial responsibility to prioritise and ensure the accuracy of ESG-related disclosures.

Companies within the European Union also need to navigate the growing body of ESG disclosure requirements. Under the European Union's Green deal, all large companies and all listed companies in the European Union must disclose their ESG performance annually, through statements which comply with the European Sustainability Reporting Standards.[4] The Sustainable Finance Disclosure Regulation (SFDR) obliges financial actors in the European Union to disclose ESG metrics at entity and product level. Sustainability-related disclosures in prospectuses are mandated by the European Securities and Markets Authority (ESMA). Companies must also demonstrate that executive pay is in line with ESG performance, and that shareholders have the right to vote on remuneration matters, according to the Shareholder Rights Directive II (SRD). Further, companies need to be careful about the claims they can make regarding their ESG performance by the EU directive against greenwashing.

There is more and more legal action on ESG matters aimed at both boards and directors. Boards need to closely monitor how legal liability is evolving through rulings such as the one against Shell in 2021.

ESG Governance Oversight: Shifting from Compliance to Proactive Governance

To improve ESG oversight, boards are moving from an approach based on compliance to one that is more proactive, engaging both on a risk and a strategy perspective of ESG. This relies on strengthening ESG capabilities either by nomination of directors with the requisite skills and experience, as well as ensuring that structures and processes are well aligned with the intersection of ESG with strategy and risk.

People: Nominating new directors, education, and seeking guidance

When it comes to reinforcing the people pillar on this topic, a useful exercise is to integrate ESG dimensions relevant to the business into the board skills

---

[4] Required by the European Union's Corporate Sustainability Reporting Directive.

mapping to identify strengths to leverage as well as to make explicit any gaps. In the latter case, the board may include this with the nomination committee's criteria for recruiting new directors. In addition to the benefits to board practice, this practice may serve as a potent signalling effect for stakeholders. Such expertise is relevant to a growing number of sectors, including renewable energy, artificial intelligence, electric vehicles, and industry transformation, which are all rapidly evolving and require specialised knowledge and insights.

To address knowledge gaps or specific competences, another important lever is ESG education for boards. This may take the form of workshops and retreats with ESG consultants, who can not only keep board members up to date with the strategic and risk ramifications of their current and future strategy, but also prompt reflection and discussions around what directors should be considering as part of their oversight role.

Structures: Expanding board and key committee responsibilities to include ESG

Not only it is essential to have the appropriate ESG expertise, these considerations need to be systematically integrated into board work through its structures and processes. There are two main ways in which boards are doing this: (1) by distributing these responsibilities into the existing committee structures, or (2) by setting up a separate ESG committee. While either approach may be warranted depending on the structure and strategy of the organisation and its board, what remains essential is that the board as a whole deliberates the resulting implications, including both material risks and business drivers.

In the first case, it is important to map each of the dimensions and how it intersects with the work of the respective committees. For example, governance issues tend to be dealt with by the nominating and governance committee, while the compensation or human resources committee usually deal with DEI issues. The audit committee is often given the responsibility for ESG disclosure and metrics. In second case, that is, when establishing a standalone ESG committee, it is a good idea to include members from other committees, such as the nominating, governance, and risk committees. This allows for a platform for in-depth discussions on ESG issues within the wider framework of strategy and risk, and can also serve to streamline board reporting on ESG matters. In more than two-thirds of S&P 100 companies, ESG oversight is spread over two or more committees, reflecting the complexity of this board topic.[5]

---

[5] Leka, L. (2022). Board Oversight of Sustainability and ESG. IFAC. https://www.ifac.org/ knowledge-gateway/supporting-international-standards/discussion/board-oversight-sustainability-and-esg#:~:text=As%20ESG%20is%20so%20broad,and%20regulations%20 and%20related%20assurance

Process: Reporting to the board on ESG issues

Data collection and reporting requires significant organisational attention and resources. To ensure that the data is meaningful and that its collection does not overburden the organisation, the board must actively engage with management to determine appropriate and salient metrics, as well as the utilisation of reliable data sources. The level of granularity as well as the cadence of reporting is also an area that management and the board should agree upon.

The information and data collected will vary based on the company's priorities, customer needs, and investor expectations. The specific needs and circumstances of each organisation will ultimately determine what is needed, as well as the frequency of discussions. This will also depend on how the discussion is structured.

Digitising ESG oversight and reporting has the potential to revolutionise the way boards oversee ESG. Data collection and analytics allow the centralisation of data into a consolidated platform in real-time and clear insights in the analysis. It also enhances traceability of data, through clear workflows to improve accountability. The benefit for boards is greater speed and precision in identifying potential issues, and their prompt attention, but also understanding linkages across topics.

Policies: Aligning ESG goals with key aspects of the company's operations

In order to ensure that company processes are aligned with ESG priorities, a review of all policies, as well as corporate governance guidelines and committee charters is important.[6] These policies should address key areas including, but not limited to, environmental impact, social responsibility, labour practices, diversity and inclusion, human rights compliance, data protection, and privacy. The allocation of responsibilities within the organisation also should be clearly documented. Regularly reviewing policies will ensure that they are aligned with the latest ESG best practices and regulatory requirements.

A critical part of embedding ESG into the organisation is having the right KPIs and linking these to the incentive plans of management teams is key to ensure their prioritisation. To effectively incorporate ESG considerations into executive pay packs, boards must establish specific, standardised, measurable, and transparent ESG performance metrics. The implementation of such metrics is helpful to prevent potential confusion or unnecessary external scrutiny.

---

[6] Ashley, J., Thompson Hine LLP, and R.V. Morrison. (2021). ESG Governance: Board and management roles and responsibilities. *Harvard Law School Forum on Corporate Governance.* https://corpgov.law.harvard.edu/2021/11/10/esg-governance-board-and-management-roles-responsibilities/

In addition to integrating ESG into its own risk process, boards also need to oversee the integration of ESG into the company's overall risk management processes. Potential ESG risks may be present in areas such as operations, supply chain, and stakeholder engagement. To effectively manage any social risk related to labour issues within supply chain, for example, it is recommended to develop robust supplier codes of conduct and engage in dialogue with relevant stakeholders.

ESG Metrics: Understanding which ESG Factors are Salient

ESG metrics reflect and demonstrate which ESG factors are most important to the business. They highlight potential risks and opportunities and align financial gains with the expectations of socially conscious investors. ESG metrics must also translate into actions are clear and trackable. There is no one-size-fits-all template for ESG metrics since they need to be carefully adapted to company-specific factors. As such, the reporting to the board may vary greatly across companies.

Selecting the right ESG metrics for the company can be overwhelming. Boards can be guided by the following principles.

1. **Determine key priorities and objectives**. Use scenario analysis to focus on the metrics that have the most impact on the business. This analysis assesses how different ESG-related events could impact the financial and operational performance of the company. It can be helpful to cross-check with competitors in the same or different industries, for example. Key priorities can be validated through collaboration with external experts.

2. **Align with company strategy**. The ESG metrics must align with the company's overall strategy. When considering accessing new markets, developing new products, enhancing brand reputation, or increasing operational efficiency, the board needs to analyse what these mean for its ESG objectives, and any potential trade-offs across objectives themselves, as well as tensions resulting from different time horizons.

3. **Identify key stakeholder concerns**. It is crucial to consider the concerns and expectations of different stakeholders, and how these play out over different scenarios. Stakeholder mapping as well as materiality matrices, are helpful tools to map the different priorities of stakeholder groups and their potential impact on the business. Boards should be actively engaging with not only investors, but also employees and customers, as well as regulators and others (e.g. end users, advocacy groups). Stakeholders often have conflicting interests, for example, investors may not prioritise social impact, which can lead to conflicts with local

community or environmental activists regarding decisions such as emissions targets. Full board discussions around how these align with board values, as well as strategy and risk, are essential in determining how to resolve such cases and commit to action.

4. **Comply with legal and regulatory requirements and ESG frameworks.** Boards must be aware of all legal or regulatory requirements that dictate which ESG metrics a business should monitor. Failure to comply with these requirements can lead to legal consequences. In this sense, it is mandatory to thoroughly research and understand the applicable laws and regulations (as discussed earlier in this chapter). There are also established ESG frameworks and standards available to guide the selection of metrics. In the following section, we elaborate on the most recognised frameworks.

5. **Ensure data availability and reliability over time.** To be useful, ESG metrics need to be collected, accessed, and gathered consistently, as well as reviewed periodically. Tracking ESG performance over time is essential for monitoring progress towards objectives. It will also help identification of trends, areas for improvement, as well as potential risks or opportunities. As already mentioned, metrics should be kept to a minimum, in order to avoid overburdening the organisation. As businesses evolve and the regulatory landscape changes, reviewing metrics to ensure continued relevance and alignment with strategic objectives is good practice.

6. **Benchmarking against peers using ESG ratings.** Examining the ESG metrics used by industry peers and competitors provides a good basis for comparison. Understanding ESG rating agencies and methodologies can assist in this benchmarking – and also serves as part of board oversight of ESG, since investors often use them to screen their investments. Rating agencies collect data on a company's ESG activities through surveys and analysis of publicly available disclosures made by the company. ESG rating is still in its early stages and despite numerous players in the field, none has yet emerged as an industry standard (refer to Table 34.1). Discrepancies among raters arise due to differences in methodologies, data sources, rating objectives, and frequency of updates. Board members need to be conversant with the different methodology types, data sources, objectives, and other relevant details that ESG raters use to determine their ratings.

It is important to be aware of conflicts of interest among some rating agencies, for example, those that also provide consulting services to the companies they rate. They offer insights into how companies can enhance their scores. Staying up to date with rating practices is therefore critical in ensuring that

Table 34.1 Sample ESG Rating Agencies

RATING AGENCY	AREA	DATA SOURCES	UPDATE
Bloomberg ESG Disclosure Score	E, S, G	• Data provided by companies • External ESG providers	Daily
Refinitiv ESG Scores	Measures performance based on E, S and G ratios. Data are grouped in ten categories: resources use, emissions, innovation, management, shareholders, CSR strategy, workforce, human rights, community and product responsibility	• Publicly available information	Bi-weekly
S&P Global Ratings ESG Evaluation	E, S, G	• Sectoral questionnaire	Annual
MSCI	Measures corporate performance using environmental ratios, as well as those regarding weapons and social issues	• Data provided by companies • Databases (governmental, scientific, NGOs) • News and media	Continuous monitoring: detailed annual analysis
ISS Governance Quality Score	Identifies risks related to corporate governance based on management structure, shareholder rights, remuneration and audit	• Data provided by companies • Media • NGOs	Annual
Sustainalytics ESG Risk Ratings	Measures company's exposure to material industry risks and risk management efficiency	• Information provided by companies • Media • NGOs	Continuous monitoring; detailed annual analysis
FTSE Russell's ESG Ratings	E, S, G	• Publicly available data	Daily
CDP	Measures involvement in minimizing climate change and transparency	• Sectoral questionnaire focusing on climate change, forest and water protection	Annual
Vigeo Eiris	Measures performance in six areas: environment, human rights, human resources, social involvement, business behavior and corporate governance. Analyzes the related reputational, human, legal and operational risks	• CSR reports, annual reports, codes of conduct, internal policies • Direct contact with companies • Stakeholder websites • Databases	Continuous monitoring

Source: Adapted from Deloitte.[7]

companies are engaging intentionally and appropriately with rating agencies, consistent with their values and objectives.

Digitising and automating ESG data collection and reporting

In many organisations, ESG data is managed by multiple systems and individuals. This complexity is further exacerbated by the fact that partners along the

---

[7] Deloitte. (2022). Comparing rating agencies and ESG methodologies. https://www2.deloitte .com/content/dam/Deloitte/ce/Documents/about-deloitte/ce_table_ratings_esg_eng.pdf.

value chain frequently have their own technology and methods. Centralisation of data using a common platform greatly aids in standardising, validating, streamlining, simplifying, and accessing collected ESG data. By ensuring that data is consistent and is comparable, common platforms can reduce the probability of costly mistakes, make verification easier, calculate integrated metrics, and track ESG KPIs. Board members can more easily track performance and trends in a timely manner, which allows for more meaningful insights to inform decision-making.

By streamlining the process, such platforms have the added benefit of reducing the reporting burden. This is key in helping boards ensure they are complying with ESG regulations, as well as inspiring investor confidence and building trust with stakeholders.

Disclosure Oversight: Managing the ESG Narrative

Investors are increasingly integrating ESG issues into their practice and decision-making. One primary driver for this is the growing body of regulatory and legal requirements for institutional investors.[8] Regulators and other key stakeholders also have increasing expectations for ESG performance data. Failing to do so puts companies at significant reputational risk. It is therefore important for boards to craft their own narrative and strategically choose disclosure platforms that meet the expectations of the stakeholders they deem most critical.

Regulators worldwide have taken decisive action to scrutinise companies' ESG activities. Starting in March 2022, the SEC enhanced climate-risk reporting requirements for all publicly traded companies in the United States. Companies are required to disclose the potential impact of extreme weather events and other physical risks on their financial performance, as well as their scope 1 and 2 GHG emissions. The EU is setting the standard for corporate sustainability reporting with the Corporate Sustainability Reporting Directive (CSRD) as discussed previously.

There is a growing demand from investors for information on how boards are fulfilling their ESG oversight responsibilities. Boards must ensure that the proxy statement includes a comprehensive and detailed description of the diligence of their efforts. Directors' skills also play a crucial role in enhancing their contribution to ESG oversight efforts. As such, investors increasingly request information on how board members acquire the skills necessary and stay up to date, including education or external expertise.

Corporate disclosures illustrate the increase in board oversight of ESG efforts, as pressure continues to mount. For example, JUST Capital tracks

---

[8] UNEP Finance Initiative. (2019). Fiduciary duty in the 21st century. https://www.unepfi.org/wordpress/wp-content/uploads/2019/10/Fiduciary-duty-21st-century-final-report.pdf

three data points to evaluate how companies prioritise and oversee ESG topics: (1) whether ESG risks and performance are linked to executive compensation; (2) whether compensation metrics include ESG KPIs; and (3) whether the board discusses environmental, social, and health and safety issues according to a formal schedule.[9] Between 2020 and 2022, companies in the Russell 1000 consistently boosted their disclosures. However, it is worth noting that board discussions and evaluations tended to focus more on environmental, social, health and safety matters, and less on linking ESG metrics to compensation. The industries with the highest percentages are oil and gas (74%), utilities (66%), energy equipment and services (58%), and chemicals (48%). In these four industries, a significant majority of companies (61%) openly disclose all three data points. This makes sense, given their environmental impact and resulting scrutiny by the public and private sectors. Investor engagement, such as Climate Action 100+, the largest climate-related investor initiative on environmental issues, likely contributes to higher disclosure levels in these industries.[10]

ESG disclosure frameworks

In recent years, voluntary ESG disclosure frameworks have emerged to assist companies in navigating their reporting obligations. Directors must familiarise themselves with these frameworks as an integral part of their duties. Many frameworks and standards have emerged due to new creations, mergers, and past collaborations. For more information, refer to Appendix 34B, which provides a short description of the key standards and frameworks for directors: the Global Reporting Initiative (GRI), the Carbon Disclosure Project (CDP), the Task Force on Climate-related Financial Disclosures (TCFD) and the Sustainability Accounting Standards Board (SASB). Since 2022, SASB has been integrated into the recently established standard-setting body, the International Sustainability Standards Board (ISSB), under the International Financial Reporting Standards (IFRS) Foundation.

ESG disclosure channels

Growing investor interest in ESG disclosures means that boards are now actively involved in overseeing ESG disclosure channels. For US companies, common channels for communication with stakeholders can include annual

[9] Just Capital. (2023). Boards are increasingly tying goals to ESG metrics as demand from shareholders rises. https://justcapital.com/reports/board-esg-oversight-increasing-as-companies-face-proxy-season/#:~:text=Our%20analysis%20found%20that%20the,%2C%20and%20Chemicals%20(48%25)

[10] Just Capital. (2023). Boards are increasingly tying goals to ESG metrics as demand from shareholders rises. https://justcapital.com/reports/board-esg-oversight-increasing-as-companies-face-proxy-season/#:~:text=Our%20analysis%20found%20that%20the,%2C%20and%20Chemicals%20(48%25)

reports, conference calls, proxy statements, ESG/CSR/impact/sustainability reports and company websites (see Table 34.2). Establishing a cohesive and consistent narrative across all chosen disclosure channels is crucial. It is essential to ensure the reliability of data, as well as the accuracy and completeness of disclosures. All types of disclosures require effective controls and procedures. Ineffective or misleading ESG disclosures can be perceived as a form of greenwashing.

S&P 500 ESG reporting and a reality check on utilities

The SEC's Enhancement and Standardization of Climate-related Disclosures for Investors, requires companies to disclose detailed climate-related information, for example, GHG emissions, climate-related risks likely to have a material impact, and progress updates on climate goals.[11]

Table 34.2 ESG Disclosure Channels

SEC annual and quarterly reporting	Companies must disclose any material issues in their SEC reporting. This means that any significant issues must be included in the risk section or management's discussion and analysis section of the report. Board directors must be aware that there are legal consequences associated with disclosing ESG information in financial filings. It is important to comply with the applicable laws and regulations when sharing such information to avoid any potential legal repercussions.
Earnings calls	Companies often use their earnings calls to highlight their ESG initiatives. By doing so, they enhance communication with investors regarding important ESG matters and effectively demonstrate how these efforts contribute to their overall value creation strategy.
Proxy statements	The proxy statement is a document mandated by the SEC. Its purpose is to equip shareholders with all the necessary information required to make well-informed decisions regarding matters discussed during annual or special stockholder meetings. Companies now recognize the importance of including ESG information in their proxy statements to directly communicate with investors and showcase their commitment to ESG practices.
ESG / CSR / impact / sustainability reports	Historically, companies have used sustainability reports as the primary means of communicating their sustainability performance and impact.
Websites	Companies often host ESG information on their websites. They have dedicated specific pages to showcase sustainability goals and initiatives. These webpages often feature links to additional sustainability resources.

---

[11] SEC. (2022). SEC proposes rules to enhance and standardize climate-related disclosures for investors. 21 March. https://www.sec.gov/news/press-release/2022-46

Following the proposal of this new rule, we investigated climate-related disclosures by S&P 500 companies. A list of words that companies might use to describe their ESG activities, particularly environmental activities (such as eco, ecological, environment, dialogue, carbon, air, greenhouse, sustainability, sustainable), was matched to words from the annual reports of S&P 500 companies (SEC Form 10-K) to ascertain the ratio of environmental words to total ESG word count. This helped to give a rough idea of how much companies talked about eco policies in their annual reports between 1 April 2021 and 31 March 2022. The research showed a gap between environmental disclosure, firm action, and public perception (see Figure 34.2).

Companies in the utilities and energy sectors talked the most about environmental issues in their annual reports. But does more disclosure on climate-related activities reassure the public that these companies will take significant action to tackle the challenges? It appears not. In the 2022 Edelman Trust Barometer Special Report (fieldwork conducted from 16 September 2022 to 3 October 2022), the industries least trusted to address the climate crisis were coal, private equity, fashion, fast food, and oil and gas.[12] The boards of these companies should be aware of the perception gap between talking and trust. Public mistrust could be due to a handful of energy and utilities companies

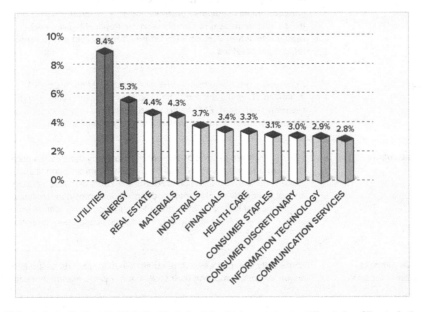

Figure 34.2   Industry Sectors that Talk the Most about the Environment are not Trusted on Climate Action

---

[12] Edelman. (2022). Edelman trust barometer. Special report: Trust and climate change. https://www.edelman.com/trust/2022-trust-barometer/special-report-trust-climate

being caught not following through on addressing environmental issues. 'Trust is a fragile thing – hard to earn, easy to lose.' The real concern is that some sectors fall short of their stakeholders' expectations.

Taking a closer look at the utilities sector, we examined the environmental disclosures and firm behaviour of the 29 utilities companies in the S&P 500 index as of 31 March 2022. We collected data and investigated whether there was a connection between current environmental disclosure and past corporate misconduct. The dataset contains information on any environmental violation of these companies between 2015 and 2021, including both civil and criminal cases settled by federal and local agencies that incorporate the costs of supplemental environmental projects related to settlement.

For each company, we aggregated the total number of cases and total penalty amount for the period and found that they were positively correlated with the length of environmental disclosure ($r = 0.4$ and 0.6 respectively). The more environmental disclosure there was, the more likely it was that there had been penalties and violations in the past, indicating that the board might have discussed environmental policies in an effort to rectify bad behaviours. If a company continues to violate regulations, extensive environmental discussion is likely to be seen as greenwashing.

We collected total returns data for 28 utilities companies (one company was omitted due to missing data) and checked whether stock returns were related to current environmental disclosure. From 1 January 2021 to 30 November 2022, the stock returns of 28 utilities companies were negatively correlated with environmental disclosure length ($r = -0.3$). The greater the length of environmental disclosure, the more likely the stock would perform poorly over that time. A longer environmental disclosure coupled with more lawbreaking activities could be interpreted as expectations of greenwashing.

We also found large variations in the utilities sector in terms of environmental disclosure. Unlike a normal distribution with a bell-shaped curve, the distribution of environmental talk is asymmetric with a long right tail (see Figure 34.3). Normally, greenwashing occurs in different ways, such as deceitful practices and boasting about sustainability. Unless companies are caught out, as happened with Volkswagen and the emissions scandal in 2015, it is hard to detect deceitful behaviour. However, if a company discusses environmental matters extensively, it might receive unwanted scrutiny for signs of greenwashing. Integrity and authenticity don't require lengthy statements. Ensuring integrity and authenticity are essential to board work on ESG.

Boards need to ensure that the ESG story is told responsibly and with integrity

There are two main facets to the board's oversight of ESG. The first is essentially about focus: what are the ESG issues that matter to the company are (in terms of risk or opportunity) – and how to best measure performance and

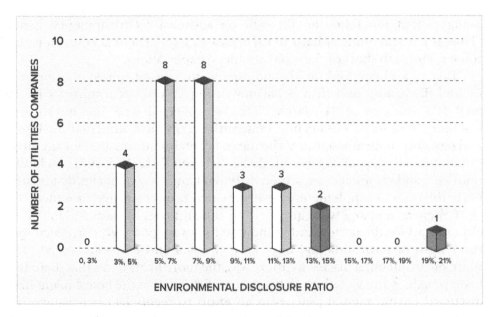

Figure 34.3   Environmental Disclosure in Annual Reports Varies in the Utilities Sector

structure accountability for these (through metrics, structures and processes, reporting). The second is deciding how to channel the relevant and accurate information to stakeholders; in other words deciding how and where to disclose ESG information and to whom. By understanding and articulating with integrity how it is doing on its ESG promises along strategic axes, the board plays a key role in keeping the organisation on course in the complex terrain of ESG commitments, reporting, and stakeholder expectations.

Annex 1: Key ESG reporting standards

The GRI Standards, developed by the Global Sustainability Standards Board (GSSB), are the pioneering global standards for sustainability reporting. The GRI offers ESG standards for the disclosure of socially significant issues that impact a company's stakeholders. GRI has been the leading provider of sustainability reporting standards since it published its initial guidelines in March 1999. 78% of the largest 250 companies by revenue and 68% of the leading businesses in 58 countries have adopted these standards.[13] The GRI Standards are a flexible system of interconnected standards with three components:

1. GRI Universal Standards: Applicable to all organisations without exception.

(continued)

---

[13] KPMG. (2022). Survey of Sustainability Reporting. October. https://assets.kpmg.com/content/dam/kpmg/se/pdf/komm/2022/Global-Survey-of-Sustainability-Reporting-2022.pdf

2. **GRI Sector Standards:** Carefully crafted standards to meet the specific requirements and address the unique environmental impacts of different sectors. They especially focus on sectors with a significant environmental footprint, like fossil fuels.
3. **GRI Topic Standards:** Focused on providing disclosures that are relevant to specific topics.

The CDP built upon GRI's concept of environmental disclosure, and enables users to measure and address risks and opportunities related to climate change, deforestation, and water security. A significant number of investors, with massive assets and procurement spend, have demanded that companies disclose their environmental data via CDP; almost 20,000 organisations did so in 2022.

The TCFD was established in December 2015 by the Group of 20 (G20) and the Financial Stability Board (FSB) to meet the increasing need for comprehensive disclosures of climate-related risks. The TCFD has developed 11 recommendations that cover four key pillars: governance, strategy, risk management, and metrics and targets. The framework effectively collects information regarding board oversight of climate-related risks and opportunities, including:

1. **Governance:** Reporting to the board and its committees about climate-related risks and opportunities should be done consistently and with clear processes in place. The frequency of these reports should be determined based on the importance of timely updates and the need for informed decision making.
2. **Strategy:** The board and its committees must take climate-related issues into account '. . . when reviewing and guiding strategy, major plans of action, risk management policies, annual budgets and business plans, as well as setting the organisation's performance objectives, monitoring implementation and performance and overseeing major capital expenditures, acquisitions and divestitures.'[14]
3. **Risk management:** The company takes the initiative to identify, assess, and effectively manage any climate-related risks that may arise.
4. **Metrics and targets:** The company utilises specific metrics and targets to address climate-related issues. The board actively oversees the company's progress towards those targets, ensuring accountability and measurable results.

The UK is set to go beyond the 'comply or explain' approach and make TCFD-consistent disclosure mandatory for both financial and non-financial sectors. The government has mandated that all premium listed companies report on their climate risk exposure, in line with the recommendations of the TCFD. This requirement took effect on 1 January 2021. By 2025, companies in the UK will be required to report on these disclosures.

Various disclosure frameworks have experienced significant consolidation in the past, reflecting the dynamic nature of the markets. The International Integrated Reporting Committee (IIRC) was established in London in 2010. The SASB was established in 2011 in San Francisco to address the need for standardised sustainability reporting in US securities disclosures. In June 2021, the IIRC merged with the SASB to form the Value Reporting

(continued)

[14] TCFD. (2023). Disclose the organization's governance around climate-related risks and opportunities. https://www.tcfdhub.org/governance/

(continued)

Foundation (VRF). The merger aimed to offer investors and companies a robust corporate reporting framework covering all enterprise value drivers and standards. The IFRS Foundation made a significant announcement at the 2021 United Nations Climate Change Conference (COP26) when it established a brand-new board called the International Sustainability Standards Board (ISSB). In November 2021, the IFRS Foundation announced that the VRF and CDSB boards would merge with its newly created ISSB board by June 2022. In addition to the aforementioned standards, the ISSB also builds upon the work of the TCFD and the World Economic Forum's Stakeholder Capitalism Metrics. The merger and integration aimed to establish a unified set of standards and drive progress in global reporting standards. The ISSB mapped out four primary goals:

1. To develop standards for a global baseline of sustainability disclosures.
2. To meet the information needs of investors.
3. To enable companies to provide comprehensive sustainability information to global capital markets.
4. To facilitate interoperability with disclosures that are jurisdiction-specific and/or aimed at broader stakeholder groups.[15]

In June 2023, the ISSB took a significant step by releasing its first standards, IFRS S1 and IFRS S2. IFRS S1 offers clear disclosure requirements that enable companies to effectively communicate with investors regarding the sustainability-related risks and opportunities they encounter in the short, medium and long term.

IFRS S2 provides clear guidelines on climate-related disclosures and is specifically intended to be used alongside IFRS S1. IFRS S2 requirements align with the 4 core pillars and 11 recommended disclosures issued by the TCFD. Companies that apply the ISSB Standards will meet the TCFD recommendations. Furthermore, IFRS S2 mandates increased disclosure, including the utilisation of carbon credits to meet net emissions targets. The ISSB actively collaborates with jurisdictions and companies to ensure the effective implementation of IFRS S1 and IFRS S2.

Appendix 34A: ESG Questions for the board to reflect on

Compliance

- Do your company's existing risk processes include the identification of ESG risks, such as lawsuits related to ESG issues against directors and senior executives?
- What types of regulatory changes are the board most concerned about? How does the board monitor the evolving regulatory landscape? How does the board anticipate where regulations on all aspects of ESG will be implemented?

---

[15] IFRS. (2023). About the International Sustainability Standards Board. https://www.ifrs.org/groups/international-sustainability-standards-board/

- Is your company under investigation by regulators? Are you actively engaging in discussions with regulators and policymakers?
- Are the directors adequately prepared to handle the new ESG regulatory demands? Is your company taking steps to ensure compliance with ESG standards, or is it just paying lip service to the idea?
- Have the directors engaged third-party accounting or law firms in the compliance process? Do your company and the board have the right technology tools in place to handle compliance processes effectively?

People, Information, Structures, and Processes

- Is our company equipped with competent individuals, appropriate governance structures, and effective processes and policies to facilitate smooth information flow regarding ESG-related strategy and risk?
- Is the board qualified to support management in executing ESG strategies and managing changing ESG risks and opportunities? How is the company communicating to investors the value that each director brings to the board?
- Is your current board and governance structure effective in proactively engaging with multiple stakeholders and fostering meaningful and effective dialogue? Is the board dedicating enough time to discussing and addressing important ESG matters on its agenda?
- Has ESG oversight been allocated to the full board or individual committees? Is the committee structure in place conducive to providing meaningful oversight and accountability for ESG issues? Does it make sense for the board to establish another committee solely dedicated to overseeing the company's ESG initiatives?
- How often does management update the board on ESG risks and opportunities? Does the board tap into the power of technology to simplify the collection and organisation of ESG data?
- Does management prioritise ESG risks and opportunities? Is the CEO truly committed to achieving ESG goals and producing tangible results, with proper incentives in place?
- Have the committee charters, governance guidelines, and other policies been updated to align with the company's ESG goals, purpose, vision, and mission?

Metrics

- How does the company determine which ESG metrics are the best fit? Has it explored different ESG standards and frameworks to ensure that it is addressing the most critical risks and issues in its industry?
- Do board members actively engage in conversations with stakeholders, and if they do, what benefits do they gain from these interactions? How do directors ensure they are aware of the opinions of significant

stakeholders and then align those perspectives with the company's governance and strategy?

- What is the main challenge your company faces with ESG data? Do you rely on both numerical metrics and qualitative information to monitor your progress?
- Is your board embracing a modern governance approach that values data-driven decisions? Have you leveraged the benefits of digitisation, automation, and platforms to efficiently handle ESG information and disclosure?

ESG Disclosure Channels

- Do ESG-related disclosures meet the expectations of various groups such as regulators, investors, employees, and activists? Which key stakeholder group wields the greatest influence over your organisation's ESG reporting and disclosure policy?
- Should your sustainability targets be presented as milestones or roadmaps with different time frames? How can you ensure that these goals are successfully achieve at each stage? Additionally, what kind of governance mechanisms are in place to monitor progress in implementing ESG initiatives over the long term?
- Does the company have strong policies and controls in place to support the development of data collection and disclosure? Are its disclosures compliant with specific frameworks or standards? Additionally, when deciding to adopt a framework or standard that includes specific metrics, has the company considered whether it is feasible to fulfil the commitments of that chosen framework or standard?
- Which communication platform should the company use for its ESG disclosures? Are the disclosures consistent across various platforms and tailored to meet the needs of different audiences? Do these disclosures effectively communicate the company's commitment to its ESG programme and how it is overseen by the board?
- Are our ESG-related disclosures, such as annual reports, websites, and CSR disclosures, legitimate and trustworthy? Have we carefully crafted them to mitigate any potential attention or criticism? Does the board have contingency plans in place to address accusations of greenwashing or potential litigation?

CHAPTER

35

Assessing and Benchmarking Governance Performance

Throughout this book we have argued that the quality of an organisation's governance is a core driver of its performance. It contributes to anchoring decision-making that is aligned with an organisation's mission and values, and is a fundamental factor for a company's lasting growth. The board of directors has a key responsibility to ensure governance quality in the organisation, with its power to ignite strategic choices, elevate openness, and boost stakeholder trust. This leads to smooth company operations grounded in transparency, accountability, and ethical integrity.

Over the past decades, I have worked with thousands of directors from all around the world who have participated in IMD's High Performance Board programme (HPB) – which is designed to elevate the board practice of non-executive board members, and is attended by participants from around the world. During each session, we conduct spontaneous polls to gather insights about their board activities and experiences. Our survey reveals intriguing insights into board effectiveness over time – and what the status of governance performance is today. It may help you benchmark where your board stands.

The survey results offer a unique opportunity to gauge what board members view as trends in board effectiveness across the four dimensions that we have been exploring throughout this book: people, information, structures and processes, and group dynamics. As we have discussed, this approach thoroughly examines the different aspects of board interactions, governance practices, and individual roles, aligning with the core concerns of investors, stakeholders, and regulatory authorities. Let's take a look at the survey results, taking each category in turn.

HPB Director Survey 2012–2023

The HPB Survey, spanning 12 years, included structured sessions, aimed at eliciting detailed and candid responses from board members. With 1,443 participants contributing it provides a substantial and rich dataset for analysis, as illustrated in Figure 35.1.

The participant demographics showed a skewed gender distribution, with 331 females (22%) and 1,156 males (78%), even considering recent sessions. Although this is not a balanced sample, it does mirror the current reality of board compositions, where men are more predominant than women, especially across some geographies.

The participants were distributed across various age groups, with the majority falling within the 51 to 55 age bracket, representing 25%. This was closely followed by the 46 to 50 age group, which made up 21%. This age distribution is reflective of board composition when cumulated across different company ownership and geographies. For example, we often have younger members of families owning businesses that participate to our programmes, thus ensuring a broad range of generational insights, as detailed in Figure 35.2.

The survey achieved a global reach, attracting participants from more than 86 countries, with a predominance of European and a strong Africa/Middle East representation, but at large, presence from across the world, including

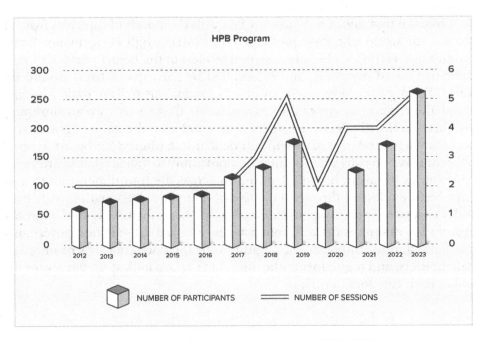

Figure 35.1   Participants of IMD's High Performance Boards Programme (2012–2023)

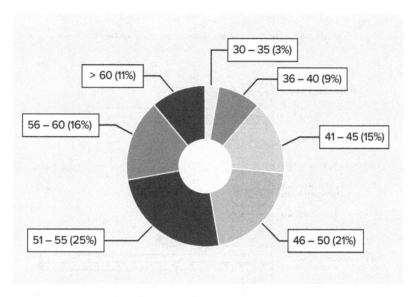

Figure 35.2   Participant Demographic by Age

Asia, the Americas, and Oceania. The top 10 nationalities constituted 61.5% of all participants.

In each session, we invited participants to share their opinions on a range of questions. When multiple surveys were conducted within the same year, we averaged the responses to provide a yearly snapshot. For the majority of the graphs presented, we have averaged these percentages across the years for a more concise overview. This approach ensures that our findings are both generalisable and relevant to a broad audience.

As a preliminary question, we systematically asked a fundamental question on perceived board effectiveness. Figure 35.3 provides insight into how board members rate their board's effectiveness. About 5% viewed their boards as highly effective, while a larger group of 24% saw them as well-balanced, a somewhat vague and uncommitted answer. Yet domination problems are ever present, with boards often not being as free as one would hope for. Of the participants, 14% raised concerns about CEO or management dominance, signalling strong governance issues. Moreover, 30% of board members surveyed reported perceptions of control by the chairman, specific shareholders, or board members, a dynamic which can hamper productive discussion in board rooms.

People Quality, Diversity, Focus, and Dedication

Figure 35.3 provides insight into how board members rate their board's effectiveness. About 5% view their boards as highly effective, while a larger group of 24% see them as well-balanced, reflecting a good mix in board composition

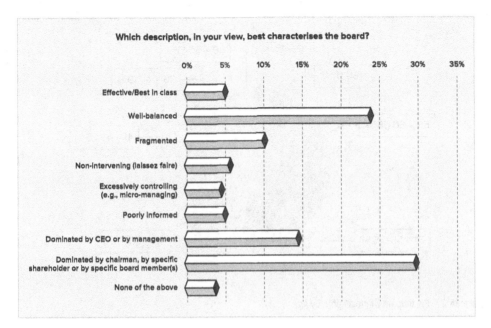

Figure 35.3   How Board Members Perceive Board Effectiveness

and decision-making. Yet 14% raise concerns about CEO or management dominance, signaling possible governance issues. Moreover, 30% of board members surveyed report perceptions of control by the chairman, certain shareholders, or specific board members, illustrating the varied governance experiences across boards.

The responses indicate that board members are increasingly recognising the importance of diversity of skills and competencies, as well as other relevant attributes and the challenge of reaching it, notably with evolution required of skills needed. This recognition appears to not yet be matched by board practice, with most directors assessing their boards as 'good', 'average', or 'with weaknesses', as shown in Figure 35.4. Given societal shifts and corresponding changes in norms and governance standards, this finding seems to correspond well with growing expectations when it comes to diversity of board composition.

As discussed, the heart of successful board work is the commitment of its members. Their active participation, thorough preparation, and insightful contributions are critical to board effectiveness. Maintaining ethical behaviour, staying true to the organisation's mission, and focusing on long-term value are typical traits of influential directors. True dedication drives boards towards real accomplishments.

Using sample data, our analysis of dedication reveals a wide range of levels in preparation and commitment among directors. The survey highlights a common theme among board members: many approach their work

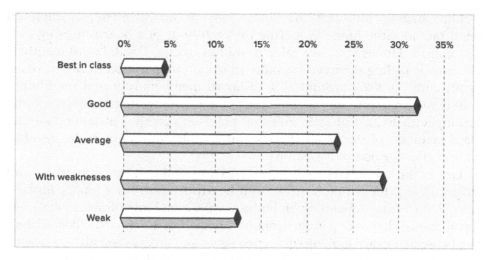

Figure 35.4   Board Composition and Diversity

with basic preparation, but often lack a deeper understanding. Figure 35.5 shows that over half of board members attend board meetings with only basic preparation, and only about 24% are perceived as being thoroughly ready for in-depth discussions in meetings. Moreover, the survey results point out a non-negligible level of concern among board members about the inadequate preparation of some their board colleagues, suggesting a possible gap in readiness and expertise within the board. Preparation is a significant driver of effective board discussion and appears to be a dimension which is consistently considered as requiring reinforcement.

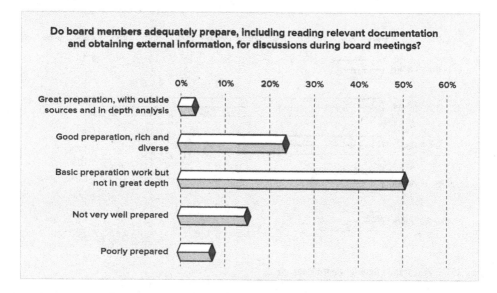

Figure 35.5   Level of Board Member Preparation for Meetings

Our analysis indicates that over 44% of board members surveyed spend one to three hours preparing for each hour of a board meeting (see Figure 35.6). However, a noticeable trend has emerged, with board members increasingly feeling the need for more thorough preparation in recent years. Significantly, in 2023, around 20% of board members reported spending 7 to 10 hours preparing for just one hour of a board meeting, nearly doubling the long-term average of 11%. This shift points to a growing awareness among board members of the detailed work and complexities required for productive and effective board discussions.

One of the key differences between executive and non-executive work (and perspectives) is their time horizon, with boards typically on a longer horizon (from 5 to 15 years depending on business type, even longer for state or family organisations). In looking at the responses related to how boards allocate their time between forward-looking versus past issues, our analysis reveals a somewhat varied perception (see Figure 35.7). However, a considerable portion of time (30–50% and 50% or greater) is deemed to be spent on future issues, suggesting that boards are prioritising their role of strategic foresight and planning.

Balanced composition, diversity, focus, and dedication, are key characteristics of directors constituting an effective board. The intersection of dedication and diversity, coupled with independence and continuous learning, equips boards to tackle challenges skilfully. Good governance is a continuous journey. It requires board members who are committed to growing their understanding of the evolving context in order to continue to enrich their perspectives. In this way, they can come to board meetings prepared to share their unique understanding with a view to driving discussions that are truly strategic to the organisation, and fully explore the implications when it comes to risk.

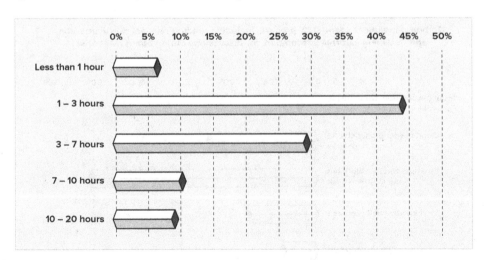

Figure 35.6   Preparation Time for Board Meetings

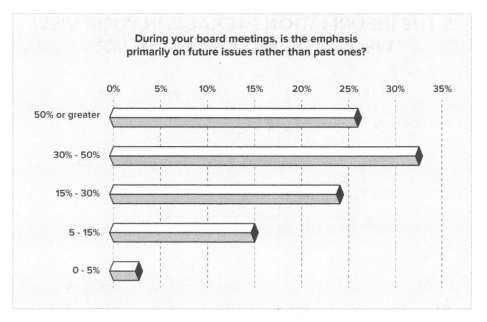

During your board meetings, is the emphasis
primarily on future issues rather than past ones?

Figure 35.7   Future Orientation of Board Meetings

Information: Designing Board Intelligence

The effectiveness of board discussions is in large part dependent on the nature and structure of the information on which it relies. Traditional management briefings are certainly essential, but a robust information framework also includes external sources, including social media, analyst reports, and informal networks. This comprehensive approach blends internal data such as financial reports and CEO updates with external viewpoints. Alongside comprehensive board briefings and detailed committee reports, diverse information sources enhance the board's understanding and inform its decision-making processes.

In examining board members' views on the information package they receive for the boards that they are on, our survey reveals that 39% agree that these are well-designed and focused (as shown in Figure 35.8). Yet this view appears to be shifting somewhat over time. In 2023, around 37% of board members surveyed expressed dissatisfaction with the design of their information package compared with the long-term average of 29%. The evolving expectations of board members when it comes to information packages may explain this trend.

For a board, getting a sense of a company's pulse is crucial – and they need to be able to understand this via their information channels. This includes engaging with a wide range of stakeholders, from shareholders, employees,

IS THE INFORMATION PACKAGE, IN YOUR VIEW, WELL-DESIGNED AND FOCUSED?

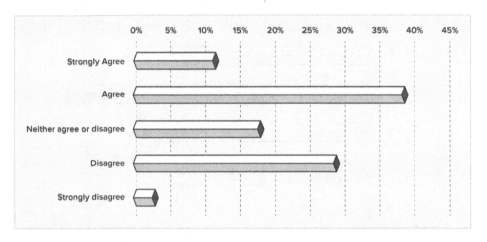

Figure 35.8   Design and Focus of Information Package

and suppliers to the wider community. To acquire this type of view and to continue to nurture the sources needed to ensure it stays informed requires more than just interaction: the board members need to ensure a diversity of communication channels and sustain a commitment to building strong relationships. Open, proactive dialogue not only nourishes its understanding and enriches its view, but also strengthens the organisation's reputation and cultivates trust among stakeholders.

Incorporating external information sources such as media outlets, analyst reports, and social media is necessary for a board's agility and ability to adapt quickly. Our analysis into board members' perspectives on external issues discloses that nearly 60% believe the information they receive is not comprehensive (see Figure 35.9). This underscores the importance of enhancing strategies for gathering and communicating external information, to ensure boards have a full grasp of the external factors influencing their decisions.

Regarding the board meeting time, our analysis unearths a somewhat troubling trend: too large a portion of board meeting time is devoted to management presentations (see Figure 35.10). More than 55% of board members declare spending more than half of their time on board presentations during board meetings! As discussed, a board needs to devote the bulk of its time to discussions, the heart of the governance process. Spending too much time on presentations both signals and creates inefficiencies on boards.

IS THE INFORMATION PRESENTED TO THE BOARD COMPLETE WHEN IT COMES TO EXTERNAL ISSUES LIKE REPUTATION ANALYSIS, CUSTOMER KNOWLEDGE, STAKEHOLDER UNDERSTANDING, TECHNOLOGICAL EVOLUTION, ETC.?

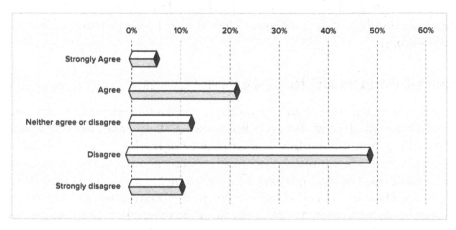

Figure 35.9   Information Adequacy regarding External Matters

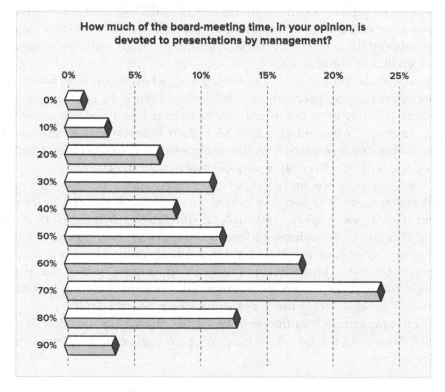

Figure 35.10   Board Meeting Time Devoted to Management Team Presentations

Informal channels, like employee interactions and discussions among board members, inject fresh perspectives and enrich views to supplement formal views being communicated by management. This mix of official internal briefings, external insights, and the spontaneous nature of informal channels enriches the data that the board is relying on for its decision-making. As such, board members need to be intentional in actively shaping information channels, drawing insights from a variety of sources, and determining that the information shared is not only pertinent but also forward-looking.

Structures and Processes: Architecting Governance Excellence

As discussed, the importance of a company's governance structure and processes in driving an effective board is immense. A sharp assessment of roles, decision-making, and ethics offers a clear picture of the board's effectiveness. Some organisations are adopting innovative strategies to strengthen their governance structures. For example, appointing a chief risk officer who reports directly to the chair of the risk committee or to the board chair demonstrates a serious approach to risk management. Another example is the creation of new board committees, such as ESG committee or cyber-security committee. While we are not advocating the creation of any of these committees per se, the point is the degree to which boards are considering what structures and processes align well with their strategy and risk process. It's important to make adjustments regularly to ensure these continue to align with the company's strategic goals and context.

How does this compare with our survey data, when it comes to how board members view the risk process? As exhibited in Figure 35.11, the responses vary: about 31% rate their board's involvement in risk as 'good'. Another 30% see it as 'average', while roughly 25% view their board's engagement in risk as 'poor'. This variety underscores the complexities of risk oversight and the differing levels of effectiveness in various governance structures.

A common concern across different organisations is how to engage around crises, notably reputation crises. We consider it normal practice to perform such an exercise (for example, a simulation) at least every couple of years. Our survey specifically looked into this issue, finding that a significant majority of respondents' boards don't regularly discuss how to respond to such a crisis (refer to Figure 35.12). This is an important gap that needs to be addressed, in order for boards to be prepared. Proactively testing behaviours and possibly creating response plans enhances a board's ability to respond quickly and appropriately in the event of a crisis, thereby minimising the likelihood of damage of the board splitting or of a fast governance deterioration under pressure.

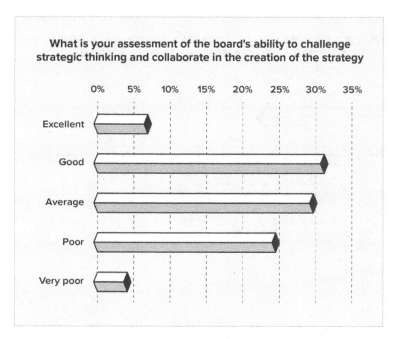

Figure 35.11   Board Risk Identification and Assessment Effectiveness

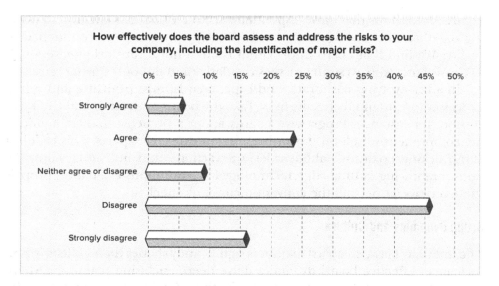

Figure 35.12   Board Engagement in Reputation Crises

A board's work on strategy is central to its effectiveness and ranges from co-creation with management, to support and oversight. Our research indicates a generally positive view of boards engaging in robust strategic thinking.

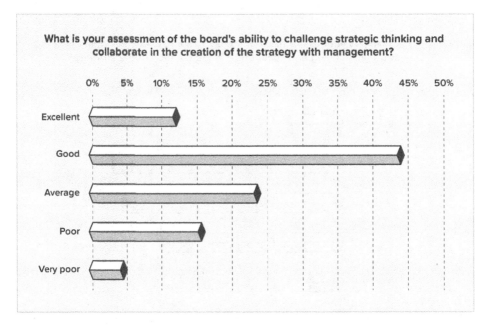

Figure 35.13   Board's Strategy Process

Figure 35.13 shows that most respondents see their board as effective in working together with management on the strategy process. Overconfidence or reality? We find that board information is often not future oriented enough to consistently address strategy issues regularly (and not only during retreats).

In a fast-evolving corporate landscape, boards must prioritise and refine processes for sustained effectiveness. Take the board evaluation and CEO succession, for instance. Progressive boards adopt a proactive stance, conducting comprehensive self-reviews or bringing in external experts. This isn't just about ticking boxes; it's about roles, interactions, and individual contributions. Embracing cutting-edge technology for continuous evaluation propels these reviews far beyond the conventional yearly check-ins.

Group Dynamics and Culture

The interplay between board members significantly shapes their collective performance. Effective board dynamics delve deep, enclosing teamwork where useful, challenge and dissent where productive, mutual respect, and the cultivation of constructive debates. A board that truly values diverse perspectives, champions collaboration, and acknowledges each member's contribution is more equipped to make balanced decisions. This kind of board doesn't just function; it thrives, turning varied opinions into strategy for success.

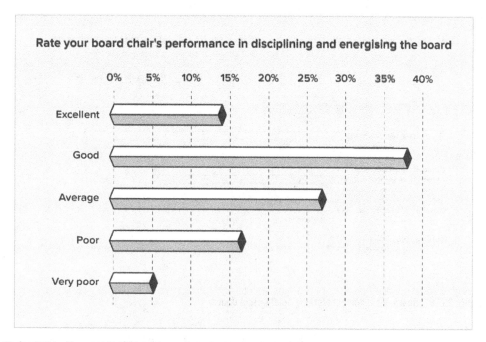

Rate your board chair's performance in disciplining and energising the board

Figure 35.14   Board Chair's Ability to Foster Successful Board Culture

The chair serves as the anchor to foster successful board culture. While a dynamic and effective culture may be partly outlined in formal guidelines (such as a board charter), it is rooted in promoting equal participation, nurturing quality discussions, and respecting diverse decision-making and conversational styles. Recognising and valuing these nuanced differences can significantly improve group dynamics, by ensuring unique perspectives are given voice and enrich the exchanges.

Figure 35.14 points to a challenging view on how the board chair's performance is assessed. While members are supportive of their chairs, we still see perceptions of underperformance that engages the question: How can we ensure meritocracy in chairing?

Figure 35.15 reveals board members' views with regard to their working relationship with management. Most respondents (about 44%) describe it as 'productive with some rare failures', suggesting smooth collaboration. A slightly smaller group (about 31%) sees potential for improvement, labelling the relationship as 'somewhat productive but could be improved'. Generally, these insights indicate that the board and senior management interactions are viewed as effective.

The interplay between the board and senior management is no doubt significant. When board dynamics are effective, marked by mutual respect and

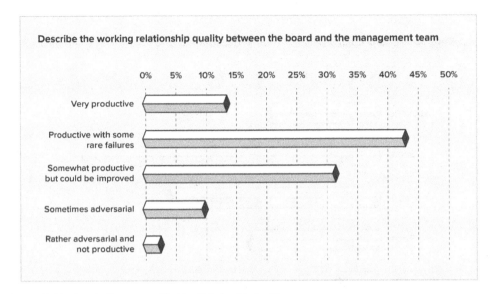

Figure 35.15   Board–Management Working Relationship Quality

clear rules, they serve as a defence against conflicts of interest. Such an environment underlines accountability and encourages a culture of openness and healthy dissent. By prioritising these elements, boards can navigate challenges and anticipate and prepare for future complexities.

A productive board culture is at the foundation of its effectiveness. Addressing board pathologies, like group-think, disruptive behaviour, and low engagement, is indispensable. Unfortunately, boards in many cases are confronted with areas of dysfunction, leading to governance shortfalls. Practices that undermine effective governance, such as distributing materials late or withholding data and information, usually point to more profound issues like trust deficits and confusion over roles. As discussed earlier, there are a number of issues underlying board dysfunction, which undermine board culture and effectiveness.

When board members were surveyed about inefficiencies they have encountered in meetings, the top three responses highlighted key areas for improvement (refer to Figure 35.16). The most common issue, cited by 23%, was a lack of discussion on enhancing board effectiveness. The second, at 20%, pointed to poorly allocated meeting time. And thirdly, 17% felt that political sensitivities were hindering meaningful conversations. These findings clearly indicate a pressing need to explore ways to boost the board's efficiency and effectiveness. Some of these issues are much more complex than others to deal with, and all require a concerted effort from the board, ideally under the leadership of the chair.

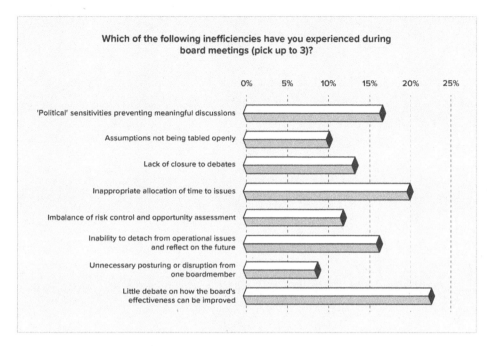

Figure 35.16   Inefficiencies Experienced by Board Members during Meetings

Conclusion: Orchestrating Governance Excellence

In the dynamic world of corporate governance, the impact of a board of directors on an organisation's ethical framework, decision-making, and long-term viability cannot be overstated. A well-functioning board is key for strategic decisions, increasing transparency, and boosting stakeholder trust. Achieving peak board performance requires a systematic approach for evaluating group dynamics, governance practices, and individual contributions. For investors, stakeholders, and regulators, evaluating the effectiveness of corporate governance is of utmost importance. This assessment is not just a routine check; it is an imperative measure of an organisation's health and future potential.

Our in-depth analysis of corporate governance focuses on areas like quality, diversity, focus and dedication of people involved, board dynamics, information design, structures and processes, and group dynamics. The survey gives other boards a good benchmark and sheds light on various viewpoints and potential improvements, stressing the need for boards to adapt to changing market conditions, improve transparency, and strategically manage information for lasting success. In summary, board effectiveness is multifaceted, with these elements coming together to orchestrate a harmonious approach to corporate governance.

Conclusion

Governance is a key driver of quality success of organisations, from start-ups all the way to multinationals and beyond, including governments and countries. Dedicated bodies such as boards and committees are principal actors of governance and of its effectiveness.

This book was inspired by my work over many years with boards around the world. For any organisation, there are four pillars to a board's effectiveness: outstanding directors with the right diversity, focus and dedication; sophisticated information architecture, internal and external, formal and informal; the long list of structures and processes, all developed with clarity and sophistication; and healthy board dynamics and culture, based on the right values, including integrity and, accountability and constructive dissent – and increasingly conviction.

These pillars of board effectiveness are nourished by the many practices developed in this book. I urge all boards and their directors to think how they can further strengthen these pillars to bring about world-class governance, and in so doing contribute to a better world.

I wish you every success in your board and governance endeavours.

Index

Note: Page references in *italics* refer to Figures; those in **bold** refer to Tables

GAAP *see* Generally Accepted Accounting
    Principles
GAME 185
Gargaro, Jr., E.A. 192
Gaussian distributions 268
gay marriage 326
GE 348
Gen Z 187
genchi genbutsu (onsite learning and
    problem-solving) 220
gender diversity 35, 214–16
gene-pool analysis 52
General Motors (GM) 133, 348, 360
Generally Accepted Accounting Principles
    (GAAP) 152
geopolitical risks and opportunities 347–64
    action in tackling 358–62, *359*, 364
    assessment 356–7
    assumptions 354
    business dimensions affected by 362–3
    director education in 353–4
    diversification 360
    geopolitical competence 350–4, 363
    geopolitical outlook 352–3
    hedging 361
    identification 355
    influence, exercising 359–60
    in-house expertise 353
    insurance 361
    losses due to 347, 348
    opportunity 361–2
    preparedness 363
    prevention 358–9
    quantification 357–8
    recruitment for 353
    stages *352*
    toolkit 354–8, *355*
German Corporate Governance Code 131
Germany, duty of care 132
Gerstner, L. 134–5
Ghosn, C. 160
Gillette 151
Glass Lewis 118
Glencore 287
Global Reporting Initiative (GRI) 300,
    342, 374
Global Sustainability Standards Board
    (GSSB) 378–80
Goh Swee Chen 247
Goldman Sachs 23, 327, 353
good judgement 31–3, 132
Good Strategy, Bad Strategy (Rumelt) 237
governance
    board–management relationship 211–12
    corporate frameworks/fraud *156*
    Corporate Governance Codes 127, 131
    Corporate Governance Statements 333

DNA 24–5, *25*
ESG 222
global challenges 19–25
group dynamics & governance culture *10*,
    16–17, 57, 72
    risk checks 87, 98–100
    subsidiary/holdings governance 271–5
    see also best practice
governance performance 383–97–99
    architecting excellence 392–4
    board intelligence 389–92
    group dynamics and culture 394–6, *395, 396*
    HPB Director Survey 2012–2023
        384–5, *384, 385*
    meeting, inefficiencies *397*
    people quality, diversity, focus, and
        dedication 385–89
    risk identification and assessment
        excellence *393*
    strategy process *394*
gray rhino risks 357
Greenhouse Gas (GHG) Protocol 300
Greenpeace 324
greenwashing 163–4, 365, 367, 377
GRI 318
GRI Standards 378–80
Griffiths, C. 192
group dynamics and governance culture (Four
    Pillars) *10*, 10–17, 57–75
    board culture 69–72
    board potential 67–8
    checklist **75**
    intra-board coalitions 62–4
    self-awareness 68–9
    traps 64
    understanding of 59–61
groupthink 68, 93
growth ratios 259
Gurr, D. 192
gut feelings 29
Guth vs. Loft Inc. (1939) 125

Hale, R. 336
Hall, E. 217
happy family traps 64
hard-to-quantify risks 104–5
Harvard Business Review 131, 150
Hayward, T. 240
hedging 106, 268, 361
Heinz 170
helpdesk software 281
Helvetica (Swiss insurance) 147
herd behaviour (groupthink) 68, 93
Herman, S. N. *218*
Hess, B. *181*
Hewlett-Packard (HP) 15–16
hidden liabilities 261